The Art of Video Production

To the memory of
Judith and Milton

The Art of Video Production

Leonard Shyles

Villanova University

SAGE Publications

Los Angeles ▪ London ▪ New Delhi ▪ Singapore

For information:

Sage Publications, Inc.
2455 Teller Road
Thousand Oaks, California 91320
E-mail: order@sagepub.com

Sage Publications Ltd.
1 Oliver's Yard
55 City Road
London EC1Y 1SP
United Kingdom

Sage Publications India Pvt. Ltd.
B-42, Panchsheel Enclave
Post Box 4109
New Delhi 110 017 India

Printed in the United States of America.

Library of Congress Cataloging-in-Publication Data

Shyles, Leonard, 1948–
The art of video production / Leonard Shyles.
    p. cm.
Includes bibliographical references and index.
ISBN-13: 978-1-4129-1675-2 (pbk.)
  1. Motion pictures—Production and direction. 2. Digital cinematography. I. Title.
PN1992.94.S54 2007
791.4302′3—dc22

                      2006028038

This book is printed on acid-free paper.

07 08 09 10 11   10 9 8 7 6 5 4 3 2 1

Acquiring Editor:	Todd R. Armstrong
Associate Editor:	Deya Saoud
Editorial Assistants:	Sarah Quesenberry and Katie Grim
Project Editor:	Astrid Virding
Copyeditor:	Gillian Dickens
Typesetter:	C&M Digitals (P) Ltd.
Proofreader:	Kevin Gleason
Indexer:	Kathy Paparchontis

BRIEF CONTENTS

CONTENTS

A Note to Students and Teachers

The Art of Video Production provides a comprehensive guide for making television programs in the digital age in both studio and field. It covers the technical aspects of the production process but also provides relevant advice and insight on the nature of the audience and the importance of audience analysis to the production process.

The book emphasizes these two areas for several reasons: First, programs that remain unseen cannot be judged successful even if they are of high quality. Therefore, one job of the producer-director is to understand a program's intended audience insofar as is possible *before* the production process begins so as to maximize the chances for winning an audience's attention; a practical advantage of knowing your audience in clear terms (i.e., demographically, culturally, or otherwise) is that it makes every production decision easier.

Second, *all* productions must operate within inevitable constraints of time, space, equipment, money, and personnel. Therefore, it is critical to make the best use of facilities, talent, and crew, to maximize efficiency, program quality, and production values. For these reasons, *The Art of Video Production* emphasizes the conceptual foundations and underlying technical principles that govern the process rather than the latest models of equipment that can surely become outdated in a year or two.

The book presents each chapter in a logical order, but each chapter is written to be self-contained. For instance, since it is not possible to see a video image in total darkness, the subjects of light and lighting design precede the chapter on using the camera. As another example, while it is clear that the book emphasizes audience analysis principles throughout, the writing chapter is designed to be understandable on its own. Therefore, both teachers and students should feel free to use the book in line with their needs. It is meant to be a flexible handbook, designed to fit your needs without forcing a lockstep order.

Chapter 1, "The Video Production Process," gives an overview of how television programs and videos are made, including a description of the preproduction, production, and postproduction phases. It also includes a detailed description of the jobs of the key personnel involved, telling what each crew member is responsible for during each phase.

Chapter 2, "Video as Communication," as mentioned, emphasizes conceptual foundations of audience analysis from both ancient and modern traditions. Chapter 3, "How Television Works," describes how radio energy makes television broadcasting possible, as well as the nature and role of both computers and telecommunications networks for producing and distributing programs. The chapter explains how sound and images may be converted into radio energy and then transmitted through space at the speed of light. The technologies used to accomplish this have undergone continuous refinement since the early 1900s, but the principles on which they are based have remained a constant since the inception of broadcasting and remain critical to understanding digital video today; without radio energy, much of the commerce in television content would be impossible. The chapter then explains how computers and telecommunications technologies have revolutionized video production, influencing all phases of the process, from shooting to editing to distribution to marketing.

Chapter 4, "Light and Lenses," explains how light interacts with lenses and how lenses and aperture settings produce their effects. Because it does not simply list a set of rules to follow about which lenses to use to achieve certain effects, you will better understand what lenses to use in *any* production situation.

One of the book's strongest features is its treatment of the aesthetic aspects of video production. For example, Chapter 5, "Lighting Equipment and Design," presents a unified rationale for lighting design beginning with a philosophy of *naturalism.* From this starting point, the chapter presents a reasoned approach to lighting in *any* production situation.

Similarly, Chapter 6, "Using the Camera," offers an aesthetic understanding of how cameras and camera mounts may be positioned for different programs. The chapter considers elements of both static and motion visuals and how images and image treatment shape meaning for audiences.

Chapter 7, "Understanding Sound and Microphones," and Chapter 8, "Audio Processing and Aesthetics," explain the physical and aesthetic nature of sound and the proper use of microphones and other sound sources to shape program content effectively for audiences.

Chapter 9, "Graphic and Set Design," addresses a fast-changing production area. While covering some of the latest approaches, including discussion of the more cutting-edge topic of computer-generated virtual sets, it again emphasizes relevant underlying principles referring to both audiences and enduring qualities of the medium. This emphasis affords you the best means of coping with rapid change.

For example, at this writing, the conversion to high-definition television (HDTV, or HD) in American homes has begun. HDTV features, among other things, a wider 16:9 *aspect ratio* in place of the still dominant 4:3 screen standard. However, regardless of which format is viewed at any given moment, it is essential for producer-directors to understand how graphic content on any television system affects audience members in broader terms than just aspect ratio differences, including brightness and contrast, scanning area and frame rate, color compatibility, pace of presentation, and so on. All these factors influence how the audience interprets what is presented; emphasizing the relationship of such factors to the audience is one of the book's strong points.

Chapter 10, "Video Processing," and Chapter 11, "Field Production," simplify and organize two major areas of rapid change in the production field. Chapter 10 builds a video switcher from the ground up, starting with the simplest transitions among video sources and advancing logically to the more complex. Then it describes how digital processing has revolutionized the way video signals are handled. The changes brought by the digital platform have market and policy implications that extend beyond the technical aspects of television. Then, Chapter 11 introduces the practical concepts of *reach, range,* and *interactivity* to explain how electronic news gathering (ENG), electronic field production (EFP), and large-scale remotes are currently accomplished.

Chapter 12, "Editing: Aesthetics and Techniques," presents both editing theory and method. First, using a fictional sitcom treatment as a starting point, the chapter applies editing concepts to an actual example, thus making theory concrete. Then it discusses the technical side of editing, including the differences between analog and digital, linear versus nonlinear, and on-line versus off-line editing. This approach makes the chapter a current and comprehensive editing primer.

The first half of Chapter 13, "Writing and Script Formats," covers the basic principles of television writing, emphasizing how characteristics of both medium and market affect the writer's task; it also describes the relationship of pictures to words, as well as the value of having a strong sense of the audience. The second half presents clear examples of several script formats, each appropriate to a different production approach. Few comprehensive production texts cover basic writing principles for television in this much depth; some neglect the topic entirely.

Chapter 14, "Producing and Directing," focuses on two different jobs. First, to simplify your understanding of what television producers do, the roles and responsibilities of the producer are examined, stressing five key factors: *space, time, material, money,* and *personnel.* Then the chapter focuses on the director's job, emphasizing how good directors make critical decisions, often with little time to spare. The chapter presents directing techniques to make your directing clear and effective.

Finally, Chapter 15, "Performing," teaches you how to put your best foot (and face) forward as a television talent, describing how technical, social, and aesthetic aspects of television influence how you look and sound, and how to prepare your best possible performance. In addition, the chapter presents a clear rationale for selecting your wardrobe and using makeup.

Several other features of the book deserve attention. First, this is one of the few if not the only comprehensive production text that features an Industry Voices section, interviews with industry professionals, freelancers, and network veterans, giving their views on the state of the art, the latest trends, and where things may be headed in the future. All were eager to talk about the impact of the transition from analog to digital platforms; many have over 30 years of industry experience. The Voices include a major network chief operations officer, a freelance writer-producer-director, a network station assistant chief engineer and director of planning, a CEO of a video and big-budget film production facility, a video and film producer-director in charge of a digital video-editing lab, and a producer for field coverage in a major market news operation. In addition to sharing their insights, they tell what they look for in an intern or employee. For any student who wants to work in today's field of electronic media or broadcasting, the Industry Voices section is a treasure trove of invaluable advice from the experts.

Each chapter also contains a Professional Pointers section of boxed material, clarifying, where necessary, some of the finer points of technical information, and a list of key terms practitioners expect you to master to be able to work alongside them in the industry. *The Art of Video Production* covers all aspects of television production in both studio and field in the digital age, offering a brief, clear, up-to-date approach to the craft.

Len Shyles
Villanova, PA

PREFACE

Why a new book on video production? Changes in the production field demand a fresh look at the process as the television industry adapts to the greatest transformation in its history: the transition from analog to digital platforms.

Television has accommodated great change before, including the conversion from black-and-white to color during the 1960s and the addition of satellite and cable to augment regular broadcast programming and distribution services. But the current transformation to digital is the most deeply altering.

The adoption of digital platforms has changed not only television technology but also production methods and markets, altering the way television programs are produced, edited, and distributed. It has fundamentally transformed the nature and function of the television industry and the movie business while increasing public access to the means of creating and sharing television content, profoundly changing the relationship of content providers and audiences forever.

From a purely physical perspective, the chief catalyst of the transformation has been the marrying together of three once disparate technologies: broadcasting, telecommunications, and digital computers. The interconnection of these infrastructures enables users with access to a camera, a computer, and the Internet to create, edit, store, transmit, retrieve, and distribute television programs and video content to millions of audience members with unprecedented ease; it is no longer necessary for producers to go to a television station to shoot, edit, and distribute television programs; in short, television production has become more decentralized and democratized.

The purpose of this book is to present modern television production methods in the digital age. It provides you with a brief, clear, conceptual view of all phases of video production in both studio and field.

The Art of Video Production differs from other production texts in two important ways. First, rather than emphasizing the latest products, it explains the underlying principles that govern their operation. Presenting how systems work and their technical characteristics, and not just the procedures for operating a particular piece of equipment, is a central focus of the book. Understanding the enduring principles by which broadcasting, telecommunication, and computer systems work insulates you from feeling that your knowledge is doomed to extinction with the introduction each year of each new equipment model.

Second, the book presents a more in-depth treatment than other production texts of audience analysis principles in production planning, stressing the value of understanding a program's topic, content, and purpose, as well as the relationship of audience analysis to your program goals. Communication concepts from both ancient and modern traditions are therefore presented to clarify how the production process may be simplified and made more manageable when informed by such principles.

To bring greater depth and perspective to these subjects, in addition to chapters on all phases of production, the book also features interviews with industry professionals. These experts make it clear that while gaining mastery of the physical aspects of the production process is essential for making successful television programs, such mastery alone is not enough; rather, it is also critical to understand the underlying relevant principles of human nature for producing quality programs that people will want to watch. In short, to be a successful producer-director, you must know how to use the physical tools of the trade, *and* you must know your audience. *The Art of Video Production* explores these principles in greater depth than other production books.

This book follows the philosophy that if you give a person a fish, you feed that person for a day, but if you *teach* a person to fish, you feed that person for a lifetime. Put more simply, a guiding principle of this book is that *there is nothing quite as practical as a good theory,* and in today's rapidly changing world, understanding is the best tool for adapting to change.

ACKNOWLEDGMENTS

I thank Villanova University for providing the atmosphere necessary for completing this project. I especially thank Ian Bush and Elvira Illiano for their editorial support during the writing of this book, Morgan Besson of the Physics Department for his review of the chapter on light and lenses (any mistakes are mine), Scott Brady and Chris Foster for the equipment demonstration photos, and Logan Thompson and Rebecca Shyles for the makeup shots.

I thank Louis Shore, Vice President for Labor Relations, Paramount Pictures, for providing interview access to personnel at CBS. Thanks also to Barry Zegel, Glen Roe, and Marc Hurd of CBS Television City in Hollywood, as well as Mark Meany of ABC Television in New York, for their help in acquiring equipment photos. I also thank Jay Dorfman of Medialand Productions in New York; Jay Fine of Steiner Studios in Brooklyn, New York; Kurt Hanson of ABC Television in New York; Bob Ross of CBS Television Network in New York; Marc Wiener of CBS-TV New York; and Paul Wilson of the Villanova University Media Lab for the interviews.

At Apple Corporation, I thank Scott Morris and Don Henderson for their support in acquiring the most up-to-date hardware, software, and screen shots and for sharing their editing expertise.

I also thank Harry Havnoonian and all the guys at Cycle Sport in Media, PA (Dennis, Drayton, and Ed), for providing access to their work as subject matter for the digital production and editing portions of the book. Thanks also to artist Don Everhart for providing the sculpture used to show how different lighting arrangements can change facial expression.

I gratefully acknowledge the comments and suggestions from the following reviewers: Chey Acuna, California State University, Los Angeles; Glenda R. Balas, University of New Mexico; Barbara Burke, University of Minnesota, Morris; Gerald M. Gibson, Elon University; Gary W. Larson, University of Nevada, Las Vegas; Nikos Metallinos, Concordia University; Rick Ricioppo, Illinois State University; and Gerald Zahavi, University at Albany, State University of New York.

At SAGE Publications, I thank Margaret Seawell for her trust, expertise, and friendship; as a professional, she continues to be a writer's dream that cares most about helping authors contribute to both teaching and education. I also thank Todd Armstrong, who stepped in with professionalism and integrity to complete the project. Thanks also to Sarah Quesenberry, Deya Saoud, Astrid Virding, and Gillian Dickens for their editorial skill, professionalism, and, above all, their good humor.

Finally, thanks to Janice Hillman, my wife, best friend, and artist, for helping to develop early sketches for many of the images that appear and my son, Daniel, for being one of my greatest inspirations sheerly through the example of his own sterling accomplishments. All of these people have made this writing experience a rewarding, often pleasurable journey.

PART 1

COMMUNICATING WITH VIDEO

Chapter 1

THE VIDEO PRODUCTION PROCESS

Why do you watch television and video? Depending on your needs and wants, television can tell you what's new, whether to take an umbrella when you go out, or where to get the best deal on a car. It can entertain you with old movies, music videos, or live drama. It tries to persuade you to buy products and even elect political candidates. You can learn to cook and find travel programs to spur interest in distant places; you can take college classes and learn about microscopic animals or distant galaxies. Moon landings and the fog of war have been televised, as well as concerts to raise money for people starving in underdeveloped countries.

Television and video enable you to see things in the comfort of your living room or on the road that would otherwise cost a lot of time, money, and effort to witness firsthand. For example, with multiple cameras, telephoto lenses, and instant replays, you can see global sporting events in greater detail than you could if you were there in person. With DVDs, video recorders, and now i-Pods, moreover, you can watch them time and time again whenever you choose.

Nowadays, you also *do* things through television. Home shopping networks have long offered you the chance to buy products after seeing them demonstrated on television; now, with an Internet connection and a computer, you can watch streaming videos and use your credit card to buy products without ever making eye contact with a traditional television screen. You can order pay-per-view programs, see and chat with friends via Webcams and instant messaging (I-M), or conduct business transactions via closed-circuit video to communicate exclusively with clients and staff. Finally, in the 2000s, it has become easier than ever to *make* television programs. Due to dramatic price reductions and therefore greater accessibility to high-quality recording and editing equipment, it is now possible for people who once thought of themselves merely as audience members to become videographers themselves.

It is no wonder, then, that more people are becoming interested in video production. But whether you want to work in the complex production environment of

Photo 1.1   This bank of monitors presents potentially dozens of video images to the director in the control room of this network affiliate facility in New York.

a modern television studio or field facility or just want to shoot your own videos and learn to edit them independently on a digital workstation in your basement, learning how can be a challenge. Where does one begin? How can you master so much complicated equipment and make successful programs?

I remember my own impressions when I entered a television studio and control room for the first time. By contemporary standards, the technology I saw there was ancient, but I felt as if I had just discovered an incredibly advanced civilization. My attention was instantly focused not on people (my future crew members) but on the many strange, new machines. In addition to the television cameras on heavy tripods, there were banks of recording and editing machines, monitors, consoles, and complicated switching devices for manipulating sounds and images. Heavily insulated cables hung on walls in coils or were strung from lights on metal grids fastened to the studio ceiling. Still others were slung across the studio floor in what seemed a hazardous mess.

Like me, you may be initially dazzled by the elaborate machinery. At first blush, it may seem that learning television and video production is mainly concerned with mastering machines. In fact, however, learning about equipment is only a small part of learning video production.

On my first day in a studio, my attention eventually shifted from the various fascinating contraptions to the crew members. I was witnessing the up-tempo activity of a production in progress. Camera operators were following directions received through headsets; an assistant director fielded questions from a separate control room; the audio operator was routing sounds from microphones and other audio sources; various other people I couldn't identify were tremendously busy—and somehow the director was coordinating all this frenzy. I began to realize the director was orchestrating the actions of the crew in much the same way that a musical conductor might lead an orchestra.

Comparing a television director and crew to a musical conductor and orchestra is a useful way to begin understanding the production process. Just as symphony conductors communicate their goals to musicians through the special language of music during rehearsals, so the television director uses jargon unique to the craft of television production to get the desired performance from the crew. Just as musicians must understand musical notation and be able to perform with special technical skill on cue, so the television crew must understand the language of video production and execute the director's commands on cue. When everything is coordinated properly, the crew functions as a graceful and cohesive unit, like an orchestra performing a musical composition. The product: a smooth, polished, well-produced, "air-quality" video.

This success cannot occur without communication, collaboration, and understanding. Video is not just a technology-centered activity but also a cooperative social activity. While the making of a video surely requires technical knowledge and skill, it also demands great people skills. Just as a musical conductor cannot perform an orchestral composition single-handed but *must* rely on successful communication with a talented group of well-trained professionals, so a television director *must* successfully communicate with a crew to produce a television program. *Lone artists need not apply.*

We can push the analogy further. Just as conductors must first learn a musical score and then communicate their concept of how it should be played to the musicians, television directors must first get the program concept clear in their own minds, then communicate it successfully (no easy trick) to the crew and talent. Only then can the program be successfully produced. For this reason, for the director, *the crew is the first audience.* Hence, even prior to production, the director must find some means of clearly articulating the program concept to the crew.

To understand this process of communication and collaboration more clearly, let's examine the basic stages of television production and the different roles played by the crew members.

THE STAGES OF VIDEO PRODUCTION

Video production is commonly discussed in terms of three principal stages: *preproduction, production,* and *postproduction.*

Preproduction

The **preproduction** stage of video production is the planning and development phase. It involves considering everything that needs to be arranged before shooting begins. These concerns can include formulating a budget, a program concept, and an overall treatment for the program. Preproduction can also involve script writing, revision, and approval; acquisition of facilities, studio space, and materials; scheduling and holding production meetings; and selecting cast and crew. In addition, agreements, release forms, contracts, permits, legal issues, and union matters are dealt with at this stage. Contingency plans to handle last-minute changes are also addressed.

Important Questions to Answer in Preproduction

➤ Is this program a worthy project to expend time, money, and effort on?
➤ What is the program's purpose?
➤ Does the program have cultural or other value?
➤ Who will be the audience(s) for it?
➤ Can this project be done with available materials?
➤ What will the script be like?
➤ How long will it take to make?
➤ Do I have enough competent personnel to crew it?
➤ What talent and facilities will I need?
➤ What will I do if some components I am now counting on fall through?
➤ What flexibility do I have to deal with unforeseen problems?
➤ What audio and video sources must I have?
➤ What rights, agreements, permissions, and release forms must I clear to avoid lawsuits?
➤ How long will the program be when it is finished and where will it air?

Preproduction must not be taken lightly. It is in this phase that the program concept is first articulated and made clear. During this phase, the director has an inner dialogue and then meets with the crew to try to answer crucial questions. If those questions are not answered satisfactorily, a project may fail before it begins, never reaching the next stage, production.

Production

The **production** stage includes all of the activities designed to produce the actual program, including setup, rehearsals, and shooting. Rehearsals include run-throughs and coordinating the use of equipment. Sets are located or built. Graphics are prepared, as are props and costumes. Lights, if needed, are hung, aimed, and focused. Cameras and all other material items are gathered and used as needed to produce the actual show. The overall quality of the show is monitored at this stage, and necessary changes are made. Reshoots are done if needed. After the show is finished, the *strike* or *teardown* is done, meaning that all the equipment is put away and the production space is cleared. In single-camera format video, all the raw footage that has been shot is turned over for editing in postproduction.

In the production stage, the trick is to remain calm, flexible, efficient, and effective, even in the face of adversity. It helps to keep the program concept clearly in mind so that you can make last-minute changes if needed and still meet your goals. This involves not only careful thought and technical mastery but also coordinated group activity—a team effort.

Postproduction

The **postproduction** stage is devoted to evaluating and editing the program. Then the marketing, publicity, distribution, and exhibition of the finished product are undertaken. Any unpaid salaries and bills are paid, and personnel involved in the production are thanked, including cast, crew, and peripheral agents who helped make the production run smoothly. Often, too, a postmortem meeting is held to discuss problems that occurred and determine how the production process might be improved in the future.

WHO DOES WHAT?

Everyone has heard of directors and producers, but their precise responsibilities in video production are not always understood. Knowing some of the differences in the roles and responsibilities of these two jobs (and those of other crew members) is invaluable to the production process.

What, then, does each team member actually do during the three stages of video production? The following sections outline a number of the major roles.

Writer. During preproduction, the **writer** works with the producer and director to develop the script and format of the show. The writer writes, edits, and revises the script until it is approved. Then, during the production stage, the writer rewrites as needed. Even in postproduction, the writer may be needed to smooth out transitions and provide supplemental material.

Producer. In preproduction, the **producer** develops the program concept, outlines the budget, and selects the crew. The producer approves the script and the director's treatment of it and supervises and coordinates personnel, scheduling, and payroll. The producer also handles all contracts and other legal matters, including the necessary permits and releases. During the production phase, the producer supervises all production activities, monitors the rehearsals, and suggests needed changes. The producer also maintains the production schedule and keeps it within budget. In postproduction, the producer supervises and approves the editing, runs the marketing and publicity effort, and pays any remaining bills.

Director. In preproduction, the **director** is involved in all meetings of the creative team and has input into the program format, content, and treatment, including the script, lighting, sets, and audio. In consultation with the producer, the director also works out crew and talent assignments. During production, the director runs the rehearsals, works with crew and talent, and (as the title implies) directs the actual shooting of the program. Finally, in postproduction, the director works with the producer to supervise the editing.

Assistant Director. In preproduction, the **assistant director** (AD) helps the director plan and develop the program. Any help the director asks for, the AD provides. During production, the AD acts like a human clock, timing segments, and also previews and readies upcoming camera shots before they go to air. The AD also helps cue other crew members to deliver needed program elements, such as music. In postproduction, the AD helps with editing, timing, and keeping track of segments.

Technical Director. In preproduction, the **technical director** (TD) works with the producer and director to select technical facilities (often abbreviated *fax*). During production, the TD operates the video switcher, the machine that permits live transitions among different video sources. If the switcher is needed during postproduction editing, the TD operates it then as well. During all phases, the TD is responsible for the technical quality of the program.

Audio Technician. In the preproduction phase, the **audio technician,** along with the producer and director, plans the audio treatment. All audio sources are prepared; microphones are selected. During production, the audio technician deploys all the audio materials for the program. At this stage, the audio board that routes all audio signals (including microphones and other audio sources) is set up. During the shoot, the audio technician operates the audio console and executes the director's audio cues. In postproduction, the audio technician helps with the editing process. Additional audio sources such as music and narration may be added at this time.

Lighting Director. During preproduction, the **lighting director** (LD) consults with the entire creative team (including the producer, director, costume designer, makeup artist, and scenic designer) to develop the best lighting approach. Since set and costume colors affect and are affected by the lighting, it is crucial to plan the lighting design *holistically,* with input from all involved about how the set and talent should look. A light plot is then developed accordingly. During production, the LD hangs, aims, and focuses the lights. Adjustments are made. Light levels are balanced. Computer-controlled lights are programmed. Then, during shooting, the LD executes any lighting changes and operates the lighting equipment (i.e., dimmer board, computer, etc.) on cue.

Scenic Designer. Like the LD, the **scenic designer** (also known as the *set designer* or the *art director*) works with the creative team in preproduction to develop the sets and set dressings. Scale drawings and floor plans are prepared illustrating where all set pieces will go. During production, the scenic designer supervises set construction and makes changes as needed.

Graphic Artist. In preproduction, the **graphic artist** consults with the creative team about the graphics that will be used and then prepares them either electronically or mechanically. These graphics can include textual material, pictorial illustrations, and complex computer-generated graphic effects. During production, the graphic artist makes any necessary changes and operates the graphic equipment on cue from the director or the AD. In postproduction, the graphic artist supplies any additional materials that may be needed during editing.

Floor Manager. During the production stage, the **floor manager** coordinates activities in the studio, feeding cues from the director to the talent. The floor manager is the director's main connection to the talent and studio crew. The floor manager also supervises set and costume changes during production.

Camera Operator. During both rehearsal and shooting, the **camera operator** prepares and operates the camera, following the cues of the director received over a headset or earpiece.

Video Technicians. During the production phase, the **video technicians** help maintain picture and transmission quality, adjusting cameras to maintain technical and aesthetic picture quality. They may also help with special effects if needed.

Talent. As you are probably aware by now, the term **talent** in television and video refers to the performers and actors. This category includes reporters, newscasters, program hosts, guests, singers, comedians—in other words, all the people who appear on camera.

Part III of this book returns to the responsibilities of the writer, producer, director, and talent, examining each role in more detail. In Part II, as we delve into the technical aspects of video production—lighting, camera operation, audio, graphics, set design, video processing, and editing—the tasks of crew members will become clearer. First, though, Part I of the text is devoted to a crucial, over-arching concept that we cannot emphasize enough: the idea that video is, above all, a form of communication.

INDUSTRY VOICES

Bob Ross

On May 11, 2005, I interviewed Bob Ross, Senior Vice President of East Coast Operations at the CBS Broadcast Center in New York City. His job title includes the letters COE, for Chief of Operations and Engineering for the CBS television network. Ross supervises network production, including live TV at CBS, and program origination for both CBS and UPN networks. His office is also home base for CBS Sports, CBS News, and production facilities for some of CBS's sister companies, including BET, where six of their shows are produced, and KingWorld, which produces Inside Edition.

L: When did you take on this position, and how did you get into this line of work?

B: About 5 years ago. I was always kind of a techie-kid. I grew up in Somersworth, NH, and earned an associate's degree from what's now called Southern Maine Technical College. From 1974–1976, I worked installing broadcasting equipment, especially cameras and tape machines, for RCA, then a very big broadcast equipment manufacturer.

Then I went to work for Westinghouse Broadcasting in Boston, at the station we still own, WBZ, as a maintenance technician, repairing equipment. I became a supervisor there. Then I worked for our station in Baltimore as the Assistant Chief Engineer and became the Director of Broadcast Operations and Engineering, sometimes called the Chief Engineer for TV Stations. I took care of the transmitters and studios, purchasing and installing equipment and upgrading the station. I came up through the technical side, then learned the operations side, meaning scheduling people, getting programs on the air, and scheduling the news departments. Today a TV station needs at least one tech type and one ops type to get everything done. Eventually, the general manager from Baltimore was transferred to Philadelphia, and he took me along to help manage KYW, the Philadelphia station. I was there when the general manager, Jonathan Klein, was promoted to president of the TV stations group. I guess I'd done a good enough job for him along the way and I became the VP of Engineering for five TV stations.

L: So you're comfortable with the principles of electricity and the math?

B: (Laughs) Yes, though I don't use it much anymore. Today the calculating I do is more financial. In this job, my department has about 525 people, a pretty large operation, and I'm managing money and people, not technology.

L: Do you like the change?

B: Yeah, I like working with people, managing, and trying to get the most out of the staff.

L: What's your take on the industry's move to digital operations?

B: It's really having an effect. Most people associate HDTV with digital, but in fact HDTV started as an analog system. This February marks the 25th anniversary of the introduction of HD to the U.S. by CBS's Joe Flaherty at the SMPTE conference in San Francisco. Since then, it's evolved into a fully digital platform, which has simplified workflow. The conversion of TV operations to a digital domain became possible when computers became powerful enough to handle audio and video information as data files, and that has allowed sweeping changes in how we function. Take editing, for example. Almost all editing now is done nonlinearly. Originally, editing was done in a linear fashion. You had to put "A" down before you could put "B" down before you could put "C" down, etc., and if you had to make a change and stick something in the middle, you had to do just about everything all over again from scratch. With computer-based editing, audio and video content is digitized and loaded into a computer, and you edit your program in any order, making different versions of it without having to reedit the whole piece. So you can have an "A" version, a "B" version, a "C" version, all slightly different, but you don't have to re-create the work, so you can make multiple versions of a show faster than you could have done one in the past.

L: Why do you need multiple versions?

B: To try to get the best telling of a story, whether it's news or entertainment. It's all about telling a story, and depending on how and when it's shown, there are advantages to having different versions. You can take the first person who speaks, and the second person who speaks, and reverse their order to tell the story better. Further, digital editing allows much faster turnaround time, and if you are tight for time, and need to get something on the air right away, digital helps a lot. It's a profound change to be able to move our signals around in digital form.

L: What about the telecommunications aspect of digitalization?

B: You couldn't manage any of this if you didn't have connectivity, and that is a by-product of not just computers, but of the telecommunications network, including the Internet. The Internet features a set of standards that allows computer files to be transferred from place to place easily, either through cables or wirelessly. Before the digital transition, unless you used a satellite, video could only be moved from point A to point B and it couldn't go any other way. Now we can transmit video using routers over the Internet to multiple locations, and this is because video can now be packaged as a file, just like a word processing file or an Excel spreadsheet. By contrast, live TV still goes through traditional TV wires and is still switched by a traditional switcher. So while we see two industries converging, with the advent of editing systems based on general-purpose computers, and telecommunications networks for moving data files around, you still have the traditional job functions; there is still a technical director, a director, and on-air talent, and what you see on the air is the result of their creativity. Video sources still include live video, where a person stands in front of a camera telling you what's going on; a reporter or talent may be in a remote truck anywhere in the world, and he or she may go to a packaged piece of video content, and then you may see what was a computer file, now played through a traditional TV switcher to get it on the air. So these industries have converged, but they have not completely merged. I've told a lot of people that in the last year. People say to me that the convergence of telecom and information technology (IT) is going to take over TV, but I disagree. The equipment used for putting TV on the air today is definitely computer-based, but traditional TV engineering and technologies and creativity have not gone away. Computers have not supplanted the traditional TV station. As the Internet gets faster, you'll be able to do more interesting things, but what you get with a traditional TV model is the creativity of the production staff, and that's not going to disappear.

L: Whose jobs have changed the most because of the move toward digital?

B: Two jobs: the traditional maintenance person and the editor. Since so much is now computer-based, today we no longer do board-level repairs, replacing individual circuits. We identify the bad board and swap it out. But the technique of figuring out which one's bad really hasn't changed even though the tools are different. As for the editing, as I said, nowadays, it's almost always nonlinear. I don't know of anyone building a linear editing suite anymore with a couple of physical tape machines and tape.

L: What does that do to the workflow and the product?

B: In addition to speeding things up, it permits repurposing of programs for different applications that were unavailable or didn't exist before. For example, take a story that breaks on the 6:00 news, say a major fire. We send a truck out and get live shots. The material can be transmitted for immediate live broadcast, or it can be taped and edited either in the truck or at the studio. Now we have a fire story for the 11:00 news. The fire may be out, but there's the story of the investigation. So we can use some of the material from the investigation coverage, with bits and pieces from the earlier story, repurposed for the 11:00 news, with fresh information. We can reedit the stuff for the next news cycle. Some stations will repurpose an entire broadcast, dropping in updated stories. Without powerful desktop computers and high storage capacity, we couldn't do that. Now with video streaming on the Internet, we can repurpose program content that originally aired on regular television for Webcasts. Almost all TV stations now have a Web presence, and many stream some or all of their newscasts, depending on how progressive they are. That's a newer form of repurposing.

L: How do issues of channel capacity influence Internet television (also called Internet protocol television, or IPTV)?

B: At CBS, we have a chief technical officer (CTO) who manages our IT network, and he deals with capacity issues. One part of his job is to shape how CBS.com is run. Some content gets a lot of hits. For example, we stream a customized version of *Survivor* just for the Internet a day after the regular broadcast. When the volume of hits surpasses a certain limit, it challenges the capacity of the system. In general, as the Internet gets faster, and broadband is delivered to more homes, we want the ability to do more live streaming video. But today, it suffers from freezes, breakups, and jitter; the quality of the content is technically degraded. But as we move toward more broadband delivery, we'll get better picture quality and reliability. At the same time, however, the industry is moving toward HD, which means even more bandwidth is needed to keep up—HDTV takes a phenomenal amount of bandwidth. Over the air, we're upping the picture quality by a lot, while the Internet guys are still in the world of VHS.

L: I use the acronym STEP to refer to four aspects of media industries currently impacted by the transition from analog to digital platforms: they are the Social, Technical, Economic, and Political dimensions. What do you think the move to digital has done to those aspects of your business?

B: Well, we've been talking about the technical side, but it's had a major impact on how we produce too. It's not yet had that great an effect on distribution, even though you can now get TV on your computer, but that's still a small, shaky, single-person viewing experience versus family or group viewing. The move toward individual and even mobile viewing (now that we have the video i-Pod) is absolutely a social impact. There are a number of people—and I've heard speeches and I don't always agree—who say that with a television equipped with digital interactive capability, you're going to be able to pop up different things on that screen related to the program for e-commerce purposes. For example, my wife and I might be watching, and she'll see a dress on a program host or sitcom talent, and she'll say, "Oh, I like that dress." Well, imagine being able to move a cursor over it and click, and find out who made it, how much it costs, and where you can order it. Well, that would mean taking a shared viewing experience and turning it into a personal shopping spree. The people that I tend to agree with say in the future—and that's not far down the road, either—you're going to have a large-screen TV set with HD, and you're going to have a computer nearby so that the shared experience can continue to happen, but you can drop off-line if you want to do that research on your computer right then or later, but not on the same screen. I think that's going to be a huge social change. I can see the wireless notebook with a stylus with Internet access to related material that, if you want to, you can go off on your own little experience, but still leave the main screen unchanged. There are people dabbling in that from a programming standpoint. So that's where you have a large network like CBS delivering millions of eyeballs, but with the flexibility to shift to the Internet experience to get more information. That's a social or marketing change we can look for soon. As for the political aspect, as I see computers, TV, newspapers, all going digital, the laws and politics around telecom will have to catch up to technology. The technology is out in front, but the political and regulatory environments are years behind, trying to figure it out.

L: How do you see the effect of digital on the film business?

B: Large-screen theatrical presentations may look the same way they do today, but in an all-electronic form. One reason for that is to eliminate the cost of having to distribute thousands of analog celluloid prints to show a film. There is a lot of money invested in traditional exhibition methods, but with the advent of technologies that can permit large-screen projection with a 70-foot diagonal image that is better than full HD as we know it, and can also be live, that will eliminate the traditional costs. You won't even need DVDs for a theater print, and you will even have mass distribution of live events all delivered from remote locations electronically. Of course, movies can also be delivered via satellite to a server and then played whenever. So the whole infrastructure of the traditional film industry, moving reels of film around—you can count the days. All these things will be electronic. Mark Cuban, owner of the Dallas Mavericks, has some theaters, and he just did a deal with Sony to put in 100-some high-quality video projectors. He's moving a theater chain to the digital world. Today, most theatrical movies are still shot on film. But in television, while half of it may look like film, it's actually electronic, using an electronic camera going to a tape machine and/or a general-purpose computer, edited on-line. About half the episodic TV today—entertainment-scripted programming—even though it looks like film when viewed on your TV screen, is actually 24-p-electronic. So as I see it, digital formats will gradually take over, because the workflow is simpler, and you can review scenes immediately. There have been some progressive people in the film business already making the change to all-digital production. The last two Star Wars movies were entirely produced on electronic 24-p platforms, with no film at all. Movies like Star Wars are good candidates for such treatment because there are so many visual effects now that are only doable on a computer. For animated features like The Incredibles and Finding Nemo, there were no cameras.

L: How have you felt about the changes you have experienced in this business?

B: For me personally, I can't think of a better time to have gotten into TV than right now. To be here for the transition to HD is—boy, am I lucky! It's very exciting. All the digital conversions, the HDTV, and what we're able to do now with picture quality is very exciting. And to have had a part in making that happen has been great.

❖───────────────────────────────

KEY TERMS

preproduction	6	audio technician	8
production	6	lighting director	8
postproduction	7	scenic designer	9
writer	7	graphic artist	9
producer	7	floor manager	9
director	8	camera operator	9
assistant director	8	video technicians	9
technical director	8	talent	9

QUESTIONS FOR REVIEW

Why is video production so dependent not just on technical expertise, but also on communication and collaboration?

What are the key tasks accomplished in each of the three stages of video production (preproduction, production, and postproduction)?

Name the major personnel involved in video production and describe each person's main responsibilities.

Chapter 2

VIDEO AS COMMUNICATION

Think of the various means that television and video offer for communicating your ideas. Television can broadcast events to virtually every household in the country, and much of the rest of the world, live as they happen. Television can also present animation, music, and sound effects. Like theater, television can show actors performing in costume and makeup, with lighting that can be altered in an instant to reflect changing moods. Like film, video can offer audiovisual effects that cannot easily be presented on stage, including flashbacks featuring instant changes of sets, talent, and costume. Video streaming on the Internet and watching videos on portable wireless devices have dramatically expanded television offerings to nontraditional platforms and places. In short, the communication options available to the television director are formidable. By combining live transmission with audiovisual capability, television has become both powerful and pervasive. It is a potent communication medium not only because of what it can do but because of how it can do it.

The potential of television and video to reach and influence audiences should challenge you to learn as much as possible about communication principles that can enhance your programs' effectiveness. This chapter describes some of those principles. The topics covered include the following:

The program concept
- Identifying the concept
- Justifying the concept

Audiences, media, and messages
- Our changing media
- Tailoring programs to audiences
- Practical advice from the past
- Modern communication research

- Information theory
- Linear and nonlinear communication models
- Message effects
- The universal audience

THE PROGRAM CONCEPT

Identifying the Concept

Before shooting any video program, you need a clear idea of the program's topic, purpose, and intended audience. You should also try to recognize the context in which your program will be shown, as well as the genre or program category (if any) into which it fits.

Context. A moment's reflection suggests that all television programs, and all messages in general, are made by some source for some audience for some purpose. If we accept this premise, it is plain that program content is by nature situated in some social or cultural *context*—it is never free-floating outside the matrix of human activity. Of course, while programs are directed toward a *target* or intended audience, they may also be seen by unintended viewers.

Understanding the social and cultural context of a television program helps you decide how it should be produced. Part of understanding a program's context includes knowing the source's reasons for making it and the audience's motivations for watching it. Knowing these things makes your program objectives clearer and simplifies all your production decisions. By grounding your program in the needs, values, and expectations of the audience, you can make your program more engaging, perhaps even compelling, and therefore more successful.

In addition, knowing about other programs that deal with similar subject matter, as well as being familiar with how other programs may have treated similar topics, is a distinct advantage. Of course, it is possible to develop a program that defies comparison to anything that has been produced before. However, producing a new program similar to past successes can increase your audience's ability to identify and accept the new material.

Topic. A program's *topic* can influence whether the program treatment should be serious or humorous, passionate or cold, light or heavy. Topics can deal with politics, history, science, literature, news, current affairs, sports and fitness, humor, cuisine, and innumerable other aspects of the human condition. The content or subject matter that can be featured in a television program is virtually endless. In most cases, however, it is possible to compare your proposed program to others that have been successful in the past to get clues about its production.

Purpose. Identifying the program's *purpose* involves specifying the goals and effects the producer wishes to achieve with an audience. For example, you can produce a program about AIDS, the purpose of which might be to inform or educate viewers about how to avoid contracting HIV. A different purpose might be to persuade viewers that more funding is needed for research, with the objective of getting the viewer to write a check for a worthy cause. For other programs, entirely different purposes may be considered, including sheer entertainment. Depending on the objective(s) of the program you are producing, your decisions regarding content and treatment can vary.

Genre. *Genre* means the basic type or category of the program: fiction or nonfiction, comedy or tragedy, period or contemporary, and so on. Many categorizations can be applied on increasingly detailed levels. For example, within the comedy genre, there may be slapstick, screwball, and highbrow, to name but a few. In the drama category, we can find westerns, cop and crime shows, and medical shows, among others. Knowing where your proposed program fits within the various program types or genres can help in planning your production.

Audience. Audience-related concerns can include *demographic* characteristics of the intended or target audience (such as age, gender, educational level, occupation, race, religion, geographical location), the audience's interests and hobbies (sometimes referred to as *lifestyle* variables), or cognitive and emotional qualities (sometimes called *psychographic* variables). The audience's experience, motivation, and abilities may also be considered. For example, if the intended audience is exclusively children ages 6 to 12, the script would probably be pitched at a different level than one intended for an adult audience.

Questions to Use in Analyzing Your Potential Audience

➤ Whom do you wish to reach?
➤ Can you describe the audience in terms of demographic, lifestyle, and psychographic variables?
➤ What benefits will the program offer the audience?
➤ Is anything known about what audience members do with their time?
➤ What have they seen before? What did they think of it?
➤ Can the audience attend to, accept, and understand the program, as well as enjoy and be moved by it, profiting from it in some way?
➤ At what level should the script be written so as not to lose the audience?
➤ What references and associations will advance the program's main idea?
➤ How hard can you work the audience members without losing them?
➤ What message(s) will the audience reject?

Justifying the Concept

The time, effort, and cost used to produce a quality television program can be great, even for short programs. If you are recording more than a family birthday party for Aunt Betty, additional costs for services of talent and crew, as well as rental and maintenance of facilities, can be high. Therefore, winning support for your project may depend on developing a proposal that justifies the concept in the eyes of a funding agent. *The proposal is a persuasive document, designed to convince a funding agent to finance your idea.*

In many cases, agents fund the video project judged most favorable after reviewing competing proposals. In the broadcasting industry, for example, relatively few pilots for network series are produced after considering many ideas that compete for resources from programming executives. In the corporate world, decisions to produce a program to motivate the sales force, or to launch new acts or products into the marketplace, are made after carefully considering needs and weighing alternatives. In educational settings, teaching modules may be produced based on the latest knowledge and information about a special topic.

How, then, can you write proposals that justify your program concept? While this question is dealt with in detail in Chapter 13, one point should be made here. Your proposal should demonstrate a significant need for the program, both from the audience's perspective and from that of the funding agent. In commercial television, desirable programs are those believed capable of attracting audiences for advertisers. In the corporate world, approved projects are those believed to offer beneficial results in generating profits, solving a problem, or satisfying a need for the company. In every case, success turns on convincing funding agents that the program will attract the desired audience.

Checklist for Developing Your Program Concept

The more you know about the funding agent, audience, topic, context, genre, and purpose of the program you are producing, the better you can determine how to assemble all production elements. There is overlap among all these factors, but each one should be considered separately. As you develop your program concept, make sure you have a clear idea of each of the following elements:

_____ *what* the message is

_____ *who* is making the program and *why*

_____ *how* the message is to be delivered

_____ *for whom* the program is being made

_____ *for what* purpose

Budget, of course, is always important to those paying the freight, and later chapters of this book will refer often to budget concerns. But it is important not to let budget issues diminish your creativity. In the beginning of the brainstorming process, imagine what the show would look and sound like if you were to have unlimited budget, facilities, personnel, and time—that is, eliminate the practical side of the equation and consider the project exclusively from a communication perspective. Later, you will have plenty of time to temper your plan in terms of practical limitations and bring yourself back to earth. *In short, in the beginning, budget issues should be secondary to concept considerations.*

AUDIENCES, MEDIA, AND MESSAGES

Our Changing Media

Audience analysis in the television field becomes more complicated as media choices and functions increase. It was once reasonable to describe the television audience as a large, undifferentiated mass of passive viewers. But just as the magazine industry, which once featured general-interest magazines such as *Saturday Evening Post* and *Life,* has evolved into a plethora of special-interest periodicals serving more highly segmented audiences, so too has the video marketplace changed; with more specialized audiences, programs are often made to serve more particular needs.

The trend toward producing more specialized programs continues right before our eyes. Today's video environment commonly offers dozens and perhaps hundreds of broadcast and cable channels featuring highly specialized content. Business, education, and government all use videos aimed at specific groups of people. Store outlets at malls and Internet suppliers such as Amazon.com, which have DVDs available for rent or purchase, offer thousands of more selections. In addition, any person with access to a computer and an Internet connection can watch both fiction and nonfiction streaming videos on innumerable Web sites.

The trend toward producing more varied programs for smaller audiences may also be helped by dramatic price reductions for high-performance video gear, making it more affordable to users who want to produce their own programs. In addition, continued miniaturization of equipment (allowing greater portability) and increases in equipment performance characteristics extend video's reach to previously inaccessible locations, adding to the feasibility of producing more specialized programs.

Finally, portable video for the solitary viewer has itself entered the mix through the advent of individual wireless video (i.e., camera-phones and video i-Pods), some featuring full-color displays, high-quality stereo sound, access to reruns, and hours of battery life. Such developments contribute to the trend toward greater fractionalization of the audience and further underscore the need to know your audience to make television programs and videos that people will value and watch.

Interactivity. In addition to audience fragmentation, **interactivity** is now common with both users and with the medium itself; viewers routinely send messages back to programmers during broadcasts. For years, thanks to the telephone, call-in shows have offered interaction with hosts and guests. Now, thanks to on-line computers linked to the phone system, home shopping networks gauge product success during the show and make programming decisions accordingly. Viewers can phone in pay-per-view orders or use on-line Web sites for e-commerce, distance-learning classes, socializing with each other, and even seeking romance. Clearly, the trend toward greater interactivity among users supplements traditional functions of video to entertain, inform, educate, and persuade. Finally, viewers-turned-program-makers interact with the medium itself, as never before, shooting and editing their own videos and then uploading them to the Web.

Convergence. The **convergence** of communication media has made interactivity possible. The transition from analog to digital platforms has made it possible to integrate three once-disparate communication technologies (telephone, computer systems, and broadcasting, including satellite, and cable television services). The convergence of these infrastructures enables program sharing and other functions, leading to the creation and distribution of content and services not possible a decade ago. In addition to increasing interactivity, convergence also creates opportunities for program makers to produce multiple versions of programs to be *repurposed* for exhibition on different media platforms in diverse venues.

The Key to New Technology: User Appeal. To succeed, new media technologies that offer programming alternatives must appeal to potential users. That is, they must come to be perceived as offering significant advantages over what they replace. An engineer's opinion of a new device is secondary, perhaps even irrelevant, to whether it will succeed in the marketplace. Doubters of this view need only recall past media inventions that have offered improved programming options but have failed as consumer products: eight-track tape, quadraphonic stereo, and video laser disks, for example. Therefore, the most powerful computer or any other program package or communication device is not the one with the greatest fidelity, storage capacity, or speed of delivery *but the one that people use.*

Tailoring Programs to Audiences

Despite technological changes brought by the digital revolution (such as increased channel capacity and greater interactivity), we human beings are still essentially the same two-eyed, one-brained communicators we have been for thousands of years. Even in a media-rich environment, the toughest part of communication is still the last few inches from the eyes and ears to the brain. Greater programming potential by itself is therefore no guarantee of programming success; television content must first be seen by an audience to be successful. With greater choices in the media environment, the need increases for programmers to know more, not less, about audiences to compete effectively.

Analyzing the linkage between audience characteristics and program appeals has been an ongoing enterprise in broadcast research for decades. Program makers, especially in commercial television, are acutely interested and relentlessly involved in trying to determine what attracts audiences, in the hopes of finding out how to maximize ratings and therefore revenue. One reason for television *spin-offs* (and film *sequels*) is that they give producers the chance to exploit formulas that have been successful in the past. When a program is a hit, often the maxim followed is, do not mess with success, but make more like it.

In addition to wanting to attract large audiences, programmers and sponsors frequently also want to attract certain *types* of audiences according to desired demographic, lifestyle, and psychographic categories. For example, the advertiser of an acne cream will want to know which types of program content attract teenagers. Similarly, the manufacturer of a denture adhesive will look for program characteristics that appeal more to senior citizens.

Broadcast audience research is a full-time and lucrative activity for such companies as Arbitron and Nielsen, Inc., which provide research data to help advertisers and programmers measure audience preferences, as well as learn the *uses* and *gratifications* specific programs offer viewers. Knowing what motivates people to watch, recall, and act on the programs they see is also important to corporations, public interest groups, political parties, public relations agencies, market research firms, and other businesses that depend on message effectiveness for their success.

Practical Advice From the Past

Arbitron and Nielsen are not the first to research audience preferences. For centuries, specialists in rhetoric and communication have analyzed the best ways of reaching audiences. In fact, many ancient principles and techniques of persuasion are still relevant to modern forms of communication.

Communication experts for centuries have suggested that the best communicators are those who know history and current affairs as well as the caprices of the human heart. They understand human emotion, memory, imagination, hope, fear, and human will. Furthermore, successful messages invariably appeal to the *rational, emotional,* and/or *ethical* dimensions of human nature. The following sections examine these three basic types of appeal.

Ethos, or Source Credibility. Ethical appeals are often the most powerful means of persuading an audience. Audience perception of **ethos** or *source credibility*—that is, the apparent ethical character or trustworthiness of a source—is strongly related to the audience's knowledge of a source's past experience and behavior. Depending on the level of expertise a source displays on a given topic, as well as the audience's knowledge of the source's past behavior and habits of character, a source may be judged by an audience to have either high or low credibility. In modern terms, ethos is also thought of as the degree of *charisma* a speaker is perceived to possess.

High levels of admiration and respect for speakers can help make their statements seem worthy of belief. This may explain why advertisers often cast doctors, or actors who have portrayed doctors, as spokespersons in commercials for headache remedies and other medicines. Since doctors can be reasonably trusted to know how to treat headaches, it is believed to be persuasive if the product endorsement appears to come from a medical expert. Frequently, the performer may wear a lab coat and appear in a set resembling a doctor's office.

To increase source credibility, people portrayed in high-stress jobs, including jackhammer operators and kindergarten teachers, may also be seen endorsing headache remedies, just as sports figures may be hired to promote muscle liniments and other pain relievers. The appeal to credibility in these cases lies not in the sources' credentials but in their experience. Beyond the selection of talent and the roles they are cast in, other production elements (props, makeup, script, etc.) are often fashioned to reflect the advertiser's desire to use high-ethos appeals to sell products.

Logos, or Reasoning Ability. Knowledge of the audience's reasoning ability or **logos** (pronounced with an "s" rather than a "z" sound at the end) is also critical in fashioning messages. To engage the audience, television advertising often uses rational appeals featuring tightly structured arguments, sometimes with one premise left out. Presenting arguments with a key part missing invites viewers to fill in the blank or make a desired inference, encouraging them to aid and abet the source in the persuasion process.

A concrete example of such an appeal is seen in the insurance company commercial where the central character has just become aware of a new insurance plan offering more comprehensive coverage than her current one. She muses in a voice-over while seen looking over some insurance brochures, "People should have the best insurance coverage they can afford. This new plan is more comprehensive than my current plan, yet costs less than I'm paying now. . . ." These lines invite the audience to complete the argument with the idea, "It's a good idea to switch plans."

Structuring video messages to engage the audience's reasoning ability is a powerful means of encouraging active participation in the communication process. It increases audience involvement and, it is hoped, leads to subsequent buying behavior.

Pathos, or Emotional Appeal. Appeals to **pathos,** or the emotional nature of the audience, work by exciting the audience's passions, feelings, and sympathies. Though whipping up strong emotions can warp the audience's reasoning ability and judgment, such appeals may nevertheless aid in the persuasion process.

The emotional life of human beings includes feelings of love, hate, fear, confidence, shame, pity, benevolence, indignation, and envy, among others. Notice how this litany describes the frequently lurid subject matter on tabloid talk shows, which capitalize on emotionally charged topics to get audience attention.

Consider, too, the many commercials that rely on raw, sensuous audiovisual stimulation, including rhythmic cutting, quick camera movements, music, color, and arresting and provocative visuals. Often such stimuli are used with the goal of having a direct effect on our bodies, not our minds, arousing us to attention. The same techniques are regularly used to arouse audience attention in provocative music videos.

Age and Message Receptivity. Understanding human experience as a function of age provides further insight into message receptivity. We know that certain programs—*Sesame Street,* to use an obvious example—succeed more with younger audiences, while others attract older audiences. Thus, video programmers need a clear idea of the age-related characteristics of the potential audience.

Over two thousand years ago, Greek philosopher Aristotle discussed human life in terms of three ages, which we can roughly label youth, the prime of life, and old age. For Aristotle, youth, compared to other stages of life, is a time of strong desires, strong sexual urges, and a relative lack of self-control. The longings of youth, said Aristotle, are "keen but not deep." The young are passionate, quick to anger, and highly resentful if slighted. They love "honor" and victory more than money. They hold a strong belief in human goodness, and they are trusting and hopeful but easily deceived. They are high-minded, not yet humbled by life. They live lives of impulse, not calculation. Finally, they are fond of friends and tend to make mistakes on the side of intensity and excess. When they injure others, it is not through malice but through insolence.

Of course, no description of youth or any other age can be completely exhaustive, nor can it apply equally to every individual in the group. It is interesting, though, to consider whether Aristotle's ancient description of youth fits popular television characters such as Bart Simpson and others watched avidly by youth audiences. What other programs or characters might appeal more to youth audiences?

By contrast, according to Aristotle, the elderly often possess qualities of extreme moderation. They "think" but never "know." All is doubtful, nothing firm. The elderly are also cynical and tend to put the worst construction on everything. They are suspicious and mistrustful as a result of sad experience. Relative to other ages, the elderly have been humbled by life. They crave the mere necessities, are not generous, and tend to be cold and calculating, with less regard for honor than expediency. Finally, unlike youth, the elderly are less concerned with what people think of them and live mainly in memory, not anticipation. In light of this profile, is it understandable why programs for the elderly are very different from programs for a youth market?

In the so-called prime of life, intermediate between youth and old age, people tend to be both confident and cautious. They judge each case by the merits of the facts, says Aristotle, and they pursue both honor and expediency. They manage to balance self-control with valor. If this is an accurate characterization, does it help us know more about designing a program for, say, 40-year-olds?

Message Construction and Style. In addition to presenting insights about the nature of the audience, communication theorists have also advanced notions about style—in other words, *how* the material is presented. Traditionally, style considerations have involved language, diction, order, and arrangement. In television production, style includes all that but extends to the many visual aspects of the set, props, costumes, makeup, graphics, and even nonverbal sound effects.

Good style also means delivering a *lively* message with *clarity* and *appropriateness.* The liveliness aspect of style (or what contemporary analysts call *dynamism*) is especially relevant to television since one of television's greatest strengths is its ability to cover events such as sports and on-the-spot news live as they happen. The liveliness aspect of video also offers the chance to demonstrate complex processes and techniques in real time, as when infomercials demonstrate how to use the latest cooking utensil or exercise equipment.

Since television is preeminent in its ability to broadcast live coverage of real events to audiences, programmers should consider how they can imbue every appropriate element of a production with liveliness. This may mean deciding when to cut to an extreme close-up of the main character's grimacing face as he struggles to escape harm or how to sequence and edit a scene in a lively and engaging way so as to maximize audience involvement.

Also, since video programs incorporate a great many audiovisual elements into a unified whole, it is helpful to consider each element in terms of how it contributes to the overall style of the program. Even the choice of decorative elements should be tempered by the totality of what else you know about a particular program's content, purpose, and likely audience reaction and comprehension.

Modern Communication Research

Building on the insights of past centuries, modern communication research offers insights about the nature of audiences and messages. Theories dealing with message construction, meaning, information transmission, message impact, audience characteristics, and persuasion can help you produce more effective programs.

For example, most modern theorists agree that defining communication as simply the transmission of information is inadequate since a message sent may not always be the same as a message received. This is partly because people do not communicate messages directly to receivers but must translate them through the use of symbols or images. In other words, messages must be *encoded* before they can be transmitted, and sometimes the encoding process itself gets in the way of successful meaning transmission. The simple parlor game of post office, where one person whispers a message to another, who then whispers it to the next player, and so on—resulting in a garbled final product—illustrates this point clearly.

In the case of video, intended meanings may also be lost because messages are often sent to viewers who may never have met the sender. To overcome this limitation, producers often use devices such as redundancy and repetition to ensure that messages and their intended meanings are successfully received. Advertisers have learned the lessons of repetition in brand-name advertising well, often repeating their central theme over and over again, through an advertising campaign, or even within a single commercial. They use redundancy techniques when they both show *and* tell about some key aspect of a new product. Of course, advertisers' commitment to audience research, which includes, it is hoped, finding out as much as possible about their target audience before constructing their appeals allows them to maximize the fit of their messages to their audience.

The following sections offer some modern communication theories and models useful for crafting video programs.

Information Theory

Information as Reduction of Uncertainty. Information theorists have defined *information* as a measure of the degree of randomness in a situation. For example, if you are watching television, and it suddenly stops working, you may not know if the problem is with the receiver or the electrical outlet (or some other cause like an unpaid utility bill). To find out, you may disconnect it and plug a working lamp in to test the outlet. Or you may plug the TV set into a different socket to troubleshoot the problem. By conducting these tests, you are reducing uncertainty in the situation, thereby gaining information.

The utility of understanding information this way is that it can help you decide what elements to include in a production based on the level of familiarity your audience is likely to have for a given subject. For instance, if you are producing a cooking show, depending on the knowledge base of your audience, it may be unnecessary to explain what "beat three large eggs" means but quite necessary to explain what "fold in three egg whites" means. If you assess your audience correctly, you can avoid the dual problems of telling them what they already know, thus boring or, worse, insulting them, or of neglecting to tell them what they might not yet know, thus leaving them confused and frustrated. Of course, knowing about information theory is no guarantee that you will correctly determine how the program should proceed, but it can alert you to consider your audience from such perspectives, perhaps resulting in a better program.

Noise as an Unintended Signal Component. Information theorists define **noise** as any part of a signal that is unintended by the source and/or distracts the receiver from apprehending the intended meaning. Noise inhibits message reception by receivers. Noise impedes communication.

Noise can take many forms. Common examples include static on the radio or whispering in a crowded movie theater. Even dirt on the television screen can constitute noise, though the dirt is perfectly silent. Noise can also include a speaker's distracting hairdo or clothing. If a speaker's odd mannerisms distract the audience from the speech, they may be considered noise from the perspective of information theory.

Linear and Nonlinear Communication Models

A *model* is a descriptive, simplified representation of some phenomenon or process. For example, maps generally model some aspect of geography. A road map may picture the highway system in some part of the world, while a precipitation map may depict the annual rainfall in the same area. Depending on what the map is intended to do, it can model any number of different aspects of what it represents.

In the communication field, theorists use models to describe, explain, and test propositions about the way messages and meanings are transmitted among senders and receivers. Communication models usually include a *channel* component to account for how much information can be put through a communication system and still be delivered accurately.

Linear models of communication emphasize the one-way flow of information from a sender to a receiver. Early broadcast media systems, such as network television and local radio, were linear in nature because they sent messages from a single source to a great number of receivers. The components of the communication model used to represent network television included a sender or transmitter, a message, a channel, and a number of receivers.

However, electronic communication phenomena can no longer be adequately rendered with such a one-way flow model. For example, a letter to the editor, a call-in television show, and a cable touch-pad that permits viewers to communicate with a program host demand that the one-way flow model be expanded to accommodate a **feedback,** or a two-way component. Such a *nonlinear* or *transactional* model better captures the process of message exchange made possible by interactive media technologies, especially systems that permit near or actual real-time two-way communication among users.

The telegraph and the public switched telephone network (PSTN) are two such systems, both born in the 19th century. The relatively recent accommodation of the PSTN to handle data transfer among computers through the use of modems and DSLs has expanded that system's range of services beyond traditional voice traffic, allowing millions of distant users to share real-time audio and video information; broadband and cell phone development have further expanded such services to wireless domains. Programmers can benefit from considering both linear and nonlinear communication models.

Recognizing the interactive relationship of the programmer and the audience has never been more important. For example, if you already possess a great deal of information about how an audience is likely to respond to a particular program, it may be unnecessary to solicit feedback. However, if a program is relatively novel and unproved, or if certain major changes are contemplated for an ongoing production, it might be wise to collect audience feedback or pilot-test your new idea to determine where strengths and weaknesses lie so that improvements can be made in line with audience suggestions. Focus group research and virtual focus group research are among the methods of collecting audience feedback to avoid disaster. Transactional communication models (both virtual and real) recognize the give-and-take or play aspect of communication—you don't play *at* people; you play *with* them.

Message Effects

Communication theorists recognize, as mentioned, that messages sent are not always messages received and that meanings are in people, not in messages. This is so in part because people bring with them to the communication setting a welter of opinions, attitudes, values, beliefs, and life experiences that may uniquely color their interpretation of messages.

Selective Perception and Retention. One stable research finding is that people tend to positively assess and accept those parts of messages they perceive to be consistent with their values, beliefs, attitudes, and opinions, and they tend to negatively assess and reject those parts of messages viewed as inconsistent. *Selective perception* and *retention,* as these tendencies are called by cognitive psychologists, are well documented in political campaign settings, where research has shown the tendency for partisan voters to assess a candidate's campaign performance in line with his or her political ideology or party membership.

Behavioral Aspects of Message Effects. Message effects may also influence behavior and action, not just perceptions. The behavioral aspect is especially important in persuasive settings, where the desired objective is to move audience members to *do* something after being exposed to a message. Persuasive appeals that influence buying and voting behavior are particularly important for television programmers.

Modern study has applied scientific research methods to build on Aristotle's notions of ethos, logos, and pathos. Much of this work has focused on experiments to try to locate the origins of source credibility. Among the variables believed to influence source credibility are message context, source attractiveness, the audience's knowledge of the source's agenda, audience incentive and level of need for attending to a particular message, and the nature of the audience's existing belief system regarding the topic of discussion.

Consistency and Balance Theories of Persuasion. As mentioned, audience predispositions, including their attitudes, opinions, beliefs, values, and life experiences, may explain why some messages succeed at influencing audiences while others fail. A number of consistency and balance theories have been advanced to account for these outcomes. For example, *congruity theory* asserts that people naturally seek consistency in the world around them to make sense of things. When they encounter messages that square well with other things they have learned and accepted and that do not contradict their basic beliefs about the nature of things, they are more likely to accept such messages. Conversely, when messages are introduced that go against the lessons they have learned over time, such messages are perceived to be dissonant and confusing, and they tend to be ignored or rejected.

Similarly, *cognitive dissonance theory* asserts that people try to reduce uncertainty and tension in their interaction with the world either by making their behavior consistent with their beliefs or by making their beliefs consistent with their behavior. By achieving consistency and balance between their behavior and their belief systems, people increase their feeling of comfort. For example, a cigarette smoker may avoid messages that describe the hazards of smoking to avoid the tension between cognition and behavior that such messages might cause. Or a car buyer who has just spent $25,000 on a new car may not wish to attend to an advertisement for the same car priced at $20,000. When messages cause tension between the cognitive and behavioral aspects of a person's life, cognitive dissonance theory suggests that individuals will seek ways to avoid either the behavior or the messages that generate discomfort.

Consistency and balance theories suggest that when predispositions toward certain topics are strong, it is extremely difficult to change audience attitudes. This may be why it is probably fruitless in most cases to try to convince die-hard political party members to vote against their party candidates in political elections or to convince Ku Klux Klan members to support minority rights legislation. In such cases, it may be wise to try to determine which audience members are less committed to such deeply ingrained values and then direct your contrary persuasive appeals to them.

Long-Term Public Communication Campaigns. While changing an audience's deeply held values through the use of persuasive communication may be difficult, must we deny the possibility that an amazing conversion may happen from time to time? Is it not possible that a change of heart can occur even in an individual who holds extreme views on some topic or whose behavior has been deeply habituated over time? While genuine conversions may be rare, it is only reasonable that we allow for them at least in principle.

The types of persuasive campaigns that try to change deeply ingrained views among audiences tend to be those that take place over long periods of time and resemble comprehensive training and education programs. Such programs tend to use *internal change agents,* or highly respected spokespersons from the ranks of the target audience, to deliver campaign messages. Not only is the persuasive appeal applied over a long period of time, but it also has cognitive and behavioral elements.

Examples of such long-term public communication campaigns using television include campaigns to get teenagers to stay off drugs ("Just say no"), drivers to stay sober and use seat belts, campers to practice fire safety, volunteers to join the army, and heart patients to alter their eating habits to lower their cholesterol. On a broader scale, China continues a national campaign to get families to have only one child. This long-term effort includes rewards for families that meet the goals of the program and disincentives for those who do not.

For video programmers, the value of audience analysis, balance and consistency theories, and the lessons from long-term public communication campaigns lies in recognizing how messages can be structured to gain desired effects with an audience. Since television is concerned in large part with convincing audiences through the use of symbolic appeals to think, feel, and act in line with programmers' messages, it is in your interest as a videographer to understand as completely as possible the nature of the audience in planning your productions.

The Universal Audience

For practical reasons, audience measurement is always incomplete. First, the actual audience for a particular program is almost never completely known since a comprehensive study is normally not done to determine, for every viewer, who has actually watched the program and with what level of interest. Furthermore, when a program is crafted for a specific audience, actual viewership may differ from the target audience profile in significant ways. Among intended audience members, some may watch for a moment and then tune away, while others may either choose not to watch at all or may remain unaware of the program's existence.

However incomplete audience data are for a given program, some programs seem to have a more universal appeal than others, consistently attracting a wider audience across demographic, psychographic, and lifestyle categories, even across generations. One such program is the *I Love Lucy* television series of the 1950s. This program has garnered the praise of critics and the loyalty of huge, diverse and enthusiastic audiences since its debut, and it has continued to enjoy both critical acclaim and rerun success in syndication for more than half a century.

When we say that a program has "universal appeal," we seem to rely on a concept of a *universal audience.* Ironically, even in an age of increasingly fractionalized audiences for more specialized programming, the notion of the universal audience has value, in that it encourages us to consider those program qualities that have enduring ethical and/or aesthetic appeal.

In the current media environment, the idea of the universal audience seems to run counter to all we have said about audience differentiation and segmentation. Recall that most of our discussion of audiences has emphasized the *particularity* of audience characteristics and how message appeals should be adapted to specific audience characteristics to maximize effectiveness. We pointed out that today's rapid proliferation of program choices and newly emerging nontraditional platforms for program exhibition makes it more necessary than ever to target more highly segmented audiences. How useful can the notion of the universal audience be in such a highly fragmented field?

Of course, not all television programs need to appeal to a universal audience to be considered worthy. However, those that do may be capturing some enduring quality about culture or objectify some ultimate truth about human nature, and they may therefore deserve to be elevated to the status of art. When such projects gain broad, universal appeal, they usually do so by revealing some truths or foibles of human nature in their themes, in a beautiful, pleasing, unified way.

Many programs never achieve such status, yet they may nevertheless be worthwhile. Many serve practical goals: to entertain, to report news, to teach language or cooking, to sell bath soap, or to instruct people on how to improve their tennis game or first aid skills.

How should we evaluate such programs? It is important to remember that while practical programs may not be intended to reveal the nature of the human condition for all time, they may still be made poorly or well. Therefore, program makers should strive to produce them according to standards of excellence in terms of what these programs say and how they say it.

Here is the main point: In planning any program, it is essential to think through carefully what your program is intended to do and then decide how best to produce it so that it communicates its message clearly to its audience. Keep this point in mind as you read later chapters, which delve into the more technical aspects of how video conveys its messages.

KEY TERMS

interactivity	21	pathos	24
convergence	21	noise	27
ethos	23	feedback	28
logos	23		

QUESTIONS FOR REVIEW

What questions do you need to answer in developing a program concept?

What attributes of the audience are especially important to video producers?

How have recent changes in technology affected the way video communicates with an audience?

What three types of audience appeal did Aristotle identify, and how are they relevant to video?

What do the modern communication concepts of *information, noise, feedback, selective perception and retention, consistency,* and *balance* have to tell us about effective video production?

Chapter 3

How Television Works

Long before computers became common to home and workplace, the telegraph, telephone, radio, television, and communication satellites, among other media marvels, put people instantly in touch with one another around the globe. Working together, these devices make global communication possible; in combination, they enable us to encode, transmit, store, retrieve, and display information in the forms of data, text, live-action images, and high-fidelity sounds, often in real time, thereby enriching communication. In contrast, the computer by itself is merely a data storage, retrieval, and processing device, utterly incapable of providing the communication functions we have come to expect from our media systems.

This chapter explains the development and function of traditional broadcasting systems that have enabled us to communicate instantly through radio and television across continents for more than a century. The chapter also explains how these systems are linked with computers through our telecommunications network, resulting in an infrastructure that makes streaming video, program sharing, and distribution possible through the Internet and e-mail channels. To understand what lies ahead in the video production field, one must understand how traditional broadcasting works and also how broadcasting is becoming integrated with computer and telecommunication systems to form our digital media network.

BROADCASTING AND THE SIGNIFICANCE OF CODE

The desire to communicate from afar is part of human nature. Long before radio and television enabled us to broadcast sounds and images instantly around the globe, we invented less powerful means to send messages to distant places. For example, we invented the megaphone, which extends the reach of the human voice, but not greatly. Other methods of communicating long-distance have included beacons, semaphore flags, drums, smoke signals, and telegraphy.

What these systems share is that they all rely on prior agreements (or codes) between senders and receivers about what various signals will mean. For example, anyone who does not know the sounds or letters associated with flag positions in semaphore will not get the message even if the flags can be clearly seen. It is the code or pattern of intelligence conveyed by the flags, not the view of the flags themselves (the physical carrier), that makes it possible to convey messages. In short, clear reception of the carrier is a necessary but not a sufficient condition for successful transmission of meaning. Successful communication relies on both unimpeded reception of a message's physical component and accurate decoding of the pattern of information (or intelligence) it contains. Of course, it is still possible to misinterpret messages after they are received, but cultural issues of meaning are not even considered until an encoded message is received and decoded.

How is intelligence carried in a message system? A common feature of communication is the need to vary some aspect of a signal to encode information. A pattern of some kind must be crafted into some physical form for a message to be generated, stored, transmitted, received, and consumed. And all patterns require some form of variation or change.

On a simpler level, consider again communication using semaphore flags. If the sender of semaphore flag signals fails to move the flags (no encoding), no message is sent even if the flags can be clearly seen. Similarly, in Morse code, if the telegrapher were to send nothing but dots at regular intervals, there would be no information to decode since there is nothing in Morse code associated with an endless series of dots.

In the technical jargon of radio and television broadcasting, the term for creating a pattern of intelligence through variation is modulation. The term modulation is synonymous for imposing a message (pattern, change, or variation) on a carrier.

Among the most pervasive, rapid, and successful systems ever developed for communicating at a distance are radio and television broadcasting. To explain the process of sending audio/visual messages via broadcasting, I first describe the physical nature of radio energy, which makes broadcasting possible, and then describe how audio signals and televised scenes are encoded, transmitted, received, and decoded. After describing traditional broadcasting, I focus on significant developments over the past half century that have extended its reach and range, including satellite broadcasting and cable television, both of which have advanced traditional broadcasting without changing its analog nature. I then describe how the more recent transition from analog to digital platforms, integrating broadcasting with computers and telecommunication networks, has brought a cornucopia of new video products, services, and opportunities to both producers and consumers.

THE PHYSICAL NATURE OF RADIO ENERGY

Among the physical phenomena that make broadcasting possible is the propagation of radio waves, or electromagnetic radiation, through space. At the simplest level, rotating a loop of copper wire in a magnetic field generates radio energy. Such rotation induces an electric current in the wire. As the wire passes through each full rotation, the intensity and direction of the flow of electrons varies in an orderly manner called a sine wave (see Figure 3.1). Figure 3.1 indicates that sine waves produced by continuous rotation feature several characteristics, which, we will see later, are also present in sound and light waves. These include **frequency** (the number of cycles per second, or cps), **period** (the time it takes for one cycle to occur), **amplitude** (the magnitude of voltage at its greatest intensity), **wavelength** (the length of one cycle in meters), and **phase** (the difference between the same points on different waves). In a vacuum, radio waves travel at the speed of light, about 186,000 miles per second, or 300,000,000 meters per second.

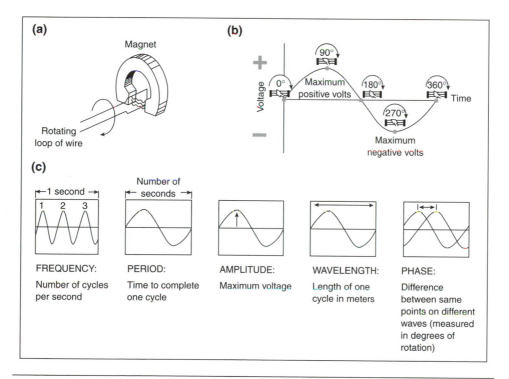

Figure 3.1   The basic sine wave of radio energy. (a) The wave is produced by a loop of wire rotating in a magnetic field. (b) One cycle of a sine wave, as the loop goes through a full (360-degree) rotation. (c) Properties of the sine wave.

PROPAGATING RADIO WAVES

In 1819, the Danish scientist Hans Oersted, while experimenting with electrical effects of magnetic fields, discovered that magnetism and electricity were related. By 1831, Michael Faraday had discovered induction, the ability of an electric current in a wire to create a similar current in a nearby wire without physical contact between them. Based on Faraday's discovery, Joseph Henry developed the first efficient electromagnet.

In 1837, Samuel F. B. Morse used Henry's discoveries about electromagnets to patent a long-distance telegraph system using electrical signals to encode messages. This method was a significant improvement over optical telegraphy systems in use at the time, which depended on telescopes and clear weather to send messages. Morse's electrical telegraphy system was more powerful and reliable than the optical systems then in use. It worked under more varied weather conditions and could send messages farther, more quickly, and more reliably than its predecessors.

As electrical telegraphy developed, it was observed that some "leakage" of electricity from telegraph wires appeared to magnetize some nearby metallic objects. This phenomenon was explained in 1865 by the English physicist James Clerk Maxwell, who presented evidence that electrical impulses emitted from wires traveled through space in a manner similar in form and speed to light waves. Maxwell called them **electromagnetic waves.** Thomas Edison tried to capitalize on this leakage phenomenon to send telegrams to people aboard moving trains. Unfortunately, the waves sent into the atmosphere by the telegraph wires were a chaotic mixture of signals leaking from other wires in the area, making the patterned dots and dashes from any particular message unintelligible.

The problem of how to separate electromagnetic waves from one another was solved by the German scientist Heinrich Hertz. In 1887, Hertz demonstrated that an electromagnetic wave using an oscillating circuit could be propagated and detected amid other waves. An oscillating circuit produces an electric current that changes direction at a stable frequency. An example of an oscillating circuit (albeit a relatively slow one compared to radio frequencies) is that found in a typical American household electrical outlet, which supplies alternating current (AC) at 60 cycles per second. In honor of Hertz's discovery, the unit called a hertz (abbreviated Hz) was adopted in the 1960s as a synonym for "cycles per second."

It was soon confirmed that a radio wave, when propagated at a stable frequency, does not mix with waves of other frequencies. In 1895, the Italian scientist Guglielmo Marconi sent the first wireless telegraph message. These early wireless messages were in the form of Morse code, using the simplest modulation technique—namely, an interrupted continuous wave (ICW). In this method of radio modulation, a continuous, alternating current, made up of a succession of identical sine waves, is broken into a series of pulses corresponding to the dots and dashes of Morse code. This is done simply by opening and closing a circuit for relatively short or long periods to turn the radio wave on or off. Thus, radio energy was used for the first time as the physical material to carry a pattern of intelligence to encode information. Although ICW is still widely used, it is limited in that it does not vary enough to carry sounds, such as music or speech. Eventually, advances in digital technology would make it possible to store enough pulses of information in binary code (patterns of 0s and 1s) to render sounds and/or images on CDs, videodisks, and computers. In Marconi's day, however, further advances were needed to permit broadcasting of audio signals.

CONVERTING SOUND INTO ELECTRICAL ENERGY

Alexander Graham Bell made possible the advance from Morse code to the sending of an electrical replica of the human voice (voice modulation). In 1876, Bell invented the telephone, which makes a current of electricity vary with changing sound waves generated by the human voice. The telephone transmits a pattern of electricity that faithfully matches a pattern of sound waves made by speech. How does this happen?

A telephone mouthpiece uses a microphone to convert sound waves (vibrations in the air) into a matching pattern of electric current. To do this, sound waves created by the voice are directed onto a thin metal diaphragm, which vibrates according to a pattern of sound waves imposed on it. A metal diaphragm (typically a thin disk of aluminum) forms the top of a cylinder containing carbon particles that can conduct electricity. When sound waves enter the mouthpiece, they cause the aluminum to vibrate so that the carbon particles are rapidly squeezed and loosened. When electricity flows through the cylinder, the current increases and decreases as the carbon particles are squeezed and released. Loud sounds cause sound waves to press hard on the diaphragm, compressing the carbon particles tightly, making it easier for electric current to flow, thus increasing the amount of electricity passing through the circuit. When the sound is low, less pressure is exerted on the carbon particles, allowing them to remain more loosely packed and making it harder for current to pass, resulting in a smaller current. In this way, the current passing through the circuit matches the pattern of sound waves striking the diaphragm. If it is a close match, an accurate replica, we call it **high fidelity** (*fidelity* means faithfulness to the original). This process of changing (modulating) sound waves into patterns of electricity is termed *transduction,* and the telephone is therefore a **transducer.**

At the receiving end, how is the electrical pattern transformed back into sound (demodulated)? The telephone is equipped with an earpiece that has a diaphragm that can freely vibrate in and out. In the center of the diaphragm is a coil of wire acting as an electromagnet. A permanent magnet surrounds the electromagnet, supplying a force against which the electromagnet pulls. As the incoming current varies in strength, so does the magnetic force of the electromagnet. Magnetic forces surrounding the diaphragm cause it to vibrate at the same rate, vibrating the surrounding air. The sound waves generated by this motion create a replica of the original sound. Figure 3.2 diagrams this process.

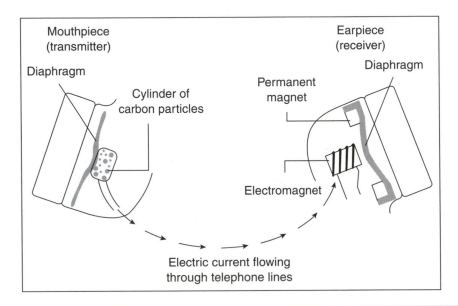

Figure 3.2   Operation of the telephone, a simple transducer. Sound entering the mouthpiece vibrates a metal diaphragm atop a cylinder of carbon particles through which an electric current is passing. This vibration produces a pattern of electric current that replicates a pattern of the sound waves. At the receiver end, the incoming current creates variations in the strength of the earpiece's electromagnet. These variations cause the receiver diaphragm to vibrate, reproducing the original sound.

The encoding and decoding processes in microphones and loudspeakers work essentially the same way as in the telephone. Standard radio and television microphones, though, are sensitive to a fuller range of the audio spectrum and therefore have higher fidelity than those found in telephones. Likewise, radio and television speakers have more power and fidelity than telephone earpieces.

MODULATING RADIO WAVES WITH AUDIO SIGNALS

The telephone makes it possible to project an electrical version of the human voice through long distances over wires and then to recover a replica of the original sound from the transmitted electricity. It soon became possible to modulate radio waves in a similar way without wires. This change resulted from the work of two electrical engineers, England's Sir John Ambrose Fleming and America's Lee De Forest.

Attenuation and Amplification

Sound waves, like radio waves, naturally dissipate as they move farther away from their source. As distance increases, the strength of a wave decreases. This phenomenon is called *attenuation*. To picture this process, imagine the effect of dropping a stone into a pond of still water. The stone causes circular waves of water to move away from the point where it hits, and as the waves move outward, they weaken. At some distance, the original disturbance attenuates to such a degree that the water remains undisturbed by the original splash.

In Fleming's day, it was already well known that electron motion produces current in a closed circuit. In the language of electrical theory, Fleming knew that a voltage applied to a metal wire conducts electrons. What Fleming discovered, however, was that an electrode inside an evacuated heated filament lamp (a glass vacuum tube) could also conduct an electric current. Fleming noticed a one-directional current between the heated filament (called the *cathode*) and the positive electrode (known as an anode or *plate*). Because it contained two elements, Fleming called the device a *diode*.

De Forest extended Fleming's work by interposing a thin metal open-meshed *grid* between the heated filament and the anode. When a separate voltage was fed to the grid, De Forest could control the magnitude of electricity flowing from the cathode to the plate. With a grid, De Forest obtained a large voltage change at the plate from just a small voltage change on the grid. Thus, by introducing a third element to Fleming's diode, De Forest's *triode* made it possible to amplify weak radio signals received from distant radio transmitters. Figure 3.3 diagrams the triode vacuum tube, the original heart of radio amplifiers. Since the 1950s, successive

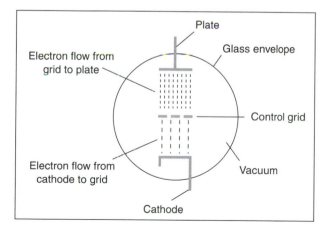

Figure 3.3   A triode vacuum tube solved the problem of amplifying radio signals. Small voltage changes on the control grid modify the electrical flow from the cathode to the plate.

generations of solid-state technologies (transistors, semiconductors, integrated circuits, and microprocessors) have replaced vacuum tubes, but the principles of amplification are the same in both tube and solid-state technologies.

Modulating the Carrier

By feeding an electrical signal converted from sound waves to the grid of a triode, relatively weak audio signals could be amplified enough to be used for radio transmissions. However, before sound waves could be transmitted to distant points without wires, the amplified audio signal had to be superimposed onto a radio frequency (RF) carrier. This is because sound waves are pressure waves and do not propagate across space at the speed of light like electromagnetic radio waves.

The RF carrier is created with an *oscillator,* an electronic circuit that produces a sine wave at a specific frequency. The RF carrier may then be modulated or made to vary by an audio signal (voice or other information) superimposed on it. In other words, the pattern imposed on the RF carrier is sound, converted into an electrical signal, supplied by a microphone or some other audio source (e.g., a CD or cassette tape).

The two most common techniques of modulating a radio wave are amplitude and frequency modulation. When an audio signal modulates the amplitude of a carrier, the process is called **amplitude modulation (AM).** When the audio signal modulates the frequency of a carrier, the process is called **frequency modulation (FM).** In AM radio, the carrier consists of a sine wave whose amplitude is made to copy the variations of an audio source. In FM radio, it is the frequency of the carrier wave that is changed by an audio source. Figure 3.4 illustrates these two common types of voice modulation in radio broadcasting.

As it turns out, FM modulation is superior to AM because it produces better fidelity with much higher noise immunity. For example, auto ignition noises and high-tension lines can cause hum and static on AM signals because those disturbances can adversely affect the amplitude of the received carrier. By contrast, FM signals are generally not affected by such impulse noises in the atmosphere.

Transmitting the Carrier

Audio signals imposed on RF carriers may be further amplified. Finally, they are fed from a transmitter to an antenna for propagation. In standard AM transmission, the range of frequencies used for radio carriers is between 535 and 1,705 kilohertz (abbreviated kHz, meaning thousands of hertz). Each channel is allocated a frequency range (or bandwidth) of 9 kHz to operate in. This means there is enough space in the radio spectrum allocated for 130 AM radio channels in any given area.

Roughly speaking, radio waves propagate in all directions unless they are intentionally altered from this pattern. The effective coverage area can radiate for

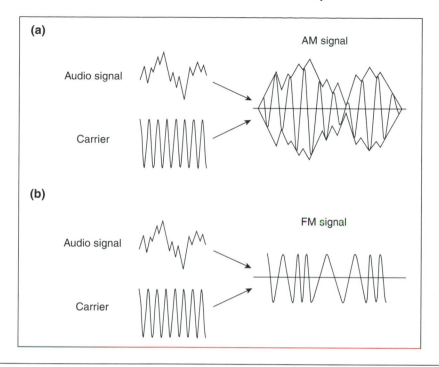

Figure 3.4 AM and FM signals. (a) In AM transmission, the audio signal modulates (varies) the amplitude of the carrier wave. (b) In FM transmission, the audio signal modulates the frequency of the carrier wave.

miles surrounding the transmitting antenna, making it possible for millions of radio sets in a coverage area to receive a signal. However, because radio signals attenuate as distance increases, they must be amplified at the receiver to make them strong enough to drive a speaker.

Demodulating the Carrier

The function of a radio receiver is to tune into a particular frequency from among those available, detect the modulated carrier operating at that frequency, and remove the audio signal from the carrier. This part of the process is known as **demodulation.** The isolated audio signal is then amplified and directed to a speaker so that the original audio information can be heard. A block diagram of the demodulation process is presented in Figure 3.5.

So far, we have provided a basic model of how audio information is transmitted via radio energy to distant points and then recovered. But how does radio energy broadcast motion images? Some preliminary facts set the stage for an explanation of the process of video transmission.

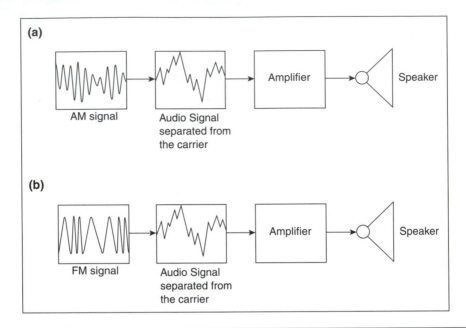

Figure 3.5   Demodulation of (a) AM signals and (b) FM signals.

CHANNEL SPACE

In using radio energy to transmit sound plus full-motion images, a greater portion of the radio spectrum (bandwidth) is needed than for sound alone. This is because there is a lot more information present in motion images plus audio than in audio alone. The need for greater bandwidth to transmit greater amounts of information is analogous to a fire department using larger diameter hoses than those used by homeowners in their gardens to deliver a greater amount of water per given unit of time.

To accommodate television's need for greater bandwidth, whereas American broadcasting allocates 9 kHz per channel for standard AM radio, television bandwidth is more than 660 times larger, or 6 MHz (6,000 kHz) per video channel. This means that one television channel contains enough bandwidth to accommodate more than 600 AM radio stations.

Determining how much radio spectrum would be allocated for each television station was done after a great deal of technical debate and testing by the National Television System Committee (NTSC). The NTSC's first objective was to suggest technical standards that would permit an acceptable level of picture quality or **resolution.** With enough resolution, the video image would be clear, convincing, and aesthetically pleasing. However, the NTSC also wanted to conserve spectrum space, using no more than necessary for each channel assignment.

The NTSC rightly viewed the radio spectrum as a limited natural resource, which it continues to be today, even though technological developments have increased its usable range. Despite these increases, the race for bandwidth by new technologies (satellites, cell phones, digital applications, etc.) is unrelenting, making it essential to allocate its use wisely.

The job of the NTSC was tricky because any increase in image detail requires a commensurate increase in bandwidth for each channel. Unfortunately, every increase in channel bandwidth reduces the total number of channels in a given portion of the spectrum.

As it turned out, the standard bandwidth for each television channel, adopted in 1941, was 6 MHz. This allowed 4.5 MHz for the AM-modulated video signal, a complex video waveform (explained later) including synchronization, scanning, blanking, and, eventually, color information. The remaining 1.5 MHz provided a guard band or buffer between adjacent channels operating in the same geographic area, to reduce interference, and space for transmitting the FM-modulated audio portion of the television signal. Figure 3.6 diagrams these original features of the television channel. Over time, ancillary signals have been embedded into existing television channels to provide supplementary services (e.g., closed-captioning for the hearing impaired, and so on). In addition, further portions of the radio spectrum have been allocated to accommodate satellite transmissions, digital video, and a spate of data, text, and interactive services.

It is interesting to note that amplitude modulation is used for the video portion and frequency modulation for the audio portion of the television signal. This is

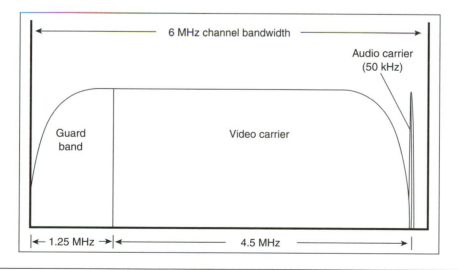

Figure 3.6 Audio and video portions of a standard 6-MHz television channel.

because FM is less subject to noise and interference than AM, making it less subject to static and therefore more suitable for audio reception. Furthermore, AM is better suited for video transmission because it exhibits fewer problems caused by multipath reception of the signal. Multipath reception occurs when the same signal reflects from obstacles such as buildings and bridges, reaching a receiving antenna from more than one path. Because the distance traveled by multipath signals is usually different, different parts of the signal arrive at the antenna at the same time. For AM signals, this causes less severe interference at the television receiver than would occur if the signals were FM.

CONVERTING LIGHT INTO ELECTRICAL ENERGY

Just as telephone and radio technologies harness natural qualities of electricity and electromagnetic radiation to transmit voice-modulated audio signals, television relies on natural phenomena of photoelectric effects, including photoconductivity and photoemissive effect, to convert light into, and back from, electrical energy.

Photoconductivity

To change light into electricity, video depends on **photoconductivity,** which occurs when light on some metals increases the flow of electricity in those metals. One of the earliest examples of photoconductivity was observed in 1873 with the metal selenium. When selenium was used in an electrical circuit, the current through it increased during exposure to light. Unfortunately for video applications, selenium responds too slowly to light to be useful for replicating natural motions. But luckily, cesium silver and other silver-based materials are excellent for such applications.

Photoemissive Effect

In the **photoemissive effect,** discovered by Hertz in 1887, visible light results from some materials' exposure to energy that may not be visible to the eye. Sources of such energy include streams of electrical energy or photons of higher-than-visible light energy, such as ultraviolet rays or X-rays. The photoemissive effect is similar to that seen in radium dials once used to make watch faces glow in the dark.

In the picture tube of a television receiver, the inside of the screen is coated with fluorescent material. When a stream of electrons strikes the screen, it glows because of the photoemissive effect. As the stream of electrons is made stronger, the portion of the screen struck by the electron stream glows more brightly. When the stream is made weaker, the glow decreases. If the stream can be modulated in accordance with the darker and brighter portions of a scene focused by the lens of a television camera, that scene can be rendered on the screen. If the re-creation process can be done quickly enough, then smooth motion can be rendered convincingly.

In monochrome (black-and-white) television receivers, the fluorescent material needs only to be able to glow with a range of brightness roughly proportional to the intensity of the stream of electrons hitting it; color is of no consequence—only brightness variations are important. However, in color television, materials that glow with different colors when streams of electrons hit them must be used. To understand this process, let us begin with the major components of the monochrome television system.

MONOCHROME VIDEO

Television cameras (see Figure 3.7) use a lens system to focus light from a scene into a **pickup tube** or, in microprocessor systems, a **charge-coupled device (CCD).** The pickup tube or CCD is the place where light reflected from a scene is converted into an electrical signal. The output is then amplified and fed to external circuits for recording, routing to closed-circuit locations, broadcast from a transmitter, or transmission via cable or satellite.

Within a studio complex featuring more than one camera, each camera is connected to a **camera control unit (CCU).** The CCU enables a technician to adjust and match camera operation for all cameras to eliminate jarring differences in how they render the same scene. In a television studio, camera operators can immediately view the video signal routed to the **viewfinder** of each camera.

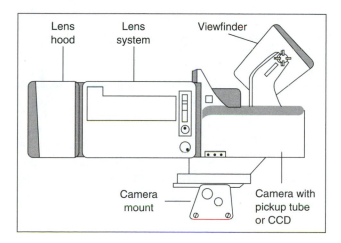

Figure 3.7   The most basic parts of a video camera.

SCANNING

Transmitting all the details of a given picture simultaneously over the same circuit would lead to a chaotic mixing of signals in a single output, resulting in an unintelligible product similar to what jigsaw puzzles tend to look like when they are dumped from their boxes. Such visual chaos is analogous to what Edison faced when he tried to send intermixed wireless telegraph signals to receivers aboard moving trains.

To maintain the fidelity of the original image seen by the camera when it is received by a television set, small areas of the picture are converted into discrete magnitudes of electric current matching the brightness information present in each portion, and then each is sent out in order. This is done so each picture element (**pixel**) can be received and converted into light without being confused with any others.

In theory, we could create a separate circuit for each area of the screen and then send all of the information at once. But such a method is impractical because it would require hundreds of thousands of separate circuits for just one video channel of NTSC video (one for each pixel) (see Photo 3.1 of the Bell Telephone receiver of

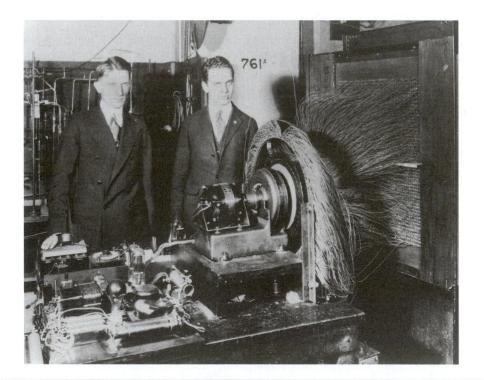

Photo 3.1   The Bell Telephone television receiver of 1927, which used thousands of separate circuits to compose a picture. What a nightmare! The impracticality of such a device prompted development of the electronic scanning method shown in Figure 3.8.

SOURCE: Property of AT&T archives. Reprinted with permission of AT&T.

1927). Instead, a *scanning* method is used to transmit the brightness information for each pixel in turn. Scanning makes it possible to use just one circuit per channel.

The original monochrome video system converted picture information into electrical signals by focusing light onto a mosaic of pixels, each composed of an individual cesium silver globule. In such a system, when a scene to be televised was focused on the mosaic, electrons became stored in each pixel in magnitudes roughly proportional to the intensity of light focused on each one. Stored electrons were then instantly attracted by an anode in the camera tube, leaving the mosaic with a copy of the original scene in the form of varying amounts of electrical charge.

In American broadcasting, the traditional NTSC video mosaic is currently composed of 525 horizontal lines, containing about 211,000 pixels. An electron gun is used to scan each line from left to right, top to bottom, in an orderly fashion. As the electron beam passes each pixel, it replaces electrons lost to the anode, enabling the video signal to exist in an external circuit. This signal is then coupled to video amplifiers for immediate transmission.

Interlaced Scanning

The human visual system detects flicker, a source of severe eye fatigue, below about 45 image presentations per second. To defeat flicker problems, the film industry has adopted a standard film speed of 24 frames per second, each illuminated twice, for a rate of 48 presentations of picture information per second. For television, a system called interlaced scanning is used to avoid flicker problems (see Figure 3.8).

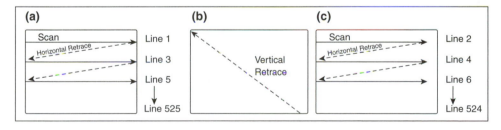

Figure 3.8 The NTSC video image is composed of 525 lines of picture information delivered 30 times per second using *interlaced scanning*. In interlaced scanning, (a) an electron beam first scans the 262.5 odd-numbered lines of the screen. (b) The beam then scans the 262.5 even-numbered lines. (c) After completing all 525 lines, a vertical retrace brings the beam to the top-left position to start the entire process all over again. During retrace, the electron beam is turned off to eliminate spurious illuminations of the screen. Each scan of 262.5 lines is called a *field* and takes 1/60 of a second. Each scan of all 525 lines is called a *frame* and takes 1/30 of a second. Therefore, NTSC scanning delivers 30 complete pictures per second of interlaced video.

Interlaced scanning takes advantage of **persistence of vision** or the tendency for an image to persist for a short period of time after a stimulus is no longer physically present to our eyes. In interlaced scanning, instead of having 525 successive sweeps of the screen, two separate scans of 262.5 lines are used. An electron beam alternately scans the odd-numbered lines of the 525 and then the even-numbered lines, thus creating the illusion of covering the entire field twice. This arrangement defeats the flicker problem, resulting for practical purposes in the appearance of smooth motion.

Each successive scan of 262.5 lines is called a **field.** Because line frequency (normal wall current, or AC power) in the United States is 60 Hz, it is convenient to scan each field in 1/60 of a second. As a result, 60 fields per second are televised, a rate fast enough to eliminate flicker. Each complete scan of all 525 lines, or two successive fields, is called a **frame.** Thus, in the traditional NTSC video system, 30 frames per second are televised.

Electromagnet coils surrounding a fixed cathode ray tube (CRT) inside the camera control the scan of the electron beam across each line. As the gun projects a stream of electrons at the tube face, varying magnetic forces generated within the coils bend it along its path. In this way, the camera performs its work without using any mechanical parts. This makes the scanning process extremely reliable.

In general terms, each time the beam finishes a line, it returns to the extreme-left position, but shifted downward to the next odd or even line, to begin scanning again. This move back is called *horizontal retrace.* When the beam finishes scanning the last line, it returns to the top-left position to begin the entire process over again. This move back is called *vertical retrace.* During each retrace, the electron beam is turned off to eliminate spurious illuminations. The signal to turn off the electron beam is called the *blanking* signal. The vertical blanking interval (VBI) and *retrace* signals, along with the synchronization information needed to keep the receiver precisely in step with the transmitter, are embedded in the overall television signal.

In reality, the VBI reduces picture detail, such that only 483 lines of the 525 transmitted are ultimately delivered with viewable picture information. However, it is during the VBI and in some other parts of the video signal that additional text and information services (e.g., closed-captioning) have found a home since the NTSC established technical standards for American television.[1]

RECEIVER OPERATION

A television set receives video, audio, and all ancillary signals needed to replicate the original televised scene and audio information. It has a loudspeaker, a phosphor-coated picture tube, an electron gun, circuits for synchronization and scanning purposes, and currently, with increasing frequency, additional equipment for receiving specialized services (i.e., set-top boxes, translators, converters). Regardless of tube size, the standard NTSC **aspect ratio** of tube height to width is three units by four units (4:3), respectively. As with the television camera, the neck of the picture tube is fitted with magnetic deflection coils that control the direction of an electron beam. The beam scans horizontal paths across the picture tube's phosphor coating.

When a television signal is received, the sound component (transmitted as FM) is routed to circuits where it is demodulated and sent to a loudspeaker. The video or AM portion of the signal is routed to the picture tube, where it directs the electron beam to emit electrons in amounts roughly in proportion to the brightness levels of the original scene. As the electron beam sweeps across the face of the picture tube, its varying intensities cause variations in the brightness of the phosphors, replicating the original scene. To synchronize the video signal so that pixels can be reassembled without mixing them up, deflection coils around the neck of the picture tube are fed horizontal and vertical sync pulses from the original video signal. These pulses control the deflection of the electron beam across the screen, thus keeping the receiver in step with the original signal.

COLOR TRANSMISSION AND RECEPTION

Color television broadcasting began after the monochrome system was already in place and millions of black-and-white sets were in use. This made it desirable to find a color system compatible with monochrome technology (hence economic and marketing constraints were at work on even the most basic engineering decisions from the beginning). To make color television compatible with monochrome transmission, color information was added to the monochrome signal without changing the 6-MHz bandwidth set aside for each TV channel. In addition, both black-and-white and color receivers were made capable of receiving both monochrome and color signals (a requirement called *backward compatibility*). This meant transmission had to be virtually identical for both monochrome and color systems.

Chrominance, Luminance, and Saturation

To transmit **chrominance** (color or hue) information, the color camera's optical system separates the light entering it into three primary colors: red, blue, and green. It is a fortunate characteristic of human vision that virtually any color can be reproduced from these additive primary colors. Furthermore, any colored light can be specified with only two additional qualities: **luminance** (or brightness) and **saturation** (or vividness). Saturation can be thought of as the degree to which a color is free from impurities, such as dilution by white light. Low-saturation colors are paler, whereas highly saturated colors are more pure and vivid.

In early color cameras, light was broken into its primary color components with filters and a set of dichroic mirrors. A dichroic mirror passes light at one wavelength while reflecting light at other wavelengths. Today, most color cameras use a prism block called a *beam splitter* to break light into its primary colors.

Once the light has been split, the separate light beams are directed into three separate pickup tubes for processing into video signals. When a CCD microprocessor is used, a silicon lattice absorbs different wavelengths of light at different depths to distinguish colors. In either case, the patterns of electrical voltage generated in an external circuit match the levels of the original pattern of light received by the camera.

Some cameras use a single imaging element with a filter to separate incoming light into its component values. Others use filters to separate light into only two colors, as well as additional microprocessors to assign values to the third color needed to reproduce the colors the camera is seeing.

In color cameras, video signals from the three pickup tubes or the CCD are combined to produce a signal containing all of the picture information to be transmitted. Signals are combined using a phase-shifting technique so that they can be transmitted in one video channel and then retrieved without confusion. The overall signal contains the audio and picture information as well as blanking and synchronization pulses, and so on. This colorplexed video signal modulates the video carrier for transmission to receivers.

Black-and-white television sets treat the color portion of the video signal as if it were part of the intended monochrome transmission. To avoid degraded reception, the scanning motions are used to mask the chrominance signal. This way, any pixels brightened by interference during one line scan are made to darken by an equal amount in the next line scan. The net effect of chrominance signal interference over successive scans is thus virtually eliminated.

The tube in the color receiver contains three electron guns that project separate beams, which deflect simultaneously in the standard interlaced scanning pattern over the face of the picture tube. One of the guns projects the red color signal, one projects blue, and the third projects green. The screen of the receiver is coated with phosphor dots that glow red, blue, or green when struck by a stream of electrons. The phosphors are uniformly distributed over the face of the picture tube, arranged in adjacent groups of three dots that form tiny triangles, each containing a phosphor dot for each color. The dots are so small that a single one cannot be distinguished by the viewer's eye. The color of any one triangle is the additive function of the varying intensities with which each dot in the triangle is made to glow by the strength of the electron beam hitting it. Virtually any color may be rendered with this method. If electrons from all three guns strike their respective dots in a triangle with the right intensity, the color of that triangle will appear white. If no electrons strike a trio of dots in a triangle, the color of that triangle will be black. In this way, black-and-white images are possible on a color receiver.

To ensure that the electron beams from the red, blue, and green guns hit only phosphor dots that glow red, blue, and green, respectively, a metal plate called a *shadow mask* is inserted close to the phosphor coating between the electron guns and screen (see Figure 3.9). The plate is pierced with more than 200,000 holes and is positioned so that it masks two of the dots in each triangle from being hit by unwanted electrons. In this way, the electron beams are confined to the phosphor dots of the proper color.

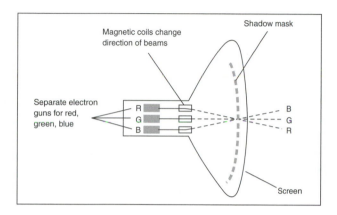

Figure 3.9   Diagram of the traditional color television receiver, showing how the shadow mask keeps the separate electron beams targeted at the proper points on the screen.

SIGNAL TRANSMISSION

Television signals may be propagated over the air from terrestrial antennas for distribution within local television markets, or they may be distributed across the country via telephone long lines using coaxial or fiber-optic cables. When such facilities are not available, convenient, or cost-effective, microwave relay links may be used to distribute television programs. Sometimes microwave delivery is not feasible due to distance, power, terrain, or other limitations; in such cases, video transmissions can be sent using satellite uplinks (covered later in this chapter). Since the 1960s, the development and growth of microwave, cable, and satellite technologies have made live television transmission and reception possible from almost any location on Earth.

The camcorder and desktop editor have more recently put production capability into the hands of the audience. Videotape recorders, computer memory chips, and video servers now enable receivers to store programs for later use and permit audiences the luxury of watching programs repeatedly and at their convenience. Special effects and digital graphics processing permit virtually endless enhancement and manipulation of video images. High-quality audio and multiple speaker configurations offer stereo and surround sound for consumers' home entertainment systems. Interactive systems enable users to engage in dialogue with program providers and with one another. Projection and big-screen video as well as flat-screen displays, including both plasma display panels (PDPs) and liquid crystal displays (LCDs), now influence homebuilders and realtors to feature entertainment theater space as a selling point in marketing homes. The remote control continues to influence the way we watch television, as well as influencing the way programmers think about how to capture our attention.

Since the advent of television, technical developments have continued to make television more engaging than it was in its infancy. Yet the core of the system still uses radio energy to broadcast television signals. However, the picture is changing right before our eyes. We are witnessing a profound transition from analog to digital platforms, as well as a convergence of broadcasting, computer, and telecommunication technologies. What is the result? An explosion of interactive information and entertainment services to American households and beyond. The new order enables us to originate our own programming if we wish. The age of interactive **digital television (DTV)** is upon us. What are some of the implications of this change?

THE ADOPTION OF A DIGITAL TELEVISION (DTV) STANDARD

On December 24, 1996, the Federal Communications Commission (FCC) announced its decision to adopt a digital television standard for a free, universally available digital broadcast television service for America. Originally, the main goal of developing an advanced television system was to provide America with higher quality video images, known as **high-definition television (HDTV or HD)**. However, rapid development of digital technologies has expanded the objectives of public interest groups, computer and television manufacturers, telecommunication providers, cable and satellite interests, filmmakers, broadcasters, and others interested in enhanced video services.

Beyond HD, the DTV age now implies expanded applications to include movies on demand, telephone and computer data delivery, interactive programming, distance learning, paging systems, home shopping and e-commerce applications, video production and editing, and so on.

Understanding the public policy and economic interests behind DTV development is key to understanding the technical configuration of the new system. Among the goals of the FCC was to adopt a "world leading digital broadcast television technology" that would

1. put more video program choices into the hands of American consumers,

2. provide better quality audio and video than that available with the NTSC system,

3. provide innovative services due to data transmission capability, and

4. offer compatibility (interoperability) between video and computer technology to spur innovation and competition.

To achieve these goals, the FCC began inquiries in 1987 into the potential for advanced television (ATV) services. At that time, industry research teams suggested more than 20 systems. In February 1993, after determining that any system to be adopted would be fully digital, four such systems were considered.

In May 1993, seven companies and institutions representing the four remaining systems formed a "grand alliance" to develop a "best of the best" single system to present to the FCC for approval. Over the next two and a half years, a final digital system was developed, tested, documented, and recommended to the FCC. In December 1996, the system was approved.

The Advanced Television System Committee (ATSC), composed of a 54-member group including television workers, television and film producers, trade associations, television and equipment manufacturers, and segments of the academic community, has endorsed the newly adopted DTV system as "the best digital broadcast television system in the world." The ATSC has characterized the system as having unmatched flexibility and ability to incorporate future improvements. However, some industry parties have voiced objections about having the government impose the standard. Some at the time questioned whether it might be better to allow market forces to dictate standards rather than have the government intervene. Some suggested having the government issue standards only for spectrum allocation, transmission, and reception, to avoid interference problems, but to leave all other conditions (e.g., frame rates, number of scanning lines, aspect ratio of the screen) open. Ultimately, the FCC decided that letting market forces determine standards would lead to the development of incompatible systems that would be too costly to consumers who might have to invest in several different receivers to gain access to different programs. Incompatible systems might also require the use of set-top boxes, translation devices, and other interface hardware and software that might slow down encoding, transmission, and decoding of data streams, thus degrading the efficiency of the entire system. In addition, the FCC reasoned that a government-mandated standard would be the best way to guarantee universal access to broadcasting services for all Americans. The FCC viewed broadcasting as unique, free, and available to nearly every American who relies on it as a primary source of information and entertainment. Because of these characteristics, the FCC reasoned that the goals of certainty and reliability take on a special significance and strengthen the case for the adoption of a government-imposed DTV standard. Finally, the FCC reasoned that allowing different standards to develop might make the conversion process from the current analog system to a fully digital service more difficult. For these reasons, letting the market drive the selection of a standard was rejected.

To make the DTV standard as industry-friendly as possible, the FCC invited standards to be developed by industry parties. In this way, it was believed the DTV system that developed would better reflect industry needs. For this reason, the standard is called "voluntary."

Characteristics of the New Standard

Like the NTSC television format, the new DTV standard calls for each television channel to occupy a 6-MHz bandwidth. To fit the more complex digital signal demands of DTV (at times with many times the picture resolution of the current NTSC format) into the same space used for current analog signals, digital compression techniques (described in more detail later) are used. However, unlike the NTSC format that uses only interlaced scanning of 525 lines at 30 frames per second on a screen three units high by four units wide, DTV remains relatively flexible on these dimensions.

For example, to promote compatibility (interoperability) with other services, including rerunning archives of NTSC programs, newer telecommunication and computer-based media, and film formats, the DTV standard can broadcast and receive both interlace-scanned programs and those produced in a new noninterlaced scanning format called **progressive scanning.** In progressive scanning, each line is scanned in order, with no skipping, at a maximum rate of 60 frames per second (double the current NTSC frame rate).

The new system accommodates both the traditional NTSC horizontal line format as well as some newer ones. Currently, the NTSC format is fixed at 525 lines of pixels distributed in a rectangular arrangement. In this design, the distance between pixels is greater horizontally than vertically. However, in the new system, a maximum of 1,080 horizontal lines of pixels will be featured in a square arrangement; that is, pixels will be equally spaced in horizontal and vertical directions. As a result, new receivers will be compatible with both NTSC format programs as well as many computer displays.

The two new line formats in the DTV standard include one with 720 horizontal lines per frame and one with 1,080 lines per frame in a 16:9 aspect ratio of width to height.

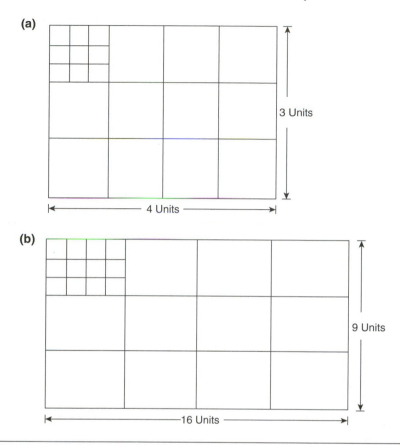

Figure 3.10   Traditional (NTSC) and DTV aspect ratios of the television screen. (a) The
traditional NTSC 4 × 3 aspect ratio (4 units wide by 3 units high), also referred to
as 1.33:1 units of width to height. (b) The expanded 16 × 9 screen size, also
referred to as 1.78:1 units of width to height. Notice that the expanded size of the
DTV screen is the square of the NTSC standard (4² × 3²). The expanded width is
nearly equal to the 1.85:1 screen format used in the movie industry.

The 16:9 aspect ratio and square pixel arrangement means that when 720 horizontal lines are being scanned (not counting those lost to blanking and retrace),
1,280 vertical lines of pixels are used, for a total of 921,600 pixels potentially contributing to the overall video image. Similarly, when 1,080 horizontal lines are
used, 1,920 vertical lines of pixels are used, for a total of 2,073,600 pixels potentially contributing to the overall image. These numbers are 5 to 10 times greater
than those associated with the NTSC format and help convey the added picture
resolution available from the new system. Several frame rates are also available
under the DTV standard, including 24, 30, and 60 frames per second, making
DTV more compatible with film, NTSC video, and computers.[2]

Finally, the 16:9 aspect ratio provided by DTV is more compatible with the format used in many films produced throughout the world, and with flexible letterboxing capability, presenting programs produced in aspect ratios different from the 16:9 format becomes easy. **Letterboxing** is a technique used to preserve the original aspect ratio of a film by blacking out portions of the screen, usually at the top and bottom. Film content is not cut from the frame. With letterboxing, the complete frame is transmitted, and no parts of the picture are left out.

In addition to these characteristics, new system capabilities include the following:

1. Layering of video and audio signals that enables multiplexing and transport of different programs simultaneously over the same channel. For example, layering makes it possible to broadcast two HD programs at the same time or "multicast" (transmit multiple data streams) several standard definition television (SDTV) programs at a visual quality better than that currently available. Current estimates claim that more than five such programs or dozens of CD-quality audio signals can be multicast simultaneously.

2. RF transmission.

3. Rapid delivery of large amounts of data (e.g., the contents of the daily newspaper could be sent in less than two seconds).

4. Capability for interactive transmission of educational materials.

5. Provision for universal closed-captioning for the deaf.

With all of these developments, it is clear that DTV will continue to expand the power, pervasiveness, and influence of television. As new configurations become available, it will become increasingly important for message makers and consumers to understand how new devices may be used to reach and influence audiences and how audiences will use them for their own ends.

Satellite communication, cellular telephones, and microwave links carrying faxes, e-mails, and computer databases all depend on wireless transmission of modulated radio signals to connect distant users. Without these infrastructures, millions now on the wireless network would be isolated from one another. As long as we use radio energy to send data representing sounds and images across space at the speed of light, it will be necessary to know how broadcasting works to have a full understanding of digital media. Understanding how broadcasting systems operate is one of the essentials.

COMPUTERS AND TELECOMMUNICATIONS IN VIDEO

In addition to understanding how broadcasting systems operate, it is also essential for you to understand how computers and telecommunications systems contribute to the video production process. Perhaps most obvious is the role of computers in creating special effects in postproduction editing (for both audio and video). Simply put, virtually all video editing is now done on computers, from network shops to small independent producers; even Hollywood has adopted digital editing for first-run films.

Less obvious is the role of these systems in video distribution, another phase of postproduction. In this application, distant users can share computer files of video programs, over both wire and wireless channels, with a computer, a fiber or phone connection, and an e-mail address. While this raises important copyright issues and underscores the vulnerability exhibitors face from media pirates, the convenience of such options makes the use of computers (combined with telecommunication channels) for rapid distribution of media products too attractive to ignore.

Computers are now also central to shooting video. For example, in the production phase, digital cameras record sounds and images as digital data, through an encoding process known as **sampling** and **quantizing** (explained later). In addition, because digital cameras record video and sound as data files, programs can be sent to computer servers immediately from multiple locations either for broadcast or further processing (i.e., editing) without losing signal quality; files can also be sent over any size channel (**broadband** or **narrowband**) either in one continuous transmission or in discrete bursts, again without signal loss. Analog video either falls short or can't do any of these things.

Besides offering videographers greater reliability, digital cameras are also lighter in weight than their analog counterparts, have longer battery life than ever before, and require lower light levels to record air-quality material. In marketing terms (a concern during every phase of production), digital encoding offers additional advantages, including the ability to embed extra information about programs regarding production dates, ratings, personnel involved, additional content (i.e., outtakes stored as separate chapter content), and other information designed to attract or advise consumers.

Clearly, computers and telecommunications channels are involved in every phase of video production from shooting and editing to distribution and marketing, making it critical to know as much as possible about how these technologies contribute to the process. The remainder of this chapter explains how computers and telecommunications infrastructures work, in both conceptual and physical terms relevant to the production setting.

Computers

How do computers enable users to create (*encode*) and display (*decode*) video information? In computers, the main substance acted on by electrical signals for coding and storing video information is silicon, a naturally occurring element.[3] When treated with other materials, silicon can be used to encode, store, and manipulate any kind of information, including video images and sound. To explain how computers make this possible, you should know first how **binary code** may be used to represent any kind of information and then, from both conceptual and physical perspectives, how computers may be used to make, store, and retrieve television programs.

Using binary code to render and store information predates modern digital computers by centuries. Simply put, binary code uses just two symbols to record information. Remember, it is essential to *vary* some aspect of a signal for it to carry a message. This is because some variation or modulation is required to impose a pattern of intelligence on any medium; otherwise, no message can be encoded.[4]

The Binary Number System

Around 1900, telegraphers began using Morse code to communicate to distant places without wires (*wireless telegraphy*) by propagating patterns of radio energy in long and short bursts to represent the letters of the alphabet. This was one of the earliest uses of binary code in a broadcast setting.

Beyond language functions, binary code can also be used to express any numerical value and perform mathematical calculations. The ability of binary code to capture both verbal and mathematical ideas is extraordinarily important because it shows how *any type and amount of information that can be expressed may be rendered into numerical code using only 0s and 1s.* In other words, although the binary number system uses only two symbols, it is completely versatile. For example, decimal numbers (so called because they use 10 symbols, from 0 through 9) may be expressed in binary form, as shown in Figure 3.11.

Notice that when the supply of digits runs out, decimal numbers move one place to the left, where they are used all over again in a new column at an increased power of 10. In binary, the same practice is followed, but with one difference: When the numbers move over, they increase in value by powers of only 2. So, as Figure 3.11 shows, the number 10 in the decimal system is expressed as 1010 in binary, where the digit "0" on the far right tells us there are no 1s, the digit next to it tells us there is one 2, the next that there are no 4s, and the last on the far left that there is one 8, for a total of 10 (decimal), and so on.

Notice that as places move from right to left in the decimal system, decimal values increase tenfold (i.e., place values go from 1s to 10s to hundreds to thousands, etc.), whereas when places move in the binary system, values increase by powers of only 2 (i.e., from 1s to 2s to 4s to 8s, etc.). Nevertheless, using binary code, it is possible to represent any number.

Binary code is difficult for human beings to use because long strings of repeating 0s and 1s can quickly challenge our perceptual systems, as the binary number representing the number 256 illustrates (see Figure 3.11). But it is just the opposite

Decimal		Binary
1 (decimal)	=	1 (binary)
2	=	10
3	=	11
4	=	100
5	=	101
6	=	110
7	=	111
8	=	1000
9	=	1001
10	=	1010
16	=	10000
32	=	100000
64	=	1000000
100	=	1100100
256	=	100000000
Etc.		

Figure 3.11   A sample of decimal numbers with their binary equivalents in each row.

for computers, which are highly compatible with a two-state system of variation, in part because electrical impulses may easily be turned on and off with the flick of a switch, just like a light bulb.

In addition to using circuits with on-off electrical signals to represent alphanumeric expressions, we can also use them to represent audiovisual content in the form of *bi*nary digi*ts* (or *bits,* as known in the computer industry). Two principles are of interest here: First, information can be processed as a series of yes-no choices in terms of binary digits (0s and 1s); second, such information can be simulated in an electrical circuit. In terms of technical advancement of computers during the early 20th century, as fate would have it, the start of World War II precipitated intense, independent computer technology development programs on both sides of the Atlantic.

How is binary code used to encode text and video? I focus first on the encoding of alphanumeric characters because so much content is available in textual form in television and other media industries (i.e., streaming video content on Web sites and, obviously, print media). Then I describe how video content may be rendered into computer code, as well as the hardware that enables today's computers to store, retrieve, and display such content.

ASCII: Why "1" Is a Beautiful Number in the Computer World

At any given moment, a binary digit (bit) has the capacity to store only one of two pieces of information, expressed as a 0 or a 1. To increase capacity, more bits are needed. So, for example, if you want to record the flavor of a cake as either chocolate or vanilla, one bit is all you need: a *0* could stand for *chocolate,* a *1* for *vanilla.* But to characterize the cake further, say in terms of both flavor (chocolate or vanilla) and type of icing (i.e., butter vs. butter free), two bits of code are required. That's because four states or conditions are in play, and that is the number that can be accommodated with two bits of code: The first bit can be 0 while the second bit is 0 (say, a chocolate cake with butter icing), the first bit can be 1 while the second bit is 0 (vanilla with butter icing), the first bit can be 0 while the second bit is 1 (chocolate/butter free), or both can be 1s (vanilla/butter free). In like manner, if three bits are used, eight conditions can be accommodated; in other words, the capacity to characterize a unique combination of conditions jumps to eight with three bits of code, as shown in the eight rows of Figure 3.12 (perhaps the column on the far left designates sugar vs. sugar free).

0	0	0
0	0	1
0	1	0
0	1	1
1	0	0
1	0	1
1	1	0
1	1	1

Figure 3.12   Eight unique combinations are possible with three bits of code.

Notice the trend. The number of unique possibilities or sets of conditions that can be characterized as the number of bits increases is equal to *2n,* where *n* is the number of bits. So, if there are three bits in use, the number of unique conditions that can be handled (the *capacity* of three bits) is 2^3 or 8. With four bits, 16 unique conditions can be captured, and so on.

The Implications of This Trend for Accommodating Text

The relationship between the number of bits of code and the capacity to code text is critical since many graphical characters must be displayed, including 26 letters in the English alphabet (52 if you count uppercase and lowercase), 10 digits, and a variety of punctuation marks (commas, periods, dollar signs, etc.).

In addition, a number of control commands provide syntax to control the layout of the graphical content, including spacing between words and sentences, tab and backspace commands, and so on. Clearly, four bits of code are not enough to handle all that since more than 16 characters are included in just one case of the alphabet alone. How many bits should be set aside for alphanumeric text?

In 1967, this question was answered in the United States when the American Standard Code for Information Interchange, or ASCII (rhymes with "gas key"), was developed. It calls for a seven-bit code standard for alphanumeric characters. With seven bits available, you can manipulate 128 unique items of information, which is enough capacity to accommodate all the letters of the alphabet (both uppercase and lowercase), all 10 digits, punctuation marks, and so on.

Adopting a single standard simplifies information exchange among computers. By using ASCII code, computers can share information without translation (a huge advantage). That is why the heading of this section calls 1 a beautiful number in the computer industry: *An agreed-on standard simplifies information sharing.*

At the time ASCII was developed, computer memory was both limited and costly, but it was obvious that a six-bit code lacked the capacity to handle alphanumeric text. So a seven-bit architecture was adopted. As it turns out, however, almost all computer systems today are based on an eight-bit architecture (each eight-bit chunk is called a *byte*); that is, information is stored in chunks of eight-bit bytes, even ASCII code.

Capturing Sound and Video With Binary Code

ASCII code is great for coding text, but it is too limited for handling sound or images. How is binary code used to capture sound?

Sound is an analog phenomenon; that is, it is a continuous stream of information, usually made up of waves of compressed air that cause the generating element of a microphone or your eardrums to vibrate sympathetically. In analog recording, physical sound vibrations are converted into a pattern of electrical signals matching the original stimulus (a process called *transduction*).

By contrast, in digital recording, or in the conversion of the voice, say, for cellular telephone transmission, binary numbers are used to represent the varying fluctuations of electricity generated by sound waves through a process of *sampling* and *quantization.* To do this, the pattern of electricity matching sound signals is converted into a digital data stream using an *analog-to-digital converter.* How does this happen?

In the sampling phase of the analog-to-digital conversion, a circuit captures instants of sound at rapid intervals on the order of thousands of times per second (see Figure 3.13). Each unit captured (each *sample*) is then converted to a number according to its amplitude at that particular moment. The number associated with

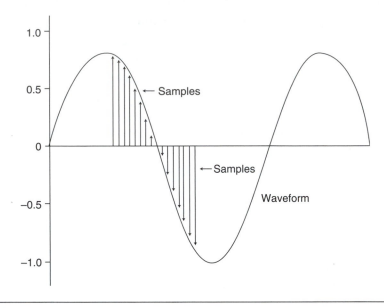

Figure 3.13 Illustration of the sampling phase of the analog-to-digital conversion.

each sample is then stored in binary form. Figure 3.13 illustrates this part of the analog-to-digital conversion process.

After the sound is sampled, another circuit takes each sampled value and quantizes it—that is, each unit is assigned a value of amplitude nearest the one that has been captured from an array of available choices. Thus, each sample is represented by the nearest allowable level of voltage the circuit is programmed to assign (see Figure 3.14). Any actual value seen to lie between two quantization steps is assigned the value closest to it.

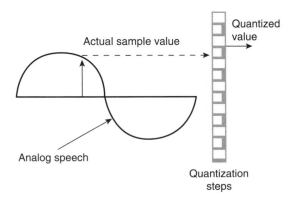

Figure 3.14 Illustration of the quantization phase of the analog-to-digital conversion.

In the case of compact disk (CD) recordings, where fidelity is of paramount importance, and transmission and bandwidth matters are not an issue, a greater number of samples quantized more finely may be used than, say, in the cell phone industry, where transmission and bandwidth issues are critical.

In all cases, once samples have been quantized, each bit of audio information is placed into a sequence called a pulse train consisting of series of 0s and 1s representing the original sound, which is, at the receiving end, converted back into electrical signals through the use of a digital-to-analog converter. It is this signal that is finally fed to your earpiece or amplifiers connected to the speakers of your stereo system or television entertainment center.

Digital image capture for both still and motion visuals is similar to the method just described for audio, but with a much larger data capacity. In the case of images, the analog information (i.e., light focused by a camera lens on a scene of interest) is converted into an electrical signal that is then coded as a digital data stream. To accomplish this, a CCD is the transducer instead of a microphone (see Figure 3.15). In a digital camera, the lens focuses light onto a CCD panel consisting of several hundred thousand (or several million) tiny light-sensitive diodes called *pixels*. Each pixel measures the amount of light hitting it, translating the brighter stimuli into higher electrical charges and the darker stimuli into lower

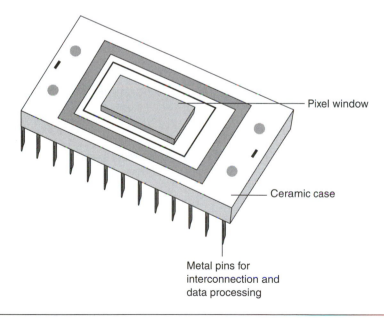

Pixel window

Ceramic case

Metal pins for
interconnection and
data processing

Figure 3.15   Schematic diagram of a charge-coupled device (CCD). A CCD these days can
contain millions of pixels. Each one converts the light energy hitting it into an
electric charge.

electrical charges. In this way, a mosaic of light intensities renders the original scene, creating a faithful black-and-white image of it.

To add color to the picture, a beam splitter (see Figure 3.16) is used to separate the light entering the camera into varying levels of red, green, and blue light (discussed earlier in this chapter). In some digital cameras (called three-chip cameras), a separate chip is used for each of these colors, from which the full color spectrum is reconstructed through an overlay process. In cameras using only one chip, selected pixels are fitted with permanent color filters. In such cameras, another computer inside the camera determines the true color of the light arriving at each pixel by interpolating information from the surrounding area. Using only one chip results in less accurate rendering of the scene to be captured but saves cost.

Digital video cameras work essentially the same way as digital still cameras, but with an additional sensor layer behind the image panel, allowing each image

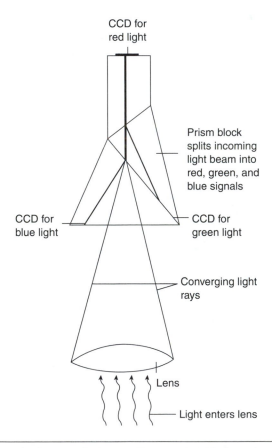

Figure 3.16 Schematic diagram of a beam splitter, a prism block used to break incoming light into three separate light beams (red, blue, and green) and to direct each one to a CCD for signal processing as a video image.

to be transferred to the second layer so that the first layer can refresh itself in order to capture a series of images in rapid succession. This process happens many times per second, creating the illusion of motion when replayed. Finally, the analog visual images are digitized essentially the same way as sound, through a process of sampling, quantizing, and coding. In the sampling stage, a number of selected instants of the analog signal (measured in MHz rather than kHz) are captured. Then each is assigned a quantized value from among an array of choices. Then, the values are coded into binary number equivalents composed of sequences of 0s and 1s. In recovering the information to make it viewable again, a reversal of this process is accomplished through a digital-to-analog conversion.

Standard Computer Architecture: ALU, CCU, Memory, Input, and Output

Once created, binary code representing content of whatever kind must be accessed properly for the content to be kept intact. If information is processed incorrectly, if sequences are apprehended out of order, or if parts of units are chunked with parts of adjacent units rather than with the ones they were originally framed with, the pattern of intelligence could be confounded, resulting in a mishmash of incomprehensible output. To avoid this, rules of syntax are imposed on the information to keep it intact.

To process code successfully, computer architecture contains five components that are necessarily segregated from one another, including a central arithmetic logic unit (ALU) to carry out mathematical calculations, a central control unit to integrate operations, a *memory* to store information and permanent instructions about how to process it, a component for entering data (an *input* component), and an *output* component for displaying data to make content accessible to users (see Figure 3.17).

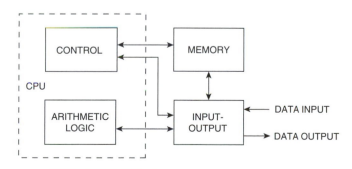

Figure 3.17   Five components of computer architecture provide accurate information processing.

Input components include such items as the keyboard and computer mouse, but those are not the only ones. Others include pressure-sensitive touch screens, such as those seen in restaurants, and plastic pens used to enter data on handheld PCs. Common output components include RGB video monitors and computer screens, printers, audio speakers, telephone earpieces, and headphones, among others.

The five-component computer architecture is still in use today. In addition, the computer's operations are performed in sequence one at a time (an imposition of temporal order to guard further against confusion), using a clock chip to order operations.

Computer systems may be programmed to control complicated and varied sets of conditions, exhibiting what has come to be called **artificial intelligence (AI).** In such systems, binary code may be used to execute an array of preset instructions designed to alter incoming information with a wide variety of practical benefits.

One application of such technology in the television industry is seen in the use of the *V-Chip,* a computer device required by FCC rules to be installed on all television sets 13 inches or larger manufactured after January 1, 2000. Thanks to digital text embedded as *header information* in most television programs, the V-Chip can read the ratings information associated with a show and then block the program from display if deemed undesirable by the user based on a set of instructions.

From Tubes to Transistors

As mentioned earlier, the ability of triode vacuum tubes to perform signal-processing functions made it a versatile electronics tool, especially in broadcasting, telecommunication industries, and computer technology. But as mentioned, vacuum tubes were not perfect; they were large, hot, electricity hogs and unreliable—they quickly burned out. When thousands of them were crammed in a box, as was often the case in early computer manufacturing, the temperature inside could soon exceed 120 degrees F. Such conditions required too much maintenance. Something better was needed. Something cooler. More reliable. Smaller. Less piggish.

By the late 1940s, alternative computer technology in the form of smaller, lighter, more reliable **semiconductors** was under development at AT&T and Bell Laboratories. Semiconductors could conduct an electric current, performing the same work as vacuum tubes but without the heat and with far less electricity consumption. Semiconductor technology gave rise to the first reliable solid-state *transistors* (called so because, depending on the electrical conditions presented to them, they acted as either a *trans*mitter or a re*sistor* of electric current).

Transistors could do everything vacuum tubes could do but without any of the tube's shortcomings—no overheating, no breakable glass or filaments, no overconsumption of electricity. Transistors were everything vacuum tubes were not—they were small, cool, light, and reliable. Their tiny size meant their electric signals had to travel only a small distance to reach their destinations; that meant a great increase in data-processing speed and efficiency.

The trend toward miniaturization put pressure on manufacturers to find ways of connecting more and more transistors for increased data processing. Manufacturers also wanted to develop ways of mass-producing transistors. Rather than making them one at a time, companies began etching them into large silicon wafers using a photoengraving process. Soon entire sets of transistors consisting of amplifiers, resistors, and capacitors were being produced together on a single substrate of semiconductor material (see Photo 3.2).

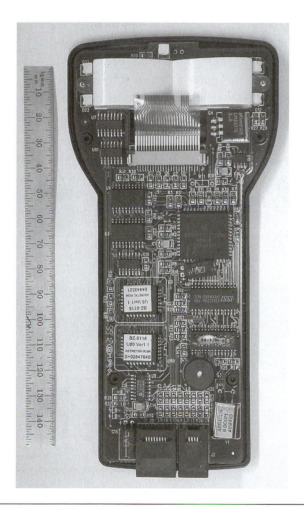

Photo 3.2   Integrated circuits such as this one, with millions of transistors, enable it to process digital information quickly.

SOURCE: Meade Autostar circuit board reprinted with permission of Richard Seymour and John Amsbaugh.

Chip Manufacturing

The leader in the field of miniaturization was Texas Instruments, which, through the efforts of its employee, Jack Kilby, conceived of a plan to produce multiple components of semiconductor material simultaneously on the same wafer. Kilby's invention, the first integrated circuit (IC), made its debut in 1959. By 1962, mass production of ICs (now called *chips*) was in full swing. Since that time, the size of each generation of transistor has decreased as their number in a single chip has increased (see Photo 3.3).

Recording television programs on computer chips requires vast amounts of data-processing capability. Without these breakthroughs in chip development and miniaturization, capturing live images with natural motion and high-fidelity sound as digital data files on computers would likely still be a dream.

Several types of computer chips are used for processing video content. Some chips are *memory* chips, designed to store information. One specific kind of memory chip, called a ROM (read-only memory) chip, acts as a permanent store

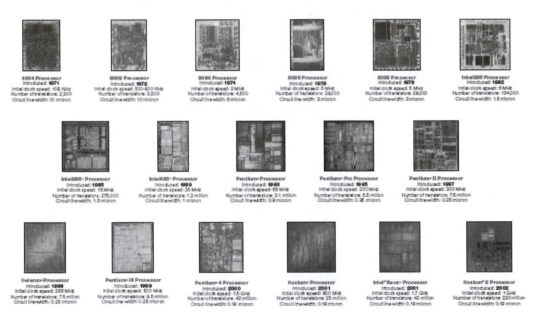

Photo 3.3   Several generations of integrated circuits show how the number of transistors on a single chip has increased over the past 20 years, enabling great increases in signal processing capability, making digital audio and video possible, among many other applications.

SOURCE: Reprinted with permission of Intel, www.intel.com/museum.

for binary code—that is, the transistor switches are set to react to electricity flowing through them the same way every time. It is like a file cabinet that simply holds the information (programs) inside.

Another type of chip is called a RAM (random-access memory) chip. RAM chips allow new information to be encoded and then deleted when no longer needed. RAM chips allow transistor switches to create different patterns of electric signals to flow, representing different types of information.

Yet another critically important type of chip is that which performs calculations and makes logical decisions that control a computer's activities in different parts of the machine. This chip is called the CPU (central processing unit) chip. Another is a clock chip that uses a quartz crystal to time operations so that all instructions are carried out one at a time in proper sequence. Together, the various chips coordinate and execute computer operations to ensure that operations go as planned.

The modern digital computer, through the use of binary code and silicon chip technology, has made it possible for individuals to *encode* a wide variety of textual and audiovisual messages that were once produced only by publishing houses, recording companies, and television studios. It is now a critical element of video production.

But the ability to *transmit* such messages is not the result of computers. Rather, it is the integration of computers with broadcasting and *telecommunication* infrastructures that permits program sharing and distribution to audiences. Without the telephone network and broadcasting technologies, computers would be incapable of sharing information across wide areas. The next section explains how computers are integrated with these older technologies to provide transmission capability for the television industry and independent producers.

Telecommunications

Video transmission occurs through the integration of computers and other digital devices with broadcasting and telecommunication technologies. Without the public switched telephone network (PSTN) and similar (i.e., private) infrastructures and broadcasting technologies, the immediate sharing of television programs among distant users would be impossible.

This section explains how video programs are transmitted. A central topic is **bandwidth,** or the capacity of a channel to move digital information from one place to another in a given period of time. I describe some of the communication technologies that transfer messages between points, including wire and cable facilities (copper, coaxial, and fiber-optic), as well as wireless facilities using radio energy (terrestrial microwave and satellite transmitters); all are currently used for transmitting broadcast programming. I also describe how digitalization increases the capacity and flexibility of telecommunication channels. The topics include packet switching, multiplexing, and signal compression, all designed to make more efficient use of available bandwidth. I also outline some of the advantages and disadvantages of digital versus analog modulation, as well as quality control issues (i.e., error correction features) designed to ensure that programs received are the same as those that are sent.

Because analog television receivers are so plentiful in the United States, it will likely be several years before we see a full transition to digital broadcasting. This is because set owners are often reluctant to invest in expensive new systems that may fail to become standard. Frequently, the adoption process is further slowed by incompatibilities across competing systems.

Of course, the digital revolution is still a work in progress. For example, twisted-pair copper wire, part of 19th-century telephone technology originally designed for analog voice traffic, is still in use today for connecting households to telephone exchange offices. At the same time, the network's switching technology has been continually upgraded (from electromechanical relays to vacuum tubes to digital solid-state equipment) to increase efficiency. Since around 1990, however, telephone companies began carrying digital content in addition to analog voice traffic through the adoption of 21st-century technologies not even dreamed of when the phone system first developed, including *T-1* and *T-3* lines, optical fiber for long-distance transmission, and digital subscriber lines (DSL), among others.

Today, the only part of the PSTN that has remained analog is the local loop (from homes to telephone exchange offices). And although existing copper wire has been successfully adapted for many digital functions (e.g., both computer data transmission and digital voice calls originating from cell phones must still be capable of reaching wire line phones through the local loop), the local infrastructure is not yet suitable for everything (i.e., broadband applications such as television-quality streaming video).

As a result, the current infrastructure still cannot deliver to most households high-speed service for real-time interactive video and other products and services requiring high capacity. Nevertheless, the eventual transition to a fully digital system for broadcasting is inevitable.

With exceptions, digital transmission is a relatively recent phenomenon. For decades, our major commercial television networks distributed thousands of hours of programming to hundreds of affiliate stations coast to coast in the form of analog video signals via high-bandwidth coaxial cable provided by the telephone company. The first such transcontinental distribution began in 1951, using AT&T coaxial cable to carry analog video signals.

But since the early 1990s, we have seen a transition from analog to digital transmission in both wire and wireless technologies. Why the change? What are the advantages of digital transmission that make it an attractive alternative for the television industry over traditional analog service?

Digital transmission was really fostered by the development and success of digital computers—as you already know, binary code is the only kind of information computers can understand. However, the conversion from analog to digital platforms in the television industry is not merely the result of pressure to conform to the needs of computers; rather, it derives from the promise of a quantum leap in *capacity* (and, by implication, profits) that comes with digital delivery of products and services.

Analog Versus Digital Signals

In the beginning of this section, I defined digital bandwidth as a measure of the amount of information that could pass through a communication channel in a given period of time. However, in the early days of broadcasting (when the term *bandwidth* was first used), bandwidth was defined not as a measure of information capacity but simply as the frequency range assigned to a specific broadcasting channel or service (e.g., short-wave radio, AM and FM radio, and, later, television).

Analog bandwidths were allocated according to both the physical limitations of the broadcasting technologies available at the time they entered service and the intended functions of those services. Some services needed wider bandwidths than others to deliver acceptable signals. For example, television channels are bigger than radio channels because they have to deliver both audio and video signals; therefore, they require greater bandwidth. Once assigned, analog spectrum allocations were fixed; that is, analog radio channels provided just radio programs, television channels provided just television programs, and so on.

Today, we live in a very different world, with deep implications for the notion of bandwidth. Digital transmission permits a more flexible and efficient use of bandwidth in both the electromagnetic spectrum and hardwire systems. First, digital transmission is more *flexible* than analog because binary code, unlike analog signals, can represent voice, text, data, images, and/or video, either alone or in combination with one another in any size channel and in any part of the frequency spectrum. Therefore, the bandwidth used to carry digital information can be any size, need not be restricted to just one type of service, and need not be limited to just one part of the spectrum. Second, digital transmission can be sent *without noise or loss of fidelity,* preserving original signal quality no matter how many times a program is transmitted. Third, digital transmissions are more *efficient* than analog because, unlike analog signals, binary code can undergo data compression without signal loss before being sent, allowing more information to be transmitted over the same channel in a given period of time.

Furthermore, analog signals require a dedicated circuit large enough to accommodate the signal being sent and must remain intact during transmission to be received successfully. By contrast, digital signals may be sent over any type of line, transmitted in parts, received out of order, and then reassembled into the original message at the receiver. For example, the digital code representing a high-bandwidth one-hour television program may take several hours to send over a low-bandwidth telephone line, but it can still be retrieved in its original form; analog signals can't survive such treatment. For all these reasons, using radio spectrum for analog signals is nowadays considered wasteful. The implications of this for the television industry, put simply, are that with increased capability, flexibility, and efficiency, *digital transmission can make greater use of available bandwidth, potentially resulting in greater profits.*

Packet Switching

As mentioned, digital signals can be broken into small bundles, intermixed with one another, transmitted out of order, and then successfully reassembled later with no loss of signal quality. They do not even require dedicated lines to carry them. This form of data handling is called **packet switching.**

Packet switching is a method of transmitting digital information in manageable units over available transmission lines. Each unit consists of a segment of the information you are sending, with *header information* or *meta-code*, which is information about the bundle itself, telling, among other things, where each should go (i.e., via e-mail) and how each should be handled once it gets there.

Packet switching allows transmission lines to be shared by millions of users, thus reducing quiescent periods, making the entire system more efficient. Messages do not need to occupy the same circuit from start to finish to survive transmission (in the language of the telephone company, packet-switched digital messages do not require *dedicated lines*). Furthermore, different messages can be sent through the same line sequentially without concern that they will be confounded with one another.

Both the traditional PSTN and the newer Integrated Services Digital Network (ISDN), introduced in the United States in 1992, use the same twisted-pair copper wire infrastructure between homes and central offices. Both were designed for continuous voice carriage. However, ISDN makes the local loop digital by connecting directly with digital technology at the central office. This means that unlike traditional analog telephone service, ISDN lines eliminate the need for digital content to undergo analog-to-digital conversions (i.e., via a modem) to be transmitted.

Unfortunately, both the traditional local loop and ISDN are circuit-switched connections that function exactly like a dedicated line—that is, when engaged, they serve just the parties connected to that line, to the exclusion of all others, even when no data are being sent. This arrangement is wasteful whenever the connection is used for data transfer rather than voice transmission (i.e., e-mailing video content or downloading Web pages) because in such instances, unlike continuous voice communication, data may be sent in bursts (or *packets*) during periods when the line connecting them is available. For this reason, data transmissions are characterized as *bursty,* meaning that transmission times may be intermixed with times of no activity. During such periods, other network users *could* be using that line for data transfer, but because it is tied up or dedicated in a circuit-switched arrangement, it is unavailable. For bursty data, it is a more efficient use of network assets to use transmission lines in a packet-switched arrangement to accommodate multiple users.

Packet switching as a mode of data transfer is generally attributed to a 1964 U.S. Department of Defense project by the Advanced Research Project Agency (ARPA), whose charge it was to develop a computer network called ARPAnet, the precursor of the Internet. By the 1980s, other networks sprang up based on the ARPAnet model. By the mid-1990s, these were absorbed into a network of networks, now called the Internet. By 1998, the number of computers connected to the Internet grew from 4 million to more than 30 million (Lu, 1998, p. 24). During that time, local-area networks (LANs) were brought on-line to connect computers in a local area to allow sharing of both data (including binary code of television programs) and hardware.

The reason the telephone company is the most desirable infrastructure for computer traffic is simple: The PSTN is the most ubiquitous system currently available for such functions. Among its most valuable assets is that it has hundreds of millions of telephones already in place providing both wire and wireless interactive (two-way) connections for information exchange.

Unfortunately, because computers process only digital code, and the phone company was originally designed to handle only analog voice traffic, many technical challenges have had to be overcome to reconcile these two essentially incompatible modes of communication. Nevertheless, the PSTN has, with adjustments, proven to be a feasible conduit for a lot of digital traffic. What makes it especially attractive is that it is the least expensive and most pervasive network available for such service. The alternative—namely, building a separate digital network of comparable magnitude—is less attractive because, among other reasons, it would be prohibitively expensive to build one with coverage comparable to that of the PSTN.

The best solution, therefore, is to develop technology to augment and adapt the extant telephone system for digital functions. And that is exactly what is being done. One way to send digital information over the analog local loop is by converting digital signals into analog sounds that can be carried over telephone lines. The first device built for this function was the modem. The term *modem* stands for modulator-demodulator. When placed between a computer terminal and a telephone line, it produces tones from carrier signals modulated by binary data, performing translation functions between them. Because the telephone system was set up for two-way communication, modems perform both modulation and demodulation processing of the tones. By way of a computer, a modem, and a telephone, users can access and share a vast array of binary-coded messages, including television programs.

Throughput

Digital bandwidth is measured by **throughput,** a measure of the amount of bandwidth carrying *meaningful* data compared to the overall information capacity of a device or channel. In digital channels, some available bandwidth is always used for nondata carriage functions (e.g., header information telling receiving computers the number and order of packets that should be received and other quality control functions). Therefore, throughput is always less than maximum capacity.

In addition, the speed of a channel is conditioned by the capacity of the receiver equipment it is "speaking" to. That is, if a fast system is sending data to a slower one, they must operate at a mutually acceptable level, which is the *fall-back rate* of the slower system. To do this, systems are equipped to monitor this aspect of their interaction, and this negotiation at the beginning of their interaction (called a *handshake*) determines the data rate that can be used. Digital systems also feature a method of checking for errors in transmission, known as a *checksum* calculation, with further cost to throughput.

In digital systems where interactivity is not possible (e.g., in compact disks or DVDs), a receiving computer cannot request that information be sent again if an error is detected. In such cases, a *forward error correction* method is used to maintain quality. In such systems, redundant information is sent for purposes of comparison. If discrepancies are detected, the system can then substitute code for data that fail to arrive intact. Some digital video satellite systems use forward error correction methods to maintain quality.

For all these reasons, raw bandwidth should not be taken as the true measure of channel capacity. Rather, quality control features in the form of meta-code must be taken into account to get a true picture of signal capacity in a digital channel.

Digital Compression

Meta-code, error correction procedures, checksum calculations, and so on are not the only issues that can alter channel capacity in digital transmission systems; the ability to compress data files before they are sent can also have an influence. But unlike the items mentioned above, which all reduce throughput, data compression actually increases it. For example, some high-bandwidth digital content (e.g., a video teleconference) can exceed a channel's (i.e., a phone line's) transmission capability. In such cases, a practical solution is to translate long strings of repeating binary code into shorter strings before they are transmitted and then include metacode telling the receiving computer how to retrieve the original content from the shorter strings. This strategy of data handling is called *digital compression.* Digital compression takes two forms: **lossy compression** and **lossless compression.** Lossy compression refers to digital compression that results in some loss of information when a data file is retrieved.

As an example of lossy compression, imagine a video teleconference featuring a static image of a group of executives seated around a table with a gray wall in the background. In this case, the video image may feature the same code for color and location for 90% of the pixels comprising the image for a significant period of time. Because much of the image is static for long periods, it makes sense to employ an image algorithm that reduces the code specifying the refresh rate of the video transmission for those parts of the signal that do not change, thus reducing significantly the bandwidth required to maintain an acceptable picture. When a motion occurs that interrupts the status of the pixels (e.g., an executive moves to the podium to give a report), the portion of the video image affected by the motion can be refreshed once again. In this example, some video information at the beginning of the new motion is lost, but the loss is insignificant. Therefore, the compression algorithm used is called *lossy* because losing certain parts of the signal is acceptable.

However, sometimes *any* signal loss resulting from compression is unacceptable. In such cases, the compression algorithm used must be capable of retrieving the original signal in its entirety. Such compression algorithms are called *lossless.*

An example of lossless compression is when a replacement algorithm specifies a short code to be used in place of a longer code, as when the letter *X* is substituted for a long and complex calculus formula appearing repeatedly in a math book. After transmission of the text file, an algorithm reverses the process so that every appearance of *X* is replaced once again by the calculus formula. Such a compression algorithm would be lossless because none of the information in the original message is lost. Lossless compression is necessary whenever any loss of the original data could be fatal to the meaning of the message.

Two compression standards have been widely adopted in the television industry: One, called *JPEG* (pronounced "jay-peg"), is named after the organization that developed both lossless and lossy versions of compression for storing and transmitting still images, the Joint Photographic Experts Group; the other, called *MPEG-2* (pronounced "em-peg 2"), is named after the organization that developed this lossy compression technique for motion visuals for both the television and film industries, the Moving Picture Experts Group.

MPEG-2 compression is similar to the video teleconference example given above. It is a form of lossy compression designed to increase throughput of video signals. However, while successfully reducing bandwidth requirements, it has negative implications for editing.

Put simply, MPEG was not developed to be edited; it was designed for preedited video intended for playback only. What makes the editing of MPEG video difficult is that compressed frames cannot be used as edit points. To offset this shortcoming, the MPEG-2 standard periodically sends a full frame of video (called a "reference frame") that can be edited. The problem is that the reference frame is generally sent only two or three times per second, which means that editors are forced make cuts fully a third or half second away from where they may want to make them. For some work, such as inserting additional footage between a commercial and a program segment, this limitation may be acceptable, but for cutting between speakers, it may cause serious synchronization problems.

To overcome this limitation, some systems allow reference frames to be recalled at selected locations. Other solutions include using a system of compression called *intraframe compression*, where each frame of video is compressed while still allowing any frame to be used as an edit point.

Video Distribution and Delivery

Since the inception of the television industry, new technologies have been added to expand distribution. Both wire and wireless technologies increase available bandwidth for distributing products and services. Cable connections include coaxial and fiber-optic cable; wireless connections include terrestrial microwave and satellite radio transmitters. Since the debut of these technologies, improvements have increased their capabilities at an impressive rate. Here I briefly describe some of these technologies and their role in video distribution and delivery.

Coaxial Cable. Coaxial cable or "coax" (rhymes with "no tax") uses two electronic conductors. One is a center copper wire sheathed in a protective layer of insulating material called a dielectric. The second is a wire mesh made of copper or aluminum wrapped around the dielectric. An outer layer of plastic shielding forms the outer body of the cable, providing insulation (see Figure 3.18). The diameter of coax cable varies from as small as .8 mm to more than 2 inches. Coaxial cable is named such because it has two wires with a common axis.

Coaxial cable makes it possible to transmit long distances with little signal loss. Its shielding reduces interference usually present in standard wiring. Its structure also makes it possible for it to handle signals well into the GHz range while minimizing spurious radiation. To offset signal loss that does occur, amplifiers (called repeaters) are added at regular intervals throughout the distribution system.

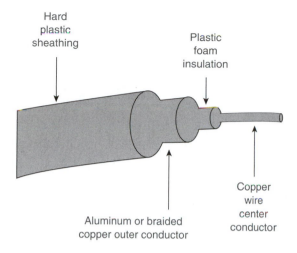

Hard
plastic
sheathing

Plastic
foam
insulation

Copper
wire
center
conductor

Aluminum or braided
copper outer conductor

Figure 3.18   Coaxial cable. Exposed view of coaxial cable used in transmitting signals for telephone and video traffic.

For decades, U.S. television networks delivered programs to their affiliates through the use of coaxial cable provided by AT&T, the nation's long-line telephone company. One reason coaxial cable has been used for this service is because it delivers high-frequency signals more efficiently than standard copper wire. Coaxial cable is now being replaced by fiber-optic cable.

Optical Fiber. Fiber-optic cable uses flexible glass in place of copper or aluminum, as well as light pulses in place of electrical signals, to transmit digital information (see Photo 3.4).

The basic principle on which fiber-optic cable operates is to use a pipe to carry light. Signals through fiber-optic cable may be encoded using either a laser light or light-emitting diode (LED) and decoded by a photodiode at the receiving end.

There are many advantages to using optical fiber in telecommunications applications. First, glass is lighter, cheaper, and more plentiful than copper or aluminum. Second, and more important, brute capacity for encoding information with light is unsurpassed by any other conduit used for message transmission. For example, because light is electromagnetic radiation ranging in the hundreds and thousands of billions of cycles per second, it offers extremely large signal capacity. Its high frequency means that it can be turned on and off quickly, making it capable of carrying a great deal of digital data in a short amount of time over a single fiber. Thus, a single glass strand of optical fiber has more than 600 times the capacity of a coaxial cable; in short, fiber-optic cable has huge bandwidth, with all of the attendant implications for economic competition, even against satellite

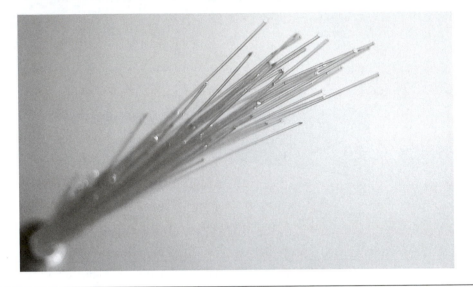

Photo 3.4   Fiber-optic cable with its light-carrying capability makes it possible to carry
tremendous bandwidth compared to other types of cable.

technology. Third, electrical interference is nonexistent in optical fiber; this means clearer signals for both audio and video. Finally, when properly installed, fiber optics cable exhibits very little signal loss (*attenuation*), so fewer amplifiers (called regenerative repeaters) are needed to maintain signal strength. These benefits are attractive to cable television companies, which long for technologies that offer virtually unlimited capacity.

Of course, optical fiber technology has its downside. First, conversion from metal to glass is labor intensive and therefore expensive. In addition, connecting and switching fiber-optic transmissions can be tricky, as the glass used in the lines must not include any impurities. Furthermore, since the frequencies of natural light are too incoherent to travel effectively through fiber, lasers or LEDs must be used. Another problem is that light waves traveling through the pipe may take slightly different paths—some travel straight down the axis of the pipe, whereas others reflect and bounce their way through. Because all these paths have different lengths, signals arrive at their destinations at slightly different times, resulting in what has come to be called *smearing* or *pulse spreading*. This factor limits the rate at which data can be sent over a line without being corrupted.

Nevertheless, the move is on to make the switch. As of 1994, the regional Bell operating companies, or RBOCs (rhymes with "car locks"), had already installed more than 2 million miles of fiber-optic cable, while the major cable television companies, all of which now use fiber in some parts of their systems, had laid over 100,000 miles (Dominick, Sherman, & Copeland, 1996, p. 126; Dominick, Sherman, & Messere, 2000, p. 68).

AT&T began installing submarine fiber-optic cable in the 1980s to supplement undersea copper telephone cables. Such deployments offer a cost-effective option for intercontinental delivery of television programs instead of satellite systems.

The service capacity of fiber-optic lines has been truly impressive. According to some experts, the upper limit of a single fiber-optic channel is about 200 Gbps, or 200 billion bits per second, enough to carry 4,000 television signals. At this rate, if all of the light spectrum that could be harnessed for optical fiber were used, the theoretical capacity would be 50,000 Gbps or 50 Tbps (terabits or trillions of bits per second), enough to supply carriage for a million television programs to a single household (imagine the reruns).

One difficulty with fiber-optic systems as they have developed over the years is their incompatibility with one another. Interconnecting fiber systems built to different specifications means that special interfaces must be designed for handing off signals from one to another.

Terrestrial Microwave Transmission. Radio transmission in the form of microwaves (in current terms, roughly from 1 to 50 GHz, practically speaking) is used to carry broadcast signals and other services in the United States.

In terrestrial microwave transmission, radio waves are sent between antennas using microwave dish antennas and/or horn-shaped metal pipes called *waveguides* (see Figure 3.19). Some of the uses of microwave bands are for long-distance

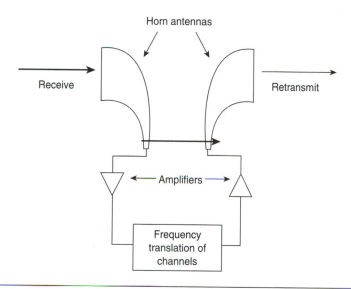

Figure 3.19   Diagram of a terrestrial microwave transmitter.

SOURCE: Adapted from A. M. Noll (1998), *Introduction to Telephones and Telephones Systems, 3/e.* Reprinted with permission from Archtech House.

NOTE: Microwave relays receive radio signals, change their frequencies, and retransmit them.

telecommunication, cable broadcasts, and cable point-to-point transmissions. As is well known in broadcasting, the nature of microwave radio energy is such that it must follow a line-of-sight path. Therefore, communication between antennas is possible only if there is an unobstructed view between them. For a microwave radio signal to cross the country, therefore, terrestrial towers must be spaced at no more than about 26 miles from one another to avoid having their signals blocked by the curvature of the Earth.

Microwave signals also dissipate relatively quickly. Therefore, to maintain signal strength, repeaters are used to amplify signals along their path. The usual practice is to beam a signal from a waveguide to a target antenna, where its frequency is shifted to a different channel to avoid jamming. Then it is amplified and sent on its way through another waveguide.

Satellites. In some situations, it is either too costly or infeasible to build a series of terrestrial microwave towers for delivering broadcasting products and services to audiences and subscribers. For example, sparsely populated rural areas are not cost-effective investments for such infrastructure, and stringing towers across oceans is simply impractical. In these cases, placing a microwave transmitter up in the sky aboard a satellite is the answer.

Satellite technology enables microwave signals to cross the ocean in one hop (see Figure 3.20). Satellites placed over the equator in **geosynchronous** orbits (meaning that they stay above the same spot on Earth at all times) must be at an altitude of 22,300 miles. When deployed this way, satellites take 24 hours to make one revolution of the Earth. Radio transmission between a satellite and a ground station is constant and reliable when the satellite maintains the same position relative to the Earth while in orbit. This is a great advantage because ground stations do not have to be moved to maintain contact and signal strength with the satellite. Satellites can then receive reliable signals, amplify them, shift them to a new

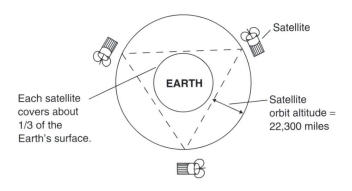

Figure 3.20   Diagram of satellites in orbit in relation to the Earth.

frequency (to avoid interference), and then retransmit them to ground stations thousands of miles away. Circuits that do this are called *transponders*.

The effective coverage area of a signal beamed to Earth from a satellite is called a *footprint* (see Figure 3.21). Access to the satellite's signal varies as a function of the size of the footprint, which is in large part determined by the satellite's transmitting power.

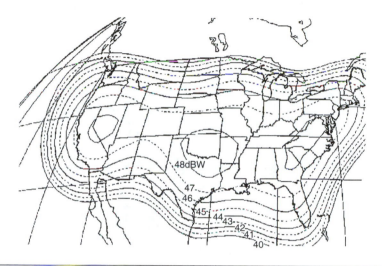

Figure 3.21   Satellite footprint showing area of strongest signal strength in the central portion of the coverage area.

One fundamental advantage of satellites over older terrestrial relay technology is that whereas repeaters on land can link one location with only two others, a satellite can link a group of program or service suppliers (e.g., television networks) to an unlimited number of ground stations in multiple locations at no extra cost. For this reason, satellites are called *distance insensitive*.

A geosynchronous satellite signal takes about ¼ second for it to travel up to and ¼ second to travel down from the satellite. Such delays, while insignificant for bursty data, can be annoying for an interactive telephone conversation. For this reason, satellites are not the best choice for voice transmission. However, they are excellent for one-way distribution of television signals (called TVRO for TV receive-only signals) among networks, cable companies, and affiliate stations. In addition, there is growth in direct-broadcast satellite (DBS) programming from program suppliers directly to homes.

Unfortunately, in reality, satellites deployed in geosynchronous orbit are not perfectly fixed in relation to the Earth; they require adjustment. To do this, noncommunication (*telemetry*) signals are traded between satellites and Earth stations to make corrections using fuel and rockets aboard the satellites. Eventually, the fuel runs out. When it does, satellites must be replaced.

Cellular Telephony

Without doubt, the success in recent years of wireless cellular telephone service has been among the most impressive developments in digital communication, with deep implications for video production and distribution.

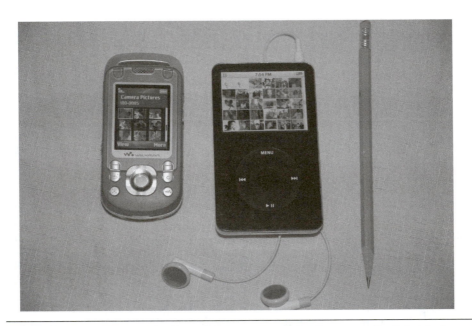

Photo 3.5   Cell phones are no longer just for phone calls. These versatile digital devices now enable users to download and watch videos wirelessly from the Internet, providing video and audio capability just like the MP-3 player (or video i-Pod) next to it.

In 1990, 6 years after cellular service began in the United States, there were 5.3 million U.S. subscribers. By 1996, that number had grown to more than 44 million. In 2006, the number of U.S. subscribers has reached over 200 million. The ability to watch streaming video wirelessly is largely the result of the successful development and deployment of cellular telephone technology.

Access to the World Wide Web via cell phones is also on the rise. It is estimated that by the end of 2001, about 100 million subscribers were accessing text-based content via their cell phones. By 2004, according to some estimates, the worldwide number of cellular wireless Web surfers had grown to more than 750 million. In America alone, some analysts have predicted that by 2006, the number of Americans with Web-enabled phones have topped 50 million.

Cell phone technology connects users to regular wire and portable (wireless) telephones using two-way radio transmission. In the early (precellular) days of mobile telephony, a few dozen channels in an area provided telephone service with a single transmitter covering a 25-mile radius. Access was limited because if a user engaged a frequency, it was unavailable for anyone else until the user completed a call. This approach quickly led to congestion problems. The introduction of the basic principles of cellular service, developed by Bell Labs in the 1940s, solved the congestion problem. By the 1970s, cellular technology became viable for widespread service.

Technical Principles. In cell service, the big improvement over early mobile telephone technology is the reuse of channels to increase access. The ability to reuse channels is due to a scheme that places a low-power transmitter or base station into a small area (called a cell) inside the larger service area (see Figure 3.22).

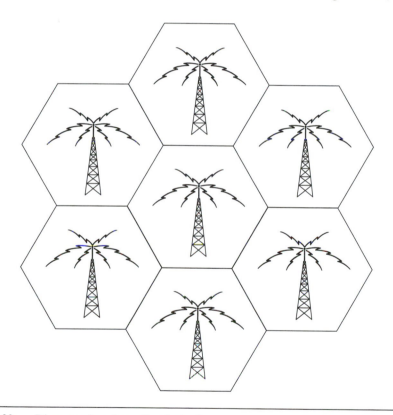

Figure 3.22   Diagram of a scheme for placing low-power transmitters into small areas for carrying phone traffic.

SOURCE: Adapted from A. M. Noll (1998), *Introduction to Telephones and Telephones Systems, 3/e*. Reprinted with permission from Archtech House.

NOTE: Cellular telephone areas are ideally shaped like hexagons. Six are placed on a circular arrangement with a seventh in the center; each has its own low-power transmitter.

Mobile Telephone Switching Office. Cells are typically 6 to 12 miles in radius. Each base station is equipped with a low-power (less than 100-watt) transmitter and is receiver-controlled by the service provider's mobile telephone switching office (MTSO). The low power of each transmitter means that the same frequency can be reused in other parts of the service area without causing interference.

The MTSO directs all call activity (see Figure 3.23). When a cell phone initiates a call, a control channel receives a signal to assign a channel pair for service; if available, the MTSO assigns one. As the cell phone moves from one cell to another, the MTSO tracks its movement through adjacent base stations, all of which can sense the signal strength of the cell phone's transmitter. The base station receiving the strongest signal assumes service. The assumption of service by an adjacent base station is called a *handoff*.

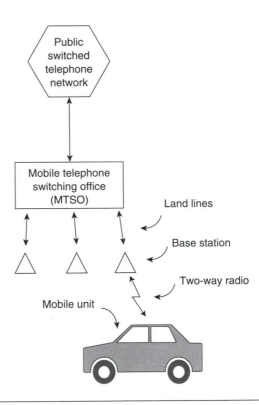

Figure 3.23   Diagram illustrating the relationship of the mobile telephone switching office (MTSO) to the public switched telephone network (PSTN).

SOURCE: Adapted from A. M. Noll (1998), *Introduction to Telephones and Telephones Systems, 3/e.* Reprinted with permission from Archtech House

NOTE: Each cell phone communicates via two-way radio with a base station. Base stations communicate over landlines with the MTSO, which maintains communication with the PSTN. Systems such as this permit wireless downloads of MP-3s and videos in addition to handling phone traffic.

To have a full understanding of how technology enables us to create, store, transmit, receive, consume, and manipulate television and other content through both wire and wireless means, it is essential to know something about broadcasting, computers, and distribution networks. All three infrastructures are critical to commerce in both mass media products and services; without all three, digital video would not be what it is today.

KEY TERMS

frequency 35	aspect ratio 49
period 35	chrominance 49
amplitude 35	luminance 49
wavelength 35	saturation 49
phase 35	digital television (DTV) 52
electromagnetic waves 36	high-definition television (HDTV or HD) 52
high fidelity 37	
transducer 37	progressive scanning 54
amplitude modulation (AM) 40	letterboxing 56
frequency modulation (FM) 40	sampling 57
demodulation 41	quantizing 57
resolution 42	broadband 57
photoconductivity 44	narrowband 57
photoemissive effect 44	binary code 58
pickup tube 45	artificial intelligence (AI) 66
charge-coupled device (CCD) 45	semiconductors 66
camera control unit (CCU) 45	bandwidth 69
viewfinder 45	packet switching 72
pixels 46	throughput 74
persistence of vision 48	lossy compression 75
field 48	lossless compression 75
frame 48	geosynchronous 80

QUESTIONS FOR REVIEW

How does signal modulation make communication at a distance possible?

Describe the process of transduction in a microphone.

How do AM and FM differ? Why are FM signals less susceptible than AM to static and interference?

Why did video engineers choose a scanning method for video signal transmission?

What components of the video signal must be sent to reproduce a coherent program at the receiver?

What are some production implications of current television technology?

What are some differences between the NTSC standard and the new DTV standard?

Describe several implications that result from integrating television technology with computers and telecommunications networks.

NOTES

1. With digital television (DTV) systems, three scanning standards have emerged, including both interlaced and progressive formats, described in more detail later.

2. Actual picture resolution and frame rates of a received video image may differ from the resolution and frame rate of the sent signal, depending on the user's needs. For example, a DTV receiver may receive an interlaced image at one level of resolution but display it differently; that is, it may play a program back at 24-p (24 frames per second, progressively scanned), even though the program may have originally been sent at 60-i (60 frames per second, interlaced scanned), performing such feats through the use of digital signal processors. Both the 480- and 1,080-line formats offer interlaced or progressive scanning.

3. Silicon-based chips for computers are the semiconductor industry standard, but industry researchers are planning for a transition away from conventional silicon transistors to nanotechnology using organic molecules and carbon-based materials as a way to increase computing power beyond what is believed possible with silicon. The transition to nanotechnology is now scheduled for 2015 (see Markoff, 2005d).

4. A thorough review of the history of computers and binary code is beyond the scope of this book. Interested readers wanting more information about these topics should read "Computers in Communication" in Shyles (2003, pp. 45–93). Excellent additional sources abound in print and on the Internet. In print, see Augarten (1984) and Petzold. On-line sources include http://goldenink .com/computersandnetworks.shtml (retrieved December 26, 2005) and http://inventors.about.com/ library/blcoindex.htm (retrieved December 26, 2005). Individuals who deserve further study include Blaise Pascal, Gottfried Leibnitz, Joseph-Marie Jacquard, Charles Babbage, George Boole, Claude Shannon, John Vincent Atanosoff, George Stibitz, Alan Turing, John Mauchly, J. Presper Eckert, John von Neumann, Jack Kilby, and John Noyce. While this list is not exhaustive, it is a great start.

5. At this writing, the Motion Picture Experts Group has MPEG versions up to MPEG-7, but it appears that the MPEG-2 standard is still among the leaders.

PART II

ELEMENTS AND TECHNIQUES OF VIDEO PRODUCTION

Chapter 4

LIGHT AND LENSES

Light is the universal currency of television—without it, no pictures would be possible. The way light falls upon a scene critically affects the way the scene appears. For these reasons, you need some basic understanding of the nature of light in order to use it to best advantage in making programs.

Similarly, since light interacts with different lenses (or lens settings) in different but predictable ways, understanding how lenses work offers you powerful advantages in planning lighting designs. For example, with the proper choice of lenses and lens settings, you can determine which objects in an image will be kept in clear view and which will be pushed out of focus, thus increasing your ability to shape the impact and meaning of every shot.

This chapter describes physical aspects of light relevant to television production, especially its interaction with lenses and filters. The topics covered are the following:

Light as radiant energy
- The law of reflection
- The inverse square law
- The role of lenses

Focusing characteristics of lenses
- Focal length
- f/number

Aesthetic effects of lenses
- Depth of field
- Perspective

Zoom lenses

Contrast and color

- White balance
- Color temperature
- Filters

LIGHT AS RADIANT ENERGY

Physicists define light as "visible electromagnetic wave radiation" or "radiant energy that can be seen" and locate it in that portion of the electromagnetic spectrum between the infrared and ultraviolet wavelengths (see Figure 4.1). Light viewed this way may be thought of as essentially the same phenomenon as radio waves, with this difference: Radio transmissions use wavelengths that may be several meters long, while wavelengths of light are only a few hundred-thousandths of a centimeter long. At these wavelengths, the energy transmitted is visible to our eyes.

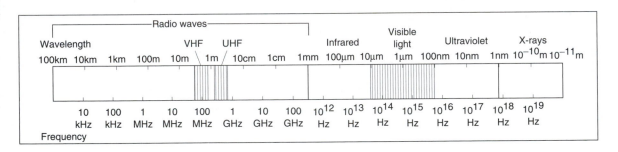

Figure 4.1   A portion of the electromagnetic spectrum showing the approximate position of visible light with respect to other kinds of waves. Note the areas used by VHF and UHF television.

We can learn much about the nature of light by looking at a simple pinhole camera, as in Figure 4.2. In this device, an image of a stationary object is formed on an image surface by light passing through a small hole in a screen. Rays of light reflecting from the object head toward the screen. Since light travels in straight lines (a quality known as *rectilinear propagation*), the light rays that do not travel exactly in the direction of the hole are blocked. The rays that do pass through the hole form an inverted image of the object. Those rays that come from the top of the object arrive at the bottom of the image surface; similarly, those that come from the bottom of the object arrive at the top of the image surface. Likewise, rays that come from the right side of the object arrive on the left side of the image surface, and those that come from the left side of the object arrive on the right side of the image surface. Some rays from all parts of the object get through. In this way, an inverted and reversed image of the entire object is formed.

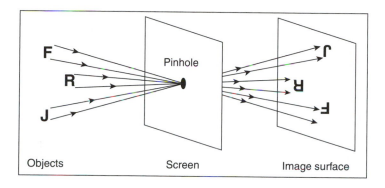

Figure 4.2   This figure demonstrates the "rectilinear propagation" quality of light; that is, the fact that light travels in straight lines.

Note also that light scales image size according to the distances from the object to the pinhole and from the pinhole to the image surface. As the image surface is moved farther from the hole, the images get larger because light from the object spreads out in space. Conversely, as the object itself is moved further from the hole, the image it casts gets smaller. Notice also that with a fixed amount of light, the brightness of the image decreases as image size increases.

The Law of Reflection

The reflection of light enables us to see the moon at night and is responsible for most of our visual experience of the world. On smooth surfaces, reflection occurs in a predictable fashion. It follows the **law of reflection,** as illustrated in Figure 4.3.

The figure shows a mirror with a ray of light striking it. The imaginary line perpendicular to the mirror, at the point where the light strikes, is called the *normal.* The ray approaching the mirror, called the incident ray, makes an angle called the *angle of incidence* with the normal. Similarly, the reflected ray makes an *angle of reflection* with the normal. Regardless of how the surface is oriented to the beam of light, *the angles of incidence and reflection are equal.*

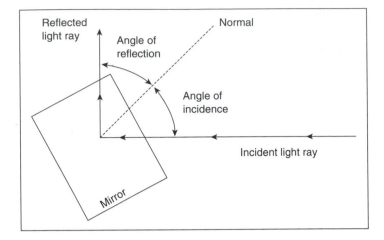

Figure 4.3　　A ray of light striking a mirror demonstrates the *law of reflection:* The angle of incidence equals the angle of reflection. Both angles are measured from the normal, the imaginary line perpendicular to the mirror at the point where the light strikes.

The law of reflection is simple but critical in planning lighting designs for television. For example, by paying attention to the law of reflection, you can direct unwanted light away from the set and the camera lens. In Chapter 5, we will see how crucial this can be.

The Inverse Square Law

As light travels away from a source, it spreads out—that is, the area that it illuminates increases. At the same time, the intensity of light falling on a given area decreases. In effect, the light beam grows wider but dimmer. To put it scientifically, *the area illuminated by a light source increases with the square of the distance from the source.* The intensity of illumination on a given area decreases at the same rate. Physicists call this principle the **inverse square law** (see Figure 4.4).

We can see the inverse square law at work when we project an image on a screen with a projector. If we move the projector farther from the screen and refocus, it does not appear as bright. Though the amount of light on the screen remains the same, it is being distributed over a larger area. This means there is now less light per unit area. In fact, the inverse square law tells us that if we double the distance from the projector to the screen, the intensity of light on the screen goes down by a factor of 4. That is, the light for a given unit area is only one quarter as bright. Remembering this property of light is important in creating lighting designs that work.

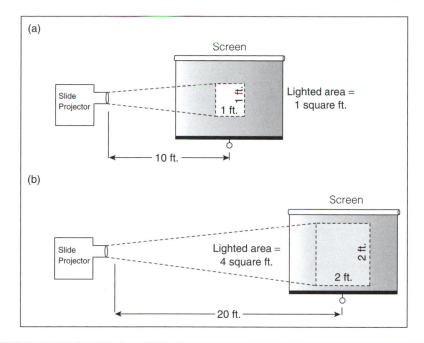

Figure 4.4   The field lit by a projector illustrates the inverse square law. Comparing the two parts, we see that the screen in part (b) is twice as far from the projector in part (a). Because the distance to the screen has been doubled, the area illuminated is four times as large (the square of 2 is 4), but the intensity of the screen's illumination is only one fourth as strong (¼ is the inverse of 4).

The Role of Lenses

Look again at Figure 4.2. As light emerges from the pinhole, it spreads out, covering a wider area, and consequently the sharpness of the image is reduced. To minimize this degradation of the image, we could keep the **aperture** of the camera—the hole through which light enters—extremely small, but that would let in so little light that a much longer exposure time would be needed. (Some photos made with an actual pinhole camera have used exposure times of several hours.) Conversely, if we increase aperture size to allow in more light, we would reduce exposure time but suffer an unacceptable loss of image sharpness.

It is only by controlling light in some way that the conflicting needs of image sharpness and sufficient light level can be met. This is the function of a lens. A lens can converge incoming light rays, making it possible to use larger apertures while still achieving sharp focus.

FOCUSING CHARACTERISTICS OF LENSES

Lenses rely on the fact that light slows down when it passes from air into a denser transparent medium such as glass. When light passes through a flat sheet of glass, all parts of the light slow down at the same time and then speed up at the same time as they exit the glass, continuing to travel in the same direction. But if the glass is curved or of varying thickness, some light rays take longer than others to get through the glass, and they change direction when they exit—in short, some of the light bends or *refracts*. Convex (outward-curving) lenses converge incoming light rays, whereas concave (inward-curving) lenses spread the rays farther apart.

When a convex lens brings light rays to a point, that point is called a **focus.** For imaging purposes, in almost all cases, more than one lens is used, and it is essential that the centers of all the lens elements lie on a straight line, called the *axis* of the lens system. If we construct an imaginary plane perpendicular to the axis at the point of focus, we call that plane the *focal plane.* It is here that one places film to receive an image in a traditional still camera.

Focal Length

The **focal length** of a lens is the distance between the center of a lens and the point at which a sharp image of an object is formed, often expressed in millimeters (mm). The factors that influence focal length or bending power of a lens include the density of the glass and the curvature of its surfaces. Lenses of shorter focal length generally have a wider **angle of view**—that is, they capture a larger horizontal and vertical area in front of the lens, whereas lenses of longer focal length have a narrower angle of view and provide a larger image size.[1]

Usually a lens receives light from various objects at a variety of distances from the lens. But the lens will focus sharply on the image plane only for rays within a certain range of distance. Therefore, some parts of the image will be in focus and some will not.

The region of space for which images are acceptably sharp is called **depth of field.** Photos 4.1a and 4.1b illustrate how depth of field can change with different aperture settings. In Photo 4.1a, the depth of field is greater than in 4.1b because the aperture is smaller in 4.1a. Why does aperture setting change depth of field? Because as aperture increases, the light entering the lens from the perimeter travels further than the light entering closer to the center, so the focal planes for the incoming rays differ, resulting in less depth of the field (and less focus) for the image shot with the larger aperture. Thus, we can say, when all other factors are kept equal, *the smaller the aperture, the greater the depth of field.*

(a) **(b)**

Photo 4.1   Two different depths of field when the same scene is shot with the same lens from the same position, but with different aperture settings. In the photo on the left (a), both the foreground and background are in focus, but in the photo on the right (b), the foreground is in focus, while the background is blurry. The photo with the deeper focus was taken using a smaller aperture, resulting in greater depth of field.

f/number

The brightness of an image is largely determined by the amount of light permitted to go through the lens. To control the amount of light entering a lens, an adjustable aperture may be used. In television and photography, an iris diaphragm serves this purpose (see Figure 4.5). The intensity of light collected is also influenced by the magnifying properties of the lens. Lenses of different focal lengths have different magnifying properties.

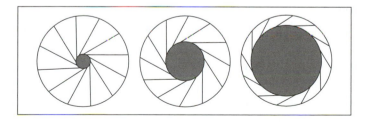

Figure 4.5   A camera's iris diaphragm opens and closes to control the amount of light entering the lens.

Because of these factors, the ratio of focal length to aperture diameter is a useful way to express information about the amount of light entering the camera. The ratio of focal length to aperture diameter is called **f/number** or, in the term often used in the video industry, **f-stop number.**

Does f/number Affect Angle of View?

It may seem that when f/number increases and aperture size decreases, there would be an accompanying decrease in angle of view. But this is not true, for a couple of reasons.

First, *stopping down* the lens—that is, raising the f/number setting to decrease the aperture size and reduce the amount of light permitted to pass through the lens—has no effect on light coming through portions of the lens close to the center. It only blocks light from portions of the lens near the perimeter. Since light from all parts of a scene strikes all parts of the lens, the lens remains able to collect light from all parts of the scene. The net effect of stopping down the lens is to attenuate light from all parts of the scene, not to eliminate light from some parts of the scene. Hence, angle of view remains constant.

Second, the close proximity of the iris to the lens permits light from the scene to be delivered to the entire focal plane regardless of how much or how little of the lens is actually used. The location of the iris with respect to the lens is analogous to the location of a window shade with respect to your eyes when you are leaning on the window sill. If you pull down the shade to a height just above your eyes, you do not change your view of the landscape outside.

As an example, if a lens has a focal length of 50 mm and an aperture or lens opening of 5 mm in diameter, the f/number or f-stop number is 10. For the same lens, if the aperture diameter is 10 mm, the f/number is 5. For any given lens, as f/number increases, aperture diameter decreases.

Knowing that f/numbers relate focal length to aperture opening is critical in the film and photography industries because, unlike the video production setting, they do not have devices like waveform monitors to judge light levels. However, even in video production, f-stop helps determine depth of field, which in turn helps control which objects in a scene will be kept in focus. Knowledge of f-stop numbers is therefore a powerful tool in refining shot composition.

AESTHETIC EFFECTS OF LENSES

Picture content is of paramount importance in television and photography. Deciding which objects to include and exclude from a scene, or determining which objects to emphasize by focusing on the foreground rather than the middle or background, can contribute much to the meaning of a program. Selecting camera angles, as well as deciding how to frame the image, will also influence the emotional impact of every shot. In many cases, the impact of lenses on these decisions can make the difference between a barely adequate production and an outstanding one.

As mentioned above, depth of field is one of the most important characteristics of lenses to consider in shaping program content. Recall that depth of field includes all of the space between the closest and farthest objects that appear to be in focus. Technically speaking, the sharpest plane of focus in the object space is unique—there is an immediate deterioration of focus as one moves away from the focal plane in either direction. But different lens settings yield different rates of fall-off of *acceptable* focus, depending on three variables:

- *Focal length.* When all other conditions are held equal, lenses with shorter focal lengths yield greater depth of field. This is because shorter focal length lenses have more bending power (greater refractive capability). Because of this greater bending power, the image planes for objects at varied distances are closer together, and the image sizes more similar, than for longer focal length lenses.

- *Camera-to-subject distance.* With other things equal, as distance from camera to subject increases, depth of field increases. This is because light rays from distant objects tend to enter the lens more nearly parallel, while light rays from objects close to the camera make greater angles relative to the axis of the lens and cross at greater angles to focus on the focal plane. For this reason, rays from close objects are still converging when they reach the lens and are not brought to focus as quickly as parallel rays entering the lens from more distant objects.

- *Aperture size.* As we already know, when all other factors are held constant, as aperture gets smaller (i.e., as f/number increases), depth of field increases. This is because rays entering the lens closer to the center converge at the focal point at smaller angles to each other than rays entering from the perimeter.

It helps to remember these principles when planning shots for television. First, controlling depth of field enables you to direct the viewer's attention to preselected parts of the picture. For example, in a product advertisement where the main shot is the product in the foreground, you may want to make all other objects in the middle and background somewhat blurry. In this case, you might choose a long focal length lens, with a large aperture setting and with the product close to the camera.

By contrast, depth of field can be increased to emphasize a grand vista. For example, the central character of a program can be seen for a long period of time riding off into a beautiful sunset, with everything in the frame appearing in focus. To do this, you might use a short focal length lens on a small aperture setting, with the main character slowly moving away.

Perspective

Lenses also help control **perspective,** or the illusion of depth in a two-dimensional picture. This illusion can be created by *linear perspective,* where apparent distance is conveyed by the relative size and location of objects. When the lines of a roadway appear to coverage at a vanishing point or the cables of a bridge appear to get smaller as distance increases, we interpret these cues as indicators of depth. Similarly, objects in the bottom of the frame that overlap other objects are usually interpreted as closer, while objects toward the top of the frame that are overlapped by other objects usually appear to be farther away. Other depth cues result from texture and focus elements. For example, more highly defined texture and detail tend to convey a sense of closeness, while hazy objects appear to be farther away.

Lenses of different focal lengths can produce strikingly different perspective cues. For example, varying focal length can alter the relative sizes of objects, changing the apparent distances between them. As Figure 4.6 shows, shorter focal length lenses expand background space, decreasing the apparent size of background objects while increasing the apparent size of nearby objects. This is because they feature a wider angle of view than is normal for the eye. Since a wider angle of view takes in more object space, objects in the background appear smaller than they appear to the unaided eye. An extreme example of this is found in images captured by what is aptly called a *fish-eye* lens.

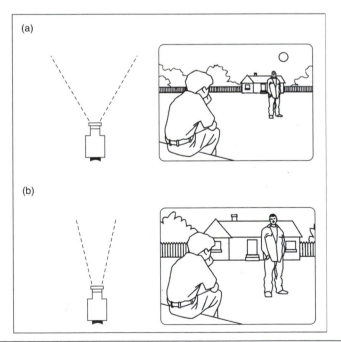

Figure 4.6   The influence of focal length on perspective. (a) A lens with a short focal length and wide angle of view takes in a good deal of background and makes objects in the background seem relatively small and far apart. (b) A lens with a long focal length and narrow angle of view not only takes in less of the background but also makes the background objects seem larger and closer together.

Conversely, longer focal length lenses tend to compress image space. This is because they have a narrower angle of view than that afforded by the eye. Since a narrower angle of view takes in less object space, this tends to magnify distant objects and decrease the apparent distance between them. A *telephoto* lens is a lens of this type used to magnify distant objects.

Knowing how to manipulate perspective as a function of focal length is important for controlling image content. It gives the director tremendous flexibility.

ZOOM LENSES

Nowadays, virtually all television cameras in both studio and field are equipped with *variable focal length lenses,* commonly known as zoom lenses. The **zoom lens** is a complex system of lens elements arranged to allow the spatial relationship of lens components to change. Zoom lenses therefore offer continuous smooth variation in focal length between two limits.

The advantage of such a system is that it permits picture composition to change as you change focal length. When you zoom in, objects in the frame become magnified as they smoothly appear to move closer to the camera. Conversely, you can decrease focal length by zooming out, thus making the objects in the frame appear to recede into the distance. Throughout these actions, if the image is in focus to begin with, focus will be maintained.

For video, zoom lenses are often composed of more than 20 elements, 8 of which may be made of highly refractive glass. In some lenses, as many as 16 different types of glass may be used. When the number of lens elements gets this high, internal reflection of light between elements increases, reducing the total amount of light that gets through the lens to the CCD. When this happens, you may need to increase light intensity to ensure adequate illumination. Furthermore, internal reflections in complex lens systems can cause ghost images and loss of contrast. To reduce such reflections, lens surfaces are given nonreflective coatings.

Steps in Focusing a Zoom Lens

➤ First, zoom in all the way on the object being pictured.
➤ Next, use the focus control to focus the lens.
➤ Then zoom out to compose the desired picture.
➤ Now the lens will remain in focus throughout the entire range of motion.
➤ Refocusing is necessary only when the distance changes from the lens to the object being pictured.

There are several advantages to using the zoom lens in television. First, it makes it possible to "move in" on subjects without physically approaching them. For example, if the subject is being interviewed, a slow zoom-in during a key answer can add visual interest and heighten audience involvement without making a camera-shy guest feel more self-conscious. Furthermore, the zoom lens permits you to frame content with precision as a program unfolds through time. For instance, in a cooking show, a zoom-in to a tight close-up of a specific ingredient or a detail of the cooking process can help clarify a demonstration. Similarly, in a drama, a zoom-out at the right moment to reveal the perpetrator of a crime can be a crucial part of the action. Zoom lenses are also especially good for large public events, such as parades and sporting events, where the work space may be confined but the coverage area is large.

Among the aesthetic disadvantages of the zoom lens (in addition to the technical problems of lower light levels) are the abnormal shifts in perspective that occur while zooming. As you zoom in, focal length increases; this means depth of field decreases, distant space compresses, and the relative size of distant objects increases. Conversely, as you zoom out, all of these effects are reversed. While these factors may not be noticed during small increments of change, they can influence the quality of the overall production. The convenience of the zoom lens should not tempt you to ignore careful placement of the cameras, a subject we will discuss in detail later.

CONTRAST AND COLOR

Besides knowing about lenses, you need to understand the camera's ability to render brightness and color information accurately when different light levels are presented. One basic characteristic of a camera is the minimum amount of light it requires to create a picture. We call this the **operating light level** of the camera, and it can vary quite a bit from one camera to another.

Cameras also differ in **contrast ratio,** which refers to the difference in brightness between the lightest and darkest possible image that the camera can produce. In color cameras, the optimal contrast range is roughly 40:1 or 50:1 (or about 4½ to 5½ f-stops). This means that the brightest possible image the camera is capable of producing is no more than 40 or 50 times brighter than the darkest, a narrower range than that of the human eye.

Knowing this helps you set limits on what can be differentiated for the viewer. For example, if you are displaying two different sets of silverware on crushed velvet, with one set on black velvet and the other on navy blue, the relatively limited contrast range of the camera may make them indistinguishable.

White Balance

Because the color camera breaks light into three separate signals (red, green, and blue), it is necessary to balance the strengths of these signals correctly to maximize accuracy in color reproduction. Accurate color is especially important in rendering flesh tones since large discrepancies in such cases look unnatural and are easily noticed.

Adjusting the levels of signal strength to enable cameras to render colors most accurately is called *setting white balance.* In a studio, setting **white balance** is done by focusing all cameras on a white card under the same lighting conditions that will be used for the production and adjusting their color at the camera control unit until an image is obtained that matches most closely the color of the original card.

Using white as a color reference for the camera makes sense because, as we already know, in light-based systems such as video, white is produced by combining all three additive primary colors of red, blue, and green in just the right amounts. Hence, if levels are set so that the video image of a white card closely matches the white of the actual card, we get accurate colors across the rest of the spectrum. Furthermore, in studio productions using more than one camera, setting white balance for each camera enables subjects and scenery to look the same across all cameras. This is critical for avoiding jarring differences in color rendition of a subject when cutting from one camera to another.

In field settings, in cases where there is no camera control unit, setting white balance is still necessary for capturing colors accurately. To do this, portable cameras have white balance controls. To set white balance in the field, focus the camera on a white card or other convenient white surface under the lighting conditions you intend to use for the shoot, and press the white balance control button. The camera will set the balance and let you know when it is ready.

In addition to setting a white balance, the camera also sets a black balance. In some cameras, black balance must be set manually, but in most cases, this is done automatically by the camera when it is capped.

Color Temperature

In normal daylight, objects are lit with radiation from all parts of the visible spectrum. It is under these conditions that we tend to fix (in our mind's eye) the colors of objects. However, the colors of objects may change under different lighting. Imagine trying to identify the colors of different crayons without the wrappings, lit only by a strong, blue, artificial light.

One reason colors of objects change under different light is that, unlike sunlight, artificial light rarely includes wavelengths from all parts of the visible spectrum. In fact, even artificial light meant to simulate natural sunlight rarely matches all the sun's spectral qualities. Therefore, when using artificial light to illuminate a scene for television, we must compensate somehow for the missing parts of the spectrum if we want to render colors accurately and convincingly.

To help do this, the dominant hues of various light sources have been classified by their **color temperature,** understood in terms of a standard scale of values expressed in degrees Kelvin or just "Kelvin" (K). By this standard, ordinary daylight is located in the range of values between 4,500 and 6,200 K (5,600 K average), with the light of a clear blue sky located as high as 10,000 to 12,000 K. Incandescent studio lights are generally located at around 2,800 to 3,200 K, and fluorescent lights range from about 4,000 to 7,000 degrees Kelvin (nowadays, there are seven different types of fluorescent bulbs, each with a different color temperature). (See Figure C.1 in the section of color plates.)

Notice that, on the Kelvin scale, bluish light has a higher color temperature than reddish light. This is the *reverse* of the way we normally use the terms *warm* and *cool* in reference to color.

The transition from reddish to bluish color as you move from the lower K numbers to the higher ones raises issues for television lighting, especially when mixtures of light are presented to the camera in the same scene. If possible, it is recommended that you avoid such mixing of light sources if you want to present an accurate rendition of skin tones, which is among the best ways of convincing your audience that your video image is rendering the colors of a scene accurately.

Video cameras are normally set for standard tungsten studio light, around the 3,200 K region. Field cameras are equipped with a color filter wheel that enables you to shoot outdoors in natural light by rotating a daylight filter into the path of the lens. However, because different light sources vary so much in color temperature, it is important to white-balance the camera in the same light that will be used for the shoot, or the camera can be confused by possibly discrepant temperatures of light entering it, making it difficult to set a white balance and difficult for the camera to render colors convincingly.

Even within the category of artificial lights, color temperatures may vary widely. While quartz studio lights operate in the 3,200 to 3,500 K range, high-intensity arc lights operate at about 6,600 K. For a more detailed listing of the various color temperatures associated with different light sources (both natural and artificial), see Table 4.1. Obviously, if a transition is made from one light source to another, rebalancing or changing filters may be required.

Filters

As the name implies, a **filter** is a device for eliminating unwanted portions of things that pass through it. Photographic filters are pieces of colored transparent material (usually glass or plastic) placed over lenses or lighting instruments to

Should You Trust Your Eyes?

If you are shooting in a bright interior space where the light quality looks very much like the sunlight outdoors, can you simply move outdoors without color balancing the camera again? Can you trust what your eyes tell you about the similarity of the light?

The short answer: no.

Compared to sunlight, incandescent light contains more orange-yellow color. This fact is not always evident to our eyes, but to a television camera, the differences are quite apparent. If you color balance with incandescent light and then go outdoors without color balancing again, the material you shoot will take on a bluish cast. Conversely, if you color balance for daylight and then come indoors without rebalancing, the indoor footage will appear more orange than it should.

What about mixing natural and artificial light? Since natural light differs so significantly from artificial, it is best to avoid illuminating a subject for video with different types of light at the same time. Doing so confuses the camera.

Table 4.1   Color Temperature Chart for Several Types of Artificial and Natural Light (Kelvin)

Light Source	Degrees Kelvin (K)
Match and candle flame	1,700–1,800
Sunrise and sunset	2,000–3,000
Tungsten bulbs (in the home)	2,500
Tungsten studio lamp (500–1,000 watt)	3,000
Quartz lamp	3,200
Fluorescent lights (various)	3,200–7,500
Tungsten lamps (2,000–10,000 watt)	3,300–3,400
Direct noonday sun	5,500
Daylight (bright sky)	5,500–6,500
Overcast daylight	6,000–7,000
Daylight (shade/cloudy)	7,000–10,000

NOTE: See also color insert C2.

absorb some wavelengths of light while permitting others to pass. Among the functions served by filters are to increase contrast between similar colors, to reduce haze, to reduce brightness in a scene, and to create special effects. Other filters are constructed to pass only wavelengths from a light source that vibrate in a particular plane or reflect at a particular angle, thus eliminating glare and certain reflections; these are called **polarizing filters.**

In addition to filters inside cameras, video often uses **gels**—formerly gelatin, but now usually plastic—placed over a light to change its color temperature to match the color temperatures of other light sources in the scene you are capturing. Matching light sources helps the camera set a white balance, making color rendition more accurate. Gels on lighting instruments can also be used to set a mood or create special effects.

It is important to control the light from sources with highly discrepant color temperatures in order to render colors (and especially skin tones) accurately. For example, if you are shooting indoors with tungsten lights near a window that is letting in natural light, you can cover the window with an amber gel (a large plastic sheet made for such purposes) that will lower the bluish light streaming in to match the K value of the indoor light, or you can put bluish gel filters over the lighting instruments to match the color temperature of the outdoor light coming through the window. Whichever solution you choose, it is better than ignoring the problem. In some cases, such solutions may not be available, in which case, you may have to decide which type of light is dominant and then set the camera's white balance accordingly to render colors accurately, especially skin tones.

KEY TERMS

law of reflection	91	zoom lens	99
inverse square law	92	operating light level	100
aperture	93	contrast ratio	100
focus	94	white balance	101
focal length	94	color temperature	102
angle of view	94	filter	102
depth of field	94	polarizing filter	103
f/number or f-stop number	96	gel	104
perspective	97		

QUESTIONS FOR REVIEW

Why is it helpful in television production to know the law of reflection and the inverse square law? Can you think of examples of how they would help the producer-director in planning productions?

What does changing the f/number setting on a lens do to the aperture size? To the angle of view?

How do focal length, camera-to-subject distance, and aperture size influence depth of field? What combination of factors maximizes depth of field and what combination limits it?

How does a zoom lens alter perspective cues as it moves in on a scene? How do perspective cues change as you zoom out?

In what way does a camera need to be "balanced" for color? Why?

N O T E

1.   Technically speaking, angle of view and focal length are not directly related. This is because almost any lens will accept light rays from any arc in front of it—an arc approaching 180 degrees. But the practical angle of view is that which provides rays that can be used to produce an image, and this is influenced by the focal length.

Chapter 5

LIGHTING EQUIPMENT AND DESIGN

In recent years, advances in video technology have made it possible to produce cameras with greater sensitivity to light than were available in the past. As a result, the basic light levels cameras need for seeing have decreased. But this change does not mean that we can be less careful in planning lighting designs. What principles can guide us in designing a sensible **light plot**—that is, a precise plan showing the types, sizes, positions, and directions of all the lights that will be used? How can lighting enhance the purpose and meaning of a television program?

In addition to providing visibility, lighting enhances the illusion of depth of objects and performers. Lighting can also add meaning, visual beauty, mood, and dramatic dimension to a scene. Lighting provides composition by incorporating shadows and highlights as well as brightness and darkness, thus avoiding giving every object seen by the camera equal status. A picture composed with light and shadow can direct the attention of the viewer to important parts of the image, selectively adding or reducing emphasis.

In creating a lighting design, the process begins by reading through the script. The script should, whenever possible, indicate set elements, talent requirements, subject matter, content, sequence of events, tone, and purpose of the program, all of which help determine lighting needs. The script might also indicate time of day, locale, and the presence of specific light sources such as sunlight or lamplight. Important information about talent movement may also be given, and this too can influence lighting decisions. The light plot is further conditioned by the physical limitations of cameras and the physical constraints of the set or the field space (for instance, ceiling height, size of studio, location and direction of the sun, etc.).

It is essential to develop light plots holistically, that is, to recognize that lighting decisions affect, and are affected by, all the physical and symbolic elements of every production. Therefore, lighting design should be viewed as an integral part of the overall production process. After surveying the common types of lighting equipment used in video production, this chapter presents a rationale and techniques for creating lighting designs that are pleasing, efficient, and consistent with program content and objectives. The topics include the following:

Lighting equipment
- Lighting grid
- Dimmer board
- Lighting instruments
- Additional lighting equipment

Fundamentals of lighting design
- Naturalistic lighting
- A sample naturalistic light plot

Departures from naturalism
- Flat lighting

Motivating light sources

Lighting in more complicated cases

Field lighting
- Procedures
- Equipment

LIGHTING EQUIPMENT

This section describes lighting equipment used in studio production. Field lighting is discussed later in the chapter. Among the items to be discussed are the lighting grid, the dimmer board, common types of lighting instruments and their components, and peripheral equipment and hardware.

Lighting Grid

The studio environment contains a **lighting grid** (see Photo 5.1) that consists of a series of parallel or cross-hatched sturdy metal bars hanging near the ceiling or affixed to the studio walls close to the ceiling. The grid provides numerous locations for hanging lighting instruments above sets and talent on the studio floor. In addition to the grid itself, electrical outlets are spaced near each bar at regular intervals to provide electrical power. Lighting grids make it easy to light sets and

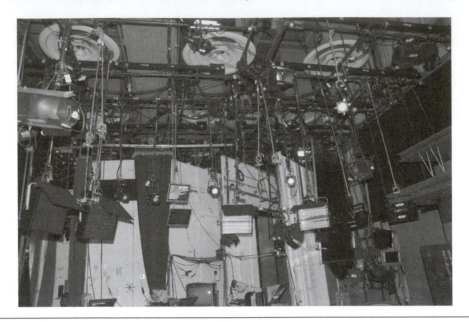

Photo 5.1   Lighting grids provide locations for hanging lighting instruments above sets and talent on the studio floor. In addition to the grid itself, electrical outlets are spaced at regular intervals to provide electrical power.

talent from above. Lighting grids also get lights and cables off the floor so that cameras can move more freely around the studio floor.

Dimmer Board

Electrical outlets are wired to a **dimmer board** (see Photo 5.2) equipped with switches and faders that permit single instruments or groups of instruments to be turned on and off instantly or faded up and down gradually. The dimmer board may be located in the studio, in the control room, or at some other remote location. Many dimmer boards permit the grouping or *ganging* together of selected instruments, which can then be manipulated with a single fader or controller. Some dimmer boards use rheostats as dimmers. Others use computer software, making them capable of executing complex instructions. Many boards provide a master switch for controlling electrical power to all instruments connected to the system.

Lighting Instruments

Among the most commonly used lighting instruments are those that provide directional sources of light, called spotlights, and those that provide more diffuse sources of light, called floodlights. The most common spotlight used in television

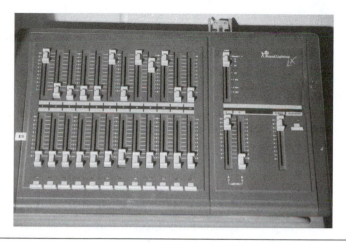

Photo 5.2   Dimmer boards enable you to control lighting instruments used in a production with both faders (for varying intensities) and switches (for turning lights on and off).

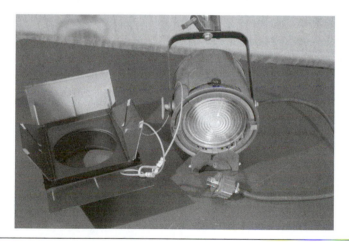

Photo 5.3   The Fresnel spotlight has a lamp, reflector, lens, and a focusing knob for controlling the spread of the light beam it produces. It comes in a variety of wattages, depending on production needs. Notice the set of *barn doors,* or black metal flaps, used to block light from parts of the studio where it is not wanted.

production is the **Fresnel spotlight** (pronounced "fra-nell"), named after the French physicist, Augustin Fresnel, who invented its special lens (see Photo 5.3). The major components of the Fresnel spotlight that enable it to serve as a directional light are its lamp, reflector, lens, and focusing apparatus.

The Fresnel lens has a plano-convex shape with stepped concentric rings enabling it to throw a beam of directional light onto the subject. A reflector located behind the lamp directs light out through the lens. Turning a focusing knob changes the spread of the beam by moving the lamp and reflector either toward or away from the lens. Focusing is made possible by mounting the lamp socket on an adjustable worm gear connected to the focusing knob at the back of the instrument housing; some instruments use a sliding mechanism to move the lamp. Either way, as the lamp is moved closer to the lens, the beam spreads out and becomes less intense as it covers more area. As the lamp is moved away from the lens, the beam narrows and becomes more intense as it *spots down* to cover less area. Hence, intensity and coverage area can be controlled.

In addition to the components mentioned above, the Fresnel spotlight is often fitted with external, adjustable, black metal flaps, called *barn doors* (shown on the left in Photo 5.3), which provide a means of controlling the spill of light from the instrument. It is also fitted with a *gel frame holder,* which permits the attachment of color filters, as well as *diffusers* or *scrims,* which are neutral-color filters for softening or reducing light intensity. Fresnel lights commonly come in 500-watt, 750-watt, 1,000-watt, and 2,000-watt power ratings, with 6-inch, 8-inch, and 10-inch lens diameters. Other ratings and sizes are also available. Selecting the appropriate instrument depends on studio size, limitations of the lighting board and power source being used, and the nature of the production.

Compared to spotlights, *floodlights* provide a more diffuse, nondirectional base light to large areas. They are often used to light large areas of scenery and backdrops (see Figure 5.1). Floodlights are often used as *fill* lights since they are used in front of talent and opposite spotlights to fill in and reduce harsh shadows that may be caused by spotlights.

(a) (b)

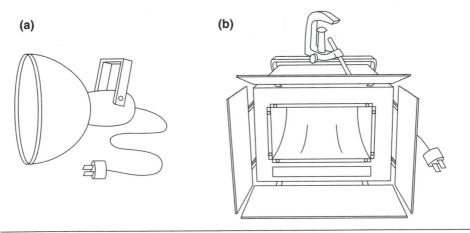

Figure 5.1 Floodlights are a broad category of lighting instruments and include (a) *scoops* and (b) *broads*. Floodlights are designed to fill in and reduce shadowy and dark areas. Some lighting manufacturers call their fill lights *soft* lights.

Floodlights are comparatively simple devices, consisting of a lamp (available in wattages comparable to those for spotlights) and a reflective surface inside the instrument housing. Because of the shape of the housing, some fill lights are called *scoops* (see Figure 5.1a). Others with a more box-like shape are called *broads* (see Figure 5.1b). Fill lights offer few options for controlling spill and intensity. Of course, if the light is attached to a dimmer, light intensity can be controlled to some extent by dimming, but the more you dim a light, the more you change its color temperature, and this can create unwanted effects in the way colors are reproduced by the camera. A better way is either to change the distance from the light to the subject or to use *scrims* or *diffusers,* which are spun-glass materials placed in front of lighting instruments to soften their intensity.

Another, more specialized type of lighting instrument, with a sharp-edged and highly controllable beam of light, is the *ellipsoidal* spotlight (see Photo 5.4), so named for the elliptical shape of the reflective surface inside the instrument housing. The ellipsoidal spotlight sends an intense beam of light through an adjustable iris that controls the diameter of the light beam. After passing through the iris gate, the light beam may be further shaped by a customized pattern insert, a metal disk with shapes cut out of it; this insert is called a *pattern* or *template.* The light is then focused by a large, compound lens. This arrangement makes the ellipsoidal spotlight useful for pattern projections onto backdrops and other surfaces.

Several other lighting instruments deserve mention. These include *strip lights, follow spots,* and *camera lights* (also called *eye lights*) (see Figure 5.2). A strip

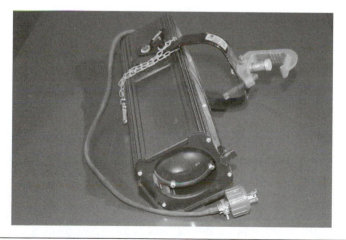

Photo 5.4   The ellipsoidal spotlight produces a well-defined beam that can be further shaped with metal pattern inserts. In this photo, the *C-clamp* used to affix the instrument to the lighting grid is clearly in view, as is the lamp's *safety chain,* used to further ensure that the lamp stays where it belongs.

(a)

(b)   (c)

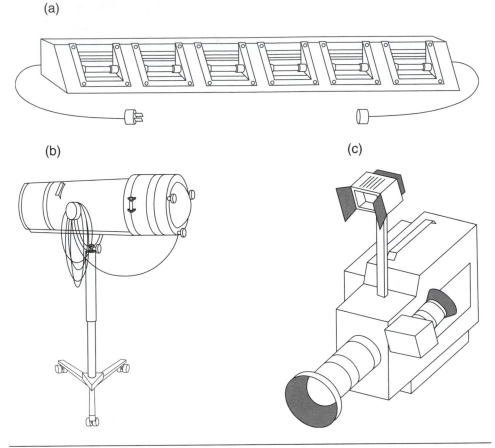

Figure 5.2   Other common types of lights include (a) strip lights, (b) follow-spot projectors, and (c) camera lights.

light is an oblong box containing a series of small lights that can be fitted with colored gels and used to light sets and backdrops. These small lights may be either hung from the lighting grid or set up on floor stands or on the ground close to the surface they are lighting, hidden by scenery and out of camera view. Strip lights are also useful for lighting sets in highly stylized productions where they can add a festive and decorative accent; for instance, they can be used on runways for fashion shows or to create traditional footlight effects for performers.

Follow spots are powerful, stand-mounted spotlights that require an operator. They are useful for following action on the set, especially in musicals and variety shows. Follow spots throw a powerful beam of light with an adjustable sharp or soft edge.

Finally, *camera lights* (or *eye lights*) are small, low-power lights mounted on top of cameras commonly used for filling in dark areas, eliminating shadows, and providing additional sparkle to talent faces and eyes.

Working With Lighting Equipment

➤ To avoid burns, wear protective gloves when working with hot lights.

➤ Unplug instruments before changing bulbs (even ones that are not hot).

➤ Even with cold bulbs, don't touch them with your bare hands. When installing them, hold them with a soft cloth, paper towel, or even the box they came in. This will keep oil from your hands from getting on the glass, which may cause the bulbs to shatter when they heat up.

➤ To avoid shocks, turn off the power at the dimmer board before connecting or disconnecting lights.

➤ If you climb a ladder to move a light, have a helper standing by who can "foot" the ladder (stabilize it with his or her foot) and take instruments out of your hands before you climb down.

➤ Make sure the ladder you use is in good condition and is approved for electrical work.

➤ When reconnecting lights to the grid, always reattach the safety chain to keep the lights from falling on people below.

➤ Before turning on lights, be sure you have not exceeded the safe power limits of the system.

➤ Periodically check the dimmer board and circuit breakers for proper functioning to avoid risk of fire if you accidentally overload the system.

➤ If you use light stands, secure them with sand bags or tie-downs, especially in high traffic areas, and put up proper warnings so that stands do not get knocked down.

➤ Electrical cables running across the floor can trip people. Secure your lighting wires, cables, and extension cords with gaffer's tape or tunnel tape to minimize hazards.

➤ Cables can be protected with cable troughs to keep them from being damaged, and they can be hidden from view with rubber mats.

➤ To keep cables from getting warm, don't bunch them together.

Additional Lighting Equipment

In addition to the lights themselves, other types of equipment are critical for rendering high-quality lighting designs. Among the more important is the **light meter** (see Photo 5.5), which measures light in terms of *lux* or *foot candles,* standard measures of light intensity falling on a given area. A foot candle refers to the light intensity produced by a standard candle (specified precisely in terms of size and material) at a distance of one foot. One lux equals about one tenth of a foot candle.

Light meters are of two types: *incident* and *reflected.* An incident light meter measures the amount of light falling on a subject. To use one correctly, aim the meter's sensor at the principal camera from the place the talent will be. A reflected light meter measures the amount of light reflecting from a subject. To use one correctly, aim the meter's sensor at the subject to get a proper reading. Light meters are useful for locating and adjusting hot spots and dark spots in a production area.

Photo 5.5   A light meter.

Remember, however, that surrounding light conditions can change from moment to moment, from camera shot to camera shot, and that extremely dark or bright backgrounds can affect the accuracy of meter readings. Remember also that different cameras may have different performance characteristics, such as different operating light levels and different contrast ranges, and may therefore perform more or less adequately in the same light. For these reasons, light meter readings alone cannot guarantee desired results.

Therefore, it is essential to check the final court of appeals, the **waveform monitor** (see Photo 5.6a), in the control room. The waveform monitor graphically displays the white and black levels in the video signal, making it possible to control brightness, which must be kept within proper limits to maintain video quality. Two controls enable you to maintain brightness levels: the *pedestal* control and the *iris* control, both of which should be adjusted while referring to the waveform display. Adjusting the pedestal and iris controls is called *shading* the camera. Aside from providing optimal contrast range, proper shading reduces or eliminates jarring brightness differences when cutting between different cameras during a show.

To set brightness levels most efficiently, it is best to use a *chip chart* (see Photo 5.7), which displays shades of gray from black to white. The darkest area on the chart is called *TV black,* and the lightest is called *TV white.* To use the chart, place it where talent will appear with the lights turned on as they would be for the actual program. Then focus the camera on a full shot of just the chart, and adjust the pedestal and iris levels so that the brightest portion of the picture registers 100 on the waveform monitor and the darkest portion of the picture registers 7.5. This procedure ensures that you are getting the proper contrast range for most situations.

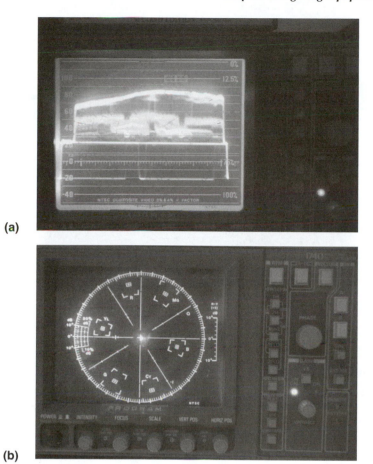

(a)

(b)

Photo 5.6   The waveform monitor is used to adjust brightness levels for cameras to reduce jarring differences across cameras and to render images with optimal contrast range and image quality. A vectorscope is used to adjust color.

Just as a waveform monitor is used to set brightness levels to ensure the best possible contrast range, a **vectorscope** is used to adjust color (see Photo 5.6b). To balance color reproduction with the vectorscope, a standard *color bar chart* may be used in the same way you would use a chip chart for adjusting contrast range. The vectorscope displays six small squares inside a circle, marking the areas where the three primary and three secondary colors should appear when colors are rendered accurately. Adjustments are made to align the colors the camera is seeing with their designated locations. When all six colors appear in their proper locations, colors seen by the camera should be accurately reproduced.

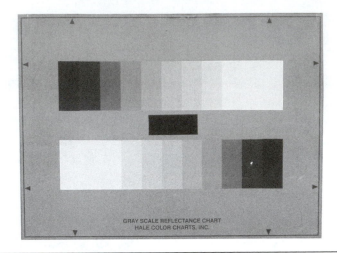

Photo 5.7   A chip chart, such as the 11-step version pictured here, is used with the waveform monitor for setting white and black levels.

Several other types of peripheral equipment are also important:

Reflector boards (see Figure 5.3)—boards or sturdy cards with bright white, silver, or even mirrored surfaces—are used to bounce light onto a subject. They find frequent application in field settings to alter the effects of sunlight.

Figure 5.3   Reflector board.

Rods and pantographs (see Figure 5.4) are expandable devices used to lower lighting instruments from the lighting grid to a desired height closer to the studio floor. Pantographs may also be used to adjust the position of mounted television monitors.

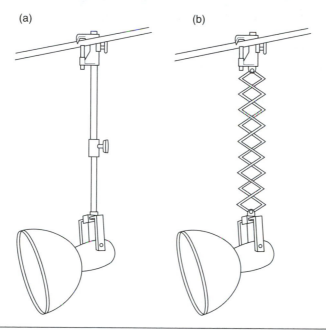

Figure 5.4   Rods (a) and pantographs (b) are used to raise and lower the heights of lighting instruments.

C-clamps (visible in Photo 5.4) are screw-down devices used to affix lighting instruments to lighting grids and stands.

Safety chains (also visible in Photo 5.4) keep instruments from falling if their C-clamps come loose.

FUNDAMENTALS OF LIGHTING DESIGN

At the simplest level, lighting design principles are usually grounded in **naturalism.** The naturalistic approach recognizes that over millions of years, we have been conditioned to see objects illuminated from above by a single main source of light. This is because we inhabit a solar system featuring only one sun, which provides our main source of light. Normal lighting, to us human beings, must be consistent with this arrangement.

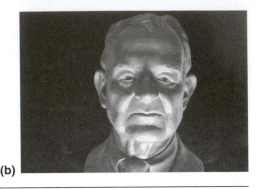

(a)　　　　　　　　　　　　　　　　　　(b)

Photo 5.8　　Two photos of the same bust illustrate (a) the natural effects of lighting from above and (b) the unnatural look caused by lighting from below. Note how this difference in lighting appears to change facial expression.

SOURCE: Reprinted with permission of Don Everhart.

Theater people recognized this principle long before the advent of television. Traditionally, stages had been lit from below, with footlights, but by the 1820s, when more powerful gas lights replaced candlelight, theater critics began to note the advantage of the chandelier. Chandeliers threw light on the faces of the actors from above, which seemed more natural. Strong footlights, on the other hand, inverted the natural shadows of the face and distorted actors' expressions.

As another example, think of children playing with a flashlight, scaring one another by aiming the light up at their faces from below their chins. Such lighting appears unnatural because it reverses the normal pattern of light and shadow on the face, subverting our normal expectations, at times creating monstrous effects. Photo 5.8 illustrates this phenomenon.

In addition to being generally located above us, the sun is also millions of miles away, and its light passes through all of the Earth's atmosphere before reaching us. As a result, some light is diffused, having been deflected repeatedly at odd angles. It therefore strikes objects in our vicinity on all sides, reducing harsh shadows. Even when the sky is extremely clear, objects rarely appear illuminated on only one side and utterly dark on the other. Rather, they appear illuminated on all sides, but with the sunward side more brightly lit than the others. On overcast days, the directionality of the sun's light can be completely eliminated, making all the light we see appear diffuse and directionless. Under such conditions, objects may appear to be illuminated evenly on all sides.

In summary, sunlight provides both the main source of "hard," directional light from above—the **key light**—as well as "softer," more diffuse (less directional) **fill light** that reduces harsh shadows throughout other parts of a scene. This arrangement constitutes a naturalistic lighting scheme. You can simulate naturalism by following this simple rule: *In the absence of compelling reasons not to, use lighting designs that imitate the way objects are lit in nature.*

Following this rule is not as easy as it sounds, for a number of reasons. First, in designing light plots for television, we cannot simulate natural light using a single instrument. We must use more than one. When a single light shines on a subject from nearby, it creates unnaturally sharp shadows since the light does not have enough distance to diffuse adequately through the atmosphere before reaching the subject. That is why designing lighting schemes is *always* a departure from "reality," even when the program is nonfiction and the artistic goal is realism.

Second, when natural shadows extend from objects on a bright day, we see *only one shadow* for each object. Duplicating this effect is difficult when lighting for video because we often use more than one light per object, and *each time we aim a light at something, we create a shadow somewhere.*

Third, in nature, the *direction* of shadows cast by objects in our field of view is consistent. That is, shadows are always cast on the side of objects opposite the sun. If a shadow from one object is cast from left to right, then shadows for all objects in the vicinity should also be from left to right. In addition, the shadows will be parallel with one another since light rays from distant light sources such as the sun are parallel. Therefore, when we use multiple instruments to light a set, we must ensure that the shadows seen on air are cast consistently, or we can quickly break the illusion.

For all these reasons, *controlling shadows is as critical a part of lighting design as controlling light.* To do this, you must know not only where the set pieces and the talent are with relation to the lights but also where the cameras are. You must also know how much of the scene the widest shot includes. Knowing the extent of the widest or *master* shot enables you to plan lighting schemes that direct unwanted shadows either off the set or beyond the reach of the cameras. Conversely, using the same principles, you can also direct shadows onto parts of the set where they are needed. Let the program purpose and content dictate these decisions.

Naturalistic lighting provides an attractive, visually satisfying, sculptural appearance of the talent and objects seen on camera, enhancing the sense of depth for the viewer. It is especially useful for stationary talent in limited performance areas in programs such as news, sports, public affairs, information, interview, talk, and audience participation (quiz and game) shows.

A Sample Naturalistic Light Plot

Let us apply the principles and use the equipment mentioned so far to light an actual program, a simple, two-camera interview program for two stationary on-air talents, a host and a guest-author.

Figure 5.5 shows a rough floor plan of the program. Notice that the talent are in the same relationship to each other as Jay Leno or David Letterman would be

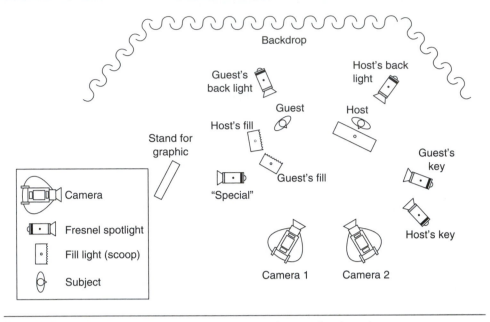

Figure 5.5   Floor plan/light plot for two-person stationary talent interview segment.

with an interview guest. The host is seated behind a desk with a microphone positioned in front. The floor plan also shows the location of two cameras, a backdrop, and a stand for a program graphic—in this case, probably a book jacket, since we are interviewing an author.

The backdrop in this case is a stretch of black fabric extending around the perimeter of the studio, from the floor to the top of the set space. Alternatively, we could use a **cyclorama** (or *cyc* for short, rhyming with "bike"), which consists of a nonblack continuous seamless opaque fabric similarly stretched around the perimeter of the studio, creating the illusion of endless depth. Cycs are often gray and may be lit with colored strip lights to create attractive backgrounds. In some studios, instead of fabric, the cyc is a smooth plaster wall, sometimes called a *hard cyc*. Cycloramas provide a smooth, unobtrusive background for the talent. When a black backdrop is used, only the talent, chairs, and desk are seen since black is invisible on television.

Our goals in naturalistic lighting will be to flatter the talent and to eliminate spurious shadows that might distract the viewer from the talk. First we determine which camera will capture shots of just the guest in close-up (the guest's *one-shot*) and which camera will carry the host. After seating the guest on the left, we decide that the guest's one-shot will be carried by Camera 2, as shown in Figure 5.5. We select Camera 2 as the guest's principal camera because Camera 2 is positioned to get a fuller front-face shot of the guest than Camera 1, which can only get profile or three-quarter guest shots. For the same reason, we use Camera 1 for the host's one-shot.

This arrangement is called *cross-shooting* because the imaginary lines from the cameras to their assigned talents cross one another. If we had used Camera 2 for the host and Camera 1 for the guest, we would have been *parallel shooting*. Parallel shooting, which provides profile and three-quarter images of each person, would have given us less intimate images. For an interview program, cross-shooting is better.

Now that we know where the cameras are with respect to the talent, we can set the lights. The key lights, with the most directional and concentrated beams, are the hardest lights on the talent. The guest's key light is positioned above and in front of the guest. It angles downward at roughly a 45-degree angle. It is also set at about a 30- to 45-degree horizontal angle from the imaginary line between the guest's head and Camera 1. The same is done for the host's key light.

These angles are a rough rule of thumb, a starting point. The vertical angle simulates sunlight, but after all, as the sun passes through the sky, it changes its angle. Therefore, we can feel free to position the lights to maximize the flattering effect we are trying to achieve. For example, if the guest is an attractive actress, a starlet, it makes sense to go for the beauty shot. We may start with a 45-degree vertical angle and see what improvements we can make by departing from that angle. Bone structures differ from person to person, as do program purposes, so it's a good idea to experiment and check the effects by looking at the line monitor.

As the brightest source of light, the key light casts the sharpest, darkest shadow on the opposite side of the guest's face (especially below the nose and chin and onto the neck). To soften this shadow, we position a fill light on the opposite side of the talent, also at horizontal and vertical angles of about 45 degrees. The fill light is more diffuse than the key light and less intense. Therefore, we may need to place it closer to the talent to achieve the right intensity. The purpose of the fill light is to reduce unnaturally sharp shadows made by the key and to illuminate the rest of the guest's face. Together, the two lights should provide a nicely sculpted image for the camera; as a lighting designer (LD), it is your job to achieve that effect.

Finally, to create the illusion of depth and to separate the image of the talent from the background, we use a **back light** to illuminate each talent's back, especially the head and shoulders. This is done by positioning a light directly behind each talent, aiming toward the camera but tilted down at about 45 to 60 degrees from the horizontal plane. It is common to tilt the back lights down toward the floor at an angle as great as 60 degrees to reduce the chance of spilling light into the camera lens. Since the back light is aiming in the direction of the camera, the extra angle is justified. To further guard against sending incident light from the back lights into the cameras, we will use spotlights with barn doors. (If you have a choice, *never use a scoop light or broad as a back light.*)

This arrangement of key, fill, and back lights on each talent constitutes a **three-point lighting** scheme and completes the basic lighting job. Three-point lighting is the bread-and-butter arrangement for stationary talent in video production. It should provide a natural, aesthetically pleasing presentation of the subject. Notice the triangular relationship of the key, fill, and back lights. Notice also that each talent's principal camera (the one that gets each talent's one-shot) is positioned between each talent's key and fill lights.

As shown in Figure 5.5, we have used a three-point lighting scheme to light each talent separately. That is, we have six lighting instruments. It is possible that, with slight adjustment, one set of lights may be enough for both talents since the guest and host are stationary and close together. The advantages of using only three instruments would be that we would use less electricity, set up in less time, and provide consistency in light locations (since both talents would receive their key light from the same place). However, disadvantages might include a lack of coverage if the guest shifts around and an increased risk that the host could cast a distracting shadow on the guest if the host moves between the guest and the key light. These disadvantages generally outweigh the advantages, so the professional approach is to use separate key, fill, and back lights for each talent whenever possible.

To determine whether the lighting is satisfactory, examine the line or program monitor, which should be checked for each camera before show time; do not trust the way things look to your eyes through direct observation. When you check camera shots on the monitor, make sure you have acceptable coverage for the talent and the set. Look for *specular highlights* (areas of extreme brightness) or unwanted shadows.

Eliminating Unwanted Shadows

Let's assume that after setting up the three-point lighting scheme shown in Figure 5.5, we found unwanted shadows on the backdrop. How could we eliminate them? There are various solutions:

- We might wash out the shadows by shining additional lights on them. This solution is not usually recommended, though, because it uses additional lighting instruments and more power.

- Another way might be to reposition the lights, placing the key lights higher than 45 degrees, causing the shadows to fall on the floor outside the range of the camera. However, this is often murder on the talent since it lights them from a higher angle, elongating shadows on faces, especially below the nose and eyebrows.

- A better solution in most cases would be to move the talent further from the background and then reset the lights.

Usually, unwanted shadows can be avoided by placing talent no closer than 6 feet from the backdrop or walls of the set. Since most people are less than 6 feet tall, this is a good rule of thumb, even for standing talent, especially if you keep the angle of attack of the lights at around 45 degrees.

We are not finished with our lighting job, however, until we have lit the book jacket for an insert shot during the interview. The light for the book jacket is known as a *special* since it performs such a singular function. Figure 5.5 shows the location of the special to the right of the stand, following the same rule of 45 degrees described for the talent. We could have placed the light for the graphic on the other side of the stand, but that might bounce reflected light from the graphic onto the set, causing unnecessary glare or hot spots.[1] We might also have placed the special light directly over the camera, but that would have increased the risk of bouncing unwanted light from the book jacket into the camera lens. Instead, our placement of the special sends unwanted reflected light off the set and away from the camera, thus lighting the book jacket without causing unnecessary problems.

Finally, if we used a cyclorama as background, we might wish to light it with some scoops or colored strip lights. (Figure 5.5 does not include this option.) Whatever lights we might use on the backdrop and other peripheral set areas, they should be separate from the lights used on the talent areas. The reason is that sets and scenery are usually more reflective than talent and costumes, so the intensity of light on them must be kept lower. Furthermore, since talent action is where the main interest most often lies, the talent generally should receive the most light. Lighting set and talent areas separately becomes even more important when performers move around since it becomes more difficult to keep annoying shadows out of camera range.

DEPARTURES FROM NATURALISM

Naturalistic lighting, as we have described it, provides the **base light,** that is, the light needed for basic visibility. It should also provide a sculptured, attractive look to talent and a sense of depth for the talent and sets. However, there are times when departures from or additions to naturalism are justified. This section considers some of the more compelling reasons to break from naturalism.

First, video, more than any other visual entertainment medium, relies for emphasis on the close-up. The close-up, as one network lighting designer put it, is the "money shot." Even sports programming now employs longer lenses and image stabilization systems to get more close-ups. In fact, some feel that even with the advent of HD and larger screens opening the possibility for a shift to a more cinematic style, featuring more panoramic and wide-angle long shots, the close-up will continue to be the most important shot in video. Hence, it is the appearance of the talent in close-up that is often the primary consideration. If the talent's appearance is improved by deviating from naturalism (for instance, by departing radically from the standard 45-degree angles), then the director may want to do so.

Second, the standard naturalistic angles can be hard on talent. While there are 24 hours in a day, only a few of them are the "magic hours" that photographers and video producers talk about—those hours when natural light comes from low-angle directions. It is sometimes desirable, therefore, to use lower lighting angles to get more pleasing effects. While lower angles do cause more shadow problems, these can usually be solved by careful placement of lights and by enlisting the help of the set designer and director. For example, if a low key light used to improve the talent's appearance causes an unwanted set shadow, the shadow may be hidden from view by the talent's own body.

Third, people don't always want to see only what is normal when they watch video. Normal is what is out the window, but special is on television. In many cases, therefore, people on video are made to look better than they might look in person, just as skies may be made to appear bluer. In short, everything may be made more attractive (or even uglier) than normal to drive home an emotional point.

Additional departures from naturalism may be dictated by the program genre. A horror story may use multiple shadows, lighting from below, as well as bizarre colors, intensities, and other special effects. In an outer-space saga, not surprisingly, other-worldly lighting may be wanted. Light and shadow can be used for dramatic emphasis, as when a climactic point is reached in a drama and the lights are killed everywhere except in one spot. Some videographers may even resort to unnatural lighting schemes just to give a distinctive look to their talent or show. All such lighting decisions should be based on the meaning of the work.

Finally, from a purely tactical perspective, some production formats militate against using naturalistic lighting schemes, especially those featuring moving talent in multicamera settings. Programs in this category commonly include situation comedies, sketch variety series, dramas, and soap operas. These programs intercut shots from several cameras in different locations, perhaps all shooting the same performer in the same performance area from different angles. Seeing cuts of the same set area or performer from different camera angles may be too jarring if highly discrepant light intensities are used. For this reason, instead of naturalistic light, a "flatter" lighting scheme is warranted.

Flat Lighting

The renowned cinematographer Karl Freund introduced a **flat lighting** technique for the *I Love Lucy* series in the 1950s. The program's producer, Al Simon, approached Freund and asked if he could "film with three or four 35-mm cameras, in front of an audience, like a stage play, without stopping, resorting to retakes only under the most dire circumstances." Freund responded, "You can't do that. Every shot requires different lighting. You couldn't photograph three or four angles at the same time and come up with a decent piece of finished film" (Andrews, 1985, p. 49).

Despite his objections, Freund developed flat lighting to deal with the problem. In order to cover talent action over almost the entire set, Freund made the light intensity uniform over the total area at all times. Set illumination was mostly from overhead. The only light from a lower level came from a portable fill light mounted just over each camera. With overhead lighting, cameras could dolly over the studio floor unobstructed. Cuts could be made from one camera to another without jarring differences in light.

Freund's system of flat lighting is still in use today, as evidenced by the use of such lighting for studio scenes in programs such as *The King of Queens* and *The Office.* In multicamera productions, the most compelling reason to use flat lighting is to minimize light-level differences when cutting between cameras shooting the same scene from very different positions. However, this does not mean that fill lights are the only acceptable tool. Spotlights may still be used for acting areas and smaller set spaces.

MOTIVATING LIGHT SOURCES

Some scripts refer to special light sources indicating time or place, called **motivating light** sources. Motivating sources may include different types of natural light (early sunrise, midday, sunset, cloudy daylight, moonlight) or artificial light (lamplight, candlelight). More exotic effects such as lightning are also motivating sources. The illumination provided in simulating such sources should be convincing but should not draw attention away from the main point of the action. The following sections offer techniques for creating some of the more common motivating light effects.

Sunlight and Sunset. Aim a highly directional beam—uncolored light from an incandescent lamp—onto an acting area or an essential piece of scenery. It should be the brightest light on the set. Use amber gels of varying grades to indicate sunset, and vary the angle of attack to match the angle of the setting sun. If more than one instrument is used for this effect, they should be parallel. The best instrument to use is a powerful concentrating instrument mounted far from the set. A follow spot or a high-powered spotlight is a good choice. If a projector is used, the spread of the beam may be controlled with a funnel, which is a cylinder fitted over the light to control unwanted spill. Use dimmers to control changes in brightness.

Moonlight. Moonlight may be rendered like sunrise and sunset, except for adjustments in intensity and color. Adding a steel blue gel with a color temperature comparable to moonlight will normally suffice. Aim the motivating spotlight at the acting area. On the other side, use spotlights in the flood-beam setting for fill, outfitted with a lighter blue gel at lower light intensity.

General Daylight. This requires a virtually shadowless, broad, general source. It should appear as light coming in from all directions. Directional light is to be avoided. Intensity should be uniform. Color regular incandescent fill lights with light steel blue gels. A large reflecting screen can help create the look of light entering through a window, as can several small floods equipped with gels of the same color. Imitating changes in daylight from dawn to sunset can be managed by progressive addition of light blue to violet to steel-colored gels. For an extremely hot day, simulate general daylight with light amber.

Fixture Lighting. In most cases, lighting fixtures that appear on camera, such as table lamps in an interior scene, are used strictly as motivating lights. Unless they contribute something dramatic, they are not used as major lighting devices for the acting area. To reduce hot spots, keep the wattages in the fixture lights to a minimum: 25 to 40 watts are usually sufficient to add a necessary accent to a scene. Light the acting areas from hidden sources.

On the other hand, fixture light can occasionally add useful illumination to a scene. Such lights are called *practicals*. An example of a practical light would be a lamp over a music stand to help the performer see the music. Frequently, the location and reflective power of the scenery will influence the use of such fixtures. To control intensity in these cases, use a dimmer. Another way to control fixture light is to cut away the back of a lampshade (on the side away from the cameras) to increase the intensity of light falling on a piece of scenery without letting the light spill directly into the camera's view.

LIGHTING IN MORE COMPLICATED CASES

How can you apply the basic principles of lighting to more complicated productions, say a sitcom or soap opera? Lighting for drama or comedy is a challenge because such programs feature talent moving through and interacting with the set, and they often require the use of motivating lights as well as lighting changes to indicate different times of day. Here are some guidelines:

Meet first with the director and the rest of the creative team, including the producer and the scene and costume designers, to study the script, floor plan, and talent needs. Determine the subject matter, treatment, and tone of the production. Take inventory of the available lighting hardware and become familiar with the space you will light.

From the script and floor plan, determine where the cameras and talent will be, and begin forming a rationale for lighting. Consider how you will provide base light. Then work on providing additional special lighting needs, including motivating lights, and any special instruments. For example, the location of doors, windows, and set pieces will help you decide where to place instruments to provide sun, moonlight, and fixture lights. Let the tone of the program indicate the mood you try to convey, such as whether the lighting should be festive or somber.

Arrange for unobstructed access of the cameras to all of the locations where they need to go to maximize shot variety. Note all camera angles and light accordingly to avoid spilling light into the camera lenses. Also note where key speeches or action take place, and make those areas a central focus of your lighting design. In areas where talent come close to the set, such as doorways, fit lights with funnels or barn doors to shape and limit their throw and to reduce or eliminate unwanted shadows (aluminum foil has served well in many such applications). Light the set areas separately from the talent positions to control shadow problems. Remember, it is generally best to keep light intensities on sets lower than they are for talent because sets tend to be more reflective than talent, and the talent is where you want the audience's attention. If appropriate, consider using flat lighting for the acting areas to keep intensities uniform over that space, thus reducing jarring differences when cutting from one camera to another.

When the light plot is complete, use the rehearsal to observe the talent as they move through the set. As they move, judge how they look on the cameras intended to cover them, both in the master shot and in close-ups. Fix any dead areas where lighting is dark and uneven. *Spike* (mark) spots on the floor with bits of masking tape where talent deliver speeches. Observe the talent on these spots and improve the lighting if needed. As the action is covered, keep watching for spots that may be too bright or too dull. Use both a light meter and the appearance of each camera shot on the program monitor to make adjustments: Move lights, tune them, or cover them with gels or scrim to color or soften them. Use all the tools available to you to make the lighting scheme convincing and appropriate to the subject matter, tone, and goal of the production.

When you are satisfied that you have a light plot that does what it is supposed to do, log the location of each instrument on a lighting grid. Note dimmer levels. If any lights are grouped together, note them. This logging of the light plot will help if lights burn out and need to be replaced quickly. The light plot should be complete enough so that if the lighting designer is sick and unable to report to work, the crew member taking his or her place can set lights for the production by referring to the floor plan, light plot, and log.

FIELD LIGHTING

Lighting in the field presents unique challenges. You may decide to use the available natural light if the shoot is outdoors. You may decide to use the available artificial light indoors. Or you may choose to supplement the location's light with lights that you bring to the shoot. If you choose to augment available light, you will need access to a power source. This may mean nothing more than bringing a light kit and extension cords and using wall current at the location. But if wall current is not available, you may need to bring a generator. If you use a light kit, bring extra lamps in case some burn out.

Procedures

Scout the location in advance, at the same time of day as the shoot. Test outlets you may wish to use to make sure they are working, and confirm whether they can handle your power needs. The purpose of scouting is to eliminate surprises.

If you decide to use available natural light outdoors, note the direction of the sun, and keep in mind that it changes as the day progresses. Weather conditions can also change, and this can cause continuity problems if you shoot the same scene on different days. If you use artificial light to offset differences, remember to use the proper light for a color temperature match. If possible, shoot at the same time any scenes that will be viewed together. If that is not possible, you may need to wait for similar weather conditions to get what you want. You may also have to get to the location at the same time on those days, so that the sun will be at roughly the same place.

If you cannot get the cooperation of nature, you may wish to consider changes in the script to accommodate shooting conditions. Obviously, flexibility is a virtue in location shooting. Either way, leave enough time in the production schedule to deal with such contingencies. If you are waiting for a rainy day to do a crucial scene, plan the rest of the shooting schedule so that you can get other things done while you watch the weather report.

If you shoot with indoor lights near a window with sunlight streaming in, shield the window to keep it from throwing off the color temperature, or cover the window with the proper filter to correct for color temperature differences. Similarly, when shooting outdoors, be aware that extremely bright sun can cause contrast ratio problems, making your talent look washed out on the sunward side and underexposed or dark on the opposite side. To correct such problems, you can shield the talent by blocking off direct sunlight with large sturdy cards called *flags* (hope for low wind) or by moving the shoot to the shady side of a building. Or you can use reflectors to fill in and reduce harsh shadows on the talent's face opposite the sun. Seek a solution that brings the picture into a tolerable contrast range.

Remember that the canons of lighting do not change from studio to field. Control of light and shadow is still the goal. If you are striving for naturalism, light from above, and control intensities and shadows. Finally, be sure to set white balance for the camera(s) you are using each time you change location or lighting so that the color rendition of your video image is acceptable and consistent from setup to setup.

Equipment

Field lighting requires the use of some unique equipment. Among the tools used in the field are portable lights; light stands; booms, clips, and braces; and flags and reflectors.

Photo 5.9   Some of the typical contents of a field lighting kit: portable lights clipped to their stands, reflector umbrellas, a flag (the black circular item to the right), a white balance card, filters (three are visible leaning against the card), and extension cords.

Portable lights offer several advantages over studio lights when doing remote shoots. First, portable lights are lighter in weight than studio lights. Second, they use normal wall current and do not require any special adapters to plug into normal wall outlets. Third, they come in kits that provide custom-designed stands for the lights so that they are easy to use. In fact, much of the equipment designed for field use is also used in studios because it is convenient. Photo 5.9 displays the basic elements of a field lighting kit.

Light stands, depending on the brand, enable you to raise lights to heights of up to 15 feet or lower them to about 2 feet. The stands are light in weight and retractable for easy storage. For especially tight spots, clips and braces are available for mounting lights. *Booms*—long, movable arms—can be rigged to make lights available in set areas where it is not desirable to see the light stand in a shot. Flags, as mentioned earlier, are clip-on black cards that attach to stands that can be placed in an area to block light from entering the set or camera. Conversely, reflectors may be used to increase the effects of sunlight on a subject by creating fill light for the side of the subject opposite the sun. Some reflectors are shaped like umbrellas (those made for artificial lights), while others are simply flat cards with a foil or highly reflective white surface.

A special outdoor light made with metal halide material is worth noting. Called an **HMI lamp,** this type of Fresnel lighting instrument provides light in the color temperature range of about 5,000 to 5,600 K, making it suitable for simulating daylight, which spans from about 4,500 to 6,200 K.

A great advantage of HMI lamps is that they do not get as hot as incandescent lights, chiefly because they work in concert with a *ballast* that serves to limit current through the lamp. HMIs are most often used in high-end electronic field production (EFP) and film productions. The latest versions of HMIs provide four to five times the illumination of an incandescent lamp of the same wattage. Among the disadvantages of HMIs is that their ballasts, which can be quite heavy, can produce a noticeable hum.

KEY TERMS

QUESTIONS FOR REVIEW

Name the standard items of lighting equipment found in a television studio.

Beyond providing visibility, what else can lighting do to enhance a video presentation?

How can understanding naturalism guide the lighting designer in planning lighting designs for television?

What aesthetic considerations and physical constraints justify departures from naturalism in planning lighting designs?

Sketch out some ideas for lighting an indoor basketball game. What could you do, for instance, to reduce problems caused by the highly reflective floor? How would you deal with the color temperatures of the lights provided at the arena?

NOTE

1. Of course, a book shot will more than likely be supplied by a computer, but then we'd miss an opportunity to talk lighting strategy.

Chapter 6

USING THE CAMERA

In use, the video camera is more than an imaging device. Besides the lens and electronics that enable the camera to register an image, the camera has additional mechanical and electronic equipment that allows you to control its position and movement and adjust image composition. These features range from mounting devices such as pedestals and body braces to viewfinders, headphone jacks, and prompters.

In addition to the camera components themselves, a video production person needs to understand the specialized language used to talk about them. "Truck left," you will hear. "Get an establishing shot and then zoom out for a reveal." In keeping with our general approach, though, this chapter will cover more than devices and language. We also discuss the design elements and aesthetic considerations that go into picture composition. The topics in this chapter include the following:

Camera mounts and camera movement

- Tripods, wheels, and dollies
- Studio pedestals
- Mounting heads
- Jibs
- Body and vehicle mounts
- The language of camera movement

Electronic components of cameras

Basic design elements of picture composition

Picture composition in video

- Framing
- Using the *z*-axis
- Focus

- Camera angle
- Types of camera shots

A final note about picture composition

CAMERA MOUNTS AND CAMERA MOVEMENT

The equipment that physically supports the camera provides stability, ease of operation, access to different locations, and smooth, controlled motion in the video image. Using appropriate mounting equipment makes camera operation safe and easy and helps you obtain the program you want. The following sections cover the basic types of mounts, the movements they facilitate, and the language used to describe camera movement.

Tripods, Wheels, and Dollies

The camera may be mounted on a **tripod,** a three-legged support with adjustable extensions, usually tipped with spikes or rubber ends for stability (see Photo 6.1). Each pod can be extended to a different length to accommodate uneven terrain. Tripods can be placed on a *spreader,* a device that limits the spread of the tripod legs so they remain stable under the weight of the camera.

For leveling the camera on uneven ground, most field tripods come equipped with a bubble level similar to that used by carpenters. If you are using a tripod without a level indicator, you can still level the camera by aligning the top or bottom edge of the image in your viewfinder with a true horizontal in your set (such as the horizon) or by dropping a plumb line into your shot and aligning it with the left or right vertical edge of the image.

For better movement, especially in the studio, tripods can be placed on wheels, using a *dolly* (see Photo 6.2). Studio tripods generally have brakes on each wheel, and they often come with wheel covers that help to protect the wheels from obstructions. The need to avoid obstructions is a major consideration, even on a studio floor that appears flat and clear. Because much of what the camera sees is shot in close-up (even in HD), small aberrations in camera movement may be magnified many times in the picture. Wheel covers help because they tend to push away obstructions such as cables rather than letting the camera roll over them. Still, it is best to have a crew member act as a cable puller.

Studio Pedestals

A more sophisticated class of camera mount is the **studio pedestal**. Studio pedestals are more versatile than tripods in that they permit you to raise and lower

Photo 6.1   A camera on a tripod.

the camera while on air. The *counterweight* pedestal uses weights to maintain a safe center of gravity as the camera moves smoothly up and down. Another type, the *pneumatic* pedestal, uses air pressure to raise and lower the camera (see Photo 6.3).

Studio pedestals also have mechanisms that set the wheels parallel to one another. The direction of the wheels (or *casters*) is controlled by a steering ring indicating the position of the wheels (see Photo 6.3), making it easy to push the camera along a predetermined course. Casters also have brakes, as well as a cable guard that functions in the same way as wheel covers to keep obstacles from getting in the way. Some automated or robotic pedestals are controlled by computers.

While studio pedestals offer many advantages, there are some drawbacks. For example, counterweight pedestals are big and heavy, especially when loaded down with equipment. When fully loaded, they may be too heavy for a single operator to handle easily. They may also function poorly if used as mounts for lighter field

Photo 6.2   A camera tripod placed on a dolly for easy movement in the studio.

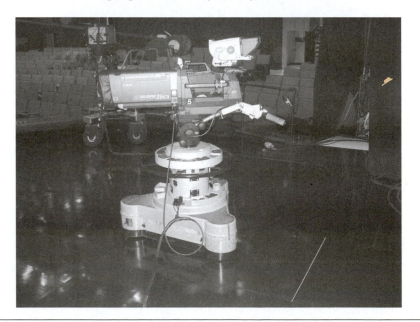

Photo 6.3   A studio pedestal.

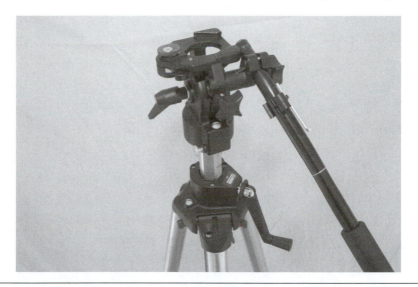

Photo 6.4   Mounting heads are used to fasten a camera to a tripod or pedestal. The mounting head in this picture is in the friction variety.

cameras for which they were not designed. Pneumatic pedestals are lighter and easier to move than their counterweight cousins, but they also have their drawbacks, such as their tendency to leak air from their pressure units. This means the air must be replaced from time to time, which requires a compressor.

Mounting Heads

A **mounting head** (see Photo 6.4) is used to fasten the camera to the tripod, pedestal, or other support device, enabling the camera to move in a controlled manner. Several major types of mounting heads deserve mention:

- *Cam friction head:* Often used with studio cameras, these heads use cylinders called cams to allow camera movement. Drag controls provide the necessary friction to keep the motion smooth and to maintain the camera's shifting center of gravity during tilting.
- *Fluid head:* Suitable for field production because of their light weight, these heads use springs in heavy oil to provide drag control.
- *Friction head:* Often used in field production, mainly on tripods, friction heads are equipped with a handle for moving the camera into a selected position. They are best suited for jobs requiring only limited movement.
- *Geared head:* Two geared wheels deliver extremely smooth movement, but this type of head is not suitable for fast adjustments.

Mounting heads can also be programmed to perform automated movements.

Photo 6.5   A studio jib arm camera mount.

Jibs

As Photo 6.5 illustrates, the studio **jib** features a counterweighted arm mounted on a heavy wheeled dolly. Jibs permit you to move the camera from roughly 1 to 20 feet above the ground or studio floor, depending on the model. With a jib, you can rotate the camera while raising or lowering it. This makes quite dramatic camera work possible. Jibs allow you to cover large vistas, and they are useful for *follow shots* (shots in which the camera follows a moving subject). Since the advent of lighter cameras, some jibs can be rigged to allow you to operate from a ground location in front of a monitor, moving the camera by remote control. However, there are some disadvantages to jibs. First, they require a large space for use and storage. Second, the camera operator may need extensive practice to master the shots you have planned.

Body and Vehicle Mounts

The move toward lighter cameras has also made it possible to mount cameras directly on the operator's body. **Body mounts** (see Photo 6.6) can vary from the simple and cheap to the sophisticated and expensive, but they generally fall into two categories: (a) shoulder mounts and (b) body braces that use a harness or belt. Shoulder mounts place most of the camera's weight on the shoulder, freeing the hands for framing and focusing work. Body braces provide greater stability than shoulder mounts but may restrict freedom of movement and may prove uncomfortable.

(b)

(a)

Photo 6.6   Body mounts include (a) shoulder-mounted cameras and (b) body braces that use a
harness or belt.

Among the most sophisticated body mounts are the *Steadicam* and the
Panaglide. These trade names refer to body mounts that permit you to cancel out,
within limits, the jarring motions of walking or running while shooting video.
They use a spring arm and stabilizers to produce smooth motion. However, they
are expensive, heavy, and require a good deal of effort to use. Nevertheless, they
allow you to get high-quality action and follow shots. If the camera needs to be
attached to a moving object such as a car or a helicopter, special camera clamps
and beanbags are also available.

The Language of Camera Movement

Camera mounts all serve the purpose of keeping the camera steady while allowing it to move in certain ways. In fact, the essence of television, in addition to
sound, pictures, and color, is movement. Unlike painting or still photography,
video images can change from moment to moment. Furthermore, whereas a
painter can paint alone, television is still largely a collaborative enterprise. For
these reasons, it is essential for both directors and camera operators to understand
the jargon used to describe camera movement.

Table 6.1 describes and illustrates the standard types of camera movement.
These are terms you need to know so well that they become automatic.

Table 6.1   Terminology for Camera Movement

Pan	Turn the camera from side to side on the mounting head while keeping the tripod or pedestal stationary. You *pan right* by moving the lens to the right as you look at the camera from the operator's point of view. Conversely, you *pan left* by moving the lens to the left from the operator's point of view.	 Pan Left
		 Tilt Down
Tilt	Tip the camera up or down on the mounting head while keeping the mount stationary. You *tilt up* by moving the lens upward. You *tilt down* by moving the lens downward.	
Cant	Take the camera off the horizontal so that the subject appears to be tilted on screen.	 Cant
Zoom	Change the focal length of a variable focal length lens while keeping the camera stationary. *Zooming in* means moving the lens elements to a narrow angle of view, making the scene appear to move closer to the viewer. *Zooming out* means moving the lens elements to a wide angle of view, making the scene appear to move further away.	 Zoom Out Zoom In
Dolly	Move the entire camera and camera mount toward or away from the subject being pictured. You *dolly in* by moving the camera and mount closer to the subject. You *dolly out* by moving the camera and mount away from the subject.	 Dolly Out
Truck	Move the entire camera and camera mount laterally with respect to the subject being pictured. You *truck right* by moving the camera and mount to the right, from the point of view of the camera operator. You *truck left* by moving the camera and mount to the left, again from the point of view of the camera operator.	 Truck Right
Arc	Combine the features of the dolly and truck to produce a curving movement. The curve can be specified to be tight or wide, toward or away, or to the right or left.	 Arc Right
Ped	Raise (ped up) or lower (ped down) the camera on its pedestal.	 Ped Up
Crane or boom	Raise or lower the entire camera on a camera crane. You can crane or boom up, and you can crane or boom down.	 Crane Up
Tongue	Move the entire camera from side to side, like trucking but with the use of a crane. You can tongue left or tongue right.	 Tongue Left and Right

ELECTRONIC COMPONENTS OF CAMERAS

Viewfinders. The studio camera is equipped with a **viewfinder** (see Photo 6.7), mounted on the operator side of the camera, to display what the camera is seeing. The viewfinder is a television monitor, usually black and white. Measuring about 7 inches diagonally in studio models, it is easy to view with both eyes from a distance of about 2 feet. In addition to showing the operator what the camera is seeing at every moment, it can switch or combine its image with those from other cameras, making it possible to see how composite images will appear on screen.

Viewfinders must be adjusted for contrast and brightness to display optimally clear images. They should also be periodically adjusted to make sure they display the same field of view as the *line monitor* (the actual program monitor). Significant discrepancies (poor *registration*) can result in poor picture composition.

In field cameras, the viewfinder is usually a 1.5-inch monochrome or color screen with a magnifying eyepiece designed to touch the face (see Photo 6.8); it can also be a small LED screen that swings into view. When used with the eyepiece, the screen is seen with one eye. In many cases, however, the eyepiece can be swung away to permit the operator to look at the screen with both eyes from a slightly greater distance. Field camera viewfinders also include status displays that indicate battery power, adequacy of the light level, and audio level, and they offer reminders and warnings about white balance and recording mode.

Zoom and Focus Controls. In studio cameras, zoom and focus controls are usually provided on the panning handles (see Photo 6.9). These controls permit you to adjust the framing and focus of the camera to compose the desired picture.

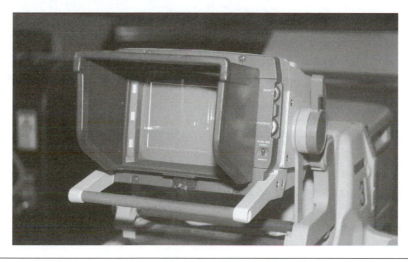

Photo 6.7   The viewfinder of a studio camera.

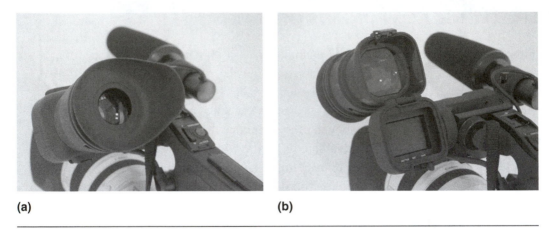

(a) **(b)**

Photo 6.8   The portable field camera features a small viewfinder (a) with an eyepiece for displaying what the camera is seeing. The viewfinder can be swung away to reveal a small monitor (b).

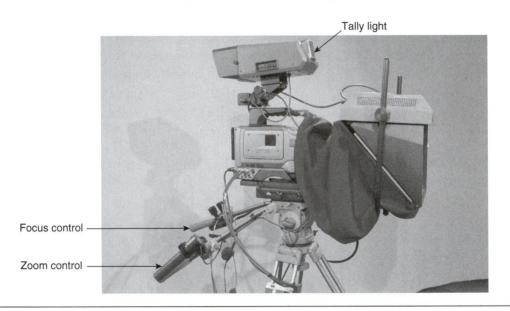

Photo 6.9   Zoom control, focus control, and tally light.

On field cameras, in contrast, the zoom control is usually a button or lever located on a grip handle. Focus may be automatic; if it is manual, it is set by manipulating a focusing ring on the lens.

Tally Lights. The **tally light** is a red light on top of the camera (see Photo 6.9). In studio or multicamera productions, it lights when that particular camera is on the air, informing the talent and crew that the camera signal is being broadcast or recorded. A smaller tally light located in back of the camera lets the operator know when the camera is on air. When the tally light goes off, the operator is free to move to compose the next shot.

In field cameras, one tally light is mounted externally, and another is located inside the viewfinder. They light when the camera is recording and go off when recording stops.

Intercoms and Headsets. Studio cameras are equipped with *intercom channels* or *headset connections* to carry voice communication among crew members, including production and technical staff. Headsets connected to these channels permit camera operators (and anyone else on headset) to hear the director's (and others') voice cues. Commercial television industry union requirements specify separate inputs for technical personnel and production personnel, even though the audio feed for these channels is identical. Some higher-end field cameras are also equipped with intercom channels.

Cue Cards. On-air talent use a variety of means to deliver scripted copy. Among the oldest is memorizing copy before show time. However, many television actors have come to rely on prompters to deliver their lines, and newscasters use such devices routinely. A *prompter* is any device used to provide script or text to on-air talent.

One of the simplest methods of prompting on-air talent is through the use of **cue cards** (see Photo 6.10), large poster cards with lines of copy written on them

Photo 6.10   The proper way to hold cue cards: next to the camera lens, with the line being read aligned with the lens.

in heavy black letters. To keep the talent oriented properly, the cue cards are usually held by a crew member right next to the camera. As lines are read, the holder moves the card to keep the appropriate text aligned with the lens.

Cards are inexpensive and immune to mechanical breakdown. However, they take time to prepare, they require a floor person to hold and change them, and they are good only for relatively short amounts of copy. Furthermore, when they are brought close to the talent (especially talent oriented directly to the camera), they may noticeably force the talent's eyes to glance off to the side of the camera lens. Conversely, when they are moved further away from the talent to reduce this effect, the extra distance can make them harder to read.

Teleprompters. The **Teleprompter** (see Photo 6.11) solves many of the problems associated with cue cards. Studio Teleprompters are electronic text display devices that place copy directly over a camera lens using two mirrors. One mirror reflects text from a monitor above or below the camera to a second mirror placed over the camera lens, which in turn reflects the copy to the talent. By placing written copy directly over the lens, Teleprompters eliminate the need for talent to glance off to the side of the camera to read. Instead, the talent can appear to have direct eye contact with the audience.

Photo 6.11   A Teleprompter. When in use, the text to be read appears right in front of the lens.

Most studio Teleprompters (capitalized because it is a trade name) use a character generator to electronically roll typed copy up or down the screen. Older ones use hard-copy news typewriters to provide script material that is then viewed by a television camera and forwarded to any prompter designed to carry it. For field use, prompters range in sophistication from a simple paper roll attached to the camera (reminiscent of cue cards) to battery-powered devices with more sophisticated displays.

In addition to the advantages already mentioned, prompters can provide identical copy to all cameras, making it possible for talent to look from one camera to another without losing their place. But, as with any other mechanical or electronic device, prompters can break down. Therefore, it is wise to have a hard copy of the script available just in case. It is even better to have well-prepared talent familiar with their assignments.

BASIC DESIGN ELEMENTS OF PICTURE COMPOSITION

Composing quality pictures for video requires both an aesthetic and a rational sense. Picture composition should be shaped by the message you wish to communicate to, as well as the effect you wish to create in, your audience. Sometimes the goal of a program is to provide information; sometimes it is to move the emotions. Deciding what to show the audience is essentially a rhetorical act.

In composing quality images for television, it is helpful to be familiar with formal canons of *static* picture composition, such as those used in photography, drawing, and painting. Line and shape, texture and pattern, color and contrast, depth and perspective, placement of key features—all these design elements are important in video production.

Line and Shape. The boundaries of objects are defined by lines. Our eyes follow naturally along dominant lines to differentiate the objects that make up the television picture. By using dominant straight and curved lines, we can direct the attention of the viewer to different parts of the video image (see Photo 6.12). We can also use lines dynamically to move the attention of the viewer from one picture to another.

In addition to marking boundaries, lines define the shape of objects for the viewer (see Photo 6.12). In a two-dimensional space, it is important to define shapes clearly if we want objects to be easily identified. Shape also helps convey a convincing sense of solidity and depth, thus helping preserve an impression of three dimensions in the videospace.

Texture. *Texture* refers to the surface qualities of objects, how rough or smooth they appear, whether they are hard or soft to the touch, and so forth. As shown in

Photo 6.12   Dominant lines define the boundaries and shapes of objects in a two-dimensional image. In video, dominant lines can help provide an impression of depth and solidity; they can also draw the viewer's attention to important parts of the image.

Photo 6.13, the video image can convey a great deal of information by differentiating objects from one another on the basis of their texture. Clearly defined textures telegraph the tactile qualities of objects and provide a sense of closeness. Less defined textures make objects look farther away.

Pattern. *Pattern* may be defined as the repetition of a design element (see Photo 6.14). Patterns tend to create rhythmic qualities and a sense of movement. Depending on how patterns are used, feelings of boredom or excitement can be instilled in the viewer.

Color and Contrast. Color can differentiate objects from one another in the video image. Conversely, if objects of the same color are close together, they may tend to merge, confusing the viewer. Color arrangement on the screen is therefore an important part of image clarity.

In addition, sharper, brighter colored objects generally appear to be closer, while less vividly colored objects appear to be more distant (see Figure C.4 in the color insert). Colors may also symbolize different psychological states: For instance, white often is used to symbolize purity, while red may indicate passion.

Contrast—that is, differences in brightness levels—also differentiates objects from one another. Closer objects tend to exhibit greater relative contrast than those further away.

Photo 6.13   Contrasting textures help to differentiate objects on screen. Note how different the smooth shiny leather top of the carriage looks compared to the horse hide or the velvet upholstry of the carriage seat.

Photo 6.14   Strong visual patterns add rhythm and a sense of movement to an image.

Depth and Perspective. As mentioned in Chapter 4, *perspective* helps create the illusion of depth through the use of converging lines. Depth is also indicated by the elements of focus and image size. Images that are small and hazy appear to be far away; those that are larger, sharper, and more detailed appear closer.

Placement of Key Elements. As shown in Photo 6.15, the key elements of a picture should be prominently placed on the screen. Secondary picture elements should support the main idea but not dominate it. Irrelevant objects should be removed from the shot.

Balance. *Balance* refers to the psychological sense of stability, steadiness, and restfulness in the video image. For example, if picture elements are distributed across the screen evenly, we tend to view the picture as more balanced than if all items are on one half of the screen and the other half is empty. Unbalanced shots tend to convey a sense of tension and discomfort. Sometimes, of course, temporary discomfort is what you want to achieve.

A simple way to create imbalance is to cant the camera, so that the subject looks tilted in the screen. Such canted angles are also called *Dutch angles.* This effect is often used to convey a sense of psychological stress or loss of control in

Photo 6.15   One key to picture composition is to place the crucial elements in prominent positions on the screen. Here the balloons dominate the foreground and middleground, with their importance reinforced by the strong, nearly horizontal axis they form across the middle of the picture. The lesser elements—the signs and cars—occupy much less prominent positions.

Photo 6.16   Dutch (*canted*) angles, with the objects tilted on the screen, can create a sense of power, tension, or other psychological effects.

a character (see Photo 6.16). On the other hand, Dutch angles can also convey a sense of power.

Achieving a sense of balance does not mean that the elements must be perfectly evenly distributed. Visual interest may be enhanced through some degree of asymmetry without disturbing the overall sense of balance.

Unity and Variety. From a purely functionalist perspective, a program has *unity* when it embodies a central theme in all of its aspects, and each of its elements seems connected in a whole. Unity also means that the content contains nothing superfluous. Put another way, a program is unified if a gaping hole results when part of it is removed.

However, incorporating unity into a program does not mean it lacks *variety*. Unity does not mean harping on the same idea the same way over and over again. Such monotony is usually boring.

Rather, *variety in unity* is the goal. In the first movement of Beethoven's *Fifth Symphony,* the famous four-note theme is repeated several hundred times, but by different instruments, at different volumes and intensities, at different tempos, and in different registers. In the same way, video presentations should express a unified theme in a variety of ways to maximize interest and effectiveness. For example, NBC's *The Tonight Show,* which has aired roughly 5 nights a week for nearly a half century, features a monologue performed every night by the host, but the jokes are not the same.

Of course, a functionalist perspective is not the only one that may serve you. More decorative approaches may also be appropriate at times. For example, music videos lean heavily on decorative impulses for their content, as do circus spectacles. In these cases, an action, shot, or sequence would not be considered superfluous simply because it was not functionally imperative. Therefore, it is important to decide which aesthetic principles you are using to judge how to shape the video content.

PICTURE COMPOSITION IN VIDEO

Now that some general principles of picture composition have been introduced, we can turn to more specific applications of these concepts in video. This section presents the specific language associated with video picture composition and aesthetics, along with examples from typical program situations.

Framing

Framing defines the area of the picture. In literal terms, the frame is the perimeter around the edge of the picture that limits your field of view. The process of framing includes deciding what will be included in each shot and what will be excluded. Framing should be influenced by the principles of static picture composition that we have just covered and also by the dynamic needs of the program from one moment to the next.

Let's go back to the two-person, stationary-talent interview situation that we introduced in Chapter 5. Assume we start with an image of host and guest (wearing a tie) sitting together in the frame (see Photo 6.17a). Now, when the host asks a question, both static and dynamic considerations suggest that we frame the next shot without the host, zeroing in on the guest for a response (see Photo 6.17b). A close-up of just the guest is desirable at this point for a number of reasons. First, from a static perspective, television close-ups are important for presenting information clearly. Second, the close-up on the guest forces the audience's attention to the guest's answer, synchronizing the video and audio and increasing intensity. Third, from a dynamic standpoint, since we have just established the relationship of the host and guest in the opening shot, we may now proceed to a close-up of the guest without losing context or continuity for the audience. However, after a while, another shot framing the host and guest together may again be needed to reestablish their relationship. Hence, framing decisions are influenced by time considerations (also called *pace*) and by shot sequences.

In addition, framing is greatly influenced by program content. For example, imagine that you are shooting a cooking show in which the opening shot shows the

(a)

(b)

Photo 6.17 Typical framing sequence for a two-person, stationary-talent interview program. The sequence begins with the host and guest together in the frame (a). When the host asks a question, the next shot (b) zooms in on the guest.

widest view of the set, including all the ingredients and utensils laid out on a table, plus the talent and an attractive backdrop. When you frame that shot, you notice on the line monitor that the front vertical face of the table takes up a quarter of the picture. You decide that part of the table is irrelevant to the program content and ought to be excluded, or at least minimized, so you tilt the camera up. Now, however, you see that the frame includes a great deal of *dead space* above the talent's head, which also is not appropriate. As a result, you correctly decide to zoom in on the table to exclude the superfluous parts of the picture. But if this close-up also excludes some of the important items on the table, you may need to make further adjustments in the shot—for example, by moving some of the items closer together or by panning across the table. In sum, good framing generally means leaving out dead space, the superfluous, and the irrelevant and including only what is motivated and essential.

Using the *z*-Axis

We designate the horizontal dimension of the picture as the *x*-axis—that is, the dimension across the screen from left to right. The vertical dimension is called the *y*-axis. Also of crucial importance is the **z-axis,** the imaginary dimension extending from foreground to background. By placing objects along the *z*-axis, we can create a three-dimensional sense of depth on the two-dimensional television screen.

As noted in Chapter 4, the overlapping of objects in the picture can help establish an illusion of depth and perspective. For example, you might place a foreground object in the lower left third of the shot, overlapping a middleground object in the center (in a different location on the *x*- and *y*-axes) and a background object in the top right third (yet another location on the *x*- and *y*-axes). This would establish a strong sense of depth. The danger is that objects toward the foreground can blot out the others. To avoid this, check the way the objects appear when framed in the video image, not just the way they look to you in actual three-dimensional space.

Focus

As you know from Chapter 4, *focus* refers to the sharpness of the objects featured in a shot, and *depth of field* is the area in which the images are acceptably sharp. Changing focus and depth of field can shift the viewer's attention from less important parts to key aspects of the video image.

When focus is changed from foreground to background elements of the picture, or vice versa, the change is called *racking focus* (Photos 6.18a and 6.18b). Racking focus shunts the viewer's attention from the one part of the video image to another.

Selective focus may also be used to stress important picture elements while de-emphasizing irrelevant, confusing, or distracting parts. Say you are conducting a serious interview with a nature expert about endangered species, and you have the

(a)   (b)

Photo 6.18   Racking focus. In these photos, the change in focus from foreground to background shunts the viewer's attention in the same way.

Photo 6.19   Selective focus. In this photo, selective focus is used to emphasize the roses in the foreground while de-emphasizing the background.

expert on camera with specimens of elephant tusks behind him. In the viewfinder, you notice that one tusk appears to be growing out of his head, making him look comical. To deal with the problem, you bring the subject closer to the camera, thus reducing depth of field (Photo 6.18 illustrates this technique). Now when you set focus on the speaker once again, the tusk is pushed out of focus, making the picture more acceptable. (Photo 6.19 illustrates a less dramatic example of selective focus.)

Camera Angle

Camera angle can greatly influence the amount of information available in a particular shot, how subjects look, and the meaning of a shot or scene. Therefore, it is essential to consider whether the camera should be lower than, higher than, or on the same level with the subject being pictured.

When the camera lens is at the same height as the subject, the picture is said to be shot at *eye level,* or on a normal camera angle. When the camera is lower than the subject, the picture is said to be shot from a *low angle.* When shot from above, the picture is said to be shot from a *high angle.*

In our cooking demonstration, for example, it may help to ped up the camera and tilt it down onto the work surface to show the cooking process more clearly (see Photo 6.20). More dramatically, if we are showing a knife-wielding villain approaching the camera, we may want to use a low angle, which will grant more strength, power, and psychological impact to the subject. Conversely, high angles generally make subjects look less threatening.

(a)　　　　　　　　**(b)**

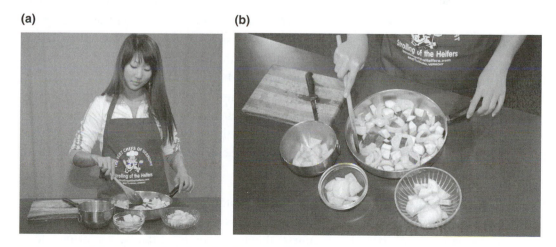

Photo 6.20　Use of appropriate camera angles to reinforce the program's subject. After showing (a) a chef at eye level, the camera dollies in, peds up, and tilts down for (b) a high angle shot of the food being prepared.

You also need to consider the impact of camera angle on shot backgrounds. Low angles usually mean that you will be including more vertical height in the background portion of your shots. In studios with low ceiling height, low-angle shots risk including the lights or other studio items that are not meant to be part of the set. Therefore, for tall talent, it may be necessary to ped up rather than shoot from below eye level. Remember also that camera angle can be changed during a production to accommodate different needs. Some pedestals even permit on-air adjustment, which can create dramatic effects.

Types of Camera Shots

Camera shots can be classified in many ways—by their function, by what they include, by the amount of screen space they allow the subject, and so on. The following sections introduce the common terminology and explain some of the reasons for choosing one type of shot rather than another.

Establishing and Master Shots. An **establishing shot** is the shot that establishes, for the audience, the relationship of talent to each other and to their setting. In our example of the two-person interview, the opening shot that shows the guest and host seated next to each other is the establishing shot. But the establishing shot does not need to be the first one in a program or a sequence. Consider, as an opening shot, a close-up of the main character's hand as it lifts a shot glass of liquor to his mouth (Figure 6.1a). As he drinks, the camera zooms out to reveal that he is at a bar. The camera continues to zoom out, showing that he is alone (Figure 6.1b). We see chairs upside down on tables throughout the bar, and finally we notice a clock on the wall reading two o'clock near a window with a neon sign flashing to indicate that it is the middle of the night (Figure 6.1c). This final shot is the establishing shot for the sequence because it establishes the setting for the character (Figure 6.1d).

A **master shot** or *cover shot,* on the other hand, is one that includes the widest shot of the set for a scene or program. It is important to know the extent of the master shot so that off-camera production elements (lights, microphones, booms, cue cards, crew members) can be placed into the set without inadvertently seeing them on camera. In some cases, a master shot can be used as an establishing shot, but often the two are different.

One-Shots and Two-Shots. As noted in Chapter 5, a **one-shot** is a frame containing one person. Similarly, a **two-shot** contains two people, a **three-shot** contains three people, and so forth. Of course, the arrangement of the person or people in the frame is highly variable. The subjects can be in tight close-up, can be far away, or can be arranged in a combination of screen distances (foreground, middleground, and background).

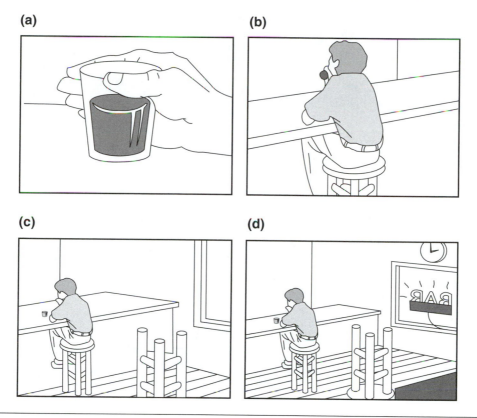

Figure 6.1 A sequence in which the camera gradually zooms out to reveal more and more of the scene. In this case, the last shot, which conveys the full setting, is the establishing shot.

Long Shots, Medium Shots, and Close-Ups. Another way of classifying shots, as shown in Photo 6.21, is by the proportion of total screen space a subject occupies in relation to the overall field of view. In a **long shot** (LS), the entire subject (head to toe) generally occupies significantly less than half the total screen space (Photo 6.21a). If the subject takes up far less than half the screen space, the shot may be called an *extreme long shot* (ELS). When the subject occupies closer to half the total screen space, we describe the shot as a **medium shot** (MS) (Photo 6.21b). Similarly, **close-ups** (CUs) and extreme close-ups (ECUs) describe frames where the subject dominates (Photo 6.21c).

In medium shots and close-ups, the subject's body is often truncated. For example, in a scene at a dentist's office, a medium shot might give most of the screen space to an image of the dental hygienist from the waist up. An extreme close-up could use most of the screen space to picture just the patient's mouth.

In one classical approach, directors begin with long shots to establish setting and relationships among characters and then move to progressively tighter shots to

Photo 6.21   Shots may be classified by the proportion of screen space the subject occupies: (a) is a long shot, (b) is a medium shot, and (c) is a close-up.

emphasize key program elements as the program unfolds. In many cases, though, other techniques may be advisable. In a murder mystery that starts with the murder, the director might want to hide the identity of the perpetrator. The program might start with a close-up of the murder weapon in use without letting the audience see the killer. In this example, wide shots would follow rather than precede the close-ups.

Head, Bust, and Waist Shots. For shots of people, a more exact terminology may be used to indicate the portion of the body that should be included. A *head shot,* obviously, is a shot of the person's head. A *bust shot* generally includes the head, shoulders, and the upper part of the chest. A *waist shot* includes everything from the waist up.

In framing such shots, be aware of exactly where the body is cut off. Shots that crop a person at a joint line—for instance, exactly at the knees, the waist, or the chin—tend to appear uncomfortable (see Figure 6.2). It is usually better to let the body's natural cutoff lines fall either clearly within the screen or beyond its bottom edge.

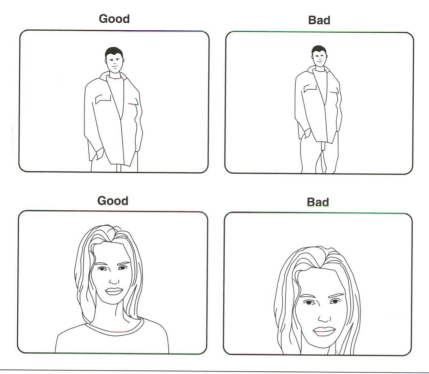

Figure 6.2   Preferred ways to frame a person on screen. Note that cropping a person exactly at a joint tends to look awkward or uncomfortable, as though the rest of the body has literally been chopped off.

Headroom, Noseroom, and Leadroom. Another framing consideration involves giving human subjects a comfortable amount of room on the screen, as illustrated in Figure 6.3. For instance, you normally want to provide enough **headroom**—that is, space between the talent's head and the top of the frame—so that the head does not appear squeezed or cramped. On the other hand, too much headroom can make the subject seem overwhelmed or lost in the picture.

In head shots taken from the side, **noseroom** refers to the screen space in front of the talent's face. In conventional composition, noseroom is generally greater than the screen space in back of the head. Restricting noseroom tends to create tension and a sense of entrapment of the subject. **Leadroom** is a similar concept applied to moving talent. If a horse and rider are moving from left to right on the screen, leadroom is the space to the right, in the direction the talent is moving.

You should determine how much headroom, noseroom, and leadroom to use depending on the effect you wish to create. Also, keep in mind that you may need to move the camera to maintain appropriate room around the subject as the picture changes.

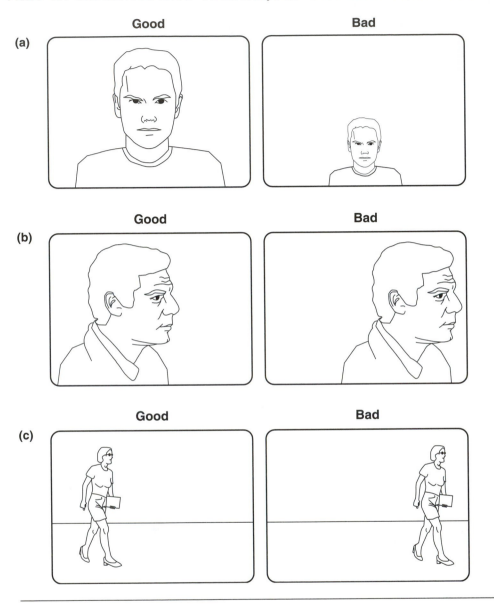

Figure 6.3   Subjects should be framed so that they have an appropriate amount of room on screen. These drawings illustrate correct and incorrect (a) headroom, (b) noseroom, and (c) leadroom.

Over-the-Shoulder Shots. When two subjects face each other, a common technique is to shoot one talent over the other's shoulder (see Photo 6.22). For example, it is common for the camera to frame a *speaker* over a *listener's* shoulder. This **over-the-shoulder (OS) shot,** as it is called, establishes the relationship between

(a)   (b)

Photo 6.22   Over-the-shoulder (OTS or OS) shot. (a) A standard OS establishing the relationship
between the talent. (b) A zoom to a close-up.

the talent, presents an intimate image of the speaker's face, and shows the audience who the speaker is talking to.

In addition, the OS can easily be changed to an even more intimate close-up of
the speaker by zooming in past the listener's shoulder. After a time, the relationship
can be reestablished by zooming out (on or off air) to recapture the back of the listener. This type of camera movement provides shot variety and visual interest,
emphasizes relationships among talent, and preserves context and unity in the videospace. Of course, a different camera can be positioned behind the speaker to carry
an OS of the listener's reactions, offering additional variety and visual interest.

Reveals and Trims. To communicate important information to your audience,
you can use camera movement to reveal or isolate important picture elements,
sometimes with dramatic effects. Imagine beginning with a high-angle one-shot of
your central character's face in extreme close-up (see Figure 6.4a). As he delivers
an especially subservient and deferential apology to someone off camera, a
slow zoom out reveals that he is hanging by a rope from a Manhattan office building, high above the street, in obvious mortal danger. This **reveal** further discloses
that the rope is being held by the person he is apologizing to. Obviously, reveals
can evoke horror, humor, and other reactions, depending on the subject matter and
sequencing.

In similar fashion, a **trim** from a wide shot to a tighter frame can be useful
when you want to emphasize a key element of the picture. In a mystery drama, you
may start with a cover shot of a crime scene as detectives file out after their preliminary investigation (see Figure 6.4b). As they leave, the camera zooms in to a

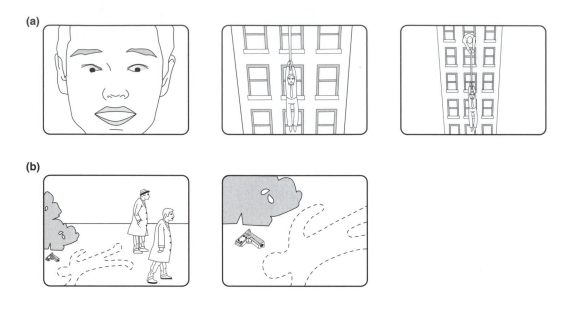

Figure 6.4   Camera movement can disclose or highlight important information. (a) A reveal, as the camera zooms out, gradually conveys the subject's peril. (b) A trim, as the camera zooms in, isolates a weapon the detectives have failed to notice.

close-up of a key piece of evidence (say, the murder weapon) that the police have missed. By trimming the shot to isolate the key item, the audience is given clues that can explain later action. As another example, in a cooking show, a shot of the chef placing the finished dish on the table could be trimmed to a close-up of the dish itself. Trim shots stress the important elements, eliminate irrelevant information, and use screen space optimally.

Point-of-View Shots. Shots that appear to be from the point of view of a particular actor are called **point-of-view (POV) shots.** For example, imagine a drama in which our main character is talking on the phone with the local police. They warn her that a desperate murderer has just escaped from a nearby prison. She is framed in a waist shot as she finishes speaking and hangs up the phone (see Figure 6.5a). Suddenly she is startled by the sound of the front door handle being jiggled from outside (see Figure 6.5b). We cut to a close-up of the door from her POV, zooming in on the door and then trimming to an extreme close-up of the handle as it moves ominously back and forth (see Figure 6.5c). Rather than simply recording the action from outside, this POV shot gains dramatic impact by taking the subjective stance of the main character, increasing the audience's identification with her.

(a) 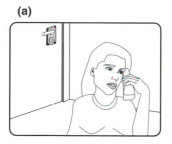 **(b)** 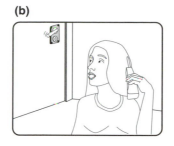 **(c)**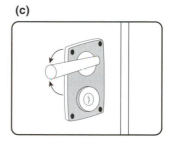

Figure 6.5   Sequence illustrating a point-of-view (POV) shot. In (a), a character gets a phone call about an escaped murderer. In (b), she hears her door handle rattle and spins around to look. In (c), the director cuts to a close-up of the ominously jiggling handle from her POV.

Working With Cameras

➢ Keep the floor clean. Because video makes extensive use of close-ups, small jolts to the camera—when it rolls over a piece of gum, for instance—may cause severe rocking of the image.

➢ Check your viewfinder registration. Faulty alignment between the viewfinder and the line monitor can spoil your picture composition.

➢ If you are using cue cards, be sure to number them. Numbers help you keep the cards in correct order. If they get out of order, they may confuse the on-air talent.

➢ With both cue cards and Teleprompters, find the correct distance from the talent. The prompts should be close enough to be readable, but not so close that viewers notice the talent's eye movement.

➢ Adjust camera angle for the needs of the program, not for the height or comfort of the operator. Check the line monitor to be sure you have framed the shot correctly.

➢ When framing a person, don't truncate the image at the edge of a body part. "Chopping" the person in an obvious way tends to make the audience uneasy.

A FINAL NOTE ABOUT PICTURE COMPOSITION

Throughout the discussion of the camera's mechanical and electrical technologies and the marvelous things people can do with them, we have come back repeatedly to the notion of program content and the fact that the program is communicating with an audience. These points deserve additional emphasis before we turn to the audio component of video production in the next chapter.

Remember, if you are directing, then you call the shots. You are the one arranging the camera work in a way that will make people either want to watch or tune out. While you must know the capabilities and limitations of sophisticated camera equipment, you also need to develop your understanding of what will enlighten and move the audience. Successful programs have a purpose. They present content clearly, with the intent to entertain, inform, and/or persuade an audience. Cameras have not yet been invented that can automatically achieve that aspect of video production.

INDUSTRY VOICES

Jay Fine

On Tuesday, July 12, 2005, I interviewed Jay Fine, CEO of Steiner Studios, located on the site of the old Brooklyn Navy Yard in downtown Brooklyn, New York. Steiner Studios is a 15-acre site consisting of a building with 285,000 square feet of space for sound stages and support areas for film and video production. There are five stages with three 16,000–square foot stages, one 22,000–square foot stage, and a 27,000–square foot stage. Jay Fine supervised the building effort, where he now manages productions of big-budget films and other projects. His expertise developed over 30 years in the television and film production business as an editor, operations manager, and senior executive for several major media corporations with global reach.

L: *Give me your bio, where you were born and raised, etc.*

J: *I'm born in Brooklyn and raised in New York, and I've been in the business for 30 years, 20 of them at NBC. I worked my way through college at NBC, as an editor, animator, and then manager, and moved into the news division. I was Senior VP of news operations and planning for NBC network news, including all of the bureaus worldwide, with a 350-person operation and a $75 million annual budget. Then in the early '90s, I moved to CBS, where I was Senior VP of East Coast Operations, with $200 million a year budget and 1,500 employees, all below-the-line activity: studios, entertainment, news, local stations, the rebuilding of the Ed Sullivan Theatre, Olympics, sports, mobile units, and anything that had to do with technology, engineering, and production. In the late '90s, I left and started several companies. One, called the FeedRoom, started with a colleague, was the first broadband news network. It's still going. Later, I moved to L.A., where I was managing director of National Teleconsultants, which designed and built media facilities around the world. They built the multichannel facility for DIRECTV in L.A.; the new ESPN Digital Technology Center, in Bristol, CT; and had projects ranging from*

Hong Kong to Australia to Washington, D.C. During that period, I met the Steiners, and they had an intriguing project. What started out as a casual relationship ended up as a full-time position, which really got into full gear about 3½ years ago. I'm happy to say that we're now sitting in the premier production facility in the U.S.

L: The footprint of the building was blank 3½ years ago because you removed some structures.

J: Right. The area had been cleared.

L: Is the building completed?

J: Almost. The north end of the building, when finished, will be an amenities area, including event space for parties, a screening room, additional catering facilities, and a commissary. The stages, dressing rooms, and offices are done, and we've been putting productions in since November. Since February we've been full.

L: Do you provide the hardware necessary for a shoot?

J: No, we don't get involved in acquisition technology. Instead, we provide large, column-free space, access to support space to build, weld, and paint. We provide lots of parking, adjacent offices, dressing rooms, with the ability to walk easily from stage to dressing room and back. It's up to the production companies and directors to decide what kind of acquisition technology they want to use. What we're seeing is that 35-mm film is still prevalent for shooting feature films, but more and more producers and directors are creating a digital intermediary (DI) for editing movies.

L: So they still shoot celluloid?

J: Yes, then it's converted to a digital format, and that's where all the postproduction occurs. The commercial industry has adopted HDTV faster than the feature film business because they're not creating something for the ages. They create programs with more immediate use and shorter shelf-life—something that looks good, can be done quickly, and cost-effectively. So HDTV technology is now used more by commercial directors. But I think over the next decade, we'll see feature film directors shifting to HDTV. Film is also an industry where things have been done a certain way for decades, so even when a viable new technology becomes available, that is no guarantee of overnight adoption. There's a learning curve, and there's the issue of how to extract the best of any given technology. Since people have been working with film, and they have their favorite film stocks that they use, they understand how to use those tools, and that's what they need to learn with HD. That takes time no matter how good the new technology is. I think the transition probably will take a decade. Cameras must do what the directors want them to do, and their product must have a certain look and feel, and they have to be adopted not just by young directors but by the veterans they come to work with. It just takes time. Users want to know, "What's in it for me? Can I get a better look? Can it be easier to do a production?" At Steiner, we also do television and still photo shoots. The advantages of HD are that results can be seen immediately. It's also less expensive (at least in theory), because you're not shooting film stock, although I'm not so sure about that when you add up the costs of the technology involved. But it is more immediate. If you're on location, people can beam the results someplace to others that need to see it. And for feature films, I think you have creative options that are different from those available with film. However, the wonderful thing about film is that it's got archival advantages over digital material. The problem with digital technology is that it's ephemeral. Recording something on a particular type of storage medium that may not exist several years from now is a conundrum for archivists. With film, if you store it at the right temperature and humidity, it'll last hundreds of years. With digital, nobody really knows for sure. But for things that need immediacy, such as commercials or television, HD is a wonderful option. It's fast, it's immediate, and it's closer and closer to film.

L: In terms of percents, what of your recent projects have been shot in house versus in the field?

J: For the average movie we've done thus far, I'd say probably 85% is shot on our sound stage, and the rest on location. Ninety percent of the movie *Fur* about the life and work of Diane Arbus, starring Nicole Kidman as Arbus, was shot on our soundstage, using a single camera. Occasionally there are additional cameras, but most of the projects have been shot in what's called feature film style, where each angle is set up differently. For big musical numbers, we have had multiple cameras. The approach is dictated by the script and what the production designer needs to do and what's going to be better, easier, and less expensive. So if you want to shoot in Times Square, and a lot of your movie takes place there, it's probably going to be less expensive to build a Times Square set on our soundstage and shoot it here. If you only need to go there for a couple of hours, then you're probably better off going on location.

L: You haven't mentioned anything about sitcoms or soap operas.

J: The jobs we support are driven by the kinds of productions that come to us. Sitcoms, soap operas, it's all fine. Currently, we like that we're doing feature films, because they have always had a hard time finding good production facilities in New York. There are only a handful of facilities that were built to be stages. And almost everything else in New York that's being used as a stage was originally built to be something else—a factory, a bakery, a radio studio—but not a soundstage. We give producers a big, clean facility with modern amenities—everything they need so they can focus on making a movie.

L: With the transition to digital, there are market, political, economic, and postproduction issues. What do you see as the major pressures on the business?

J: Again, for commercial producers, there are significant economic and time pressures because commercials frequently need fast turnaround, so HD provides advantages for videographers. But film has always given productions a different kind of feel. Nowadays, however, some say you can get that kind of feel from HD. I remember years ago, a director had said to me, "Film is funny, video isn't." So, for others, there are emotional issues with different acquisition media. With features, I think it's more of an issue of what kind of movie you're making. If you're doing a special effects movie with a lot of postprocessing, keeping things in the digital domain probably makes sense. But if you're making a love story or some narrative movie, which doesn't really have a lot of special effects and is more about the characters and cinematography, then I think a director is going to stay with film.

L: How has the digital transition in the postproduction environment changed the business side of production?

J: First of all, most of my comments prior to this focused on big-budget feature films, not small independent movies. For big-budget movies, I think digital might actually add cost because there's more you can do creatively. But for low-budget independent filmmaking, the new HD digital technology, which provides you with a 24-p frame rate, wide screen, reasonably good quality, and immediacy to instant dailies, lowers entry barriers. You can buy a Macintosh with basic editing software that's probably more sophisticated than anything I started out with in the industry 30 years ago. And programs like Final Cut Pro and Avid, which are now industry standards for postproduction, allow you to edit on the computer, and transfer it to whatever distribution medium you want. And that's the nice thing for people who have great ideas but not a lot of money. The Producers was shot on 35-mm film and edited digitally. They assembled what they were shooting each day so they could see it and make sure they had what they needed. Then they've moved to a postproduction facility to combine all the elements they shot here.

L: What does the digital transition do to the hiring process?

J: With digital, it's easier to get along with fewer people because there's less mechanical work to do. But there are risks: Disks can be contaminated with viruses, and there are more risks for piracy and theft. These are the same issues you'd have with any computer. But digital allows work to be done more quickly. The bottom line is when it comes to shooting and editing, it's really not about the technology, it's about talent. The talented operator can work with scissors and a rewind or a computer. But someone with a computer doesn't always have an eye, doesn't necessarily know how pictures should go together, or how to frame a shot, or adjust lighting to generate an emotional response. For that, you have to understand human nature and what grabs an audience.

L: You touched on the issue of piracy.

J: Piracy is a real problem. It's going to have to be dealt with legally and socially. I have friends who are with the MPAA, and I tell them how I'm walking down the street seeing people with supermarket carts pulling DVDs out of a basket—movies that had been released the day before or, in some cases, movies that had not yet been released. These aren't DVDs of movies made by having someone go to the theater with a camera to shoot the screen; these are movies somehow pirated from in-house. Movie studios have stepped up security, and theaters are more diligent about policing cameras in theaters, which becomes trickier with cell phone mini-cams. And I think you're seeing the effects of these technical realities in policy choices with respect to release windows. For example, when a movie is released into a theater today, it may no longer be weeks or months before a DVD is released—in some cases, it may be released on DVD simultaneously. I think the issue is if people are going to pirate a movie and sell it, you may as well have the legitimate version out there to sell so that the pirates themselves are undercut by owners adopting earlier release dates. I have friends in the business spending all of their time wrestling with this issue.

L: Now that the video i-Pod is available, have you considered the issue of the tiny and the large in terms of production aesthetics?

J: Directors have thought about this for years. Feature films end up on TV, and until recently, the TV format was 4:3 while the film format is closer to 16:9. So for films going to TV quickly, directors intentionally framed the main characters in the center of the image. There are also postproduction techniques for panning, scanning, and compressing images so that you get the main activity in that 4:3 format. But now that home TV is becoming wider format—16:9 is becoming more prevalent in the home—I think there's less concern about aspect ratio. In terms of screen size, I think most producer-directors would focus on the primary use. For producers making commercials, maybe they're thinking about how it's going to look on several different formats and screen sizes. But for feature films, I think people think about how it looks on the big screen. Home theaters are still getting bigger. And now, it's not only the display but also the sound system. Sound is important to the whole film experience, and for a few hundred dollars, you can get a modest 5.1 surround sound system with subwoofer for home use. A small room can have that theater kind of feel. For more money, there's obviously more realism. But sound enriches viewing. The quality of display is also improving—it's not just the aspect ratio or screen size, although years ago, studies showed that the aspect ratio had the greatest impact on how people rated the quality of something: Widescreen was perceived as better than 4:3. But manufacturing technology has improved, broadband technology has become better, compression algorithms are constantly improving, and *there's an expectation of higher quality in the home. One thing is certain: Consumer electronics companies will have products to sell for the next few years.*

L: *Who works at Steiner Studios? Who are you hiring, and what would you advise college students finishing their degrees in this field to maximize their market value?*

J: *We have a very small staff—it's here to run the building and manage the stages. Most of the people who work here are employees of the various production companies. So if someone was looking to get a foothold in the business, they would really need to focus on people who make the movies, and they need also to figure out for themselves where they think they can add value. This business is a meritocracy. That is, you may have a good education, and you may even have good family connections. But at the end of the day, almost everyone is judged on their contribution to the production. If you're good and helpful to the others around you, you'll get your next job. If you're just OK, you may not get your next job. It's very Darwinian. And the people you meet at the top have spent a lot of years honing their craft, learning different parts of the business, and learning how to work as a team. Above all, you need to determine what you do well that others don't do as well—what do you do better than others? Focus on that. Work at it every day. If you think you want to be a director, you should be making movies every day; you should be writing every day. You should be looking and doing every day, not just talking about it. It's a business of doing, and it's very demanding, and the hours are long, and except for people at the top, the pay isn't very good. It can also be boring at times. So you have to be very committed. The people in the business are wonderful, very creative. They energize you in terms of how to look at things. There are some very smart people in this business, and if you want to be part of it, then you have to operate at that level. The sooner you start, the sooner you can make mistakes and start moving up and determine if this is the right business for you.*

KEY TERMS

QUESTIONS FOR REVIEW

How do different camera mounts affect camera movement in both studio and field?

What terms do directors use to request different camera moves from the camera operator?

What electronic camera components help the camera operator compose video images?

What are the advantages and shortcomings of the various prompting devices available in video production? How should cue cards be set up for talent oriented directly to the camera?

What static design elements should be considered when composing pictures for the camera?

What dynamic considerations affect picture composition, sequence, and pace?

In addition to terms such as *close-up, medium shot,* and *long shot,* what other terminology might be used to specify precisely how you want shots of talent to look?

Chapter 7

UNDERSTANDING SOUND AND MICROPHONES

Sound has always been part of the video medium. Since the 1980s, however, audio in television has improved significantly. This is because television receivers are now offered with high-quality audio technology. Many newer sets feature multiple speakers with full-range audio, stereo, and surround sound options. This is a great advance over the tiny single speaker that was once the norm.

But the importance of sound in television does not depend only on the nature of the equipment. It is also due to differences in the way we perceive sound and pictures. Think about what attracts your attention to a program when your attention is elsewhere. If you are turned away at the start of a program, it is the sound that draws your attention, because your ears (unlike your eyes) can pick up signals from all directions. That is why, from a production standpoint, it makes sense to bring the audio in either simultaneously with or slightly before the video. Moreover, the ear can focus on many sounds at once, providing a powerful means of setting a scene quickly.

Another perceptual difference is that our eyes are more forgiving than our ears when noise enters the signal. (Remember from Chapter 1 that noise is any unwanted material that interferes with the desired content.) Our vision is coarser and more tolerant of defects in detail than our sense of hearing. For example, we can hear differences in quality between analog cassette and a CD, but not between live versus recorded video. In short, noise is more obvious to the ear than to the eye, making sound quality extremely important.

One purpose of this chapter is to describe the physical nature of sound and our perception of it. Another is to explain how microphones work and how they are used to capture sound for video production. The topics include the following:

The nature of sound

- The sound wave
- The sound envelope

Microphones: basic types and characteristics

- Generating elements
- Performance characteristics
- Pickup patterns

Microphone selection

- Audio design principles
- Visible mics
- Off-camera mics
- Wireless mics
- Other technical considerations

Stereo and surround sound

- Problems in stereo miking
- Surround sound

THE NATURE OF SOUND

The Sound Wave

Sound is the vibration of molecules caused by the motion of a physical object. Most often, the vibration consists of the transfer of energy from one air molecule to another. However, sound may result from the motion of a physical object in the presence of any molecular medium with some degree of elasticity (including gases, liquids, and solids). Elasticity refers to the tendency of a molecule to bounce back to its original position after bumping into one nearby. In the presence of air, a hammer hitting a concrete block, a guitar string being plucked, a violin being bowed, or vocal cords being moved by a column of air in your windpipe can all cause nearby air molecules to bump into one another, sending air pressure waves of sound out from a source.

When sound travels through air, molecules that are disturbed do not travel the entire distance from the source to the furthest point the sound reaches. Rather, they bump into one another, transferring energy from one molecule to the next. In this way, each molecule moves only a small distance. This is similar to the action you observe when a cue ball strikes a row of billiard balls, leaving the cue ball near the first ball it strikes but transferring the energy from the cue ball to each one in line, causing the last in line to move without ever having come in contact with the cue ball. It is the *energy* from the cue ball that moves through the row, not the cue ball itself.

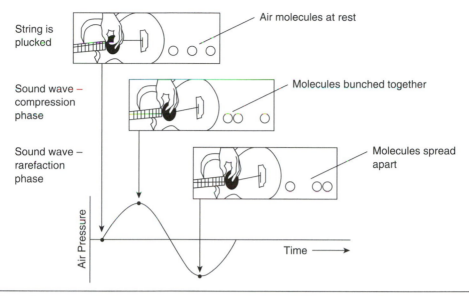

Figure 7.1   The compression and rarefaction phases of a sound wave.

For example, when a guitar string is plucked, air molecules closest to the string are disturbed by its rapid back-and-forth motion. This movement is called *vibration* or *oscillation*. As the string vibrates, a sound wave is propagated as air molecules transfer energy to adjacent molecules. If you are in range, air molecules vibrating sympathetically with the guitar string strike your ear drums, causing you to hear the sound. The motion from one molecule to the next imitates the original vibrations of the sound source, matching the rate of motion of the string.

As the string moves, it compresses nearby air molecules in the direction the string is moving. This *compression phase* consists of a bunching together of air molecules, increasing the density of air in the direction the string is moving. As the string moves back, it sends a compression reaction in the opposite direction, causing molecules to pull further apart in the initial direction. This thinning of air molecules in the initial direction is called a *rarefaction phase*. Alternating compressions and rarefactions can be pictured as the same kind of sine wave we described for radio energy in Chapter 2, and the wave features the same components of frequency, amplitude, wavelength, and phase (see Figure 7.1). Actually, this explanation does not take into account the added vibration of the body of the guitar, which vibrates sympathetically with the guitar string. The guitar body acts as an amplifier as it vibrates a greater volume of air than the string can do alone.

Frequency and Pitch. The *frequency* of a sound wave refers to the number of times per second that it completes a cycle from compression to rarefaction. Using the same notation used to describe radio waves, audio frequency is measured by the number of cycles per second (cps) or hertz (Hz). For example, if the rate of vibration of a guitar string is 50 cycles per second, we designate its frequency as 50 cps or 50 Hz. Similarly, a sound wave of 10,000 cycles per second is 10,000 Hz, or 10 kilohertz (10 kHz).

The normal range of human hearing is roughly from 20 Hz to 16 kHz. Our perception of a sound changes according to its frequency. We hear a difference in **pitch** such that as frequency changes, so does the perceived highness or lowness of the sound. At higher frequencies, sounds are thinner and more shrill; at lower frequencies, sounds are deeper. For example, the low notes of a bass fiddle range between 20 and 100 Hz, while the high notes of a piccolo can go above 3,500 Hz. The faster an object vibrates, the higher the pitch.

Amplitude and Loudness. When an object vibrates in any elastic medium, molecules surrounding the object do also if the vibration is intense enough. The more intense the vibration, the greater the pressure exerted on the surrounding medium, and the greater the number of molecules set in motion. The magnitude of intensity is known as the *amplitude,* more commonly known as *volume.*

As amplitude increases, loudness increases. For example, an opera singer singing a note of constant pitch (say 262 Hz, known as middle C) can vary the intensity from loud to soft by regulating the volume of air passing across the vocal cords. Keeping the amount of air relatively small produces a soft note (low volume); conversely, increasing the amount of air flow raises the volume making the note louder.

We can discern a broad range of variations in loudness. For example, we can hear both a whisper and a cannon shot from a distance of 10 meters. The cannon shot may be 10 million times louder than the whisper. We call variations in loudness that we can hear *dynamic range.* Because dynamic range is so broad, we use a logarithmic scale of values known as the *decibel scale* to measure and express differences in loudness efficiently.

Basically, the **decibel** (dB) is a unit of measurement that expresses logarithmically a ratio between two sound levels or two electrical power levels associated with different sounds. People tend to perceive that a sound has "doubled" in volume when it has increased by about 3 dBs, whereas a 1-dB change is barely distinguishable. For comparing volume levels of different signals, broadcasting stations use as their standard a decibel value known as the **volume unit** (VU), measured by a *VU meter.* (See Chapter 8 for a discussion of how the VU meter is used.)

Frequency and Loudness. The relationship between amplitude and our perception of loudness is complicated: Our ability to hear sound across the entire frequency spectrum is not uniform. Of course, hearing may be affected by such factors as age, health, and exposure levels to sound over time. But in general, we are more sensitive to sound in the middle range of audible frequencies, from about 300 to 3,500 Hz, than we are to either the low end (*bass*) or high end (*treble*). Therefore, while your audio equipment might present the full range of audio frequencies at equal volume, our subjective perception of sound presented this way tends to favor the midrange frequencies. This means that midrange sound masks other portions of the spectrum presented at equal volume. Because of *masking,* it is sometimes necessary to vary volume levels according to our sensitivity to different frequencies. When we electronically alter the volumes of certain frequencies to increase or eliminate masking, we call that process *equalization.*

Wavelength and Phase. As with light and radio waves, the wavelength of a sound is inversely related to its frequency. *Wavelength* is the distance traveled by one complete cycle of compression and rarefaction. Lower frequencies have longer wavelengths, and higher frequencies have shorter wavelengths.

Sound waves also have a *phase* component, which refers to the time relationship between two or more sound waves at a given moment in their cycles. For example, if two sound waves of identical frequency are propagated at the same instant, their compression and rarefaction phases will coincide. The two waves will be received perfectly in phase with one another at a point equidistant from their sources, assuming they travel through media of equal density. The important point is that *received waves that are in phase reinforce one another—the sound you hear gets louder.* They yield a net gain in amplitude (called *constructive interference*) equal to the sum of their individual amplitudes at a given instant. Conversely, waves of the same frequency received perfectly out of phase with one another exhibit an opposite effect called *destructive interference,* the net result of which is a canceling of their amplitudes. *The sound you hear gets lower, possibly even resulting in silence* (see Figure 7.2).

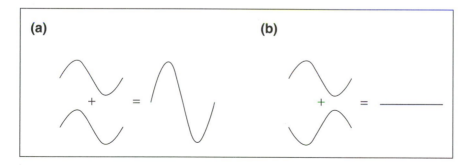

Figure 7.2   Interference of two sound waves. (a) Illustrates constructive interference when waves are in phase. The two waves reinforce each other, creating a louder sound. (b) Illustrates destructive interference when the waves are out of phase. The two waves cancel each other out.

Of course, neither situation occurs very often. Sound waves usually propagate from different sources at different times and at different wavelengths, so they are rarely perfectly in or out of phase with one another. But interference factors are nevertheless critical to sound design, especially concerning microphone placement and talent proximity, and especially when recording in stereo.

Waveforms and Timbre. *Timbre* refers to the unique sound quality that comes from variations in frequencies that accompany most tones that we hear. Timbre is defined as that quality of auditory sensation that enables us to judge that two sounds of the same loudness and pitch are dissimilar. For example, while a guitar string vibrating at 262 Hz matches the frequency of middle C on a properly tuned piano, you would have no trouble distinguishing the guitar's C from the piano's. Why is this? It is because most sounds are not pure tones; rather, they contain additional frequencies generated uniquely by the source producing the original tone and perhaps by surrounding media with which the original tone interacts. In musical terms, these additional frequencies are known as *harmonics* (tones that are exact multiples of a fundamental tone) and *overtones* (tones that are not multiples of the fundamental). In fact, the richness of our auditory experience is largely due to overtones and harmonics. Recall that human hearing extends to 16 kHz. Yet the frequency of the highest piano note is only 4,186 Hz, leaving about 12 kHz just for harmonics and overtones. Obviously, harmonics and overtones account for a major segment of the audio spectrum, at least as far as music is concerned.

When a single piano note is struck, instead of generating a simple sine wave at a single frequency, the sum of harmonics and overtones generated by the fundamental tone yields a complex *waveform* (see Figure 7.3) that uniquely identifies it as having come from a piano. A guitar has its own unique harmonic structure yielding its own unique waveform. A clarinet has another. In short, complex harmonic structure makes notes of the same pitch have different timbres. It is timbre that makes it difficult to confuse the sound that comes from Bruce Springsteen's throat with that of Placido Domingo, even when they sing the same note.

Figure 7.3   Sample of a complex waveform as it appears on an oscilloscope. This form was produced by sounding the first A above middle C (frequency 440 Hz) on a standard piano keyboard.

The Sound Envelope

Our perception of a sound is also affected by its **sound envelope,** or the characteristic way it begins, sustains, and ends (see Figure 7.4). The start of a sound is known as the *attack* phase. The attack phase for the sound of a violin string that is bowed is different from one that is plucked. The difference is in duration, amplitude, and timbre. The same note created by striking a bell exhibits yet a different attack than either of the methods used to make the note on a violin.

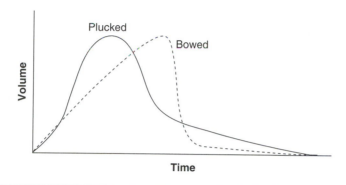

Figure 7.4   Two sound waves of the same frequency with different sound envelopes. Compared to the wave shown by the solid line, the wave represented by the dashed line has a slower attack phase, a shorter sustain phase, and a sharper decay phase.

The *sustain* phase refers to the time it lasts after the attack. Amplitude and duration of the sustain phase may vary. Some sounds take longer than others to reach a stable level after the attack phase, and some take longer to die out. The final stage is the *decay* phase. This refers to the character of a sound as it begins to become inaudible.

Sound envelopes can convey important information about the nature and origin of different sounds. Knowing about them helps in shaping sound in the editing process. For example, intentionally chopping off or reversing attack and decay stages of a person's speech can radically alter the sounds you hear. To hear the effect of altering the sound envelope, record a person reading words backwards onto audiotape. Then play the tape in reverse. Part of the reason the words still do not sound normal is because the attack and decay phases have been reversed.

MICROPHONES: BASIC TYPES AND CHARACTERISTICS

When sound waves are directed at a pressure-sensitive element, causing it to vibrate in the presence of a magnetic or electric field, a pattern of electricity matching the waveform of the original sound is generated. This is how a microphone (or *mic* for short) converts sound energy into electrical energy. Some microphone elements are shaped like a thin disk or diaphragm made of Mylar or aluminum. Others are shaped like a piece of ribbon. In all cases, sound vibrations directed at the element are changed into an analogous[1] pattern of electrical energy.

This process is the same as that described for the telephone microphone in Chapter 2, except that the telephone may use a cruder element of carbon particles to convert sound waves to a pattern of electricity. The telephone mic is considered crude because it is designed only for discrimination of speech; its pickup element responds only to audio frequencies from 300 to 3,000 Hz. By contrast, professional broadcast-quality mics are sensitive to audio frequencies over the full range of human hearing (20 Hz–16 kHz) and beyond.

Microphones are classified according to the types of generating elements they use, their performance characteristics, and their pickup patterns (directional characteristics). Each of these aspects of microphones is discussed in turn below.

Generating Elements

Microphones may be classified according to three types of generating elements: capacitor, dynamic, and ribbon.

Capacitor Microphones. Capacitor microphones (also called *condenser* microphones) use a capacitor as a generating element. A capacitor is any two electrical conductors (usually thin metal plates that can store an electrical charge) separated by a thin layer of air or insulating material. A change in voltage results when one of the plates moves. In a capacitor microphone, a sound-sensitive diaphragm is used as one of the two plates (see Figure 7.5a). When exposed to sound, the narrow airspace between the two plates changes in direct relationship to the original sound waves, changing the amount of electricity in its circuit accordingly. The pattern of voltage variations matches that of the original sound waves.

Because capacitor mics use a capacitor instead of a magnet to induce an electric current, they must have a power supply to charge the capacitor. There is, however, a special type of capacitor mic called an *electret* microphone. These mics have their capacitor elements permanently charged during the manufacturing process and therefore do not need power to maintain a charge. Other capacitor microphones receive power either from a supply built into the body of the microphone housing or, more commonly, from a supply external to the mic. In some cases, power can be delivered to the mic over the same cable that carries the audio signal to the recording console or mixer. This is referred to as a *phantom power supply*. The required voltage is available to a capacitor mic plugged into the input but not to other types of mics that do not require power.

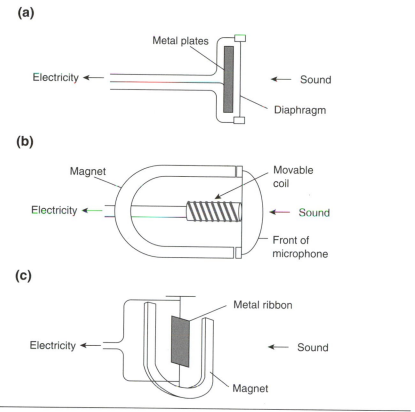

Figure 7.5   Three different types of microphone-generating element: (a) a capacitor mic, (b) a dynamic mic, and (c) a ribbon mic.

Since capacitor microphones (electret or otherwise) produce such a small voltage output, they must boost their electrical signals to usable levels. To do this, a *powered preamplifier* is used. The preamplifier (or preamp) is located inside the microphone housing and receives its power either from an internal battery (as is the case with many electret mics) or from a remotely located power supply.

Dynamic Microphones. The dynamic microphone is also called a *moving coil microphone.* It gets its name because it uses an extremely thin Mylar or aluminum diaphragm attached to a movable coil of wire suspended in the magnetic field of a permanent magnet (see Figure 7.5b). The diaphragm vibrates when subjected to air pressure waves supplied by a sound source. As the vibrating diaphragm moves the coil, an electrical voltage is induced that matches the original sound pattern.

Ribbon Microphones. In place of a diaphragm or wire coil, ribbon microphones use an extremely thin and light corrugated metal strip suspended in a powerful magnetic field (see Figure 7.5c). Air pressure waves vibrate the metal ribbon, inducing a voltage pattern that matches the original sound wave. Ribbon micro-phones are also called *velocity microphones* because the voltage generated as the ribbon cuts through the magnetic field is the electrical equivalent of the velocity of the air molecules themselves.

Performance Characteristics

The range of frequencies that a microphone is sensitive to is its *frequency response.* Manufacturers supply a *specification (spec) sheet* for every microphone containing a graph of that mic's response curve. The response curve plots dB gain on the ver-tical axis against frequency range on the horizontal axis (see Figure 7.6). The flat part of the curve indicates the frequency range where audio response for that microphone is constant. The ends of the curve indicate the limits of the mic's sen-sitivity. The spec sheet also shows where the mic has "peaks" or "roll-offs." *Peaks* are portions of the frequency spectrum where audio sensitivities increase; *roll-offs* are portions where sensitivity diminishes.

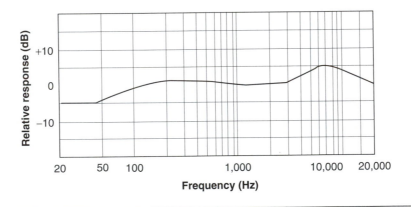

Figure 7.6   Response curve for a typical wireless lavaliere mic.

Mics differ in their frequency response and also in their general ruggedness and durability. Here is a brief summary of the usual performance characteristics of the three different types of mics:

• *Capacitor mics.* Because of their electrostatic design, capacitor mics gen-erally deliver the highest quality sound across the entire frequency spectrum. They reproduce more detailed sound and are quicker than other mics in responding to sudden changes in sound (such as quick attacks and decays). However, because their generating element is made of an extremely thin sheet of metal or metal-coated plastic, they are less rugged than dynamic microphones. In addition, they are not as impervious to extreme weather conditions. Nevertheless, they do find application in field settings.

- *Dynamic mics.* Dynamic mics, by virtue of their construction, are among the most rugged and durable of all professional microphones. Their ability to withstand physical shocks and severe weather (both temperature and humidity variations) makes them a fine choice for field productions. In terms of frequency response, dynamic mics discriminate high-frequency sound more clearly than other types of mics.

- *Ribbon mics.* Ribbon mics are the most fragile of all professional microphones and, for this reason, are not recommended for field use. In terms of frequency response, ribbon mics produce a warm, rich, mellow sound, which is excellent for studio announcing and musical presentations. However, because ribbon mics are activated by sound velocity, they may be especially affected by sudden sharp sounds. In fact, loud sneezes or coughs directed into a ribbon mic at close range can permanently damage it.

All mics, regardless of type, can encounter noise problems from outdoor wind. Moreover, sibilant vocal sounds, such as the letter *S,* can create a wind effect in any setting, and the consonants *B, P,* and *T* can cause "popping" noises. Some speakers are harder to mic than others because of the way they say these letters. Proper mic technique, however, can help eliminate such problems. Popping sounds can be almost completely eliminated by keeping the talent at a distance of about 12 inches from the mic. A better technique involves placing the mic somewhat to the side of the person speaking, or slightly off-axis to the direction of speech. For close miking in studio situations, *pop filters* are used to cover the mic head. In more extreme or windy outdoor situations, foam windscreens or other sophisticated devices are used (see Photo 7.1).

To offset sound problems caused by rough handling, some mics are designed with their diaphragms doubly insulated from their housing. In addition, a mic may be placed in a *shock mount,* which suspends the microphone in a protective housing to isolate it from mechanical vibration.

Pickup Patterns

The pickup pattern of a microphone refers to the direction(s) from which it is sensitive to sound. There are three basic patterns:

- If a mic is sensitive to sound from mainly one direction, its pickup pattern is *unidirectional.* Often, a unidirectional mic is referred to as a **cardioid mic** because the typical pickup pattern is somewhat heart shaped. Depending on how concentrated

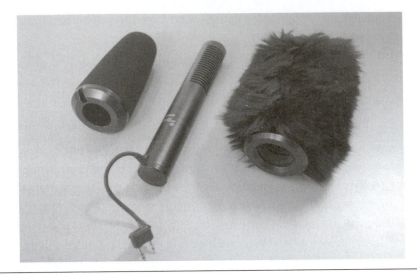

Photo 7.1   To reduce the noise caused by wind in field productions, mics come equipped with foam windscreens and *fuzzies* (also called windjammers). While these devices do not eliminate wind noise, they help reduce it considerably.

the pattern is, cardioid mics may be further classified as *supercardioid, hypercardioid,* or *ultracardioid,* each of which describes progressively more directional sensitivity.

- Mics with pickup patterns in two opposite directions are called *bidirectional.* Their pickup pattern resembles a figure 8.

- Finally, if a mic is equally sensitive to sound from all directions, its pickup pattern is said to be *omnidirectional* or *nondirectional.*

These types of pickup patterns are illustrated in Figure 7.7, which shows each pattern on a *polar diagram,* a concentric circle graph marked off with pie-shaped segments. The microphone is at the center of the graph, and each circle farther from the center represents a drop in microphone sensitivity. Polar diagrams can also indicate the effective distance of a microphone. Such information can help you determine how far talent can be from the mic and still be "on mic" or maintain "presence" (a sense of closeness).

MICROPHONE SELECTION

Selecting a microphone and positioning it for use should be based on the job you need it to do, as well as on equipment availability. For example, for a roundtable discussion with several participants, simplicity (or limited equipment availability) might dictate a single, stationary, omnidirectional mic, placed in the center of the

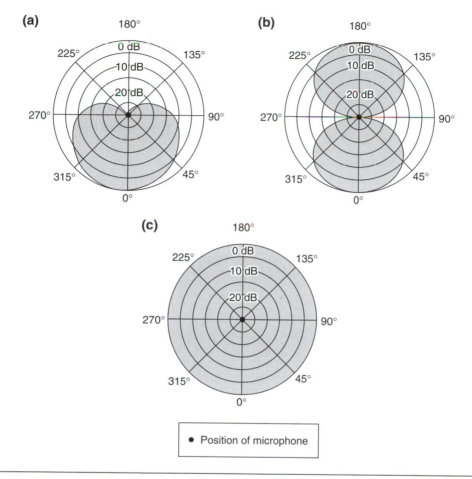

Figure 7.7   Polar diagrams showing three basic microphone pickup patterns: (a) unidirectional
or cardioid pattern, (b) bidirectional pattern, and (c) omnidirectional or
nondirectional pattern.

table (see Figure 7.8). If, however, you are covering a sports event with an
announcer, a color commentator, and much unwanted crowd noise, you should
consider using a separate unidirectional mic for each speaker. These would help
limit sound to just their two voices. But for the same event, if you decided to
include crowd noise, you could hang some additional omnidirectional mics near
the crowd. For a host-guest interview (again, with limited equipment availability),
perhaps a bidirectional single mic might be the best choice. However, if the host's
voice is significantly louder than the guest's (or vice versa), if possible, you should
use two cardioid mics with a great deal of separation, allowing you to set different audio levels.

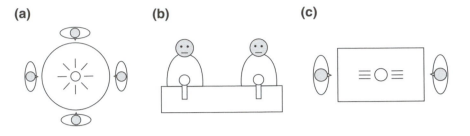

Figure 7.8   Typical microphone selections for different situations. (a) For a roundtable discussion, a single omnidirectional mic in the center of the table. (b) For two sports announcers calling a game, separate unidirectional mics. (c) For a host-guest interview with two talents seated at opposite ends of a table, a single bidirectional mic.

From these simple examples, you can see that there is much to consider in deciding what microphones to use and how they should be deployed. Audio design means more than just placing mics in the vicinity of your talent and going on the air. Add the questions of whether sound will be monophonic or stereo, whether the mics should be visible or not, whether the talent is stationary or moving, and you have many issues to consider. The following sections describe strategies for selecting microphones to meet specific program objectives. Keep in mind that a particular mic may have various applications, but it is likely to be better for some jobs than for others.

Audio Design Principles

On-Camera Versus Off-Camera Mics. Generally, when talent is oriented directly to the camera, as in news, interview, talk, game, quiz, variety, and audience participation shows, it is acceptable (though not required) that microphones be visible on camera. It may be desirable to display a host's mic as a way of imparting authority.

By contrast, in programs featuring talent oriented *in*directly to the camera (soap opera, drama, situation comedy), visible mics are often a production error, breaking the show's illusion. Of course, not all on-air personnel in news look at the camera, and not all talent in sketch comedy avoid it, but most of the time, talent orientation to the camera is a strong indicator of whether it is proper for mics to be visible. From this comes the first consideration of audio design: *Decide whether mics should be seen on camera or not.*

Stationary Versus Mobile Mics. After deciding whether mics should be visible, determine whether they should be stationary. One factor that often influences this decision is talent movement. However, if the talent moves, that does not necessarily mean that his or her mic must go along for the ride. The critical factor is to *put mics where the sounds are that must be captured.*

For example, if you are miking a drama, and your talent moves across the studio floor but speaks in only one location, you may mic just that one location, perhaps with a hanging mic over the speaking area or concealed in the area where the speech takes place. On the other hand, if your talent has a frenzied scene, moving around the set while delivering key speeches, you may need a mobile mic, perhaps a mic on a boom or a wireless mic concealed on the talent's body.

Whatever you do, base your strategy on both production values and on equipment and personnel availability. Remember that in most cases, simplicity is a virtue. It is not necessary to mic every talent location, just those where sound must be picked up. Only by careful study of the script, floor plan, facilities, and lists of crew and talent can you know how to proceed.

Visible Mics

If it is acceptable, desirable, believable, or plausible for mics to be seen, there are a number of alternatives. These include personal microphones worn on the clothing (most often in the upper chest area) or held in the hand. Other visible mics include those on desks, stands, and tables.

Lavaliere (Lapel) Mics. The **lavaliere** or **lapel mic** (see Photo 7.2), as the name implies, is clipped to the front of the talent's clothing, in the chest area, close to but below the talent's mouth. It may be fastened to a tie, jacket lapel, dress, or blouse. Because it is positioned well below the chin, the speaker does not talk directly into it. Therefore, the lavaliere mic (or *lav* for short) is usually omnidirectional. In addition, many lavs have a built-in high-frequency boost to compensate for the loss of high frequencies, which tend to travel more in straight lines than other frequencies.

Photo 7.2   Talent wearing a lapel (lavaliere) microphone.

Virtually all lavs are of the electret capacitor type. This enables them to be made quite small and unobtrusive. The battery pack and cable connector can be worn behind or to the side of the talent, out of camera range.

Lavs offer many advantages. Since they are small, they can be easily placed on the talent without getting in the way. Their size also makes them easy to conceal under talent's clothing, so they can be used for either on-camera or off-camera applications. With the mic clipped to clothing, the talent's hands are free, and the talent can move without worrying about getting out of microphone range. Of course, lavs are great for stationary interviews as well.

However, there are disadvantages. Since lavs are designed for close, single-voice work, their frequency response is not ideal for musical performance. Moreover, their small size allows lavs to be easily damaged (especially their fragile mic cable). They may also be easily misplaced or lost. Furthermore, while their small size makes them easy to conceal under clothing, poor placement can result in muffled sound. Even quiet activities, such as holding a book close to the chest, can muffle speech or cause unacceptable noise. In addition, vigorous movement can cause distracting noise because the mic can jostle and rub against clothing or bang against jewelry. Vigorous motion can even cause lavs wired to the body to pull loose.

For these reasons, it is best to have the audio operator secure the lavs on the talent and then caution the talent about possible problems. For talent engaged in vigorous movement, it is better to avoid using wire lavs altogether. Wireless lavs are available for this type of movement, though they remain subject to many of the other problems with lavs. Aerobic exercise programs use wireless lavs with great success because the producers give a good deal of thought to securing them to the body properly and keeping noise problems to a minimum.

Headset Mics. Often used by sports broadcasters and pop singers, **headset mics** (see Photo 7.3) allow the users to position the mic extremely close to the mouth while maintaining constant distance even when the head is turning. They also free up the users' hands as well as the workspace in front. Headset mics may be unidirectional to limit background sound or omnidirectional to include it. Because the mouth is so close to the pickup element, the headset mic often has a built-in pop filter to reduce unwanted blowing sounds caused by breathing, as well as popping sounds from consonants such as *B, P,* and *T.*

Headset mics equipped with headphones can be fed two separate audio signals, such as program audio through one ear and director's cues through the other. Thickly padded headphones enable the wearer to hear production cues in the presence of crowd noise. Some models feature a "cough switch" to enable the user to turn off the mic when desired.

Photo 7.3   Talent wearing a headset mic.

Hand Mics. The **hand mics** (see Photo 7.4) afford mobility and control to program hosts who use them on audience participation programs, as well as to news and weather reporters in the field. Singers use hand mics to enhance their performance by bringing the mic closer to the mouth for quiet passages and moving it away during climactic parts. Some use the mic as a prop, tossing it from hand to hand, even swinging it by the cord to excite the audience, but this kind of treatment can damage the equipment.

Photo 7.4   Talent sharing a handheld mic.

If you use a hand mic, you carry much of the responsibility for sound quality. For example, you must be aware of the mic's ability to pick up sound sources at different distances. As with all microphones, as distance increases, mic sensitivity decreases. Furthermore, if the mic is the conventional wire type, you need to know the extent of the area you can move without yanking and damaging the cable. As an interviewer, be aware of the relative volume of your voice compared to that of your subject. Favor the softer voice with closer placement. Also, in turn taking, try to move the mic between speakers at the proper time to avoid clipping opening or closing remarks. Finally, if you are interviewing someone easily intimidated by the microphone, you may need to comfort the speaker beforehand to reduce his or her anxiety.

A wide variety of hand mics with different performance characteristics are available. Some have omnidirectional pickup patterns; others are unidirectional. The more rugged ones for field production use dynamic pickup elements; however, electrets and ribbon hand mics are also available.

Desk Mics. Also known as table mics, **desk mics** are often simply hand mics clipped to desk stands (see Photo 7.5). They are generally visible, stationary mics suitable for talent seated at a desk or table or standing at a podium. Desk mics are frequently used in news and panel shows. Desk stands vary from fixed, static supports with a heavy base to the gooseneck variety with a clamp for quick, easy attachment to a podium or lectern at a news conference.

Since desk mics are most often used for speech, dynamic mics are a good choice for this function. Their ruggedness also makes them especially well suited to desk use, where they may be inadvertently knocked around.

Photo 7.5   Talent using a desk mic.

Handling Mics

➢ Even ruggedly designed mics should be treated gently. Don't bang them around. Don't drop them. When you want to get one out of your hand, place it down carefully in a safe place, out of harm's way.

➢ To see if a mic is on, speak into it or scratch softly across the screen of the pickup element. Do not blow into it.

➢ Respect for the integrity of the equipment includes the mic cables. If they get tangled or caught on furniture or other obstructions, don't yank them to free them. Untangle them gently.

➢ When you walk with a mic in one hand, hold the cable with the other hand to avoid pulling the cable with the mic, which can damage the connector.

➢ After a production session, disconnect mics and store them in their boxes or pouches to protect them from loss or damage. When storing cables, to minimize tangling, instead of coiling them, use the ribbon method (see Figure 7.9). This means forming a loop going in one direction, then one in the opposite direction, like a figure 8 pattern. This way, the entire cable can be deployed with a gentle toss without tangling. This approach will save valuable production time.

➢ Avoid the ugly look of a tangled mass of wires by dressing the cables. This means taping them unobtrusively along a table edge or other convenient surface, out of camera view and out of harm's way.

➢ Even if a cable is concealed under a rug on the set, tape it down to minimize the chance of tripping someone.

➢ To keep users from disrupting desk mics, tape the mics into position if possible. Instruct the talent not to touch the mics or tap on the table or desk. If mics must be shared among speakers (not the best situation, but it does happen), shock mount them, and instruct users to pass them gently.

Stand Mics. Desk and hand mics can be mounted on floor stands (see Photo 7.6). Stand mics are a good option for stationary performers when it is appropriate for the mic to be visible (as with singers, standup comics, and announcers). The mic and stand can also become props for the performer, who can move them around, lean on them, tilt them, disconnect the mic from the stand, reconnect it, and so forth. The major advantage of the mic stand is that it leaves the performer's hands free while fixing the location of the mic precisely. The major disadvantage is that it can limit movement.

Mic stands come in various shapes, from straight vertical stands to those with goosenecks. There are also stands with crossbars for supporting additional mics—useful, for instance, for a single performer who plays the guitar while singing. In this case, a single stand can accommodate separate mics to pick up guitar and voice.

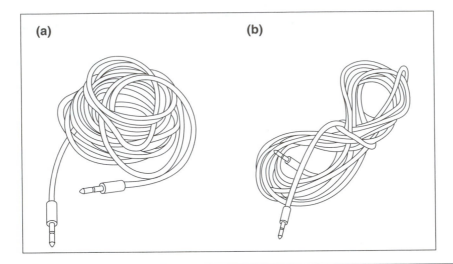

Figure 7.9   Two ways to store cables: (a) coiling, which often produces tangles, and (b) the ribbon method, a better alternative that eliminates tangling.

Photo 7.7   A hanging mic. Note that the mic can be as close to the talent as necessary, as long as it is not in the shot.

Photo 7.6   Talent positioned in front of a mic stand.

Off-Camera Mics

Off-camera mics may be mobile or stationary, off the set or concealed on the set, hanging, attached to a boom, or held by a crew member. This section discusses some of the more common off-camera mics in terms of their chief uses.

Hanging Mics. Any mic hung over a set, even a hand mic or a lav used in this fashion, is a **hanging mic.** The main function of such mics is to provide microphone coverage for a stationary performance area. Usually, they are hung out of camera range (see Photo 7.7). Examples of production situations that can be carried by hanging mics include a talent speaking while demonstrating an exercise or preparing a recipe, a writer performing a poetry reading, or two actors playing out a scene of a chance meeting at a bus stop. A major advantage of hanging mics is that they enable audio coverage of talent without mic wires. Disadvantages are that they cover sound only in a limited performance area and can cause annoying shadows on talent and set pieces.

The preferred pickup pattern for a hanging mic is cardioid rather than omnidirectional. This is because omnidirectional mics tend to pick up reflected sound from the ceiling as well as extraneous noise. To keep the mic out of camera range, hang it while watching the widest camera shot (the master shot) on the line monitor. Lower the mic into the set until you see it enter the master shot, and then pull it up enough to lose it from the shot.

After hanging the mic, be sure to check audio levels for all personnel who are to use it. Be sure the mic is sensitive enough to handle the job. For example, a tall talent close to the mic may have enough presence, but a shorter talent may not and may need to be miked separately. Under no circumstances should you accept an audio check from one user as proof that all is well. Check everyone's level before you approve the setup.

Concealed Mics. Hidden anywhere on the set, such as in a vase of flowers, under a sheet of newspaper, or taped to the edge of a table or to a telephone handset, **concealed mics** are usually stationary, but it is conceivable for a wireless lav to be transported to different locations taped to a cordless phone or worn under talent clothing. Of course, any live mic is subject to unwanted noise. If you conceal a mic under a sheet of newspaper, don't move or crumple it unless you want to hear a remarkably loud sound of rustling newspaper!

Lavs make good candidates for concealed mics because they are small. If they require cables, dress them appropriately so they don't draw undue attention. Often a simple throw rug can hide the mic wire.

Boom Mics. Just as with lights, *booms*—essentially long arms—are useful for keeping technical apparatus out of camera range. **Boom mics** can be set up in various ways, and booms may be either mobile or stationary. In the simplest form,

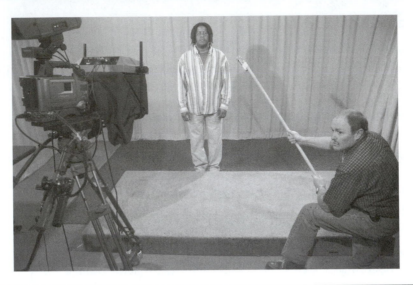

Photo 7.8   A talent miked with a fishpole boom.

a boom mic may be nothing more than a stick with a mic on the end of it held by a crew member. This type, known as a *fishpole boom* (see Photo 7.8), can be held above or below the talent out of camera range to augment spotty coverage of an area, and it can be moved as the sound source moves.

A *tripod boom* or *giraffe boom* (see Figure 7.10) may also be used to support a mic if a crew member is not available or if it is better to secure the mic in a fixed position. The tripod boom is an excellent choice for covering a fixed audio source, but it cannot move along with a mobile sound source.

A more sophisticated device is the *perambulator boom* (see Photo 7.9), a wheeled device that allows an operator to move a mic into and around a set from out of camera range using a set of pulleys and extenders. The mic can be rotated to cover more than one talent position, and the height of the boom arm can be adjusted. Some perambulator booms provide a platform with a seat for the boom operator. From this position, the operator can silently pan, tilt, extend, and retract the boom arm during production. Some perambulator booms provide a Video monitor to help the operator judge how close the mic can get to the sound source without being seen on camera. The operator may wear a headset to hear the director's cues and program audio or even other crew members. The entire boom may be moved on its wheels by a second crew member. Perambulator booms are frequently used for drama productions such as soap operas and sitcoms.

Mobile booms provide programs with natural *sound perspective,* which refers to the agreement between video and audio distance in program content. In normal sound

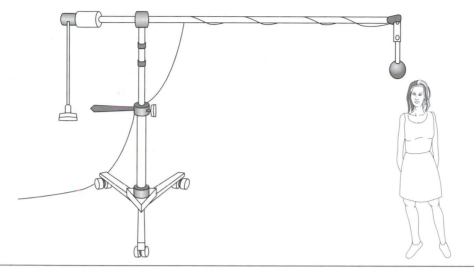

Figure 7.10   A giraffe boom is a good means of miking talent in a stationary performance area with an off-camera mic without requiring the use of additional crew.

perspective, video close-ups are accompanied by close miking, while long shots are accompanied by more distant miking. The boom operator provides this by bringing the mic closer to the talent when framing is tight and moving the mic away when the shot widens. Violations of sound perspective can be disconcerting to the audience.

Photo 7.9   A perambulator boom.

The disadvantages of boom mics include the fact that they take up a lot of space and require up to two skilled crew members to operate them. More important, a perennial problem with all boom mics is unwanted shadows. To avoid or minimize this problem, integrate booms from the side of the set *opposite* the key lights. This will at least avoid the harshest shadows. Above all, plan where booms will go *while* you are planning the lighting scheme. (See Table 7.1 for a brief summary of mic problems and ways to solve them.)

Long-Distance Mics. Microphones that pick up sound from great distance offer another means of covering on-camera talent without burdening them with cables. In outdoor settings, long-distance mic coverage is sometimes essential. The **shotgun mic** has been developed to serve these needs (see Photo 7.10).

Table 7.1   Some Microphone Problems and Their Common Solutions

Problem	*Solution*
"Popping" sounds or too much sibilance in talent's voice	Keep the talent at a distance of about 12 inches from the mic. Position the mic somewhat to the side of the speaker or at a slight angle so that the speaker talks across the mic rather than directly into it. Or, if the mic must be close to the mouth, cover the mic head with a pop filter.
Outdoor wind noise	Use a pop filter or a foam windscreen.
Audio transition difficulties when talent moves around the set	Use a boom mic or a wireless mic attached to the talent's clothing. If you must use stationary mics, use the same model in each performance area and check that the mics provide uniform coverage.
Interference between mics in close proximity to one another	Either put the mics as close together as possible so they receive sound simultaneously from the same source (*dual redundancy setup*) or place them at least three times the distance from one another as each is from its source (the *three-to-one rule* for multiple mic setups).
Shadows from hanging mics or boom mics	Position the mics out of the direct path of lights, especially key lights with a hard directional throw. For example, put the boom mics on the opposite side of the set from the key lights. Better yet, plan ahead in preproduction so that you can integrate the mic setup with the light plot.
Hum or other noise from power lines	Hanging mics especially may pick up hum from power lines that are improperly grounded or shielded. Try running the cables away from and perpendicular to the power lines. If this problem can't be fixed, find another way to mic the area.

Finding application in sports coverage and on-the-scene news coverage, the shotgun mic uses an interference tube to attenuate sound from all directions except the one in which it is aimed.

A **parabolic mic** uses an omnidirectional or unidirectional mic at the focal point of a concave parabolic reflector, with the mic's pickup element facing the center of the reflector (see Photo 7.11). The concave surface of the dish is then aimed at a sound source, and collected sound is reflected into the microphone from

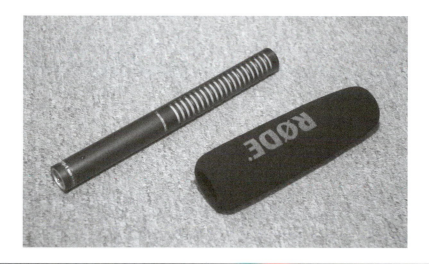

Photo 7.10   A shotgun mic with a foam cover for reducing wind noise.

Photo 7.11   A parabolic mic.

SOURCE: Photo courtesy of Telinga.

the direction the dish is facing. A headset can be used in conjunction with the mic to locate the optimal position. Finally, a **super beam mic** consists of a row of microphone elements that pick up sound from distant sources.

The advantage of highly directional mics is that they permit audio coverage without being seen on air and without restricting talent movement with mic cables. However, there are some drawbacks. The greater the directionality of a mic, the more its frequency response tends to be compromised. The flat part of the response curve—the part showing the frequency range where audio response is constant—tends to be narrower than for less directional mics.

Moreover, because of the shotgun mic's construction, it becomes less directional with lower frequency sound, especially wavelengths that are longer than the length of the tube. This means that at low frequencies, it fails to discriminate sound from unwanted directions. The same is true for parabolic mics.

In addition, for all long-distance mics, since sound travels slower than light, the video of a speaker's face (especially mouth movements) can appear out of sync with the words the talent is saying. For this reason, it is sometimes better to use a concealed mic near the talent.

Pressure-Zone Mics. A special type of mic designed to pick up sound from different sources at varied distances with roughly equal volume and clarity is the **pressure-zone mic** (PZM), also called a *boundary* mic (see Photo 7.12). The PZM uses a pickup element (usually an electret transducer) pointed at a hard, flat, built-in plate. This makes the PZM most sensitive to sound reflected from the plate, instead of from direct and indirect waves from sources, walls, and other reflective surfaces at different distances. The PZM's design reduces reverberation and muddiness caused by time differences between sounds received directly from sources and those reflected from nearby surfaces. It results in cleaner audio since additive and subtractive phase shifts (constructive and destructive interference) are greatly reduced.

PZMs may have either omnidirectional or directional pickup patterns, with an open and spacious acoustic quality. Their pickup pattern can be altered somewhat with the use of *blocks* designed to obstruct unwanted sounds from selected areas.

The disadvantages of PZMs result from their ability to treat all received sound roughly equally. For example, if the mic is on a table, tapping with a pencil or rustling papers will be picked up just as clearly as speakers' voices. For these reasons, some experts restrict PZMs to specific off-camera uses—for instance, hanging them above the set merely to pick up ambiance. Others dismiss PZMs entirely, finding that better results are obtained from conventional mics in almost every situation.

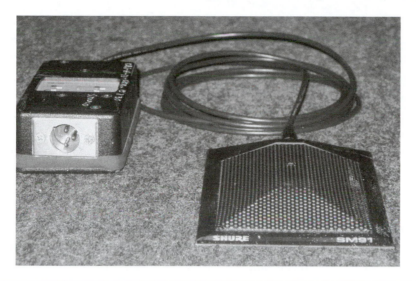

Photo 7.12   A pressure-zone mic.

Wireless Mics

Wireless mics (see Photo 7.13), as we have already mentioned, dispense with cables that can hamper a talent's movement. Performers in both indoor and outdoor settings have used wireless mics—astronaut moon walkers, race car drivers, rock climbers, rock musicians. Wireless mics can be hand mics, headset mics, or any other kind, and they can be positioned either on camera or off.

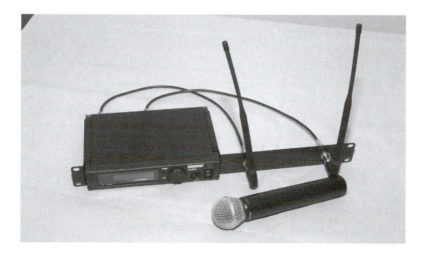

Photo 7.13   This wireless mic has an FM receiver featuring two antennas that receives radio signals from a transmitter that may be concealed on the talent's body.

The wireless mic system consists of a battery-powered FM radio transmitter (usually concealed somewhere on the talent's body) that sends a radio signal from the mic to a receiver connected to an audio console, to loudspeakers, or to any other desired output. Since wireless mics convert an audio signal into a radio signal, they are sometimes called *RF (radio frequency) mics.* When a lavaliere mic is used, the transmitter is often worn as a separate unit. In some hand mics, however, the RF transmitter may be built into the mic itself.

The receiver for the mic's RF signal can be located several hundred feet away from the transmitter. Of course, because it uses a broadcast signal, the wireless mic is subject to interference problems from surrounding conditions and from nearby transmitters. To secure an optimal signal, it is wise to verify what radio frequencies are already in use in your area so that you can choose equipment that operates on different frequencies. Signals from wireless mics are also subject to problems from perspiration, which can shunt signals straight to ground. To avoid this problem, keep the transmitter protected from sweat. In addition, it is helpful to keep the antenna vertical and clear of obstructions.

Tunable wireless mics allow you to tune to a frequency that is not already being used in the area. They are especially useful in situations where more than one wireless is being used in the same production at the same time.

In recent years, wireless mics have become one of the most versatile audio instruments in the director's arsenal. Their advanced technology makes them easy to conceal. They have well-defined pickup patterns and excellent resistance to wind and clothing rustle. These advances, coupled with the fact that they can be tuned to different frequencies, make them excellent instruments in both studio and field.

Other Technical Considerations

Proximity Effect. When a sound source is placed close to a directional microphone, frequency response increases in the low portion of the audio range. This is because, compared to higher frequencies, low-frequency sound exhibits a greater pressure differential between sound reaching the front and sound reaching the rear of the generating element. This difference, known as a *proximity effect,* causes bass response to rise. The result can be muddiness in the bass response and masking of higher frequencies. To reduce proximity effect, many mics have a feature known as *bass roll-off,* which limits bass frequencies below a certain point.

Microphone Impedance. *Impedance* (symbolized with a *Z*) refers to the amount of electrical resistance in a circuit. It is measured in ohms, which are units of electrical resistance. Mics with impedance levels below 600 ohms are considered low-impedance (low-Z) mics. Those above 10,000 ohms are considered high-impedance (high-Z) mics. Low-Z microphones are less prone to noise, such as interference from fluorescent lights and static from nearby motors. Low-Z mics can also be used with longer mic cables without significant signal loss.

It is critical to *match impedances between mics and the equipment to which they are connected.* If there is a mismatch, serious audio distortion may result. Mismatches can be corrected by using a matching transformer.

Balanced Versus Unbalanced Lines. Cables used to carry audio signals from microphones to their destinations (amplifiers, loudspeakers, tape recorders, consoles) may be either *balanced* or *unbalanced.* Balanced cable consists of two conductors and a shield that acts as a ground. Unbalanced cable has just one conductor and a shield that serves double duty as ground and conductor. The advantage of balanced cable is that it is less prone to electrical noise. Adapters are available to connect these two types of lines to one another if necessary.

Connectors. Microphone connectors link mics with cables or two cables to each other. Most professionals prefer a three-pin connector called an *XLR* to transmit audio signals along balanced lines. The *X* stands for the ground or shield; *L* designates the lead wire; *R* designates the return wire. Adapters are available to connect XLR cables to two-pin alternatives if necessary. Some of the more popular audio cables are pictured in Photo 7.14.

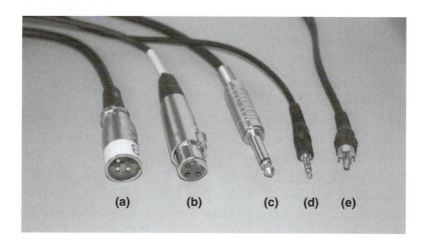

Photo 7.14   From left to right are XLR cable terminals (a and b), followed by unbalanced cables (a phone plug, an RCA phone cable, and a mini-plug; c, d, and e).

Open and Close Miking of Musical Performances

Live music requires that all the sounds of the ensemble be captured. To do this, two different techniques may be used: *open* (or *distant*) miking, in which mics are placed far enough from the sound source so that most or all of the ensemble's sound is picked up and blended by the same mic(s), or *close* miking, in which each individual voice, instrument, or sound section is separately captured by a directional microphone placed very close to it.

In the open miking approach, omnidirectional mics are often used, and the result is a blended, airy sound carrying room reflections. In the close miking technique, the directional mics capture a drier, more direct sound, with little or no reflected sound and a great deal of separation among various instruments and voices. The advantage of close miking is that more control can be exercised over the music since there is a great deal of separation among the elements; the disadvantage is that the lack of reflected sound reduces the sense of sonic space. Most musical recording is done with close miking techniques, but to compensate for the absence of reflected sound, reverb and pan circuits (see Chapter 8) are often used in the postproduction mixing.

STEREO AND SURROUND SOUND

Discussion thus far has been limited to monophonic audio production. This is because, in reality, all individual microphones are monophonic devices. Some "stereo mics," as they are called, contain two pickup elements oriented in different directions in the same housing. These mics provide little spatial separation and therefore limited stereo effect. But more robust stereo sound can be achieved in other ways. Chapter 8 will discuss multitrack stereo recordings and methods of altering sound electronically. Here, we will look at ways of producing stereo effects by careful placement of regular microphones in the production environment.

Stereophonic sound exploits the fact that we have two ears located in slightly different places, resulting in what is called *binaural hearing.* Binaural hearing enables us to experience minute differences in the intensity and the arrival time of the sounds that we hear. These differences add a sense of location and depth to our hearing. Stereo sound simulates binaural hearing by feeding two separate audio channels (left and right channels) with slightly different audio information to increase our sense of the *sound space* or *audiospace*—that is, the sound qualities of depth and location. Microphones may be used to create stereo effects by carefully fixing their orientation to sound sources, as well as to each other, in the audiospace. The basic principle is to place mics so as to imitate binaural hearing.

One way to mic stereophonically (the *spaced technique*) is to place two omnidirectional or cardioid mics (or several, if need be) perpendicular to a sound source so that sound arrives at the pickup elements at slightly different times and at slightly different volumes (see Figure 7.11a). The problem with this, of course, is the threat of phase problems (constructive and destructive interference) when

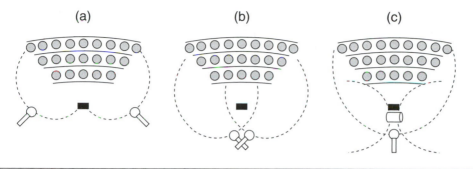

Figure 7.11   Three techniques for stereo miking an orchestra performance: (a) the spaced technique, (b) X-Y miking, and (c) mid-side miking.

these signals are combined in monophonic speakers in home receivers. To offset *stereo-to-mono incompatibility,* as this problem is called, the distance from mic to mic should be at least triple the distance of each audio source to its assigned mic (the *three-to-one rule*). Test equipment is available to display phase relationships so that mic placement can be adjusted to minimize such interference.

To ensure stereo-to-mono compatibility, a different stereo miking technique, called *X-Y miking* or *coincident miking,* may be used. X-Y miking uses two directional mics located close to each other (but not touching) in the center of the audiospace, crossed at roughly right angles, with their pickup elements on the same vertical axis (see Figure 7.11b). This minimizes phase differences but still discriminates sound intensity for left and right channels enough to create stereo effects. The angle between the two mics should be dictated by the width of the sound source.

Finally, a miking technique called *mid-side (M-S) miking* is available for creating stereo effects. This technique uses a bidirectional mic in close combination with a directional mic. The directional mic is aimed toward the center of the sound source. The bidirectional mic is placed parallel to the sound, covering the left and right sides of the audiospace (see Figure 7.11c). Audio outputs from this arrangement are then fed to an audio circuit designed to use phase differences to feed left and right channels.

Problems in Stereo Miking

Recall from Chapter 5 that flat lighting was developed to minimize jarring light-level differences when cutting between cameras shooting the same scene from highly discrepant positions. Similarly, it is important to design audio to minimize sonic discrepancies when cutting between cameras. This means not violating viewer expectations regarding the location of sound sources.

Matching sounds to pictures can be particularly difficult when using stereophonic miking formats. For example, imagine an opening shot of a character appearing in the left half of the screen. Initially, it makes sense for that character's voice to come predominantly from the left channel. However, if the next shot captures the same character in the right half, does that mean the voice must now come from the right channel, or will that switch be too jarring? Do all camera angle changes require similar changes in sound perspective? Many experts would say no. The question then becomes, "When should stereo sound perspective change?" The answer: when it makes sense, when it is plausible, and when it enhances the program purpose. Such change should be avoided when it destroys continuity.

To avoid the problem altogether, it may be wise to feature voices of main characters in the center of the audiospace regardless of where they appear on screen. This is in fact what is done with dialogue in surround sound audio.[2]

Surround Sound

A welcome audio development for television home entertainment centers is **surround sound.** Surround sound uses four or five speakers to create a 360-degree sound perspective (see Figure 7.12). The five-speaker layout uses three speakers in

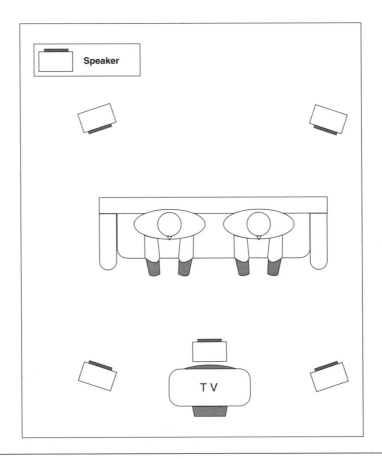

Figure 7.12   A five-speaker surround sound layout.

the front, including one centered on or under the television set to carry dialogue, and one on either side to provide normal left- and right-channel stereo for music, sound effects, and ambiance/environment. Two rear speakers may carry low-power simulated reflected sound, or they may be fully powered equivalents of the front. A system called the *Dolby MP (Motion Picture) matrix process* feeds a four-channel soundtrack to the speakers to create the overall effect. Three channels feed the front (left, center, and right), and one feeds the rear.

Stereo miking techniques are used for recording in surround sound. When surround sound audio is delivered to a normal two-speaker stereo system, the four channels are collapsed into two. Of course, the audio perspective problems outlined for stereo miking remain an issue for surround sound audio.

KEY TERMS

pitch	170	hanging mic	187
decibel	170	concealed mic	187
volume unit	170	boom mic	187
sound envelope	173	shotgun mic	190
cardioid mic	177	parabolic mic	191
lavaliere (lapel) mic	181	super beam mic	192
headset mic	182	pressure-zone mic	192
hand mic	183	surround sound	198
desk mic	184		

QUESTIONS FOR REVIEW

What are some of the similarities and differences among sound, light, and radio waves?

How are frequency and loudness related?

What are the effects of constructive and destructive interference, and how do they affect microphone placement in television production?

When mics are classified by generating element, what are the three basic types, and what are the typical performance characteristics of each type?

What are some of the main differences between miking a soap opera and miking a talk show?

What factors might you consider in miking an aerobics video on location at the beach? Assume you have a host (exercising vigorously), several other performers behind her, music, a live audience, and natural beach sound in the background. What mics might you use and where would you put them?

NOTES

1. The term *analogous* is appropriate here because all microphones are analog devices even in the digital age. The signals captured by a microphone may be digitized *after* they are received, but they are initially captured as analog signals.

2. Of course, audience analysis concerns should shape all of your production decisions. Recognizing how production techniques affect audience expectations, including entertainment value, credibility, and persuasiveness, can only help you in meeting your program objectives.

Chapter 8

AUDIO PROCESSING AND AESTHETICS

With our understanding of microphones from Chapter 7, we move on to the storing and mixing of sound for video production. In addition to the sounds picked up by microphones, television often incorporates prerecorded audio material from magnetic tape (both analog and digital), compact disks (CDs), digital video disks (DVDs), computer hard drives (chip technologies), and even film and videotape soundtracks. Remember that audio is often the first part of a program to catch the audience's attention. Think about the way an opening theme song immediately identifies a program.

The content available from audio sources includes speech, music, and sound effects. A vast archive of sound, spanning many decades, is available for use in video programs.

This chapter describes the major audio storage media used in video production, briefly explains how they work, and suggests how to use them efficiently and effectively. The topics include the following:

Using sound from audio sources

- Optical disks
- Analog audiotape
- Digital audiotape
- Computer disk and chip technologies
- Videotape and film soundtracks

Audio consoles

- Input levels and channels
- Volume and gain controls
- Cueing and monitoring sources
- Other functions of the audio console
- Computer editing
- Patching

Sound effects

Applying audio principles in actual settings

- A multicamera studio setting
- A single-camera field setting

USING SOUND FROM AUDIO SOURCES

Audio storage media used in television production include optical disks, audiotape (both analog and digital), computer technologies, and videotape and film sound-tracks. While most of today's recording and production work in the television industry is done digitally (from small shops to the network level), it is a mistake to ignore analog sound recording and production. This is because a vast archive of material is available on analog storage media, including both tape (audio and video) and film; therefore, this chapter covers both analog and digital audio.

Optical Disks

Optical disks include both CDs and DVDs (sometimes called digital "versatile" disks because some DVDs may also be used to store audio and still images).

Both CDs and DVDs use a laser to retrieve audio content. Hence, there is virtually no wear when playing them; when treated properly, they retain their high-quality sound indefinitely. They also have less background noise and a better dynamic range than analog audio sources.

By assigning a discrete value to each bit of sound sampled rather than using a continuous stream of information, the CD's digital coding allows rapid random access and retrieval of desired segments. Storage on a CD can therefore be likened to an efficient filing system, where every sampled sound has its own unique address, making it possible to locate each one quickly and easily.

A Legal Note About Digital Technology

Compact disk technology's biggest advantage is also the source of its biggest weakness. Because digital copies have the same signal quality as the original, there is great incentive for pirates to dub copies illegally for sale. This is a copyright violation since it cheats the original creators out of profits legally due them. To help combat copyright infringement, technology has been developed called the Serial Copy Management System (SCMS) to make it impossible to dub more than one digital copy of an original CD. It is an ongoing concern to continue upgrading and improving SCMS as users develop methods of defeating it. Unlimited analog copying is still possible even when this technology is used.

Digital audio recorded on optical disks can be copied (*dubbed* or *duped*) repeatedly without losing signal quality. Another advantage is that audio data can be transmitted over telecommunications lines, without signal loss, to multiple locations simultaneously, arriving in pristine condition. None of these things can be done with analog recordings.

Digital coding offers further advantages over analog systems. For example, a player can be programmed to play selections in random order. In addition, **cueing** is simple and requires little attention or skill. Many players offer a *pause* feature, which holds a selection in cue before playing it; a *review* feature, which lets you check the start and end times of a given selection; an *auto space* feature, which lets you add seconds of silence between selections; a menu feature, which can display the title of the selection being played as well as identifying the artist and production date; and a *volume check* feature, which lets you locate the loudest span of a few seconds on the entire disk (useful for setting sound levels during a broadcast or during postproduction operations). Furthermore, there is virtually no startup time before selections begin, and you can make noiseless transitions between program segments.

Audiotape

While recordable (rewritable) CD systems are available, many CDs store audio content but do not allow you to change what is on them; these are called "read-only," meaning that they cannot be used for recording. By contrast, magnetic tape (both analog and digital) permits you to store *and* record audio content. In record mode, audiotape recorders have an erase head that comes in contact with the tape right before it is exposed to a recording signal, erasing prior signals so that the tape may be used over and over again. The ability to erase and rerecord audio material on the same tape makes audiotape very useful for video production.

As mentioned, audiotape comes in both analog and digital varieties. Both consist of a thin Mylar ribbon coated with magnetic particles that can store signals supplied, for example, by a microphone.

Analog Recording

In the analog variety, as audiotape travels past the record head, its magnetic particles arrange into patterns that match the magnetic field presented to it, preserving an analog signal copy of the original sound.

Many sizes and grades of analog audiotape are available. The major recording formats include open-reel tape and cassettes.

Open-Reel Tape. Also called reel-to-reel tape, **open-reel tape** is a thin ribbon of magnetic tape wound onto a spool (see Figure 8.1a). Tape lengths, widths, and

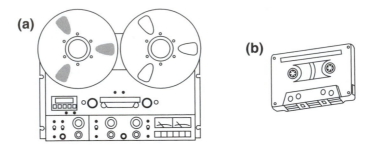

Figure 8.1   Two formats of analog audiotape include (a) open-reel tape and (b) cassette.

thicknesses vary. For single-track monaural and two-track stereo recording, the standard tape width is ¼ inch. But for multitrack recording, ½-inch, 1-inch, and even 2-inch tape may be used.

As mentioned, tape thickness also varies. In general, the thicker the tape, the less susceptible it is to stretching, breaking, or creasing. Thicker tape is also less subject to *print-through,* or the tendency for a signal from one layer to transfer a copy of itself to an adjacent layer on the spool. However, the thicker the tape, the shorter the length that can fit on a reel, and the shorter the playing time.

Tape thickness is measured in *mils,* or thousandths of an inch. So, for example, a 7-inch reel can hold 1,200 feet of 1½-mil tape, providing about 30 minutes of recording time, assuming the tape travels through the tape head at 7½ inches per second. Broadcasters generally use 1½-mil tape to minimize problems from breaking and stretching.

Tape speeds also vary. Machines can move the tape at speeds of 3¾ inches per second (ips), 7½ ips, 15 ips, or 30 ips. The faster the tape speed, the better the fidelity and the better the **signal-to-noise (S/N) ratio,** or relative strength of the intended signal to the amount of interference that accompanies it. Improved S/N ratio means that lower level signals can be recorded, providing greater dynamic range. S/N ratio improves with tape speed because the faster the tape moves, the more tape area there is to handle a given amount of content. In other words, the audio information is more spread out on the tape at higher speeds, making it easier for pickup devices to read the signal. Studios normally use tape speeds of 7½ or 15 ips.

Open-reel analog tape is still used for multitrack recording and for providing long pieces of audio content (i.e., background music) for studio productions; in addition, radio stations and audio production facilities still use it for archiving program material, even in the digital age.

Tape Cassettes. Despite the transition to digital technology, analog cassette recorders/players are still useful for some production functions.[1] **Cassettes** use a reel-to-reel format encased in a plastic housing to keep the tape free from dirt (see Figure 8.1b). Cassettes permit record and playback functions in two directions (unlike CDs, cassettes have a flip side). Cassettes also use narrow tape (about ⅛ inch wide) and slower speed (1⅞ ips) than open-reel tape, yielding longer playing time. Cassette recorder-players work from batteries as well as normal AC wall current.

Depending on tape length, cassette playing time commonly varies from 30 to 60 to 90 to 120 minutes. The 120-minute length is not recommended, however, because of unreliable tape speed; the thinness of this tape (¼ mil) makes it difficult for the tape to be grabbed by a dirty pinch roller. Such cassettes also exhibit sluggish fast-forward and tape rewind, and the tape's thinness makes it fragile and more subject to damage. Shorter length tapes use ½-mil tape, which avoids many of these problems.

While small size, light weight, portability, and ease of handling make cassettes useful almost anywhere, they have drawbacks. Since the cassette system encases the tape inside a small cartridge, it makes program material difficult to cue and edit. Moreover, the narrow gauge and slow speed of cassettes can limit their ability to produce broadcast-quality sound. Analog cassettes have poorer fidelity and a higher S/N ratio than other tape formats.

Improvements in tape coatings have made cassettes more useful in professional applications. There are four grades of magnetic coating available for audiocassettes. In order of increasing quality, these are ferric oxide (Type I, also called *normal* tape), chromium tape (Type II, or *high bias*), ferrichrome (Type III, or *intermediate bias,* a rarely used variety), and metal particle (Type IV, also known as *high bias*). *For best recording quality, be sure to set the recorder's tape-select switch to match the type of tape you are using.*

Digital Audiotape (DAT)

Digital audiotape (DAT) is a superior form of recording compared to analog tape because it offers a wider dynamic range and lower noise level on playback. There are several formats available, each incompatible with the others. One records and plays back using a stationary tape head on a reel-to-reel machine. Another uses a cassette with a rotating head. Yet another uses videocassettes for audio-only recording. Even within these categories, incompatible formats abound. The following sections briefly describe each category's major features as well as some of their advantages and disadvantages.

Stationary Head Audio Recording. Within this category of DAT recorders, there are two formats that have won a level of popularity worth mentioning: *digital audio stationary head* (DASH) and *professional digital* (abbreviated PD or Pro Digi). Both use ¼-inch and ½-inch open-reel tape to record digital audio and an analog reference track for editing purposes. Unlike DASH, the PD format also uses 1-inch tape for 32-channel recording. Mechanical editing may be done with an analog track that accompanies the digital version of the audio content. Electronic editing with time code is also possible.

Rotary Head Audio Recording. Instead of a stationary head, rotary digital audio recording (R-DAT) uses a spinning recording head. The head's rotation increases the capacity of the tape to encode information in a limited space, making it possible to produce digital stereo at lower cost using smaller cassettes. Unfortunately, this renders the R-DAT format incompatible with all stationary formats. In addition, because of the rotating head technology, R-DAT tape can only be edited electronically.

R-DAT tape is of the metal particle variety, and it is the same width and thickness as that used in standard cassettes. However, the length of the tape is generally half that contained in analog cassettes, and the cassettes themselves are smaller.

Two rotary formats, called *modular digital multitrack* (MDM), use videotape to store digital audio. One such system, called Alesis ADAT,[2] uses S-VHS videocassettes to record audio material, while the other, called Tascam DA-88, uses 8-mm videotape. The advantage of using MDM systems is that the machines are capable of recording eight tracks of audio information and can be interconnected to yield up to 128 tracks. Also, the audio can be integrated with videotapes with virtually no signal loss. Unfortunately, the different MDM systems use different videocassettes, making them incompatible with one another and with other formats.

Aside from making it possible to record sound with a superb S/N ratio (making it close to noise-free recording), DAT recorders also permit accurate cueing and rapid search capability. In addition, they provide **SMPTE time code** (see Chapter 12) for frame-accurate integration with video for postproduction editing.

It is likely that tape-based systems of digital audio recording will not survive the move to computer-based systems and will be phased out; nevertheless, it is useful to have some basic familiarity with such systems if you come into contact with them while working in the production field.

Computer Disk and Chip Technologies

In recent years, digital audio recording has moved on to devices with no moving parts whatsoever, using solid-state memory sticks and cards for tapeless digital recording and storage. One advantage of such devices over tape-based devices is that no mechanical breakdowns are possible from recording heads wearing out or transports malfunctioning. Another is that the audio is recorded as computer files, which can be easily transferred to a PC with a USB cable for immediate editing. Yet another advantage is that unlike tape-based technologies, where data are stored on a linear ribbon, making locating specific moments of program material tedious, tapeless storage virtually eliminates this problem by using computer disks with random-access capability.

As mentioned, one of the greatest advantages of computer-based recording is the ability to perform **nonlinear editing.** Instead of having to assemble edits in linear fashion as with tape-based media, you can manipulate segments with the same flexibility now available for word processing. In short, if you wish to insert a sound somewhere in the sound stream, the computer shifts (or *ripples*) the location of edited segments to make room for it without disturbing the overall order or obliterating any sounds already laid down, just as word-processing programs do for words. In addition, when such changes are made, signal quality does not suffer since all the audio information is digitally coded.

However, no technology is without its limitations, and computer-based systems are no exception. The drawback here is the demand for large-capacity hard drives to handle the workload (now on the order of terabytes and higher). For example, the amount of disk space required for 20 minutes of monaural sound (or 10 minutes of stereo) is about 150 Mbytes. This means that several disks may be needed for longer productions featuring multitrack audio segments.

Several tapeless recording devices and disk-based storage systems deserve mention, including those that use flash memory cards or sticks, hard drives with removable memory cards, and optical disks (CDs and DVDs) in various formats (mini or regular format).

One such system useful for live studio productions is the digital cart machine (DCM), which uses optical disks to record and play back desired audio selections instantly. When the DCM is connected to a computer, you can create a series of selections for playback. The DCM is especially well suited to applications where a particular sound effect is needed at a precise moment (i.e., a car crash or gunshot) that may be recued quickly for repeated playback.

Both optical mini-disks and flash memory sticks are useful for storing and playing about an hour of high-quality audio, also accessible through a USB cable connected to your computer. For higher capacity storage, you need go no further than your Apple i-Pod (see Photo 8.1), which, depending on the model you have, can store hundreds of hours of audio or videos and still images, all accessible for your video productions through the use of a USB or Firewire cable. Once desired material is downloaded to your computer, it can be edited through the use of a digital editing program. Finally, both standard as well as rewritable CDs and DVDs are now available for storing and playing back audio content.

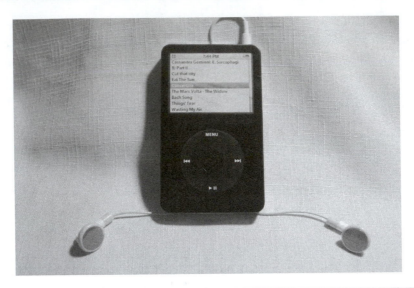

Photo 8.1   This MP-3 player, known better by the name *i-Pod,* can store hundreds of hours of audio content, as well as videos and still images. The earbuds are designed for individual listening, but downloading to other players for sharing content is easily done through the use of a USB cable.

All of these tapeless devices offer random access; many display playlist information telling such things as the amount of time for each selection, the time left for the current selection, and, in some cases, the name of the artist and the dates of production.

Musical Instrument Digital Iinterface. With computers and electronic keyboards, synthesized sound can now be precisely fitted to video content with a *musical instrument digital interface* or *MIDI* (see Photo 8.2). Using a computer as a central control, MIDI permits you to manipulate collected samples of sounds (music, speech, or sound effects) with an array of audio sources, including keyboards. When processed through a MIDI, each sound's qualities, such as frequency, volume, duration, timbre, tempo, attack, and decay, become infinitely manipulable. Because MIDI technology may be integrated with SMPTE time code, layers of sound can be made to fit precisely with video footage.

Even beyond the use of music, MIDI has had a significant impact on television production. For example, MIDI can assign vocal and sound effect samples to individual keys on a keyboard. By playing those keys, you can provide a customized soundtrack for any program.

MIDI's advantages include ease of editing. If you don't like a particular sound, it can be changed back to its prior voicing (arrangement) with a keystroke. In addition,

Photo 8.2   The MIDI pictured here integrates sound supplied from the keyboard with many stored in the computer hard drive to provide endless opportunities to customize your audio tracks.

all of the sonic image can be produced in pristine condition repeatedly without signal loss. Furthermore, there is no time wasted rewinding tape since all sound is stored using microprocessors; the computer memory offers instant random access.

MIDI's disadvantages include the need, in some cases, to provide separate synthesizers for each voice. Furthermore, MIDIs can suffer "lag" problems (or a loss of precise time agreement among sources) if too much data are processed at once. Finally, fast playing can sometimes outrun the MIDI's ability to keep up with the sound stream. MIDIs can also be expensive.

Videotape and Film Soundtracks

Traditional videotape and film contain soundtracks useful in television production. Analog videotape comes in several formats, including ½-inch cassette and 8-mm varieties, among others. In general, analog videotape features several tracks of information: a video track, one or more audio tracks, and a control track that acts like the sprocket holes on a reel of film to synchronize playback and editing functions. In some cases, there may also be tracks for time code and video scanning information. As you probably already know, among the most popular analog video tape formats are Betacam and VHS.

Three ½-inch formats with four audio tracks include Betacam SP, MII, and Super VHS. Two of the audio tracks are used for sound, and the others may be used for control track and time code. Finally, the 8-mm format has two audio tracks and an FM carrier audio track in the video waveform for time code.

In film, there are two basic types of sound formats: *optical* and *magnetic* soundtracks. In the optical format, a light shines through a track near the edge of the film, passing different amounts of light in accordance with an original sound stream. During playback on a projector, as the film advances, the modulated light that gets through is converted into electrical energy by a photoelectric cell. Then a loudspeaker converts it to sound. In the magnetic format, sound is recorded on a magnetic stripe running along one edge of the film. The magnetic stripe acts essentially like audiotape. During playback, a soundhead reads the signal and converts it into a replica of the original sound.

AUDIO CONSOLES

With so many audio sources available for television (for both live broadcast and production), how are they made ready for use at the instant they are needed, and how are they blended seamlessly into an air-quality broadcast or soundtrack? These are the functions of the **audio console** (see Photo 8.3).

Photo 8.3   A high-end audio console for television production studio work at one of the local network affiliates in New York.

Audio consoles (also called *audio mixing boards* or *audio mixers*) serve several purposes:

- Providing access to each audio source
- Providing volume control
- Allowing cueing and monitoring of each source before it is used
- Allowing you to modify each source during production
- Blending and mixing various sources during production
- Providing an air-quality output signal

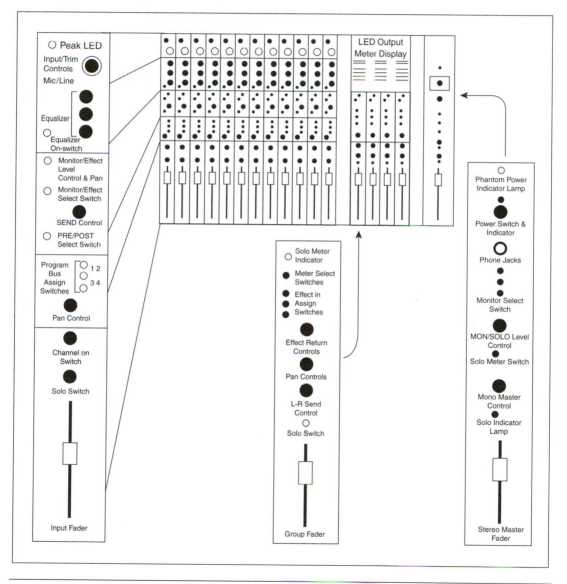

Figure 8.2   Diagram of an audio console featuring many of the components needed to control and shape sound in a typical studio production.

Input Levels and Channels

Audio consoles receive input signals from numerous sources. As it turns out, all sources fall into two categories of voltage level. Microphones, which deliver signals measured in millivolts (mV), or thousandths of a volt, are designated *low-level* sources. *High-level* sources are audio sources with much stronger signals (in the range of one volt or more). This distinction is important because audio consoles accommodate the two categories differently. Microphone signals must be boosted by a preamplifier; other sources do not need such a boost. Therefore, you need to assign the input sources to the proper channels on the console.

Some consoles permit you to use any channel for any type of source as long as you choose the input level properly. Usually, you identify a source as either high or low level by flipping a switch, clicking a dial, or pushing a button. The switch, dial, or button that does this is usually labeled *mic/line* (see Figure 8.2). By selecting "mic" position, you are telling the audio console to engage a preamplifier for that channel. By selecting "line," you are telling the console to bypass that channel's preamp.

Other consoles hardwire specific channels to accept only one type of source. (Hardwiring means making a permanent connection between two terminals inside a piece of equipment.) For these consoles, a "mic" channel is always a mic channel and must not be used for anything else. Similarly, a "line" channel is just for nonmicrophone audio sources.

If, by mistake, a mic is connected to a line channel, a low signal will result, and this will not become air quality no matter how high the volume is set for that mic. Conversely, if a nonmic audio source is mistakenly *patched* (temporarily connected) into a mic channel, it will be too loud and distortion will result.

To make life easy, especially if you have a lot of sources, you can use masking tape to label each channel. Write on the tape the name of the talent (for instance, "H" for host, "G" for guest). Then you can locate the correct channel for each source at a glance.

Simplifying further, you can arrange the assignment of channels in the same left-to-right order in which the talent appear on screen.

Volume and Gain Controls

When audio signals are each connected to the console through individual input channels, you can control the sources with either a *switch* or a *fader.* Switches allow you to open or close channels *instantly,* like turning a light on or off. For instance, you can use a switch to "hit" music or "kill" mics. By contrast, faders allow you to gain or lose volume *gradually,* like slowly raising or dimming the house lights in a theater. Thus, faders enable you to "sneak music under" or "cross-fade mics." Faders are also used to set volume levels, stabilizing the volume for each source at any level you want. During a program, faders can be adjusted as needed.

Faders may be adjusted to increase or decrease output volume to cancel out respective decreases or increases in source volume. This is known as *riding the gain.* Riding the gain may become necessary if a talent suddenly shouts or whispers during a speech or when music has great range in dynamics and features both soft and loud passages. Of course, there may be times when you wish to feature such dynamic changes rather than canceling them out—it all depends on the purpose of the program and the wishes of the director.

To monitor volume, consoles are equipped with a visual volume display, the **VU (volume unit) meter** (in both analog and digital versions) (see Figure 8.3). The VU meter displays volume intensity leaving the console. It is calibrated in both volume units (decibels) and (in the case of a transmitter) *percentage of modulation.* It is important to avoid overmodulation, which can cause distortion in the overall audio signal. Of course, it is also important to keep levels from being too low. Generally, levels of 80% to 100% modulation are considered to be *up full* and acceptable. Levels of 40% to 60% modulation are *under* and are still audible (good for background music). Levels below that may be *in the mud,* or too low for broadcast quality.

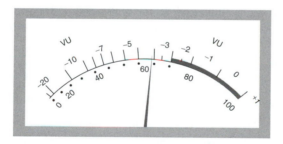

Figure 8.3   This analog VU meter shows both volume units (the outer scale) and percentage of modulation (the inner scale). Zero on the VU scale equals 100% modulation, which means the maximum amount the sound system can properly handle. The audio level should generally be kept between 80% and 100% modulation; that is, between –2 and 0 VU.

It is necessary to *calibrate* the audio console so that both the console and the recording device you are using (e.g., a video tape recorder) receive audio signals roughly the same. Most consoles offer a built-in *oscillator tone* that may be used to generate pure tones (sine waves) for recording test audio and for calibrating the console.

To calibrate an analog console, do the following: First, push all faders to zero. Then turn on the tone generator in the console (most boards are equipped with 1,000-Hz tones for this purpose). Then bring up the console's master fader to the

Photo 8.4   This VU meter also indicates audio levels, but it does so not with a needle but with an LED display.

zero point on its VU meter (0 VU units represents 100% modulation). Finally, adjust the volume control in the recorder so its VU meter matches that of the console master fader. You are now calibrated.

Calibrating levels on a digital console is different from this, in that most digital consoles do not have a standard 0 VU setting (see Photo 8.4). Instead, digital consoles are calibrated in *decibels full scale* (dBFS), designed to avoid clipping and distortion problems unique to digital audio. To avoid such clipping and distortion, it is recommended that the 0 VU setting be aligned to a level of −12 dBFS, to allow enough *headroom* so that signals will not exceed the dynamic range of the input being sent through the console.

If a VU meter's needle occasionally goes into the red zone above 100% modulation, there is no need to worry. However, if it remains there or enters the red zone the majority of the time, you may be either *pinning the needle* or *peaking* the volume, and this can cause distortion and overmodulation. To avoid these problems, the level should be lowered.

But if you are feeding the console more than one source, how do you know which one is too high? The VU meter is not sensitive to *which* source may be the culprit. It only knows that the overall sound is too loud. One way to find out is to take levels for each audio source individually. To do this, turn off every source except the one you wish to set a level for, and with the source playing, set that level. Then turn off that source and set a level for the next one. Do this for each source separately. Then, during production, ride the gain to maintain desired levels.

Although consoles provide a separate channel for every source, all the sources are eventually sent to a *master gain control.* The master gain control is simply a single fader that controls every source flowing through the board simultaneously and sets the volume level for the overall output. Some consoles also have *submaster gain controls* (or several submasters), which are used to control a subgroup of sources with a single fader. For example, if you had three mics covering the string section of an orchestra and three others on the percussion, you could feed each group of mics to a separate submaster, allowing you to balance the strings with the percussion by using just two faders. Some other features commonly found on audio consoles are listed in Table 8.1.

Table 8.1   Some Common Features of Audio Consoles

Input System Functions

Trim: provides gain control to boost low-level sources to make them more usable; attenuates high-level sources to avoid distortion.

Pad: lowers or prevents power overload when trim is not enough. Useful especially with mics in the vicinity of very loud sources (for instance, in front of a rock group's guitar amp).

Phantom power: provides power to condenser mics, eliminating the need for a battery or external power supply.

Equalizer: alters volume level for portions of the frequency range to eliminate or enhance the psycho-acoustic quality of the sound.

Filter: a specialized equalizer used to eliminate certain portions of the frequency range.

Pan: varies relative loudness delivered to selected output channels to change the "location" of sound sources in the audiospace.

Reverb: sends a source to a signal processor, which returns it a short time later to be fed through the console again, causing an echo-like effect.

Prefader listen (PFL or SOLO): enables you to hear one channel without having to shut off others. Using PFL turns off other channels feeding the monitor without affecting the actual output of the program.

Output System Functions

Bus: a board component that isolates or groups a signal with several others before sending them out of the board. This may be done to set a final volume level on a source before combining it with others. For instance, drums and backup vocals may be mixed together before they are mixed with lead vocal.

Pan pot: varies relative levels being fed to two output buses.

Reverb: adds an echo-like effect to the output audio.

Cueing and Monitoring Sources

Aside from monitoring sources when they are *on* air, you may also need to locate audio material, take levels, and cue sources during a show but *off* the air, so they can be ready to use when the director asks for them. To do this, you choose the *cue* setting for the appropriate channels.

The cue setting shunts the channel's feed to an audition loudspeaker and away from the program audio. To *audition* an audio source means to listen to it without putting it on the air. Actually, the audition loudspeaker may not be all that loud. It may be a puny control room audio monitor or even a speaker inside your headset. But in cue mode, you can safely select the program material you wish to use and then set its volume level with the fader and VU meter.

Other Functions of the Audio Console

In addition to the system functions already discussed, many consoles have a *talk-back* channel that enables control room personnel to communicate with the studio and other locations. Talkback is also called the *PA* or *SA,* acronyms that stand for public address and studio address, respectively.

A *foldback* feature is also provided to send selected audio feeds to either small, specialized monitor speakers located very near the performer or to headphones or an earpiece (an IFB or interruptible foldback circuit) worn by the talent. This allows studio talent to hear important audio material, such as sound effects cues or music for lip-synching. This feature is necessary because studio speakers are normally turned off whenever there are live mics in the studio. (If left on, studio speakers might create undesirable **feedback,** the loud squealing noise [not to be confused with foldback], caused by mics picking up their own signals from nearby speakers.)

Computer Editing

Computer disk recording transforms sound into a data file by assigning discrete values to samples of the sound stream. Once data are entered into the computer's hard drive as a bit stream, the audio can be randomly accessed, retrieved, and altered at a **digital audio workstation** (DAW). Of course, a digital video editing system can easily double as a DAW depending on how it is used. The options available on the DAW allow you to change the order of sound segments as in conventional editing. Many programs also enable you to reverse sounds so that they can be played backwards. Sounds from disparate sources can be combined. Sound envelopes can be altered. Volume and frequency can be changed. Tempo can be altered without changing frequency. The possibilities are endless.

Making audio corrections, changes, and additions in postproduction is known as **audio sweetening** and may best be done in an audio production studio. A properly outfitted audio production studio might contain, in addition to a DAW, two or more multitrack tape recorders, a digital cart machine, a couple of audiocassette player/ recorders, a couple of CD and DVD players, a keyboard and a MIDI, a standard mixing console, a standard patchboard (explained below), a computer router, a clock, and speakers for hearing playbacks.

Patching

In the event of equipment failure or the need to use equipment not normally connected to the console (such as an additional CD player), a system of *patching* may be used to bypass, replace, or add to regular audio signal routes. A **patch panel** (also known as a *patch bay* or *patchboard*) is a board that allows you to connect any audio source with any output destination (see Photo 8.5). Traditionally, the connections were made with patch cords, which resemble telephone switchboard cables with identical jacks on each end. Today, a computer (called a *router*) is often used instead. Either way, the concept is the same—namely, to provide a flexible means of connecting any audio source to any destination.

Three types of patch panels are used: *open, normalled,* and *half-normalled.* In an open system, no outputs are connected to any inputs until they are patched with a patch cord. By contrast, a normalled system hardwires specific outputs to specific inputs without patch cords. In a normalled system, inserting a patch cord disconnects the normal connection. The advantage of the normalled arrangement is

Photo 8.5   Patch panels such as this one allow you to connect any audio source with any output destination with the use of removable cables.

that it saves time in cases where the work schedule is predictable and regular but still allows flexibility in an emergency.

In a half-normalled system, hardwire connections are interrupted only by inserting a jack into the *input* (bottom) hole. Inserting a jack into the output hole does not disturb the normal connection. The advantage of the half-normalled arrangement is that it allows you to feed a signal to an additional external source (such as a tape recorder) without disturbing its normal destination.

Aside from the advantages of being able to bypass, replace, or add to regular equipment, patch panels also permit you to arrange sources conveniently on the audio console. For example, patching makes it easy to match the left-to-right order of microphone faders on the audio console to the left-to-right order of talent on screen, thus making the job of monitoring their levels that much easier.

One advantage of using computers to patch or route sources to destinations instead of physical cables is that it avoids problems that are possible with mechanical connections: Worn-out cables can lead to unreliable connections; too many cables can be confusing to trace; physical cables take more time to arrange than computer routing.

Using Patch Panels

➢ Set microphone faders to zero while patching, to avoid surges that can damage equipment.

➢ Don't patch input to input or output to output.

➢ Patching mic-level signals into line-level holes will result in a weak signal; conversely, patching line-level signals into mic-level holes will result in distortion. Both these arrangements should therefore be avoided.

➢ To avoid feedback, don't patch an output back into its own input.

➢ When setting up a patch panel, arrange sources on the panel by function to avoid confusion. For example, put all mics in one section of the board, all tapes in another section, and all film soundtracks in another.

SOUND EFFECTS

Sounds that are not music or speech may be called **sound effects** (abbreviated **SFX**). Sound effects enhance video programs by providing clues about location and context. They add valuable description. They also identify, intensify, and emphasize key action; supply transitional devices; and provide symbolic meaning.

For example, to establish locale, there is hardly a better way to convey a cityscape than to inject sounds of car horns, police sirens, and the general din of traffic noise into a program's soundtrack. Similarly, a tropical setting can easily, cheaply, and quickly be conveyed with sounds of birds and monkeys.

Sound that supports action on screen provides context. For example, when we see a window close, the sound of the window moving through the sash, followed by the contact it makes when it completes its motion, confirms the action. Moreover, the loudness of these noises adds meaning to the action, perhaps communicating important information about the emotional state of the character closing the window.

Sound effects libraries are available for purchase. When such sound effects are prepared for use, they are often transferred to digital carts or other storage media (the hard drive of a PC). However, sounds may also be mechanically created in the studio or recorded live on location, and these custom sound effects often allow a closer match to the action on camera.

In postproduction, *automatic dialog replacement* (ADR) may be needed to enhance audio that was recorded poorly during production. ADR can be an exacting process requiring talent to repeat lines while watching themselves on a television screen as they try to match the pace and intensity of their initial speeches. Similarly, sound effects may sometimes be required to be rerecorded in postproduction to enhance the original sounds. This is done using a *Foley* stage, named after its originator. Foley stages contain apparatus and gear for producing sounds such as footsteps and door slams designed to coincide with their visuals.

With the use of MIDIs or DAWs, custom sound effects can be sampled and modified to fit specific needs. Files of effects can be stored and used repeatedly during production and postproduction. Experienced television and radio sound technicians have come up with an amazing variety of ways to create sound effects with simple materials, and the accompanying Professional Pointers feature lists a few of them. Even in our digital age, you'll find that these tricks will come in handy.

Creating Simple Sound Effects

➢ Airplane: For a propeller aircraft, hold cardboard in contact with the blades of an electric fan. For a jet, place a mic at the end of a vacuum cleaner tube.

➢ Breaking bones: Chew hard candy close to a mic, or break the candy with pliers.

➢ Babbling brook: Blow bubbles through a straw into a glass of water.

➢ Engines and electric motors: Run a vacuum cleaner, a blender, or a Cuisinart near the mic.

➢ Fire: Crumple cellophane. For crackling, crush heavier paper suddenly.

➢ Footsteps: Fill a trough with gravel and walk in it.

➢ Ice cracking: Crumple a Styrofoam cup.

➢ Rain: Pour sand through a tube onto cellophane.

➢ Snow crunching: Squeeze corn starch.

➢ Thunder: Rattle sheet metal.

APPLYING AUDIO PRINCIPLES IN ACTUAL SETTINGS

Let's apply the audio knowledge we've gained to multicamera and single-camera productions in studio and field, respectively. The purpose of this exercise is to sketch how one thinks about audio design during preproduction, production, and postproduction. The discussion is not intended to be exhaustive. Since every project has its own unique objectives and challenges, this is merely a way to get a sense of how to approach the projects you will encounter.

A Multicamera Studio Setting

Multicamera recording feeds signals from several mics and cameras to a single videotape recorder (see Figure 8.4). Programs broadcast live and recorded live on tape use this format. Programs frequently done like this include sports, awards shows, public affairs, talk and interview, sitcoms and soaps, and specials such as pageants and concerts.

Let's consider the simple two-person stationary talent interview we have been using as a running example. You may recall we were using two cameras for this program. The program features a host and guest. For the sake of discussion, we'll consider a variation of the show that includes an off-camera announcer.

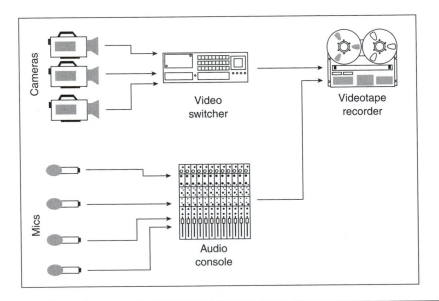

Figure 8.4   In this arrangement for a multicamera studio production, several cameras feed into a video switcher and several mics into an audio console. Then the audio and video signals are recorded together on a videotape recorder.

Preproduction. To execute the audio portion of this program, we begin by studying the script, floor plan, light plot, set, and other materials (including the facilities or "fax" lists) to determine what sounds will be needed and how they will be supplied. With two talent (host and guest), it is possible to use a variety of mics to capture their words. Assume that we decide to use two lavaliere mics, one clipped to the host and one to the guest. For the off-camera announcer, we decide to use a mic on a stand. This provides a means of picking up the announcer's voice but does so without requiring the announcer to touch the mic, thus minimizing unnecessary noise that might come from handling. It also frees up the announcer's hands for holding script materials.

We also decide we want opening theme music (*intro* music) and different closing music (*outro* music). From the fax list, we see that we have at our disposal both a CD player and a cassette player. To avoid having to change CDs or tapes during the show, when we may have plenty of other matters to attend to, we decide to use the CD player for the opening and the cassette player for the close.

We notice that the script features an announcer **voice-over** (VO) during the opening music, explaining the guest's name and the program topic. The director informs us that she does not want the music to interfere with the announcer, so we decide to bring the music up full at first and then lower it under the announcer's voice.

As soon as the announcer finishes the opening speech, we will kill his mic and then bring the music up full again, right before opening the host's mic for his opening speech. Then, just as the host begins to speak, we will slowly fade the music out. This will give shape to the audio portion of the program, avoid dead air, and telescope the sound from the host with that of the music. *Telescoping* means slightly overlapping audio sources to eliminate dead spots in the audio track, giving a seamless quality to the program audio.

As for closing music, the director asks that we make it coincide exactly with the closing credits, so that as the credits begin and end, so does the music. To do this, we time the closing credits during rehearsal, determining that they last 20 seconds. We select a 30-second piece of music. To have the music end exactly as the last credit rolls off and the screen fades to black, we backtime the music. In this case, **backtiming** means subtracting the time of an audio or video segment from the total program time so that the segment can be made to end exactly when the program ends. For our purposes, we will roll the music 30 seconds before the end of the show, but we will not fade up the channel carrying the music on the audio console until the credits begin. This is known as *deadpotting*. As soon as the credits appear, we will fade up the music—gradually so that it won't sound odd if it becomes audible in the midst of a musical phrase.

Finally, we consider Murphy's law—namely, what will we do on the day of production if the CD player suddenly breaks down? To fortify our program against the possibility of equipment failure (or unavailability), we decide to dub the CD material we have selected onto a cassette. In fact, we further decide to get both intro and outro music on CD if possible in case the cassette player fails. We obtain several backup mics and cables for the same reason. We hold a final preproduction meeting to make sure all personnel are familiar with their assignments.

Production. We seat the host and guest and place mics on them. Since the guest sits to the host's left and therefore looks to the right to see the host, we cheat the lav slightly to the guest's right side to favor the orientation of the guest's mouth. Conversely, since the host looks to the left, we clip the host's lav to the host's left. After the mics are in place, we calibrate the console and then have each talent speak into his or her live mic while all other mics are turned off. As each talent speaks, the audio operator takes a level. When each level is set, the audio operator places a piece of masking tape on each channel and labels it to identify the talent delegated to that source.

Each nonmicrophone audio source is then cued, levels are taken, and the appropriate channels on the audio board are tagged. When this process is completed for all audio sources, the audio operator fades the master gain to zero (to cut the noise level in the control room during other preparation), informs the director that audio is ready, and stands by.

During run-throughs, we see if everything is working. If all is well, then either the show is broadcast or it is put on tape for later use.

Postproduction. After the show is completed, it is time to strike the studio. This means all equipment must be put away. Audio cables are disconnected, tape labels are pulled up from the audio board, faders are placed at zero, audio sources are removed from their players, mics are put away, and the studio is cleared of all production materials. If the program has been taped for later use, the strike begins only after the director has made sure that a videotape has in fact been recorded and that it is of acceptable quality.

If audio sweetening is needed (say, adding a voiceover announcing a change in guest for the following week's program), it is wise to prepare it during production. For example, you may want to use the same announcer to preserve a seamless quality to the show.

A Single-Camera Field Setting

Elaborate field configurations feed video signals from several cameras and audio signals from several microphones to several video tape recorders. However, many programs shot in the field use a single camera. In the single-camera production style, the lone video signal, along with one or more audio signals from one or more microphones, is fed to a single recorder. When several mics are used with a single camera, an audio mixer (see Photo 8.6) is needed to feed the audio signals to the recorder. In the field, the audio mixer takes the place of the studio console.

Photo 8.6   An audio mixer can feed several audio sources to a single recorder in the field.

Let's consider a program that features a series of one-on-one interviews with several subjects, as well as a panel session with five people sitting in a semicircle around a table. We will use one camera and several microphones, and we have an audio mixer to feed all of the mics into one recorder.

Preproduction. In general, the single-camera production format differs from the multicamera approach in that various angles and perspectives at given locations are shot in separate takes. For instance, in our interview segments, video images of the host's reactions to subjects' comments will probably be shot separately to be used as "cutaways," which provide smooth transitions between segments. Assuming we will have a number of such interrupted starts and stops in the video and sound recording, consistency of sound will be especially important because it can help unify the entire program.

To achieve sound unity in the one-on-one interviews, we want to maintain consistent mic distances at consistent volume levels. For this reason, we decide to conduct all the interviews in a single location, and we plan to set up the camera, chairs, and microphones only once. We decide to use lavaliere mics (electrets) on each interviewee. We bring windscreens for the mics if we intend to record out-doors, and we also make sure to pack cables, extra batteries, mic clips, and gaffer's tape to secure the cables. For the panel discussion, we decide that three desk mics will be appropriate, and we pack the necessary desk stands to use with them.

We determine that the background noise of the site is something we wish to include. This natural sound, or **nat sound** as it is called (also known as ambient sound or room tone), will add sonic texture, help identify the location for the audience, and help smooth out the transitions when segments are shot out of sequence. To capture nat sound, we decide that the lavs we use in the interviews will be omnidirectional. (If we wanted to exclude nat sound, directional mics would be the better choice.) We also pack a separate recorder to record additional nat sound, thus ensuring that it can exist on an audio track separate from any voices.

Production. On the day of the shoot, we arrive early enough to set up the equipment to execute the one-on-one interviews and the panel discussion. The lights, camera, recorder, audio mixer, mics, and cables are arranged. We tape loose cables with gaffer's tape to keep personnel in the area from tripping over them.

After positioning each interviewee and setting up his or her mic, we take sound levels to verify that everything is working. To record the nat sound, we start the separate tape recorder before each interview and let it run throughout the interview. We also verify that SMPTE time code is being recorded for editing purposes.

For the panel discussion, we repeat the same procedures, this time setting up the desk mics. We make sure to space them properly to avoid interference problems, and we instruct panel members to keep incidental noise to a minimum. When the panel is assembled, we take levels. Then we record sound before, during, and after the interviews. After the last field footage is shot, we thank all personnel for their participation, strike the equipment, pack, and head back to the editing suite to assemble the program.

Postproduction. At this stage, we play back our recordings (voices and nat sound) and supplement them, if necessary, with other sounds captured during the shoot. We can also add background music, sound effects, or voice-overs with explanatory narration. All of these supplements help eliminate dead air and improve transitions in addition to adding needed narration or story details.

However, if we add music or sound effects, it should be done only after much consideration. For example, will music contribute aesthetically to the program, or would silence contribute more? If we add music, how does it fit the mood of the show? We also question whether the music should contain lyrics. In most cases, lyrics under a voice-over are distracting and should be avoided. While much of this thinking should occur in the preproduction stage, it may not be until postproduction that decisions about audio sweetening are finalized.

At the postproduction stage, sound levels also become critical. If we have recorded principal audio and nat sound at full volume but now want to add narration or other sound, we may need to lower the volume of the field audio to make the new sound audible. We will return to these considerations in Chapter 12 when we discuss editing in more detail.

KEY TERMS

cueing   203

open-reel tape   203

signal-to-noise (S/N) ratio   204

cassettes   204

digital audiotape   205

SMPTE time code   206

nonlinear editing   207

audio console   210

VU (volume unit) meter   213

feedback   216

digital audio workstation
(DAW)   216

audio sweetening   216

patch panel   217

sound effects   218

voice-over   221

backtiming   221

nat sound   223

QUESTIONS FOR REVIEW

How do CDs and DVDs store audio information? What are the implications of this for video production?

How does digital coding differ from analog coding, and what advantages does digital coding offer?

What advantages and disadvantages do tape-based media offer over CDs and DVDs?

How does nonlinear editing differ from linear editing?

What are the functions of the audio console, and how can they help you in shaping the audio materials for a video production?

What is the difference between foldback and feedback?

What are some of the factors you need to consider in using nat sound or sound effects?

NOTES

1. However, high-end recording machines (e.g., *Nagra* recorders) that use reels or solid-state digital storage (memory sticks and flash cards) have largely replaced analog cassette recorders for field production. For example, *Marantz,* the longstanding leader in mid-level audio recorders for journalists, is now using digital storage cards.

2. ADAT and the other digital audiotape (DAT) formats named in this section are being replaced by the computer-based digital audio workstation (DAW). However, ADAT is still widely used in the recording industry. Although it is a tape-based format, the term *ADAT* now refers to the Alesis ADAT HD-24, the next step in digital multitrack audio recording. It uses hard disk recording as opposed to the traditional tape-based ADAT.

Chapter 9

GRAPHIC AND SET DESIGN

Earlier in this book, the term *fabricate* was used to describe the creation of video content. The dictionary associates *fabricate* with terms such as *make, assemble, construct, manufacture,* and *shape.* However, the term *fabrication,* a close cousin, is also related to such terms as *fable, fakery, fiction, figment,* and *deceit.*

Just as musical instrument digital interfaces (MIDIs) and digital audio workstations now enable you to take natural sound and alter it to fit the needs of a particular project, computers can be used to change visual images of events captured by the camera to fit the whim of the editor. By now, it is well known that computer graphics technology can readily alter subject matter. Furthermore, just as MIDIs can generate sound without having to collect it from any natural source, computer graphics technology can help you create images from scratch without collecting them from the outside world. Today, video artists, using nothing but their imagination and a computer graphics or video editing program, can generate and store images (including animated ones) that can be fully integrated with regular broadcast signals.

As technology continues to enable you to erase the line between fact and fiction, new questions emerge about what images presented on television are "real." The question of fakery is particularly worrisome for journalists, whose job is to report news events faithfully. Not just journalists, however, but everyone involved in video needs to be aware of the ethical challenges raised by today's technologies.

Keep the question of "real" versus "fake" in mind as you read this chapter and the next. This chapter begins with the topic of video graphics and moves on to set design. Basically, graphics include any two-dimensional visual design presented on video. Sets, of course, are three-dimensional, but many of their parts that are visible on television are two-dimensional and therefore graphic in nature. In fact, new digital graphics systems are making it possible to substitute virtual sets for actual physical ones. Hence, more than ever, design principles used in preparing graphics apply to sets as well.

The topics included in this chapter are as follows:

Graphic design

- Camera graphics
- Noncamera (computer-generated) graphics
- Digitizing video images

Principles for creating air-quality graphics

- Aspect ratio
- Scanning area and essential area
- Brightness and contrast issues
- Color context and compatibility
- The role of graphic design in setting tone and style
- Preparing mechanical artwork

Set design

- Scenery styles

Basic set elements

- Floor treatments
- Hanging units
- Standard set pieces
- Properties, furniture, and set dressings

Production phases in set design

- Preproduction
- Production and postproduction

Electronic and mechanical effects in set design

- Electronic effects
- Mechanical effects
- Choosing between electronic and mechanical effects

GRAPHIC DESIGN

Graphic design is the part of video production concerned with the creation and use of two-dimensional visual images. Under this definition, any screen image of a two-dimensional display may be considered a graphic. Graphics include texts, pictures, and any combinations of the two.

The scope of graphic subject matter is infinite. Maps, charts, lists, graphs and other data displays, reproductions of signs and icons, pictures (of people, places, and things), drawings, sketches, paintings, cartoons, even animated streaming videos—all can be rendered graphically for television.

Camera Graphics

There are many ways you can convey graphic information on video. For example, a camera aimed at a lighted card mounted with a photograph is one of the oldest and simplest methods of providing graphic material for television. Such camera or studio cards have also been used to present titles and credits; in news programs, camera shots of weather maps and other set pieces have long been a graphic staple of television.

Computer-Generated Graphics

More recently, computers have taken the lead in providing video graphics. Depending on the software they use, computer graphics workstations operate at different levels of sophistication in terms of their image-rendering capability, flexibility, speed, efficiency, and storage capacity. Some use a camera to capture graphic content that can then be digitized and manipulated by the graphic artist. Others internally generate and store material for later use. The following sections describe several such devices.

Character Generator. One of the most widely used electronic computer graphics devices is the **character generator** (CG) (see Photo 9.1). The CG resembles a desktop computer; it has a keyboard for typing letters and numbers on the screen in various fonts (type styles), colors, and sizes. Some CGs permit hundreds of pages of

Photo 9.1   A character generator.

text to be stored and retrieved as needed; others have more limited capacity. Some CGs allow you to enhance the lettering you select with drop shadow and border effects, as well as backgrounds, underlining, and other edging options. Another popular option available is an **antialiasing** function, which softens the crude staircasing effect (*jaggies*) seen in diagonal lines and curved lettering. CGs equipped with antialiasing software create a blur around curves to reduce unwanted jaggies. Many CGs center text automatically when you display a page. Many offer the options of flashing text on the screen, "crawling" messages horizontally, or vertically rolling the messages up or down at variable speeds (*scroll* function). A screen cursor indicates the location of the next character to be typed, just as in word-processing programs.

Character-generated text can be combined with other video sources to create composite graphics. One such application is the placement of text at the bottom of the screen, over a camera shot, to identify on-air talent (see Photo 9.2). Such text identifications (usually names, titles, and affiliations) are called **lower-thirds** because they typically occupy the lower third of the screen space. CG lower-thirds are a good way to identify an on-air talent in a well-composed bust shot without blotting out the face. By contrast, cluttered or "busy" CG composite images, where lettering blots out important picture information, can distract viewers and are generally considered not "air quality."

Other common uses of CG text include centering a title over a program's opening shot, which can be provided by a camera or other source, and rolling credits at the end of a show.

Photo 9.2   A lower-third used to identify on-air talent.

Digitizing Video Images

Digitizing video signals allows you to manipulate graphic content easily. When a video frame is digitized from a broadcast signal, videotape, photograph, or other source, the continuous-wave energy is sampled, and discrete values are assigned to each sampled unit. In this way, each pixel is, in effect, assigned its own computer address, making it possible to change the color and brightness values assigned to it independently from any other.

Digitizing requires a massive amount of computer memory (on the order of multiple gigabytes), but it enables virtually endless manipulation and control of video images. You can change their color, size, and shape, and location. Furthermore, digital video can be reproduced repeatedly without signal loss, and it can be transmitted over telephone lines to multiple receivers. For example, Weather Service International (WSI) collects satellite images of weather patterns and distributes them to subscribers over telephone lines. TV station subscribers can then combine these images with camera shots of talent in front of a studio weather map, text, and other pictures for local weather reports.

Electronic Still Store. Another graphics device in widespread use is the **electronic still store** (ESS) system (see Photo 9.3). The ESS enables you to save digitized single frames of video from any source (tape, camera shots, even CG composites already mixed with other video) and file them on a high-capacity disk for later use. Electronic still store machines are also called **frame grabbers.**

Photo 9.3   An electronic still store (ESS) system.

Some ESS systems can store only about a hundred pages of images, while others can store tens of thousands. Some offer immediate access to thousands of pictures, any one of which can be retrieved in a fraction of a second. Some machines permit you to display image sequences in real time or in slow or fast motion. One common use of the ESS system is to display sports figures' pictures along with their vital statistics during games. Different displays can be prepared for each player and filed by number for immediate retrieval.

Captured images can come from a television camera focused on a graphic or other object placed on a copy stand or other sources. For example, a machine resembling a photocopier, called a **flatbed scanner,** can digitize two-dimensional graphics, including print photographs, which can then be captured and stored on ESS. News departments frequently use ESS with videotape, live camera shots, and CG text to create composite images for later presentation. These composites may be further combined with other images when routed through a video switcher, as described in the next chapter.

Video Paintbox Programs. One way to eliminate the need for copyright permission is to create your own images using a video **paintbox**/editing system. Some systems permit you to create video graphics out of whole cloth, without going to any external source whatsoever, using a *stylus* and a *bit pad* (see Photo 9.4).

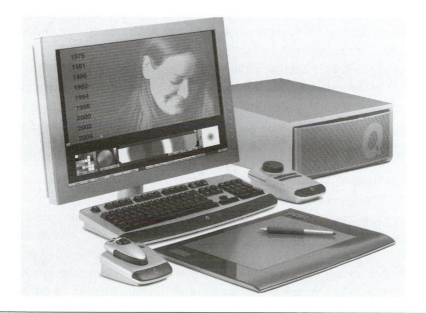

Photo 9.4   A video paintbox system. Notice the bitpad and stylus used for drawing.

The stylus functions as an electronic paintbrush, pen, or pencil; the bit pad is the equivalent of the artist's canvas. Many programs offer an array of pull-down menus (the computer's counterpart to the artist's palette) for you to select drawing options. By clicking on menu icons, you can choose various stroke widths, colors, and so on. Some machines allow drawing directly on the screen itself. When your work is finished, you can save it on disk for later use or combine it with other graphics (i.e., text from a CG).

Many systems offer **computer-aided design** (CAD) programs with complicated graphics options. With some, you can designate several points on the pad and then have the computer connect them with lines. You can fill in areas defined by those lines with a selected color or part of another image. The entire process and final results may be displayed on the screen. Other CAD and graphics options commonly include the following:

- *Sizing,* where the computer increases or decreases the overall size of an object or shape on the screen
- *Rotation,* where the artwork appears to rotate on the *x*-, *y*-, or *z*-axis, either appearing to bring one edge closer to the viewer or merely canting the image from the horizontal
- *Cutting and pasting,* where artwork may be removed intact to another portion of the screen. It may also be made to occupy a smaller space, thus enabling you to work on other drawings while keeping earlier material in view.
- *Posterization,* where the artwork is transformed by the computer in terms of only high and low luminance values. In other words, the middle values of light are eliminated, giving the artwork the look of a poster.
- *Cycling,* a simple form of animation, where an image (or series of images) appears animated as its color or brightness is made to change in a repetitive sequence. Cycling finds application in weather graphics where a simple cartoon image of the sun (often with a happy face and sunglasses) appears to shine at different intensities, thus increasing visual interest.

Three-Dimensional Graphics and Computer Animation. Graphics programs continue to gain speed and versatility. Three-dimensional modeling now enables you to present sequences of visual images that imitate what three-dimensional objects would look like if they were turning and moving in space. Pixar's hit movies, from *Toy Story* to *Cars,* use nothing but computer software for generating all of the images.

To do three-dimensional modeling, the computer first generates mathematical values that represent selected points on an object from a number of different perspectives. This information is then used to create images of the object from different viewpoints in sequence. Of course, this is not a simple task; it requires millions of calculations at extraordinary speed to present a convincing appearance of objects moving in real time. Machines that can do this are still at the high end of the computer graphics market.[1]

In addition to color and the illusion of depth, computers outfitted with *ray-tracing programs* provide an endless variety of surface characteristics such as texture (smoothness or roughness), pattern, degrees of opacity-transparency, reflection, and naturalistic light and shadow effects that vary the amount of illumination that different parts of objects appear to receive, as well as varying the apparent angle, direction, and strength of shadows objects appear to cast. When animated in real time, forms featured in computer-generated graphics can be made to look so real that it may be difficult to tell whether their images were captured from preexisting things or not.

Such computer programs require a lot of time to render animated sequences. Some sequences may be rendered one frame at a time off-line during pre- or post-production and then edited together. Fast machines can render some sequences on-line. After a beginning image, a final image, and several interim images are identified, the computer fills in the rest; when shown at 30 frames per second, in standard NTSC (National Television System Committee) format, they can be called *real-time animation.*

Some effects possible with more advanced computer animation programs include *morphing,* in which one picture changes into another through a barely perceptible series of intermediate steps. Other effects available from affordable desktop systems include *page turns, curls, flips, pushes, squeezes, fractal, fog, blur effects,* and many others. Photo 9.5 shows some of the possibilities.

Digital Still Cameras. Digital still cameras offer another source for video images, providing static images captured digitally on widely available flash sticks and memory cards. Such images can be transferred directly into video still storage. For example, digital video authoring and editing systems such as Final Cut Pro and Avid enable you to download and store such content for immediate integration into video programs through a USB cable.

PRINCIPLES FOR CREATING AIR-QUALITY GRAPHICS

No matter what tools you use to create graphic images for video, it is important to design the images properly so they can be effective on television. Successful design requires understanding the video system's capabilities and limitations. What looks good to the naked eye may or may not succeed on television.

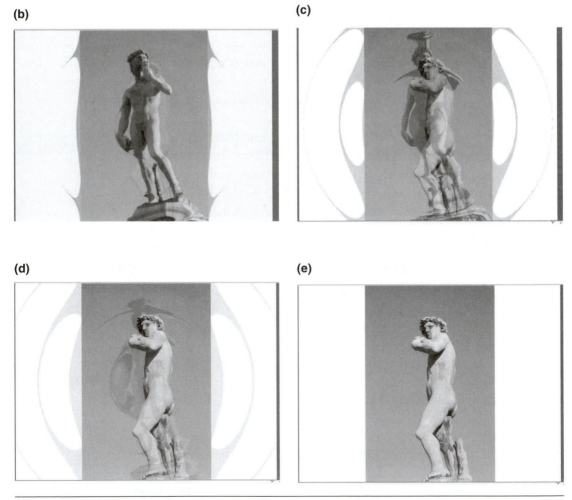

Photo 9.5   These image sequences (sequence a-e, f-j, k-n, and o-r) illustrate just a few of the digital effects possible with desktop editing systems.

(f)

(g)

(h)

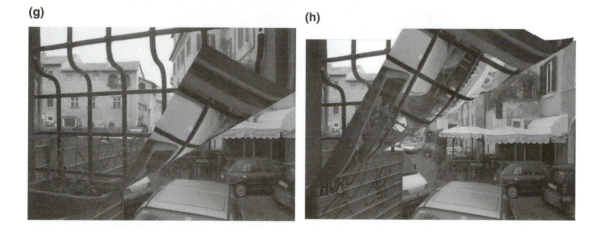

(i)

(j)

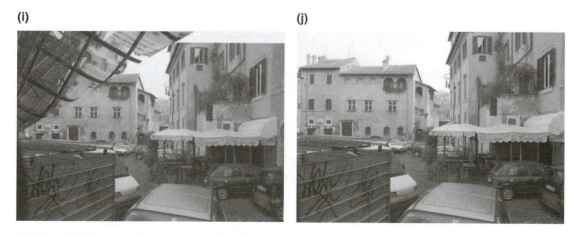

Photo 9.5 (Continued)

(k)

(l)

(m)

(n)

(o)

Photo 9.5 (Continued)

(p)

(q)

(r)

Photo 9.5 (Continued)

Compared to film or photography, the traditional NTSC television picture is a *low-resolution* image with 525 lines of picture detail, a screen space with a fixed 4:3 ratio of width to height, and a contrast range narrower than that available to your eye. We are currently in a transitional period as television advances from this traditional set of standards to a new HD format, featuring a different ratio of screen width to height of 16:9, closer to the standard used in the film industry. In addition, HD has more picture detail, with between 5 to 10 times the pixels in more lines, and offers both progressive and interlaced scanning methods to present pictures. The quality of the graphics you use is critically influenced by these and other factors.

Aspect Ratio

Successful graphics should conform to the rectangular television screen shape. Traditionally, that shape, regardless of screen size, has been fixed at a ratio of width to height of four units to three units, designated as 4:3 *aspect ratio*. On any given receiver, aspect ratio does not change from shot to shot or from program to program. Therefore, regardless of the material being shown, if it is to fit the screen without leaving dead space or unwanted border, it must always conform to a given screen's aspect ratio.

With the recent adoption of a digital television (DTV) standard (also called *HD* for *high definition, "hi-def,"* or *HDTV*), the aspect ratio of television is changing from the traditional 4:3 to 16:9 (or slightly wider than 5:3) units of width to height. HDTV is also increasing picture resolution significantly. Since HD will produce higher resolution images on a wider screen, it will open up new graphic possibilities. For now, however, the NTSC format is still quite dominant.

In an ideal production world, all television graphics would be in the proper aspect ratio. But sometimes it is necessary or desirable to use graphics, particularly photographs, that do not conform. Such materials may have originated from news archives or other sources where video aspect ratio was not a concern.

To make use of such materials on television, you can show the entire image in a static shot with the dead space of the border visible (see Figure 9.1a) and matte the border of the image with a color to make it more attractive. If you do this, try to fit the color you select to the tone of the production or at least make the border less obtrusive.

In severe cases where more border than image is displayed, this approach is not recommended. In such cases, try cropping the image so that you fill the screen space with just the most important information, perhaps eliminating border entirely (Figure 9.1b).

Another approach is to feature the graphic with camera movement (panning, tilting, or zooming) on the image while on air (Figure 9.1c). This is more complicated than cropping to a static frame and may require practice with the camera to achieve smoothness of motion and proper pace. The biggest problems tend to be jerky camera movement, movement off the graphic entirely, and the tendency to use irrelevant or unnecessary movement that can be distracting. If you have the time and want to eliminate all these problems, you can scan the image into a video editing system and prepare panning, tilting, and/or zooming shots of the desired graphic to your heart's content, presenting it flawlessly later.

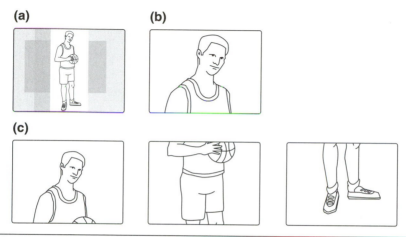

Figure 9.1   Methods of treating an image that does not fit the TV aspect ratio: (a) showing the entire image but matting the dead spaces of the screen with a color, (b) cropping the image to a shape more suitable to the screen, and (c) moving the camera to capture the image in successive frames—in this case, by beginning with a shot of the head and then tilting the camera gradually downward.

Either way, effective movement can support your show's meaning. It may, for example, include reveals of important information. When done properly, such movement provides visual variety, can heighten audience involvement, and emphasizes key aspects of the program. Keep in mind that if you do this with a camera, live in studio, executing this technique may require the cooperation of more than just the camera operator. You may need to pace the movements you have planned to the voice-over of an announcer. You may need card pullers or other personnel to integrate the moves into the rest of the program. This may mean quite a bit of rehearsal. However, the results can be both effective and engaging.

Scanning Area and Essential Area

Since there is always some signal loss during transmission because of masking of the perimeter of the home receiver and misalignment between the camera's *scanning area* (the total area scanned by the television camera) and that of the home receiver, it is important to confine essential information to the part of the screen that will reach the home receiver intact. To do this, video professionals designate an "essential" or safe title area. Roughly, the **essential area** of the television screen is the central rectangle of space comprising about two thirds of the total area covered by the camera (see Figure 9.2). Graphic information—particularly important facts such as phone numbers for viewers to call, titles, and credits—should be confined to the essential area.

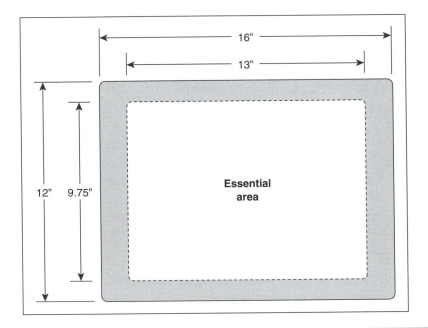

Figure 9.2   The essential area for TV screens. The measure shown here apply to 4:3 aspect ratio screens, this one with a 20-inch diagonal, but the proportions are the same for other NTSC screen sizes. For wide-screen formats the essential area is roughly the same, with 2/3 of screen space for essential area.

Designing Text for a Video Screen

➢ To accommodate the relatively low resolution of the current television screen, keep typefaces simple—avoid complicated serifs and overly thin and/or fancy letterforms (see Figure 9.3).

➢ As a rule of thumb, make the text legible at a distance 16 times the height of the monitor. For example, if the monitor is 12 inches high, type should be readable at a distance of up to 16 feet.

➢ When possible, enhance the clarity of letterforms by using drop shadows and/or borders, which help distinguish text from its background.

➢ Organize the layout of words into blocks of related material so that meanings are easy to grasp.

➢ When combining text with pictures, don't place the text over extremely intricate backgrounds. In short, avoid busy visuals.

Figure 9.3 (a) Appropriate text styles for a TV screen. These fonts are relatively easy to read on a TV screen. (b) Some fonts are much harder to read on screen and should not be issued.

Brightness and Contrast Issues

Regardless of subject matter, clear, discernible graphics require enough contrast among elements to enable the viewer to distinguish them from one another. This is true in any visual medium, but particularly in video, with its relatively low resolution and limited range of brightness.

In terms of light reflectance, the brightness range of the television system varies from *TV white,* which is at best only about 70% reflectance value for monochrome receivers (with a pure white set equal to 100%), to *TV black,* which is about 3% reflectance value (with a pure black set at 0% reflectance). For color systems, the whitest TV white is only about 60% reflectance.

If we divide the brightness range, from 3% reflectance at one end to 60% to 70% reflectance at the other, into distinct steps, we get the **television gray scale** (see Photo 5.7 in Chapter 5). The gray scale shown is broken into 11 steps; however, in the industry, you may also encounter 9-, 7-, or even 5-step scales.

One use of the gray scale is to determine differences in reflectance values between lettering and backgrounds. Most experts agree that, to ensure legibility, *the minimum spread between text and background should be two gray-scale steps.* Obviously, this is only a rule of thumb, since two steps on a 5-step scale may be much wider than 2 steps on an 11-step scale.

What if the text and background are different colors? In that case, can contrast be ignored? The answer is no, because different colors may have identical luminance (brightness) values. Therefore, to differentiate elements of the graphic image from one another, it is not enough to distinguish them by color—they must also be different in brightness. A waveform monitor, which provides a graphic display of light reflectance levels for different colors, can help you judge whether the elements of your graphics have enough variation in luminance values to make them air quality.

Color Context and Compatibility

Colors tend to change appearance depending on their surroundings. A light color generally appears even lighter when viewed against a dark background. Furthermore, light foreground elements appear to come forward more than dark ones, and they may appear larger simply as a result of their color (see Photo C3 in the section of color plates).

In addition, some color combinations tend to create more eye fatigue than others, and some are harder to reproduce on television, even for the best-quality cameras. For example, the red-blue color combination is said to be particularly fatiguing, and red is among the more difficult colors to render accurately.

Finally, different colors may have different cultural and psychological associations that may affect the tone of a program. For example, red is frequently associated with hot emotions such as anger and rage, as well as with meanings of warning and danger, while blue is often associated with emotions such as sadness and cooler feelings. Of course, color associations are not forever fixed this way; they may change depending on program content and culture.

Graphic Design Sets Tone and Style

Graphic design contributes significantly to a program's look and feel, tone and style. For example, a program's title is often the first thing seen by the audience. Therefore, the design of the title, in addition to simply stating it, offers the producer an invaluable opportunity to include enticing information about the show. Imagine the contribution made to a horror movie by a title that looks as if it were printed with candle wax drippings. Compare MTV's graphics with those of CNN.

If done tastefully, the entire graphic presentation—including the selection of pictures, illustrations, and other visuals, fonts, colors, sizes, layouts, and the pace—can convey a great deal of information to the audience about what lies ahead, while adding thematic unity to the entire production. In all cases, preview all visuals to verify that they look the way you want.

> ## Questions to Ask Yourself When Producing Graphics
>
> ➢ How does each graphic function in the overall program?
> ➢ Does each graphic convey the central concept, theme, or a significant aspect of the show?
> ➢ Will the content inform, entertain, educate, and/or persuade your audience, or will it cause boredom?
> ➢ Worse, does it insult the audience's intelligence? Does it confuse?
> ➢ Do any of the graphics cause problems with pace?
> ➢ Is each graphic being shown at the right point of the show, in the right place, and for the right amount of time?
> ➢ Can you accomplish the goal with better means?

Preparing Mechanical Artwork

Even in a graphics world dominated by electronically generated computer images, it is worthwhile to know how to prepare mechanical artwork. Many television talent still use physical cards to convey key program content. For example, both Jay Leno and David Letterman frequently use display cards to present comedy bits from their desks on their late-night television shows. The following sections briefly describe several methods for preparing mechanical studio graphics for your productions.

Studio or Camera Cards. These sturdy sheets of card stock are either held in the hand by talent or supported by an easel or card stand. **Studio** or **camera cards** can feature text and/or pictorial content. A manageable material for such cards is 11 × 14-inch (or slightly wider for HD's 16:9 format) rectangular illustration board or foam core. These sizes are large enough to support most artwork but not so large that they tip over card stands or overwhelm talents' ability to handle the cards comfortably. The space on this size of card can be easily captured by most studio cameras, without forcing the camera either to dolly out beyond the range of most studios or dolly in so tight that transitions become difficult.

Illustration board and foam core (or *art cards,* as they are sometimes called) can be purchased at reasonable cost in large sheets from most art supply stores. They can be cut to size with a cutting machine or a matte knife.

Mounting Artwork on Studio Cards. All mechanical artwork, including photographs, drawings, charts, and graphs, should be mounted on flat studio cards before being displayed on television. Do not rely on the ordinary paper stock when displaying images for the camera—in most cases, unmounted pictures will be too flimsy to stay flat, making it harder to achieve uniform lighting and focus.

How should artwork be mounted on studio cards? There are several methods to use and some that should never be used. Recommended methods include using rubber cement, spray adhesive, and peel-and-stick adhesive sheets, all available in art supply stores. These choices result in flat, smooth artwork that is extremely long lasting if not permanent.

When using rubber cement, lay out the work to be mounted and outline the area the artwork will occupy on the studio card lightly with pencil. Place the artwork to be mounted face down on a sheet of newspaper or other expendable surface, and coat it entirely with a thin layer of cement. Then do the same to the surface of the studio card. *Go slightly beyond the area the artwork will occupy on the card.* When the shiny appearance of the cement disappears (after a minute or so), apply one edge of the artwork to the place on the card where you want it. Then carefully lay down the rest of the artwork without trapping bubbles of air. You may use a roller to make this part of the job easier. Set the card aside for a few minutes until the cement is completely dry. Remove excess cement with an eraser or with the side of your finger. The card should now be ready for display and should last a long time without coming loose or curling up.

When using spray adhesive, after laying out the artwork and outlining the area as above, place it face down on a clean expendable surface such as newspaper and spray the back of the artwork with adhesive. *Do not spray the card.* Then carefully place the artwork on the card and use a roller to press it into place. Work from the edge or center of the artwork to avoid trapping air bubbles. Set the card aside for a few minutes until the adhesive is completely dry. The card should now be ready for display, and the spray adhesive is permanent.

Adhesive sheets are also easy to use. First, cut the adhesive sheet to the proper size. Then peel the sheet to reveal the adhesive material. Next, rub the adhesive material onto the surface where you wish to fix the graphic. Finally, put the graphic in place and rub it down to fix it.

Avoid using glues that cause the artwork to buckle and wrinkle. Also, do not use tape ("invisible" or any other kind) to fix artwork to studio cards. The tape shows, is unreliable, fails to eliminate buckling and warping, and for all these reasons produces an ugly effect. To ensure air-quality graphics, use the recommended adhesives.

When using studio cards, remember to number them (in pencil) so they can be easily arranged if they get out of order. Studio cards may be identified with numbered tabs of masking tape, making them easy to arrange and pull if needed during production.

Remember, too, to preview all visuals to confirm that they look acceptable on air. One of the simplest problems to correct when previewing graphics is the *keystoned* graphic. A keystoned graphic is one (usually text) in which the material looks as if it is running uphill or downhill when you want it to appear perfectly horizontal.

To fix this, while watching a shot of the card on the line monitor, have the card puller pitch the left or right edge of the card closer or further from the camera until it looks right (see Figure 9.4). In most cases, this will be all you need to do to solve the problem. May all of your graphic problems be this simple to fix.

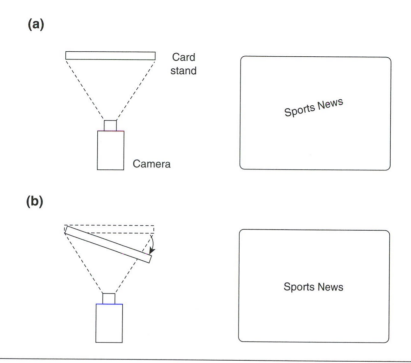

Figure 9.4 Correcting a keystone effect. (a) The original position of camera and card stand produces keystoning; on screen, the text appears to be running uphill. (b) The effect is corrected by rotating the right edge of the stand closer to the camera.

SET DESIGN

The term *sets* refers to all of the scenery, backgrounds, and furnishings intended to be seen by the television camera, including items associated with interior locales, such as walls and floors, fireplaces, bookcases, doors, and staircases, and items associated with exterior locales, such as park benches, trees, storefronts, street lamps, and even mountain views. Furniture items and larger pieces brought in to fill out a scene are called set **properties,** or **props,** for short. Smaller items, including embellishments such as lamps, books on bookshelves, and pictures hanging on walls, are called *set dressings.* There are also *hand props,* which consist of items held in the hand by on-air talent, such as telephones, guns, cooking and eating utensils, and so forth.

The function of a set is to provide scenery that supports, enhances, and evokes the program's tone and purpose. Needless to say, the set should permit ease of access, and it should be durable so that it doesn't come loose or fall apart during production.

Good set design must be shaped by what is *possible,* as well as what is *desirable.* For example, when shooting a video about environmental issues, you may want the talent to stand in front of a mountain. In Montana, this may be easy to arrange. However, if the story is being shot in Indiana, the shot might require substantial costs for transporting the talent and crew to the desired location. Beyond such natural settings, time, money, labor, and carpentry talent, as well as access to materials, are often important constraints on set design.

It is the task of the producer-director to determine how the set should look. In the beginning of the set design process, the concept phase, it is best to proceed without regard for what is available. *The first concern should be to design the set on paper or in model form in line with the program's central concept or theme, without regard for what is possible.* Brainstorm. Ask yourself what the program is about and what its overall mood is. What degree of reality or unreality are you trying to capture? If you had unlimited resources, what would the ideal set look like? Only after deciding what the "best" set(s) might be should you allow limitations of time, money, materials, and effort to temper your plan.

Categories of Scenery Style

The main categories of scenery style include the following:

1. *Realistic.* Sets designed in a realistic style use authentic (or authentic-appearing) set pieces, such as sinks that may have running water, refrigerators that may actually keep food cold, doors with doorbells that ring, and pianos that are tuned and can be played. Realism imitates nature so that the sets appear authentic from the camera's point of view. When a well-known site is reproduced realistically, the set is called a *replica.* Realism is often the style used in constructing sets for sitcoms, soap operas, and network series drama (see Photo 9.6).

2. *Representational.* Representational sets support and characterize the program material but are not authentic. For example, to convey a playroom setting, a children's show might paint pictures of windows and flower pots on a set wall rather than use real window inserts (called *plugs*) and real flower pots. Or a news special about the space program might hang several models of lunar modules, space shuttles, and space probes around the studio to indicate the program's subject matter (see Photo 9.7).

Photo 9.6   A realistic set for a soap opera. Notice the furniture and set dressings are actual
pieces of furniture and accessories one might find in someone's home.

Photo 9.7   A representational set for a production of *Urinetown*. This stylized representation
of a fictional city's public restroom facility can also be seen as a fantasy set.

3. *Abstract-symbolic.* Abstract-symbolic sets merely suggest a setting with
   few elements actually present (see Photo 9.8). For example, a shadow of
   repeating vertical stripes projected on a neutral back wall might be used to

Photo 9.8   An abstract-symbolic set for a fiction drama episode.

indicate a jail cell; a desk and phone might be all that is used to indicate an office. With appropriate sound effects, such settings can be very suggestive. Obviously, abstract-symbolic sets can save a great deal of time, effort, and money. They can also be quite open, making it easy for cameras to gain access to a number of different shooting angles. However, the sparseness of the set pieces can also limit the number of desirable angles.

4. *Fantasy.* Sets that bear little resemblance to reality can be labeled fantasy sets. These can consist of bizarre, surreal, or unreal scenic elements and may include stylized renderings that merely suggest locations. For example, science fiction programs, dream sequences in dramas, and sets for music videos can all be appropriate program possibilities for fantasy sets.

5. *Neutral.* Neutral sets, which provide a blank backdrop or nondescript locale, are designed to maximize attention on the talent. For example, a blank wall or uniformly lighted cyclorama provides a neutral setting for a poetry reading or dramatic speech. **Cameo lighting,** in which the talent is presented in completely black surroundings (see Photo 9.9), is an extreme example of a neutral setting. **Limbo lighting** presents the talent in a setting consisting of a single uniform color, giving the illusion of infinite distance (see Photo 9.10). Neutral sets can be made more interesting by using light and color variations as set elements for little cost in terms of time and money (see Photo 9.11).

Photo 9.9   Cameo lighting.

Photo 9.10   Limbo lighting.

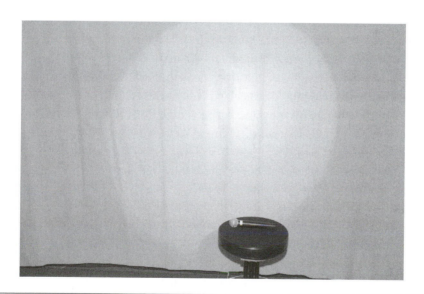

Photo 9.11   Light as a set element.

These scenery styles are just several points on a continuum. In practice, the sets you develop will likely combine stylistic elements from across the spectrum from realistic to pure fantasy. Again, the first concern should be what you want and need to support the central concept of the scene or program, tempered later by what is available, feasible, and affordable.

BASIC SET ELEMENTS

Since sets include all parts of the scene captured by the camera, there are many elements to deal with. Let's look at a few of them in more detail, working from the bottom up.

Floor Treatments

The Floor Itself. Because the floor may be seen by the camera, it must be thought of as a set element. It may be painted or covered with material such as carpeting or tile, depending on the program's needs. For example, a living room set in a soap opera or a sitcom may include carpets, rugs, or floor mats; a playroom setting for a children's show may use flamboyant painted patterns or drawings with loud colors; an outdoor scene may require grass, bricks, or sand.

In preparing the floor for a video production, from the simplest to the most decorative treatments, ease of access of cameras, equipment, and personnel is a top priority. You should also be able to install and remove floor dressings quickly and easily.

If the plain floor is seen on camera, dress cables to hide them from view. If you use wire mics, when possible, run cables behind talent, along the edge of the cyclorama or along the edge of the floor near the wall, to keep them out of view. This leaves the floor looking cleaner and less cluttered.

In general, when using rugs and carpets, tape down the edges to keep camera dollies from bunching them up if the camera rolls over them. Taping mats and rugs also keeps them from skidding. Sometimes rugs, mats, and carpets may be used to hide cables. (Still, electrical wires and cables hidden this way should first be secured with tunnel tape or protective plastic guard piping to keep them from damage in high-traffic areas.)

If you use tile or linoleum, make sure they can be easily installed and removed without leaving glue or cement behind. Tile can often be laid down without any adhesive at all. If you tape the outer edge in place, cameras and booms can have unimpeded access. After the production, removal is quick and easy.

Water-based paint permits floor decoration without interfering with camera movement. The cleanup, though, takes time and effort, and therefore the use of paint as a floor treatment may be more trouble than it is worth. If the floor must be quickly restored to its prior condition for an upcoming production, you may want to consider other alternatives.

If you use dirt or sand to simulate exterior locales, lay down a sheet of plastic first to make cleanup easier. Remember that flooring of this sort will limit the access of cameras and booms.

Platforms or Risers. The platforms that permit you to elevate sets and talent from the floor are **risers.** Among other things, they bring seated talent to eye level with the camera lens (see Photo 9.12). This makes life easier for camera operators. Risers may also be used to distribute talent to different parts of the video space for visibility or dramatic effect—for instance, by creating tiers for singers in music groups.

Risers are usually constructed of either ½-inch or ¾-inch plywood on frames of 2 × 4-inch or 2 × 12-inch stock lumber, depending on the amount of weight the platform is intended to hold. Riser heights usually vary from 2 inches to 12 inches but can go higher. In most cases, risers are covered with carpeting to reduce noise when talent walks on them. To reduce noise levels further, the hollow inside the riser may be stuffed with foam.

Risers can also be constructed from polystyrene blocks covered with ¼-inch plywood. These may be painted black or carpeted. This type of construction results in much lighter set pieces, though they are less durable than the heavier plywood variety. When carpeted, these are also quieter.

Most risers are made in 4-foot squares or in 4 × 8-foot pieces, so they can be used in modular fashion. They can be configured in different layouts on the floor or stacked on one another. These modular units are also easier to remove than larger sections when it is time to tear down the set after production.

Photo 9.12   Risers elevate talent to the level of the camera lens. Even a low riser can be a substantial help.

Risers may be placed on casters for easy movement. Sets may be placed on wheeled risers and then easily moved around. When in use, however, wheeled risers should be stabilized with wedges and sandbags.

Hanging Units

Cycloramas. *Cycloramas* (or *cycs;* rhymes with "bikes") provide a seamless background around the perimeter of the studio. To keep the cyc taut, small lead weights may be used in the hem of the cyc near the floor, or ties may attach the bottom of the cyc to a ground pipe laid along the perimeter of the studio floor. To blend the bottom edge of the cyc with the floor, a *ground row* may be used (see Figure 9.5). If the floor, cyc, and ground row are the same color (neutral gray is often preferred), the illusion of an infinite backdrop can be achieved.

Some cycs have a lightly woven curtain of gauzy material, called a *scrim,* hung in front of them to diffuse light hitting the cyc, further softening the overall appearance of the backdrop. A gray cyc can be illuminated in a variety of colors,

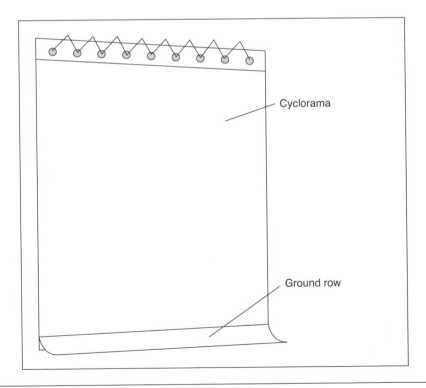

Figure 9.5   A ground row helps to blend the bottom edge of a cyclorama into the floor.

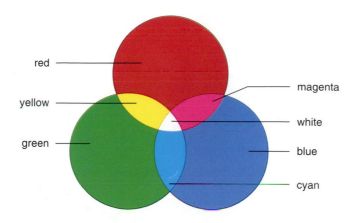

C1: For colored light, all colors can be rendered when mixing different amounts of the primaries red, green, and blue (i.e., mixing red and green colored light yields yellow).

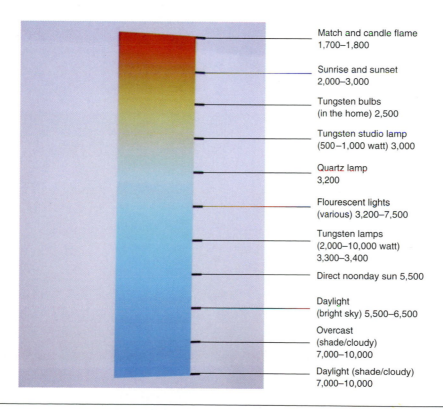

C2: Color temperature chart for common types of artificial and natural light expressed in degrees Kalvin. (See Table 4.1 on page 103.)

C3: In video, brightly colored, sharp, strongly textured, high-contrast objects often appear closer than those that are duller or fuzzier. In this photo, notice how the stone's rough texture and contrasting light and shadow strengthen its dominance in the foreground, whereas the building on the left receeds into the background with less detail.

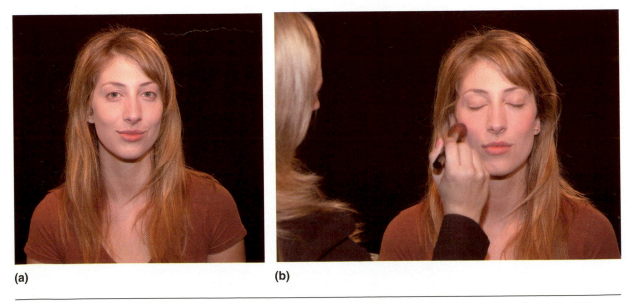

(a)   **(b)**

C4: Some of the steps in applying makeup for video talent. (a) The talent after adding foundation to control unwanted shine, with powder added to "set" the foundation. (b) Rouge is applied. (c, d) Eye shadow and eye liner are added. (e) Lip liner will be followed by lipstick. (f) Talent after final application of powder.

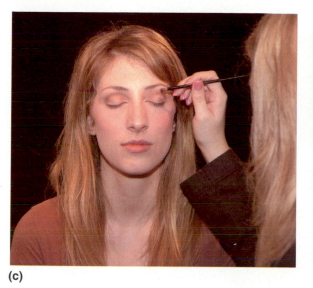

(c)

(d)

(e)

(f)

C5: A beauty kit for video makeup, used for both male and female talent. Included are lip colors, foundations, and powders. There is also eye makeup, including mascara and shadow, and an assortment of brushes, pencils, and more.

making it a flexible option for many production needs. In such cases, strip lights may be positioned between the ground row and the cyc itself, so the lights are kept out of the camera's view. Pattern projections can also be used to add detail.

A different kind of cyclorama, called a *hard cyc,* also offers an appearance of infinite space. A hard cyc is a smooth plaster wall that curves into the studio floor, providing a seamless backdrop for the camera (see Figure 9.6).

Black Velour Curtain. A black velour curtain may be hung like a cyclorama, but without lights or scrim. Such a curtain may be pulled along a metal track around the perimeter of the studio to provide a black background for talent. This

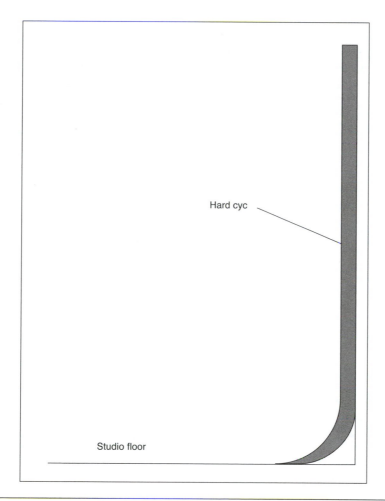

Hard cyc

Studio floor

Figure 9.6   A hard cyc, made of plaster, curves from the studio wall into the floor so that wall and floor merge seamlessly on screen.

arrangement is ideal when using cameo lighting since the curtain absorbs reflected light and directs all of the audience's attention to the talent. Black velour also makes it unnecessary to pull the curtain taut to obtain a smooth, uniform background. To achieve a total cameo lighting effect with black velour curtain, you can add a black floor covering to make the floor vanish.

Canvas Drops. Wide rolls of painted canvas are called *canvas drops,* which can be hung from the studio grid on a roll and lowered into a set using fly lines (see Figure 9.7). A number of different drops can be used during a production to provide various painted scenes. As a scene ends, the fly lines can be used to roll up the drop to reveal a new drop intended for the next scene. Drops can be repainted for use in other productions.

Seamless Paper. A cheaper way to provide colored or painted backgrounds is with *seamless paper,* which comes in 9 × 36-foot rolls in many colors. By taping it to a studio wall or stapling it to a row of flats (described in the next section), you can provide attractive backgrounds quickly. With a small amount of paper, you can

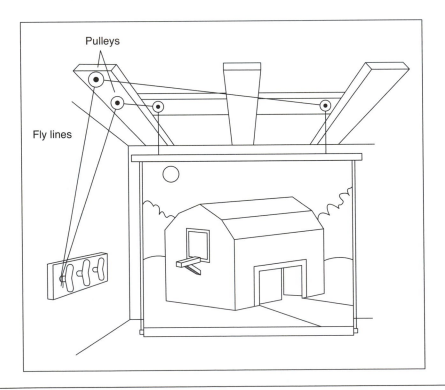

Figure 9.7   A scene painted on a canvas drop can provide an appropriate background for a set.

supply different backgrounds for stationary talent, such as on-air reporters or announcers. When used appropriately, a variety of colored backgrounds can add visual interest to your productions while creating the illusion that talent are in different locales.

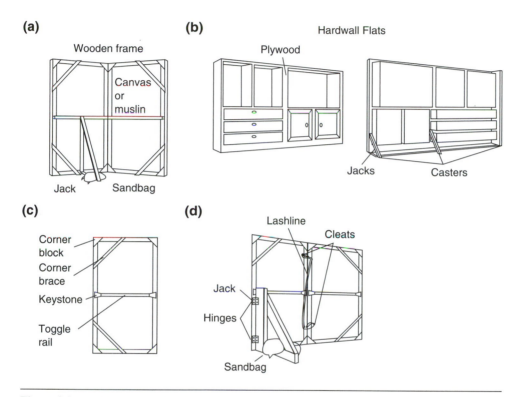

Figure 9.8   Flats. (a) Softwall flat. (b) Hardwall flat. (c) Carpentry elements of a typical flat. (d) Items used to join and support flats.

Standard Set Pieces

To form backgrounds such as interior or exterior walls, studio sets rely on standard pieces called **flats** (see Figure 9.8). Flats may be either *softwall* or *hardwall.* Each has its advantages and disadvantages.

Softwall flats are generally composed of either 1 × 3-inch or 2 × 4-inch wood frames measuring 4 feet in width by 8, 10, or 12 feet in height, depending on production needs and studio ceiling height. The frames are covered with stretched canvas or muslin stapled into place. Flats are then attached to one another to make various backgrounds. The cloth face of a softwall flat can be painted (and repainted) to fit the tone of the production.

Hardwall flats use plywood, particle board, or wood paneling (usually ⅛ or ¼ inch thick) instead of cloth. This makes them more durable and less flimsy than softwall flats; they are less likely to shake when doors are slammed or give way if a talent or piece of equipment moves into them. However, the wood face of a hardwall flat makes it heavy, often requiring more than one person to set it up.

Simple carpentry techniques keep flats from sagging, falling apart, or losing their right angles. *Corner blocks* and *braces,* as well as *keystones* and *toggle rails,* are used to make flats sturdy (see Figure 9.8c and d). Corner blocks are plywood triangles nailed to the frame joints running *with* the grain of the flat. Corner braces are strips of wood (1-by-3s) nailed across *adjacent* joint members. Keystones are small blocks of wood used to nail *parallel* frame members to a wood strip (the toggle rail) running between them to add stability.

In addition to a frame and a covering, flats need hardware to connect them together and a support element to stand them up perpendicular to the floor. Several methods are commonly used to connect flats to one another (see Figure 9.8d). One uses *lashlines* and *cleats* by running a rope back and forth between metal hooks fastened to the frames of adjacent flats from top to bottom, where the rope may be tied off. Another method uses *pin* and *hinge-type* hardware to fit adjacent flats together. Yet another fastens adjacent flats together with *C-clamps.* When joined, well-made flats should not show visible breaks between one another from the camera's perspective.

Support for flats to keep them standing perpendicular to the floor is provided by **jacks** or **braces** (see Figure 9.8). The jack or brace is a triangular wood or metal unit joined at a right angle to the back of the flat with either a clamp or a pin and hinge. Then sandbags are placed over the bottom section of the unit to secure it in place. Bracing is not required for every flat, but it should be used where the most weight or stress will be felt, as at doorways and corners.

Hardwall flats may be permanently joined together with hinges. When two flats are so joined, they are called *twofold flats* (Figure 9.9a). When three flats

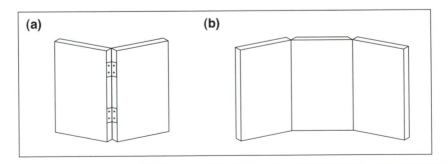

Figure 9.9   Flats can be permanently joined to create freestanding set elements: (a) a twofold flat and (b) a threefold flat.

are so joined, they are called *threefold flats* (Figure 9.9b). The advantage of twofold and threefold flats is that they are freestanding and therefore do not require bracing when partially opened. This makes them quick to set up. They can also serve different functions, including representing a corner or three walls of a room. The problem with them is that they can be quite heavy and difficult to move. For this reason, they are sometimes placed on casters. They also take up a good deal of storage space. Some flats have sections cut out of them to accommodate door, window, and fireplace inserts (*plugs*). If not made properly, door and window plugs can lead to problems (or unintended comedic effects) if they malfunction. For this reason, it is best to leave the construction of such items to professional set designers.

Besides flats, other freestanding set pieces include *columns, screens, gobos, and polecats.* These set elements help break the studio space into areas designated for different activities.

- Columns come in four varieties: *pillars, pylons, periaktoi* (plural; singular is *periaktos*), and *sweeps* (see Figure 9.10). All may be constructed from wooden forms and covered with painted cardboard. A pillar is a standard cylinder-shaped column. A pylon is a three-sided column that may be painted a different color on each side and turned to present different painted surfaces to the camera, making it suitable for a variety of production needs. Periaktoi are pylons mounted on wheels to make scene changes even more convenient. Sweeps are columns shaped in the form of partial hollow cylinders, making it possible to display either their inside or outside surfaces to the camera. Sweeps can be used to soften corners in flats or to add decorative touches. Columns can be used as door frames or to define the edge of a set in representational, abstract, or fantasy treatments.

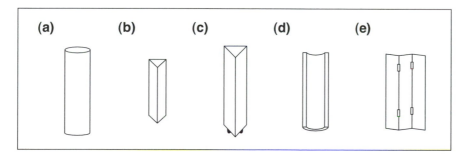

Figure 9.10   Freestanding pieces include (a) pillar, (b) pylon, (c) periaktos, (d) sweep, and (e) screen.

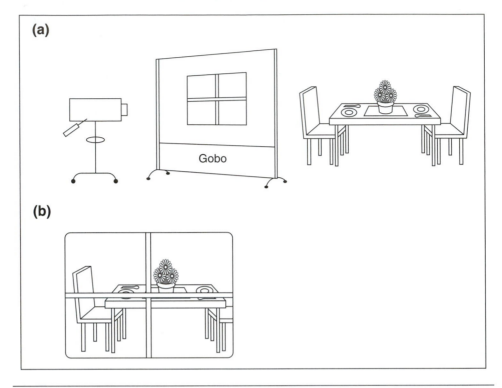

Figure 9.11   Use of a gobo. (a) Shooting a scene through a gobo. (b) The scene as it appears on screen.

• Screens (see Figure 9.10e) also divide the studio space into separate areas for different purposes. Screens may be made of wood or covered in fabric but should not be too shiny or patterned too intricately.

• Gobos are foreground set pieces through which the camera can shoot a scene (see Figure 9.11). For example, a window frame (with or without the glass) might be set up in front of a camera to give the impression that the audience is peering into a dining room set from outside a house. Gobos emphasize depth by including foreground and background elements in the same shot.

• Polecats, spring-loaded rods that extend from floor to ceiling, can be used to support other set graphics.

Properties, Furniture, and Set Dressings

When selecting furniture, remember that talent may have to interact with it. Be sure it works! This means chairs should not creak or collapse, beds should not sag beyond belief, tables should not wobble, and doors and drawers to cabinets should function properly. Get stuff that is truly serviceable and test it. At the same time, keep in mind that heavy, bulky furniture can be both difficult to store and a real problem if it must be moved frequently. If you can get away with lighter and smaller, rather than heavier and bigger, do so.

Furthermore, establish size and style requirements for the furniture you wish to use. Keep in mind that there are hundreds if not thousands of types of chairs in this world. Some are huge, overstuffed lounge chairs, while others are stiff-backed skimpy wood things resembling little more than glorified stools. Be discerning about the needs of your show and select items appropriate to the program you are producing. For example, in interview shows, swivel chairs are often a distraction because they invite erratic movement from talent.

Some items of furniture simply look better on camera than others. Intricate patterns on upholstery might create annoying moiré patterns when seen by the camera. Some pieces might be either too reflective or too dull.

Props and set dressings should all contribute to the program's thematic unity. For example, in a televised production of the play *Death of a Salesman,* Willy Loman's sample case might be authentic and actually quite heavy. Of course, this does not mean you should use an authentic pistol for a shootout! Rather, the gun must appear authentic *to the camera.* Use what works. Look at the set dressings and props in close-up on the line monitor to see if they do the job.

PRODUCTION PHASES IN SET DESIGN

Preproduction

To develop successful set designs, preparation is critical. In preproduction, as with lighting design, the script is your road map. Read the script from start to finish and list the things you will need item by item as they come up. Then construct a scale floor plan.

In some cases, you may move from the paper-and-pencil stage (lists and floor plan) to a miniature 3-D model of the set you are contemplating. Working small is a low-risk way to simulate the actual set. Like the carpenter's adage "Measure twice and cut once," using floor plan diagrams and small-scale models saves time and money. The following sections describe some advantages and details of this process.

The Scale Floor Plan. The floor plan is an aerial view of the set (see Figure 9.12a; see Figure 9.12b for a photo of the actual set). The advantage of a *scale* floor plan is that all items are shown in proportional size to one another. This makes it

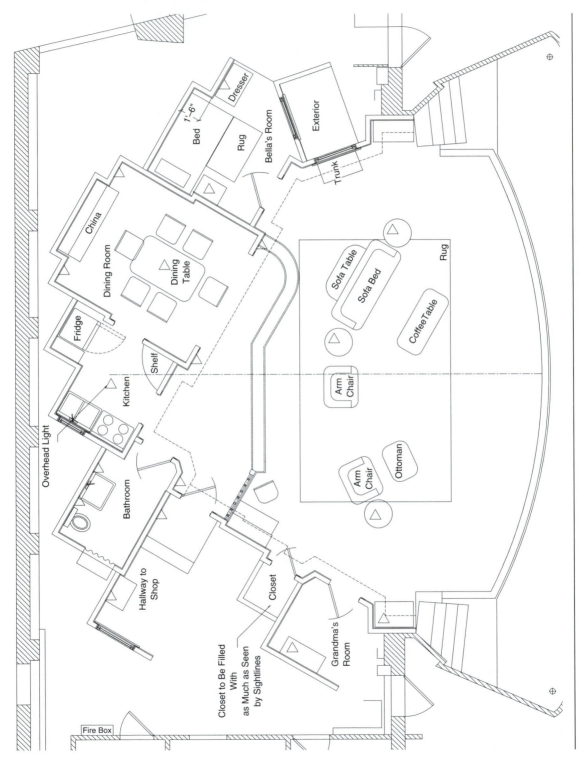

Figure 9.12a A scale floor plan for *Lost in Yonkers*. This plan shows an opulent home interior.

Fire Box

Overhead Light

Closet to Be Filled With as Much as Seen by Sightlines

Hallway to Shop

Bathroom

Kitchen

Fridge

Shelf

China

Dining Room

Dining Table

Bed

Rug

Dresser

1'–6"

Bella's Room

Closet

Grandma's Room

Exterior

Trunk

Sofa Table

Sofa Bed

Arm Chair

Coffee Table

Arm Chair

Ottoman

Rug

Figure 9.12b   The set for *Lost in Yonkers,* showing an opulent home interior.

SOURCE: Reprinted with permission of Paul Wonsek.

possible to determine whether the desired layout is feasible. Floor plans should also include the location of the studio doors, walls, lighting grid, and any other elements worth knowing about (location of the lighting board, electrical outlets, control room entrance, clearance from flats to walls, and so forth).

The conventional scale of floor plans is ¼ inch = 1 foot. However, as long as you clearly label the floor plan, you can make it any scale you want. In metric units, floor plan scale is normally 1 cm = 1 meter.

The floor plan is an invaluable tool for crew members whose job it is to set up scenery and props. It also helps in setting lights. The director uses it to block talent and to confirm that cameras and other equipment can gain unimpeded access where needed. The audio operator uses it to plan microphone connections, locations, and cable needs.

The floor plan diagram may be drawn with the lighting grid imposed on it, or you may prefer to use an acetate overlay (a transparent sheet) that permits you to see the floor plan with or without the lighting grid. After the lighting design and floor plan are finalized, copies can be distributed to the director and crew for setup and rehearsal.

Of course, to make the floor plan successful, it is essential to have accurate scale representations of all set pieces, as well as the major production items that will occupy space in the studio, including cameras and booms. This will require measuring every item or consulting an inventory list already on file. The list can then be used to draw items on the floor plan. For even cleaner results, you can create a stencil of each item and use that for drawing on the floor plan. An even better option is to use one of the CAD (computer-aided design) programs now available for such work.

Models. Miniature *models* of sets enable you to see and show others how a new set will look on the air before it is built. You can paint and repaint the model to modify the color scheme. Texture, fabrics, and other aesthetic factors can also be tried and approved or scrapped at this stage. Even camera angles and relationships among set elements can be envisioned. Again, there are CAD programs for architects and theater designers that can serve this process well.

If you do build a physical model, use balsa wood, construction paper, cardboard, and doll house furniture to create the model (see Photo 9.13). All of this can be done with a minimum investment of time and money. Of course, if preproduction is hurried, there may be little time to spend in the sketch and model phase. In such cases, it is a judgment call to decide how the preproduction time should best be spent. Picture the cost-benefit ratio of working with and without sketches and models. CAD designs may be sufficient. Imagine how the budget will be spent if errors are made with full-size sets, and weigh that against the costs of time spent constructing models.

Photo 9.13   A model of the set used for a production of *Urinetown.*

Sets and the Videospace

As with all other aspects of video production, it is relatively unimportant what the set looks like through direct observation—the key is how it looks on screen. Direct imitation of reality is often just a starting point. For set design, this means you will probably adjust your initial layout after seeing how your master shots and close-ups look on the line monitor as you block talent and cameras through the set.

Here are some common differences between the normal arrangements of daily life and those of video sets:

1. In real life, walls frequently meet at right angles, but video sets frequently feature walls meeting at much larger angles (such as 135 degrees) to allow easy camera access.

2. In real life, furniture is inches from walls, but in video, the furniture and talent positions could be as much as 6 feet or more from any walls or flats. This distance helps keep talent shadows from falling on the set. Also, it keeps set lights separate from performance area lights—an important consideration because sets tend to be more reflective than talent and because you generally want the talent lit with higher intensities than sets.

3. In real life, interior locales are bounded on all sides by walls, but in video, you can achieve realism even if you are shooting into an *open set*—that is, a set defined by a number of major set pieces but without a continuous background of walls or flats. Open sets allow you to position cameras to shoot from many different angles; talent are less restricted than in closed sets, lighting is easier, and the set itself is often simpler, making setup and strike less work. One disadvantage of open sets, however, is that there may be fewer shots available featuring set pieces in the background, and this can reduce visual interest.

4. In real life, furniture and wall decorations are often placed where they are likely to promote the most utility, but in video, they may be positioned to maximize a key shot. For example, it might be foolish to hang a painting at the talent's true eye-height if, by doing so, it is lost from the frame of a key shot. Similarly, while the space between a dresser and a bed might be several feet in the real world, on television, it might be better to push them closer together to avoid dead space when the talent reaches from the bed to get something.

5. In real life, the eye can adjust for great differences in brightness between people and the backgrounds in which they are seen, but in video, if brightness values on backgrounds exceed those on talent by more than several magnitudes, the iris of the camera lens can close down so far that the talent's face will look too dark. In general, brightness differences between talent and backgrounds should not exceed three or four gray-scale steps.

Production and Postproduction

After being designed and approved, sets are erected for rehearsal and production. Test the set during rehearsal. Block talent through each shot sequence and make final adjustments by watching the rehearsal on the line monitor. At this stage, all aspects of the set's contribution to the program should be assessed, including color, layout, and ease of access by crew and talent. Dead spots can be eliminated by moving talent and set pieces closer together. Glare can be reduced by changing the lighting, turning the offending surface slightly away from the camera, or treating it with dulling spray. In some cases, rubbing the surface with a bar of soap can eliminate the problem.

If the set must be struck for another production and then reset the following day, mark the position of each set piece with masking tape, if possible. You might also record video or still photos of the set to help in its reconstruction. After the production is completed, label all set pieces and props before storing them so they can be retrieved easily if needed.

ELECTRONIC AND MECHANICAL EFFECTS IN SET DESIGN

Electronic Effects

Electronic overlay technology has made it possible to create electronic "sets" or set elements that can be combined with live studio action on a prepared background. One of the most common methods is a technology that has been used for many years: **chroma key.**

Chroma key[2] technology exploits the fact that the camera's color signal can be used to select where part of a picture may be replaced with an external video source. That is, if the camera picture shows a green background, and nothing else in the picture is green, an external video source can be electronically substituted for the green portion each time the camera scans in green. For example, if a talent is shot standing in front of a green screen, and a second camera shoots a forest scene featuring a cascading waterfall and a river bed with trees and rocks, the forest scene can be substituted for the green background, making it appear as if the talent is standing in the forest. The same technique is used to show a weather map behind a TV weatherperson. Each time the electron gun in the camera scans a green signal, that portion of the picture is replaced by the external video source.

The reason green happens to be one of the popular industry standards for chroma key effects is that green is generally not present in flesh tones, making it easier for the technology to switch between video signals when talent is on camera. Other colors can also be used.

With chroma key, a virtually infinite variety of backgrounds can be made to appear as electronic overlays. In recent years, moreover, computer graphics technologies have made it possible to layer many more images more intricately into video signals. While this topic is dealt with in greater detail in the next chapter, we should note here that multilayered digital images can now be combined with other video signals, making the final product quite complex. Some music videos are produced as virtual cybersets that never existed in physical space.

Mechanical Effects

Though multilayered electronic key effects are increasingly used to provide sets for video, we should not overlook the numerous mechanical means for embellishing sets. Table 9.1 lists a number of such effects and how they are created. A thorough treatment of mechanical special effects in video, including pyrotechnics and breakaway furniture, is available in Wilkie (1979).

Table 9.1   Some Common Mechanical Effects in Video Production

Effect	*Method*	*Notes and Cautions*
Fire and smoke	To convey a working fireplace, industrial setting, or cooking stove, use a few drops of oil on a burning charcoal tablet.	Use extreme caution. Have a fire extinguisher on site. Protect surfaces with metal trays.
Flickering flame	Cut slits in a black strip of paper. Rotate the paper in front of a studio light aimed at a fireplace plug. Inside the fireplace, hide a flashlight for additional illumination. Hide short pieces of colored silk in the fireplace and blow them up from below with a small fan.	
Fog	(a) Rent a smoke machine to simulate fog in the studio. Use patchy lighting and mild air movement.	Option (a) can cause breathing problems for the crew and talent.
	(b) Use fog filters or a stretched nylon stocking over the camera lens. Or, for static shots, place a white card a foot in front of the lens. Cut a circular hole in the card, just large enough to leave a slight border around the shot. Then light the card from behind the camera to cause it to flare slightly.	
	(c) Tape a sheet of glass or plastic wrap, smeared with petroleum jelly, over the lens.	
Lightning	Discharge flash units from behind the set. For a more convincing illusion, add thunder sound effects.	
Mist	Drop pieces of dry ice in hot water. This will create heavy white clouds that hug the floor and hide it from view. Keeping the area cool and damp makes the effect last longer. Dry ice machines are also available.	The mist is composed mostly of water. Dry ice should be handled with gloves.
Rain	(a) You can use real water to simulate rain trickling on a window. Use a trough to catch the water.	Supply and cleanup of real water in the studio can be

(Continued)

Table 9.1 (Continued)

	(b) A more convenient variation is to use a rain drum, a cylinder about a foot in diameter covered in black paper with white "raindrops" painted on it. While someone turns the drum, shoot footage of it slightly out of focus. Then superimpose this footage over the scene.	more trouble than the effect is worth. It can also be dangerous because of the electrical equipment. Consider shooting rain footage elsewhere against a black background and superimposing it electronically.
Snow	(a) Buy plastic granular material or paper confetti at a theatrical supply house. Have crew members throw it up so that it falls down in front of the camera. Augment its motion with a wind machine.	Remember to light the area through which your "snow" is falling so that it can be seen on camera.
	(b) As another option, cut a canvas cloth with slits and have crew members hold it above the scene. Place the plastic grains or confetti on the canvas and shake it back and forth to make the "snow" fall through.	
	(c) For snow on the ground, use fine sawdust from white soft woods. For extra whiteness, sprinkle it with talcum powder, plaster, or flour. Add some glitter for sparkle.	Be careful that an accumulation on the floor doesn't impede the camera wheels. If you use flour in badly ventilated areas, you may cause a dust explosion.
Steam	Cold-water humidifiers create water vapor that looks like a forceful flow of steam. For a gentle flow, dry ice can be used.	
Wind	Wind machines are fans made to operate quietly. They come in various sizes and operate at different speeds. For a light breeze, small conventional fans can be used, and aiming the fan at the talent's hair can provide just the accent you need.	With conventional fans, watch mic placement to avoid noise problems.

Choosing Between Electronic and Mechanical Effects

The choice of electronic or mechanical effects to create or modify sets should be based on the same considerations involved in all production issues: the ability to meet production goals, feasibility, and cost. For example, it might be easy to create blur and fog effects or simulate snowfall with computer equipment. In other situations, though, computer effects could be expensive, could take a long time to create, and might even be disappointing in their final results. Base your choice on a cost-benefit analysis—whether you are getting what you want for a price you can afford—not simply on a desire to use the hottest tools.

In some cases, old-fashioned mechanical effects may be the best resource. On the other hand, computer effects can sometimes be easier and cheaper than their mechanical alternatives. Kevin Costner might have saved a lot of money making the film *Waterworld* if he had used state-of-the-art overlay and matte techniques to simulate underwater environments rather than building expensive life-size sets on location in the ocean, where some sank during production. In short, no one route is best all the time.

INDUSTRY VOICES

Jay Dorfman

On June 26, 2005, I interviewed Jay Dorfman, principal at Medialand Productions, an independent video production company based in New York City. Jay's production career began in the late '70s working as a copywriter for local radio in Poughkeepsie, New York. In 1980, he was hired as a creative director/producer/writer for MTV right before they launched their broadcast network. Jay's expertise in all phases of independent video production developed over a quarter century working for major media outlets and other large corporations.

L: *You've been an independent video producer for over 25 years. Who are some of your current clients?*

J: *In the last year or so I've worked with AOL, the new Napster, MCI WorldCom, Condé Nast, Filipacchi, Time Inc. Most are contemplating the migration of their media content from analogue to digital broadcast. In general, I deal with companies that own content, as in publishing companies like Condé Nast, who want to move their brands, media, and content into TV and digital media, and companies that own distribution channels, like AOL, MTV, and Napster, and want to acquire or develop original content for new media platforms. Condé Nast just hired a senior VP of broadcast development to move such brands as Lucky, Allure, Cargo, Wired, and Epicurean from publishing into emerging technologies like voice on demand, digital wireless broadcast, and on-line media.*

L: *Would it be a colossal understatement to say that much has changed since you started?*

J: *Yeah. It's quite different. Some currently big companies didn't even exist when I started. AOL and Napster are brand-new digital companies, and they had no business model. Among the ones that did exist, many are adjusting to completely new paradigms, taking what they currently own and adapting it to audiences seeking content away from the traditional broadcast media.*

L: *How has your job changed in 25 years? What did you use to do that you don't do anymore, and what do you do now that you never did?*

J: The major shift has been in the tools for creating images and content—the production tools. When we started in the late '70s, we were using analog tools, including linear editing equipment like ¾-inch U-matic tape, which was the standard. In that format, editing meant you had to dub selected segments of tape from a master reel onto a new tape, and if anything was in need of change after that, you frequently had to redo all the editing, which obviously could be very labor intensive and time-consuming. Then, around the mid-eighties, Avid introduced digital video editing, and became the standard. That greatly changed the way small production companies created content. Suddenly the tools needed to bring a project from start to finish were within your own studio walls, and the whole process sped up significantly. You no longer had to hire a studio to finish things, which had been very expensive. Gone was the need to spend lots of money to rent expensive production time. Scheduling was no longer an issue as it once was. Now you could turn out a far superior product on your own time, and in your own studio. And with nonlinear editing, you could explore the television medium relatively endlessly. You could plug in more variables while editing, and could make a great number of versions of a program quickly. Now, cut to 10 years after that, when Apple's editing software Final Cut Pro (FCP) came along. FCP was the next huge shift because it made the whole process much more affordable and therefore more accessible. FCP made an incredible difference in the economic model for production companies and indie filmmakers because it sold for a thousand dollars. You could buy a Mac with enough memory and hard drive so you could effectively have an up-and-running production house for between ten and fifteen thousand dollars. Before FCP, that was not possible for less than sixty to a hundred thousand dollars. Soon after that, high-quality prosumer digital cameras became available for several thousand dollars, and that put great imaging ability in the hands of producers for lower cost than ever. Comparable-quality cameras just a decade earlier were in the fifty-thousand dollar-plus range, and that often meant you had to hire a director of photography. Now you can own the camera for, say, five grand, and you can own the editorial capability and engage in virtually endless experimentation. As a result, a lot of new techniques could be explored. Accessibility brought many new untrained users into the process. They were inventing new looks and feels that were not around before. Grassroots producing at times led to new styles—a lot of the early MTV stuff with impulsive quick cutting and handheld guerilla-looking content resulted from people without formal training getting into the act. So you could see a strong connection between tools and content development when prices came down, and portability, memory, and hard drive space for editing went up. On the content and distribution side, the MTVs and cable networks opened the door for younger producers in boutique studios who could offer a constant flow of fresh ideas. Of course, all this development also brought with it a lot of questionable material too, from every Joe Blow who didn't have a clue.

L: How has your marketing plan changed as a result of such developments?

J: First, there are now a lot more people in the business. So companies that once came to you for work were now looking at cheaper alternatives and new strategies for accomplishing their goals. In short, the production business became more competitive. Second, many of the large production houses have gone under, including National Video, a huge studio in Times Square for over 20 years. Post Perfect is another one that went under. They became dinosaurs overnight, relying on traditional business models. In this new mix, one way to stay in business is to do more than just service work. You used to get calls to produce an on-air branding campaign, a marketing tape, or an up-front presentation, and that work still exists, but because there are a lot more people serving those clients, it has become more important to pay attention to who the main players are in the changes that have occurred. So when AOL, Napster, and MTV launched new broadband networks, they created a whole new distribution flow aiming to serve audiences who may not be watching television as much. So, for a company like Condé Nast which is looking to migrate to new places, I can bring them in to talk to AOL with concepts and content unique to the Internet and on-line sites. That's a new function I can serve in the new digital space. For example, AOL is doing a series of reality TV shows, produced as 3- to 5-minute streams each week for on-line users. In addition to developing TV content to be displayed on computer screens via the Internet, other devices are also serving as viewing platforms, including more substantial plasma screens with clearer video, as well as smaller portable devices like video i-Pods. There's also video on demand, wireless video, and PDAs, and programs featuring unique content are being customized to all these new platforms. To adapt programs to all these new platforms, as a producer, there are unique technical and economic constraints to recognize in addition to unique audience characteristics. For example, right now, when producing programs for the Internet or wireless, because it's in an early experimental stage, production budgets are lower than they are for programs for high-definition television or traditional broadcast. So as a producer, you have to work cheaper, and the emphasis on image quality is more relaxed. In addition, with smaller cameras and less resolution, there may be different aesthetics regarding how much camera movement is acceptable. If you're shooting a music concert with two cameras for AOL sessions, you may want to use less quick cutting and panning because it doesn't play that well on the Internet when you download and stream. You tend to shoot with a different style when producing content for different platforms.

L: Is color also an issue?

J: Sometimes if color ends up being squeezed down to a cell phone screen, less color may transfer, but I haven't seen much on that issue. Most of the production concern deals with movement of the image, the panning and cutting for streaming video on the Net.

L: With all the channels and choices increasing, what does that do to audience interest for programs?

J: I think the MTVs of the world are astutely aware that a large portion of the viewing time of their target audiences is spent on-line rather than on broadcast channels. So generating on-line content becomes paramount. You have to generate more content than ever before, and it usually takes the form of additional background material, somewhat along the lines of the behind-the-scenes segments included on DVDs. In terms of producing video content for the music business, this is a good time to recognize the need to find ways to revive audience interest in music. Because of the ease of piracy and file sharing, music has become commoditized, something we all expect to get for free. It is not viewed as precious and as valuable as it once was. It's easy to get, so producers, record labels, artists, and management are being forced to rethink the image and the content of what they produce, so they can once again create something viewed to be of value to their audience. We can compare the changes brought by the digital distribution of music to the commodity of electricity or other utilities like making water easily available to users through indoor plumbing. Before electricity flowed out of the walls of every American home, electricity was viewed as relatively precious. The way we lit our homes before electricity was with candles. When electricity became available, we began viewing candles no longer as a utility for lighting the home but as a romantic, nostalgic throwback. There are some similarities with the way we see recorded music today. Digital music now streams out of every Internet source, and i-Pods carry tens of thousands of songs. And it's possible to get it all for free through file sharing. The question now is, "How will record labels, artists, and management create an aura of interest around what people are able to get for free so that people will once again be willing and happy to pay for it?" In the past, we had record albums, liner notes, album art, and we viewed these elements as precious to examine. In the current climate, what will it take for today's music consumer to come to view some functional equivalents of these elements as valuable enough to buy? How do you take the streaming of music, which has become a commodity like tap water or electricity, and bring it back to the metaphor of the candle, where it can be viewed as being romantic and having intrinsic value, something users are happy to pay for? That's the challenge in the digital age.

L: Perhaps what the bottled water industry did in creating a market for water is a good object lesson for the music industry. It successfully competed against what was a free commodity—namely, tap water, available from every spigot in American homes—and marketed an alternative product to consumers who became willing to pay for it by exploiting the proposition that it would be cleaner and healthier than the thing it was intended to replace.

J: And consumers were willing to pay for it because it became branded and labeled, and that brought with it a sort of guaranteed quality. In the music business, there is a similar argument emerging that people who use file-sharing services are not getting guaranteed quality; that often the tracks aren't up to CD quality, are perhaps not authentic, or are not accurately credited to the correct artist. But with i-Tunes and other industry providers, the idea is that you know what you're buying—it's branded, so you get a sense that there's a company behind the product, introducing you to what's late-and-breaking, and that the company will go out of its way to create alternative tracks along with the better quality audio. It's their last-ditch attempt to save themselves by creating content not available through free file sharing.

L: When it comes to producing content for the new media platforms, especially on-line, and portable wireless displays, how have you managed to structure your business to adapt to the new markets?

J: Digital broadband is a new area for creating content, but it also presents a shift in the very concept of the audience. Audiences want more plentiful content, delivered with much greater immediacy. Content has a much shorter shelf-life. If you're pitching to companies with traditional business models, they can present strong obstacles to development, especially with respect to marketing, not just content and subject matter. We worked for Napster, the new legal Napster, within the model that went after subscribers who wanted downloaded music. I proposed to them that we could do the same thing with streaming video. So we spent the summer shooting behind-the-scenes music clips at several of the Warped Tours around the country. We shot video and streamed it to the Web. But once we shot it, we had to deal with Napster's legal department and then with the record labels, because there was suddenly content but no laws or agreements about how that content would be used. We had the technology, and the markets, but no policy guidelines to work with. The record labels had contracts with artists in terms of the music, but now that we had video streams, the questions became, "How would this be used by Napster? Who owned royalties?" The new content opened up a slew of questions regarding the legalities. It was a whole new world of policy issues.

L: What was decided?

J: Eventually it was agreed that the clips would be used as 1- to 2-minute bits and thus be considered more promotion than content. They were used to promote upcoming record releases. The point is that in entering a scenario where the rules are all brand new or nonexistent, you have to deal not only with issues of production techniques conducive to exhibiting on-line content but with legal ramifications of who owns the content, what its purpose is, who owns the licensing rights, and how the artists' best interests may or may not be served by the sale of such new materials. Steve Jobs and Napster had to hammer out agreements resulting from the way new technology changed traditional business models. So now, when someone creates new video content, is it perceived as clips to help promote the artist and sell more music, or do the clips themselves have intrinsic monetary value? The truth is, all the companies involved are still trying to find their way. Most of the traditional companies are still losing a great deal of money. i-Tunes has sold several million cuts, but that's actually small potatoes compared to the way unit sales were in the analog world.

L: What advice would you give to a young person who wants to break into the business?

J: In every aspect of production, the only things that remain essential are to develop good ideas and the ability to write, conceptualize, and come up with fresh approaches that take into consideration the nature of the audience, technology, and market forces for executing them. For people with those sorts of understandings, there are a lot of opportunities out there.

KEY TERMS

character generator	228	television gray scale	241
antialiasing	229	studio (camera) card	243
lower-third	229	properties (props)	245
electronic still store	230	cameo lighting	248
frame grabber	230	limbo lighting	248
flatbed scanner	231	riser	251
paintbox	231	flat	255
computer-aided design	232	jack (brace)	256
essential area	240	chroma key	264

QUESTIONS FOR REVIEW

Describe the types of visual material included in the term *graphics.*

Besides the character generator, what other digital graphics devices are available?

How do aspect ratio, essential area, color, contrast, and resolution issues influence the way graphics aref prepared for video?

Give some examples of ways in which graphics can influence the tone and style of the programs in which they appear.

What kinds of elements and treatments are available for use on the studio floor?

What are some standard backdrops and set pieces?

What factors should you consider in choosing props, set furniture, and dressings?

Describe the typical stages involved in designing a set.

What is the chroma key effect?

N O T E S

1. Each image produced for Pixar's latest hit, *Cars,* reportedly took 17 hours of computer time to render. At 24 or 30 images per second, it is easy to see why hundreds of computers are needed to get the job done for a 90-minute film.

2. The term *key* in this context should not be confused with a key light. In the current context, keying is an electronic effect that inserts an image or part of an image from one video source into another. Besides chroma key, there are also matte keying and insert keying; all of these are discussed in greater detail in the next chapter.

Chapter 10

VIDEO PROCESSING

As Chapter 9 made clear, you have a great (and growing) variety of sources for video images—not only the camera but also sources such as character generators, still store systems, digital effects generators, and full-blown digital editing systems. All these can help you create dazzling visual displays.

But how are the outputs from this rich variety of video sources made ready for use precisely when needed? For programs produced in real time, including both live broadcasts and programs taped live for later use, the device that routes, controls, and shapes video images during production is the **video switcher.** The switcher does with video images what the audio console does with sound. The crew member who operates the video switcher is called the *technical director* (TD).

Video switchers, in conjunction with digital servers and editing systems, may also be used for programs assembled in postproduction. Because such programs enjoy freedom from the instant time demands of live television, postproduction switchers may differ from production switchers, both in terms of how they are built (their internal architecture) and how they are configured with other video sources. Nevertheless, both production and postproduction switchers perform essentially the same functions: to provide special effects and smooth transitions among video sources used in a production and to output the finished product. In this way, the video switcher transforms a grab bag of video snippets into a cohesive program.

At first glance, the video switcher looks quite intimidating. Most have rows of buttons (called *buses*) accompanied by several levers or toggles. There may also be clusters of other buttons, switches, knobs, and even digital readouts. With all these items available to shape incoming video signals, it is little wonder the novice might get confused. However, understanding this piece of equipment (even high-end versions) is really not difficult.

This chapter explains how the TD operates the video switcher during live broadcasts, beginning with the most basic transitions and progressing to more exotic special effects. In addition, we discuss several peripheral devices needed for the proper functioning of the switcher. To illustrate how switchers work, we will "build" one from scratch. The switcher we construct will be just one among several common types. The goal here is to learn general principles, not to memorize specific buttons to push, since different switchers delegate functions in different ways. The switchers you encounter on the job may look very similar to the one described in this chapter, or they may look different, but in either case the basic principles of operation will be the same. The topics covered in this chapter include the following:

The video switcher

- Simple transitions: cuts or takes
- Mixing video signals
- From mixes to special effects
- Key effects
- Wipe effects

More complex effects and transitions

- Mix/effects banks
- Cascading: multiple M/E systems
- Computer-assisted switchers

Digital video effects generators

THE VIDEO SWITCHER

Simple Transitions: Cuts or Takes

The simplest transition between any two video sources—for instance, between two cameras or between a camera and a videotape—is the **cut** or **take.** A cut or take (synonyms in this context) is an instant transition from one source to another. The hardware used to accomplish a take is a *program button* on the switcher. If takes were the only change ever used, the switcher would need just one row of buttons, called a **program bus** (see Figure 10.1), on which each button represents a particular video source.

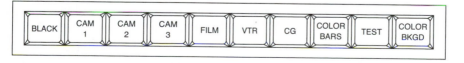

Figure 10.1   A program bus.

Let's examine how to use the program bus by *taking* the image seen by Camera 1 and using it for an instant replacement of *video black* on the **program** or **line monitor** (see Figure 10.2a), the monitor that shows the actual output that the audience will see. The director accomplishes a take by giving a ready cue and then a command to the TD as follows: "Ready one. Take one." Upon hearing the ready cue, the TD poises a finger on the button labeled CAM 1. Then, at the "take" command, the TD pushes the button. It's that simple. When the button is pushed, the scene being pictured by Camera 1 is instantly displayed on the line monitor, as in Figure 10.2b. Note that video black is an internal video source generated by the switcher itself.

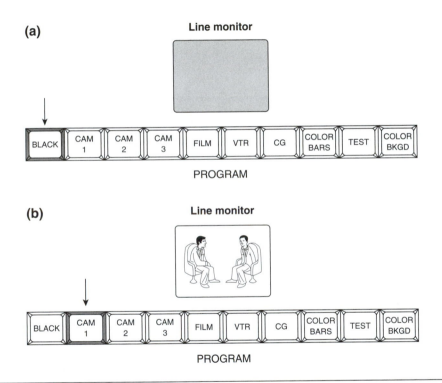

Figure 10.2 Using the program bus for a simple take. (a) The *black* button on the program bus is pushed, and the line monitor shows black. (b) When the CAM 1 button is pushed, the line monitor shows the scene being shot by Camera 1.

Usually, the buttons on the program bus are uniquely colored red (or some other bright color) to indicate that when they are pushed, they send video sources to your actual program. In short, these buttons are "hot," the "real deal," and when one of them is pressed, the source wired to it becomes part of your program.

Also notice that each button is labeled to indicate the video source it represents. For example, the first button on the left is labeled BLACK. The next button is labeled CAM 1. Then we see buttons marked CAM 2 and CAM 3. Additional sources include FILM, VTR for a videotape recorder, CG for a character generator, and COLOR BARS, TEST, and COLOR BKGD (color background) for additional internal signals generated by the switcher itself. Of course, the bus can be expanded to include even more sources, such as other cameras, satellite feeds, and digital video effects.

It is helpful for the TD and director to have the output of each video source displayed on a separate, labeled monitor in front of the switcher console (see Figure 10.3). Seeing a bank of source monitors enables the director to call the next shot simply by looking up and selecting a source. Until recently, the individual sources were displayed on smaller black-and-white monitors, while the program monitor was larger and in color. The latest technology update in control room displays is the installation of very large flat-panel computer monitors. This advance creates a video wall, where the individual video sources can be sized, shaded, and positioned to match the unique needs of a particular production or the whims of the production personnel.

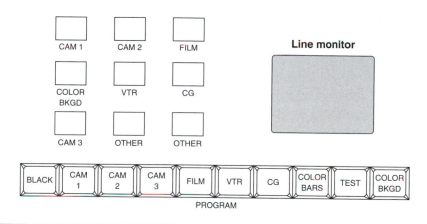

Figure 10.3   A bank of source monitors added to the program bus and the line monitor.

The bank of sources, however they are displayed, may be likened to an artist's palette, from which paints may be selected to use on a canvas. Just as the artist dabs a brush into various paints and transfers them to the canvas, the TD presses buttons on the video switcher and transfers images from source monitors to the line monitor. In this sense, source monitors are an electronic palette, the video switcher is an electronic brush, and the line monitor is the electronic canvas.

Synchronous and Nonsynchronous Sources. Actually, takes are not exactly instant because full frames of video are not available continuously—remember, they begin only every 30th of a second (or 60 times per second in one of the new Advanced Television System modes). While these are very short times in the context of a video presentation, the time issue is still a critical factor because video signals coming from different sources are not generally precisely in step (*synchronized*) with one another.

To put signals from different video sources in phase with one another, in-house sources may be fed through a synchronizer. This permits transitions among signals from purely electronic sources such as cameras, switchers, and CGs to be glitch free and stable. Some sources (e.g., analog videotape machines), which are less stable because of their mechanical components, generally use a machine called a **time base corrector** (TBC) to smooth out jitters, thereby creating an output as stable as purely electronic sources. For sources external to the studio facility, such as a satellite, microwave, or network feed, a **frame synchronizer** may be used to synchronize different sources. The frame synchronizer delays incoming video until it can be output in-phase with the in-house sources. The term *genlock* is used to refer to the ability of a device to synchronize various video signals to one another. Genlocking means adjusting various outputs so that their signals are synchronized.

When signals from various sources are fed to the video switcher, the actual moment of switching is delayed electronically so that it occurs only during the vertical interval of the scanning process. Hence, you will sometimes hear the term *vertical interval switching.* This additional function helps stabilize signals so they may be switched cleanly.

Mixing Video Signals

Fades. Instead of using instant cuts between sources, you may want to make a gradual change from one source to another. For instance, when you are starting a program, you may wish to go gradually from black to a nonblack visual. Such slow transitions to or from black are called **fades.** Instead of pushing a button, fades require the gradual moving of a *lever* or *toggle*. Also, as Figure 10.4 illustrates, we need a second bus, called a **preview** or **preset bus.** We also add a color preview monitor to display video sources punched up on the preview bus.

The preview or preset bus contains the same sources as the program bus in the same order. The main difference between them is that sources punched on the program bus are *always on air,* while sources punched on preview are *always off air.* A source displayed on preview is like the on-deck batter in a baseball game— ready to participate but not yet involved in the action.

Figure 10.4 shows what would happen in a fade from black to Camera 2. The process begins with *black on all lines*—that is, video black on both the program and preview buses. On hearing the cue "Ready fade two" from the director, the TD punches the button labeled CAM 2 on the preview bus, causing the image seen by

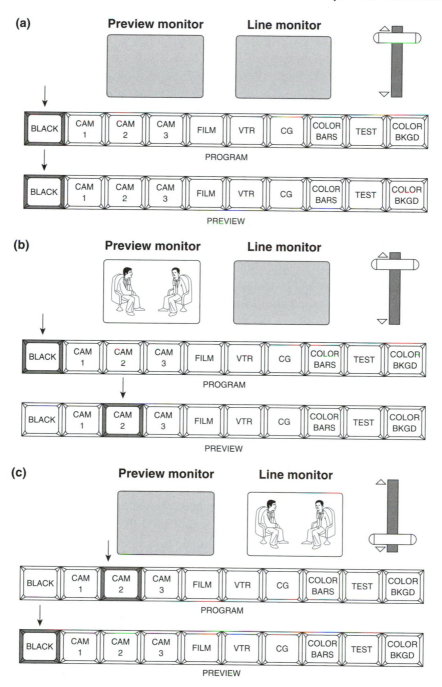

Figure 10.4 A simple fade using the program bus, preview monitor, and line monitor.
(a) Black on all lines. (b) When CAM 2 is punched on the preview bus, the image
from Camera 2 appears on the preview monitor. (c) As the lever is moved down,
the scene from Camera 2 gradually appears on the line monitor, and the preview
monitor fades to black.

Camera 2 to appear on the preview monitor. Then, on hearing the command "Fade two," the TD moves the lever through its entire range of motion. As the lever moves, the scene being pictured by Camera 2 gradually transfers to the line monitor, while video black gradually disappears. The speed of movement involves an aesthetic judgment, which may be worked out with the director during rehearsal.[1]

Most switchers are made so that when the toggle completes its full range of motion, the two sources manipulated (in this case, video black and the feed from Camera 2) switch places or *flip-flop*—that is, video black now flips to the preview bus and monitor, and the shot on Camera 2 goes to the line bus and monitor. This makes it easy to fade back to black simply by moving the toggle through its full range of motion once again with no additional setup.

One advantage of a separate preview monitor is that it enables the director, TD, and assistant or associate director (AD) to see and refine upcoming shots before they are put on air. Such refinements might include instructing the camera operator to frame or focus the shot better. Making final adjustments in a shot while it is still on preview is called **shot sweetening.**

Dissolves. The same mechanics are involved when making gradual transitions from nonblack sources to other nonblack sources, except we do not call such transitions fades. Instead, such changes are called **dissolves.** As an example of a dissolve, imagine that you have Camera 1, providing a close-up of a singer's face in the left two thirds of the screen, punched up on the program bus. Camera 2, punched up on the preview bus, shows a long shot of the singer's whole body in the right third of the screen. At the appropriate moment, you can move the toggle to make a slow dissolve from one source to the other, giving the viewer a nicely composed transition from the tight image of the singer's face to the long shot of the same subject. As the change is taking place, you can instruct the camera operator with the long shot to begin zooming in slowly on the subject while centering up. This could be done in tempo with the music to create a smooth fluid effect.

Superimpositions. Still another mix of images, called a **superimposition** (or *super*), can be made by leaving the toggle in the halfway position. That is, after the move of the toggle begins, do not go all the way through. Instead, leave it about half the distance through the entire range of motion. This will make the images from both sources remain on the line monitor at about one half the picture strength for each. In our singer example, a super would result in a close-up of the singer's face in the left two thirds of the screen and a complete body shot of the singer in the right third.

When using supers or slow dissolves to create video compositions and transitions on screen, you need a clear idea of what you want your cameras to do. Otherwise, you may end up with mixes that are cluttered or unbalanced. Or your supers and dissolves may lack visual interest because they feature essentially the same visual content from only slightly different angles. To get the most out of your video mixes, plan shots that use the screen space to its fullest potential. The camera work can be improved by having camera operators watch the line monitor in the studio while building shots and executing movements. Also, some camera viewfinders have an external feature that can carry the line-out signal so that the camera operators can see composite images in their viewfinders. In either case, rehearse camera moves to familiarize the crew with what you are trying to achieve.

From Mixes to Special Effects

Thus far, we have designed our video switcher to execute transitions and mixes among several video sources. However, the pictures we have described have not exceeded the signal strength of a single source. In other words, even when composite images from more than one source were used, the total combined signal strength of the signals we mixed on the line monitor never exceeded 100%.

In the early days of television, such mixes were the only means available for combining video sources, and some drawbacks were obvious. For instance, when supers were used to place titles and credits over program video, the composite images left a ghostly and transparent appearance for the lettering as well as for the talent and set shots. The lettering was sometimes difficult to read, and there was a dimming of the overall shot. By today's standards, that image quality is unacceptable.

To provide a more robust signal featuring full picture strength for different sources in a composite image, a **special effects generator** (SEG) has been added to the video switcher. The SEG enables the switcher to insert images electronically from one source over another while maintaining full signal strength for all remaining portions. Replacing part of one signal with part of another is called **keying.**

Figure 10.5 shows additions to our switcher to allow keying. Notice the groups of *effects* and *key control* buttons in a part of the SEG called the *effects keyer*. Figure 10.5 also shows a *key bus* above the program bus and an *effects transition control group* to the right of the program and preview buses. A digital timer, called the *auto transition rate,* has also been added at the top right of the switcher console to control the time it takes for selected transitions to occur. Of course, the locations of these new components may differ from one switcher to another.

Key Effects

With a setup such as the one in Figure 10.5, pushing KEY in the effects transition control group tells the SEG to activate the key mode. Then several different types of keying become possible.

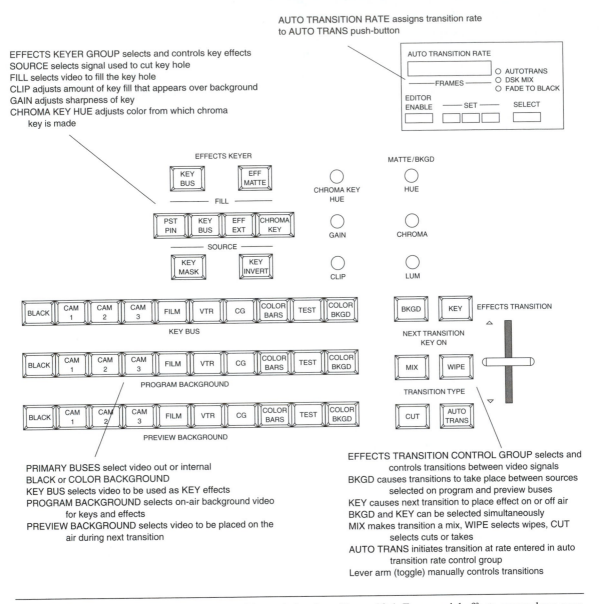

Figure 10.5   A further development of the video switcher from Figure 10.4. Four special effects groups have now been added.

Luminance or Insert Keying. In **luminance keying** (also called **insert keying**), background video is electronically replaced at full picture strength by a second video source. The area replaced by the insert is defined by brightness or luminance differences of the key source signal.

Luminance keying is frequently used to insert titles from a CG. Such sources usually feature white letters on a black field. When the SEG scans the image, it finds the bright portions (the letters) and uses them to replace the corresponding parts of the background.

As part of the effects keyer, Figure 10.5 shows two buttons for controlling the key level. The **clip** button determines what level of source video brightness is used to cut the key image onto the background. If lettering looks too thin and wavering or overly thick and bleeding around the edges, the clip level may be adjusted. The **gain** button, on the other hand, controls how transparent or solid the key image is. When using key effects, it is wise to readjust the clip and gain controls as lighting conditions change. Some switchers are equipped with a memory to make such adjustments automatically.

Let's set up a luminance key of a lower-third ID from the character generator over a bust shot of an interview guest on Camera 1. Imagine that Camera 1's bust shot is already on the line (the button for Camera 1, marked CAM 1, is punched up on the program bus). To prepare the key, we punch the source to be keyed (in this case, the CG text) on the key bus above the program bus and the source it is to be keyed over (in this case, Camera 1) on the program bus (delegated to backgrounds). We also press KEY BUS on the effects keyer and BKGD on the effects transition control group.

The TD now waits for a ready cue and a command from the director. On hearing the cue "Ready key CG over one," the TD poises a finger on the CUT button from the effects transition control group. Then, on hearing the command "Key CG over one," the TD presses the CUT button. This takes the camera shot of talent, now with the lower-third keyed over it, on the air (see Figure 10.6).

Of course, before taking the insert to air, it is wise to preview it in order to decide whether it is air quality. Previewing allows you to sweeten the insert by adjusting clip and gain control. Once a key is on preview, you also have the option of gradually

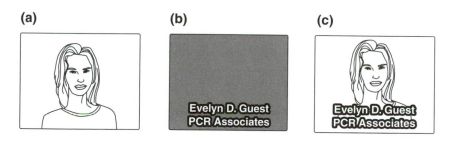

Figure 10.6　Luminance (insert) keying of a lower-third ID. (a) The talent's bust shot on the line monitor. (b) The lower-third ID prepared on the source (CG) monitor. (c) The key executed, combining the two images.

inserting the key with the toggle instead of "popping" it on air instantly. To add the effect gradually, you would select the MIX button in the effects transition control group instead of the CUT button. Then use the toggle to add the key. As an alternative to the toggle, the AUTO TRANS button would allow you to execute gradual transitions with the push of a button. In such cases, the duration of the transition is controlled by the auto transition rate, displayed in frames per second (see the top right part of Figure 10.5).

The specific procedure we have just followed for setting up a luminance key is not identical across all brands or models of switchers, but the general process is the same. Most switchers also allow you to add shot variety and visual interest by *undercutting* or *overcutting* inserts. Undercutting is done by cutting among various sources on the program bus, delegated to backgrounds, while keeping the same key source (in our example, the CG) on the air. Conversely, overcutting is done by cutting among various sources on the key bus, delegated to key sources, while keeping the same background image on the air. For example, while credits are rolling from a CG at the end of a show, an undercut might be used to cut from a shot of the host and guest chatting on one camera to a close-up of the guest reacting on another camera. Similarly, just before fading to black as the show ends, an overcut might replace the keyed credits with an image of the show's title.

Most switchers feature some other luminance or insert keying options as well. For example, a KEY INVERT button (shown in Figure 10.5) reverses the luminance values of the key source, so that dark areas become the portion of the source keyed rather than the light portions. To become familiar with the options available on any switcher you may use, it is helpful to experiment with the key source, background, and fill. To learn fast, practice and study the manual that comes with the switcher, but above all, practice. Finally, keep in mind that some options on the switcher you are using may not be installed exactly as described in the manual. If your switcher at times seems to have a mind of its own, you may need to talk with the engineering department.

Chroma Key Effects. As mentioned in Chapter 9, chroma key effects replace a camera signal of a preselected hue with a signal from an external source. For example, if a weatherperson stands in front of a green background, the appropriate weather graphics feed can be electronically inserted behind the talent in place of it (see Photo 10.1).

Setting up a chroma key effect takes several steps. Usually, the source to be substituted (most often a background scene) must be punched up on either the preview or program bus, and the source carried by the chroma key camera must also be selected. On our switcher shown in Figure 10.5, we would select the BKGD and KEY buttons from the effects transition control group. Next, we would select CHROMA KEY as the key source and KEY BUS as the fill on the effects keyer. Most switchers also allow you to adjust the chroma key hue, gain, and clip controls in order to clean up the effect before it goes to air.

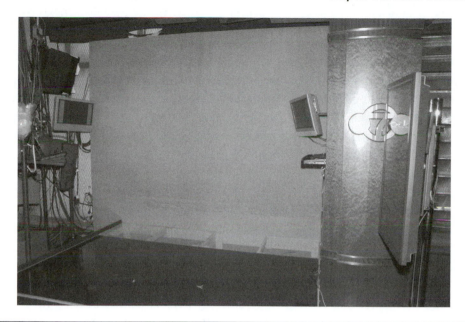

Photo 10.1   On this news set, the blank screen is the chroma key screen. On the air, the blank space can be filled with any appropriate graphics feed. This type of screen is typically used by weatherpersons, among others.

To take the effect to air, you would use the same procedure as for luminance keying. Of course, you could dissolve or fade the chroma key picture by either punching the MIX button on the effects transition control group and then using the toggle or by using the AUTO TRANS button.

Ensuring Good Chroma Key Effects

➤ Consider carefully the wardrobe of the talent. Avoid using clothing with colors that might confuse the signal. For instance, if the chroma key color you have selected is blue, the talent should not wear blue.

➤ Keep the lighting on the chroma key background relatively bright and uniform. Keep shadows off it if possible.

➤ Keep the talent an appropriate distance from the background. In addition to the problem of shadows, if talent stands too close to the background, light reflected from the backdrop can cast the chroma key color onto the back of the talent's head. This might confuse the signal and cause tearing, a wavering of the signal between sources.

➤ As another way to offset tearing, backlight the talent with pale yellow or amber gels. These tend to create better color separation, especially in the case of dark-haired talent.

Digital innovations in chroma key technology have improved the appearance of the chroma key signal. One such innovation is a *shadow key,* which senses shadow detail in a foreground object and casts it into the background portion of the overall picture. Another innovation involves the change from a *hard key,* where objects appear with a hard edge against the chroma key background, to a *soft key,* where foreground objects appear to have a softer, more natural outline in the overall picture. Soft chroma key eliminates the impression that foreground objects have been pasted onto the background. The softer appearance is made possible by a digital gain control that permits the scanning signal to be sampled in proportion to the color and luminance values presented. This move to digital sampling also permits more realistic rendering of translucent and transparent objects, such as glass, water, and smoke, making them look more fully integrated into the overall picture.

Matte Keying. Color can be added to key sources by using a *matte key* feature. Whereas in a luminance key, the area of screen space cut by the key source is filled with the key source's own content, a matte key adds an extra effect by filling the space with a selected color. Matte colors are often used to fill characters from a CG.

Internal Versus External Keying. When a portion of a background is cut out and replaced by video defining the key area, we call that type of key insert a *normal, self,* or *internal* key. However, it is possible to have a key source define an area to be keyed over but then provide a third source to fill in the space. Such a key insert is called an *external* key. To create external keys, the switcher needs an external key button, shown in Figure 10.5 with the label EFF EXT.

For external keys, three signals must be selected: first, a background scene into which the key effect is to be inserted; second, a key source that cuts a hole into the background (called the **keyhole**); and third, a *fill video signal* to fill in the keyhole. Matte color signals may be considered a form of external keying since the color signal comes from a source other than that used to provide the shape of the key that is inserted. However, more elaborate external keys may be provided by cameras or video sources designated as the external source. For example, if the switcher is set up to accept a videotape source as an external key, footage of a fire can be used to fill lettering keyed from a CG over a background shot, creating the effect that the lettering itself is made of fire (see Figure 10.7).

Downstream Key. Most switchers include a special keying function called a **downstream key,** often abbreviated *DSK* (see Figure 10.8). Downstream keying enables you to insert titles and other text immediately before the composed signal leaves the switcher. The advantage of the downstream keyer is that it permits a final manipulation of the video signal—for instance, adding a title, lower-third, or

(a)   **(b)**

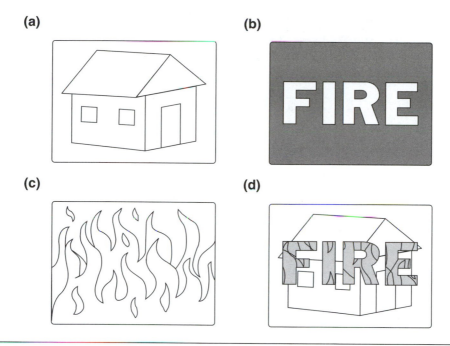

(c)   **(d)**

Figure 10.7   External keying. (a) A background shot of a house. (b) The *keyhole*—in this case, the word *FIRE* prepared on a character generator. (c) Videotape of an actual fire. (d) The key executed. Now the letters, filled with flames, are keyed over the house.

closing credits—without occupying a bus. This frees a bus to serve other functions, thus adding greater flexibility to the switcher. In news and sports productions, DSK is used for lower-thirds, where text must be inserted over pictures already composed from several sources. *Border, outline,* and *drop shadow* buttons enable DSK lettering to be edged with selected outlines to better distinguish it from its background. Figure 10.8 also shows a DSK MATTE button that allows you to matte-color DSK text. Switchers with DSK are often equipped with a master fader (labeled FADE TO BLACK in the figure) to lose the DSK graphic along with the entire video signal when, for example, the program ends.

Wipe Effects

A **wipe** is a transition between sources in which one image seems to move across another and "wipe" it off the screen. The effects transition control group usually features a WIPE button, which, when activated, permits you to create such transitions. In a *background wipe,* for example, one image appears to obliterate the image beneath it. Wipes can be made in a variety of patterns, including circles, diamonds, stripes, rectangles, and squares. Figure 10.8 shows two *pattern control*

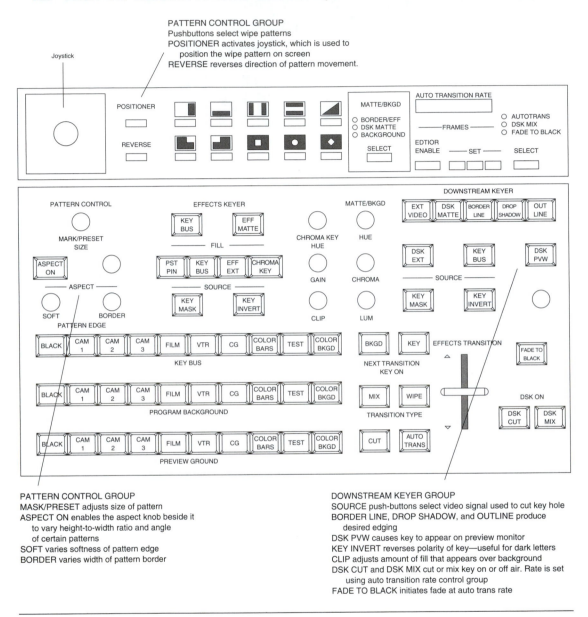

PATTERN CONTROL GROUP
Pushbuttons select wipe patterns
POSITIONER activates joystick, which is used to
    position the wipe pattern on screen
REVERSE reverses direction of pattern movement.

PATTERN CONTROL GROUP
MASK/PRESET adjusts size of pattern
ASPECT ON enables the aspect knob beside it
    to vary height-to-width ratio and angle
    of certain patterns
SOFT varies softness of pattern edge
BORDER varies width of pattern border

DOWNSTREAM KEYER GROUP
SOURCE push-buttons select video signal used to cut key hole
BORDER LINE, DROP SHADOW, and OUTLINE produce
    desired edging
DSK PVW causes key to appear on preview monitor
KEY INVERT reverses polarity of key—useful for dark letters
CLIP adjusts amount of fill that appears over background
DSK CUT and DSK MIX cut or mix key on or off air. Rate is set
    using auto transition rate control group
FADE TO BLACK initiates fade at auto trans rate

Figure 10.8   The video switcher from earlier figures, with the addition of a downstream keyer group and two pattern control groups. The downstream keyer selects and controls downstream key effects. The pattern control groups select and adjust wipe patterns.

groups of buttons, an upper one that indicates the available patterns and a lower one for additional shaping and control of the selected patterns.

Wipes may be used to indicate a change of time or place. Wipe transitions were used frequently in the 1970s hit series *Happy Days* and in Tim Allen's 1990s hit series *Home Improvement* to signal scene changes. In *Happy Days,* intricate comic checkerboard wipes were often used to punch up the transitions from Arnold's malt shop to Fonzie's place to the Cunningham residence. By the 1990s, the *Home Improvement* production designers were able to create much more intricate and clever wipes.

Using the toggle, a horizontal wipe can be stopped halfway to set up a split screen between two sources. Figure 10.9 shows two common uses of the split screen: (a) to carry a phone conversation between two talents portrayed as being in two different places and (b) to set up a corner wipe of a talent using sign language during a televised speech. The same corner wipe may be used to carry news graphics behind newscasters.

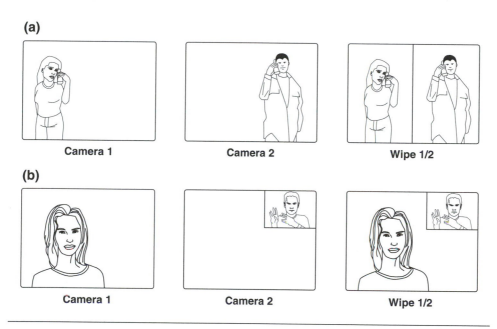

(a)

| Camera 1 | Camera 2 | Wipe 1/2 |

(b)

| Camera 1 | Camera 2 | Wipe 1/2 |

Figure 10.9 Typical uses of a wipe effect with a split screen. (a) Two people speaking to each other on the phone, shown first in separate shots and then together on a split screen. (b) A speaker captured with Camera 1 while Camera 2 provides a shot of the sign language interpreter; a corner wipe then puts the two together on screen.

Several features of the wipe pattern may be adjusted. For example, the BORDER knob shown in Figure 10.8 would permit you to add a border and adjust its width around the wipe pattern. The edge of the border could be made soft or hard with the SOFT control. In the MATTE/BKGD control group, the HUE, CHROMA, and LUM controls would allow you to adjust the color, intensity, and brightness of the border. Using the lower pattern control group, you could adjust the height-to-width ratio of selected patterns, such as rectangles and diamonds, by selecting the ASPECT ON button and then adjusting the ASPECT control knob. The white areas on the pattern symbols of the console indicate where the wipe will overcut the screen image. However, selecting REVERSE from the upper pattern control group would reverse this, so that the black areas on the pattern symbols would indicate where the overcut would be. Selecting REVERSE would also change the direction of the wipe. Finally, selecting the POSITIONER button in the upper pattern control group would activate the *joystick,* permitting you to move the pattern anywhere on the screen.

Most switchers provide these options for controlling and shaping the wipe patterns that you select, though the knobs and buttons may not be located in exactly the same places as shown in our sample switcher. Actually, the switcher we have "built" in this chapter is based on the GVG 100, one of the most popular compact models, manufactured by the Grass Valley Group in Grass Valley, California. See the box "Additional Switcher Options" for a list of some other features available on the GVG 100 and on a number of other switchers.

Additional Switcher Options

Besides the effects described in the text, many switchers offer the following features:

- *Spotlight.* A highlight effect produced by supering full-strength video shaped by a wipe pattern over an attenuated signal from the same source.

- *Key mask.* A key function that enables you to use a wipe pattern to prevent undesirable parts of a key source from cutting a shape into the background video.

- *Editor.* A control system (often computerized) that permits you to control videotape machines, the switcher, and other devices from a single control panel. Editors make it easier to produce ready-to-air programs from numerous sources.

MORE COMPLEX EFFECTS AND TRANSITIONS

In the switcher we have been describing, the program, preview, and key buses, plus a single toggle, are adequate to handle changes between one video source and another, including takes, fades, dissolves, and supers, as well as limited transitions between sources involving special effects compositions. But what happens if we want to take or dissolve from a super directly to another preset super or between wipes featuring multiple sources? The above system, though quite impressive, is simply not enough for such transitions. Let's look, then, at features needed for more complex effects.

Mix/Effects Banks

To handle more complex transitions involving multiple sources, more advanced switchers add a set of buses above the program bus called a **mix/effects bank** (M/E bank), with its own toggle. Figure 10.10 presents a simplified diagram of such an arrangement.

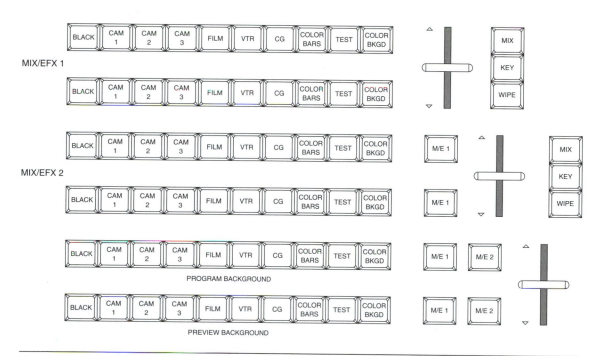

Figure 10.10 Diagram of two mix/effects banks above the program and preview buses on the video switcher.

Generally, mix/effects levers differ from program/preview levers in that direction matters. That is, on M/E banks, if the lever is in the "up" position, it routes the video source punched on the top mix bus, whereas if it is in the "down" position, it routes the signal punched on the bottom. In short, there is no flip-flop capability to the mix/effects lever.[2] Therefore, we must differentiate the two mix buses, calling them, for example, M/E 1 and M/E 2.

Notice that the buses in the M/E bank repeat the same set of video sources, in the same order, as they appear in the program and preview buses. However, Figure 10.10 adds M/E buttons beside the program and preview buses so that you can feed whatever signals you mix or compose on the mix/effects bank to either the program or preview bus or both. We call the mix/effects buttons *delegation buttons* because they route video sources from one part of the switcher to another *but do not carry unique video sources of their own.*

Using the mix/effects bank, you can set up a super, for example, along with other effects such as wipes. By punching appropriate buttons on the preview bus, you can sweeten these effects with the mix/effects toggle. (When the mix/effects toggle moves through roughly half its range of motion, both buses on the M/E bank are routed at about 50% picture strength to the preview bus.) When you like what you see and you want to cut to the super you have created, you can simply press the M/E button on the program bus.

Cascading: Multiple M/E Systems

In high-end switchers, there may be two or even three M/E banks. In such models, additional mix/effects delegation buttons are added to the end of some M/E banks, as well as to the program and preview buses, to route composite video signals in an orderly manner. Other toggles are also provided. Switchers with more than one M/E bank are said to have *multiple M/E systems*. Photo 10.2 shows a compact high-end switcher.

Switchers with multiple M/E systems can produce highly complex video images. A video effect composed from two or three sources on one M/E bank (for example, a camera shot of a studio talent standing in front of a chroma key background with a

Photo 10.2   This high-end video switcher features several mix/effects banks for composing complex images and taking them to air.

lower-third CG text) can serve as a single-source feed to another M/E bank. Combining this output from the M/E banks with still other sources at the program/ preview part of the switcher can create an extremely complicated output.

Switchers with multiple M/E systems work according to a **cascading** principle, whereby the composite video signal flows from the top M/E bank downward, much like a stream of water flowing downstream. Switchers that route the output of one M/E bank to another for further processing before it is finally sent to the program bus are said to be capable of *double reentry*. The cascading architecture of multiple M/E system switchers explains how the downstream keyer got its name: Some signals are made to flow downstream but not up.

One effect possible with multiple M/E system switchers is the *quad-split,* in which the screen is split into four quadrants, each carrying a different video source. The quad-split is often used in news and public affairs programs to carry video of several individuals located in different cities discussing a debate topic. The four sources are often separated by a thin wipe border (see Figure 10.11). Another effect is *layering,* which combines multiple key and wipe effects to build a complex image. For example, a quad-split image of four speakers can form the background picture for a chroma key insert in an over-the-shoulder shot of a studio news anchor. As each

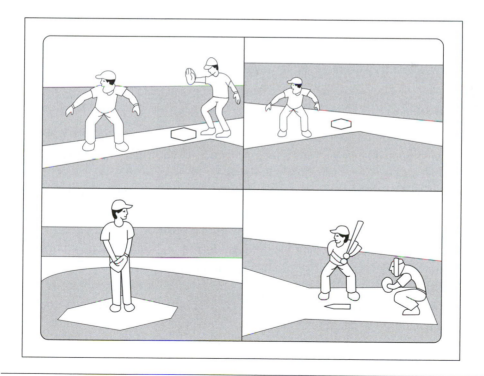

Figure 10.11   A quad-split.

Figure 10.12   A layered use of a quad-split; separate shots of four interviewees are combined into a single chroma key insert behind the news anchor, who turns to "face" them.

speaker answers questions, lower-third graphics may be keyed into the appropriate quadrants to identify each speaker (see Figure 10.12).

Computer-Assisted Switchers

Computers are commonly used to set up and execute complicated transitions. Programmable switchers can store long sequences of transitions and execute them according to a strict time schedule precise to the 30th (or 60th) of a second (that is, *frame accurate*). To execute a sequence on the air using a computer-assisted switcher, it is first entered into the computer's memory during preproduction. Then it can be set in motion by the TD during show time with the push of a single button.

Computer-assisted switchers also find application in postproduction work where the instant time demands of live production are not a factor. Such switchers can be easily integrated with digital editing systems for precise postproduction tasks, where the emphasis is on creative transitions and effects. In this role, computer-controlled switchers handle transitions among many digital video sources, including digital video effects generators, edit units, and digital audio workstations (DAWs).

When used this way, the computer can preroll tape machines before taking material from them, as well as load and use material from still-store machines and graphic paint boxes. Because computers can coordinate switching among many sources, programmable switchers are becoming more common, adding a robotic quality to the production environment. Of course, the computers that control complex switching functions are themselves incapable of making decisions. They must be programmed to do their work, and it is people who still must do that.

Postproduction switchers often differ from their production counterparts in their internal design or architecture. The production switchers we have described use a *linear architecture,* which produces the cascading principle in which signals move downstream from one bank to another for successive manipulations. By contrast, many postproduction switchers work according to a *parallel architecture,* whereby the manipulation of the video signal occurs, roughly speaking, all in one place. This difference makes it possible for postproduction switchers to program complex transitions and special effects with only one M/E bank and to execute them all with the push of one button.

DIGITAL VIDEO EFFECTS GENERATORS

Digital video effects (DVE) machines are computers that turn video signals (both analog and digital) into digital graphics. Once captured, the images are subject to virtually infinite manipulation without losing signal quality. When used as a video source and routed to the video switcher, the effects possible with a DVE can be integrated into those available from the switcher itself, resulting in an impressive product. Switchers built to accept only analog signals must be outfitted with *black-box interfaces* to accept digital signals (and vice versa). Some examples of the most common DVE image manipulations include the following:

- *Slide effects.* One video source appears to slide to one side, revealing another source that appears to be hiding underneath.

- *Freeze frame effects.* The screen displays a series of static frames of an original live image.

- *Zoom, bounce, spin, squeeze, and other motion effects.* An image appears to change from full size down to zero size or expand from zero to full size (*zoom*); behaves like a ball, bouncing from one screen edge to another while being compressed by the bounce (*bounce*); tumbles and rotates in selected directions (*spin*); or expands or compresses as it moves through different size changes and screen locations (*squeeze*).

- *Position and perspective changes.* An image appears to pan and tilt from its starting position, stretch either vertically or horizontally, or twist, bend, or lean in different directions.

- *Posterization* or *solarization.* The luminance values of an image are reduced to a limited range of values, giving the image the high-contrast look of some poster art.

- *Mosaic and tiling effects.* An image is broken into a number of squares resembling tiles, reducing picture clarity while creating a stylized pattern of the original image.

Many of these effects are bound by time constraints. For example, if a speech is to be punctuated by a digital effect used as a transition to the next speech, and the time between utterances is 3 seconds, it is critical to tell all of the machines involved when to execute each of their functions so that everything works as planned. Some systems alert the TD with a beep when a sequence of commands does not add up. Other systems are not that smart. Depending on the system you use, you will need to be more or less vigilant about time factors when programming sequences.

Though digital video effects are tempting, programs featuring dazzling sequences of effects for their own sake will probably not sustain an audience's interest very long. Avoid the temptation of using digital effects just to use them. When considering a fancy special effect or graphic display, ask yourself, "How would this enhance my program or move it forward?" "Is this effect motivated by my program purpose and content?" If the answer to these questions is no, it is probably wise to exclude the effect. *When in doubt, leave it out.*

INDUSTRY VOICES

Kurt Hanson

On October 26, 2005, I interviewed Kurt Hanson, chief engineer for WABC-TV in New York, which produces local news and sports broadcasts for the number one market, including Live With Regis and Kelly weekdays. Kurt shares his view of the business from both the technical and production sides; both are interdependent. His views on the transition from analog to digital platforms are especially informative.

L: *Let's start with a short bio.*

K: *I'm chief engineer at WABC-TV, where I've been for 9 years. I started here as a mainte-nance engineer, then was promoted to chief engineer overseeing all technical opera-tions. Before that, I worked for the FOX affiliate, WTIC in Hartford, Connecticut. I had* also worked for WTIC AM/FM in Hartford, and I've done freelance work for ESPN in places throughout central Connecticut and Massachusetts. My first job was for the ABC station in Springfield, Massachusetts, where I grew up. I went to the University of Hartford, graduating with an electrical engineering degree.

L: What is your normal day like?

K: Here at WABC it's dealing with production—news and our nationally syndicated program "Live With Regis and Kelly." I deal with all the technical issues that come up: making sure we have the appropriate staff (camera people, audio engineers, technical directors) to operate the equipment properly. I also oversee the maintenance engineers. If something breaks or if there's a problem, we make sure it gets fixed quickly. We try to keep the station running smoothly and technically clean so that the video is as good looking and sounding as possible.

L: What changes have you seen in your career?

K: From a technical perspective, the change from black and white to color was a huge transition; we also went from monaural sound to stereo, and from tape-based acquisition to disk-based or RAM-based acquisition. Now we're going from analog to digital platforms, and that is, by far, the biggest transition that broadcasting has ever gone through, far greater than mono to stereo, even more complex than black and white to color. With those earlier changes, we had backward compatibility with the equipment. But there is no backward compatibility with the analog-to-digital conversion. We're taking almost all our infrastructure and throwing it away and starting over. So I am in a position to rebuild the ABC flagship station in New York, which has just been an incredible project both from within the studio to the transmitter facilities in what was the World Trade Center, and is now in the Empire State Building, and our various microwave receiver sites around the tristate area. It's been a phenomenal opportunity for me.

L: You look at it as a challenge.

K: Yes. There have been many frustrations. For example, with analog, everything is hardware-based. You've got a box designed to do a specific function: I'm a camera—that's all I do. I'm a tape machine, that's all I do. I'm a character generator, that's all I do. I'm a graphics still-store system: My only job is to recall and record graphics. Now everything is software driven. So you have computers pretty much running everything. So instead of dealing with hardware problems, which were generally few and far between, you're dealing with software glitches, where fixing something may be nothing more than a reboot of the system, or it could be tougher to troubleshoot. Our video server system for the news department replaces what used to be several tape-based edit rooms with racks of tape machines for recording feeds and for playback. Now we have replaced all that with video servers, which are computers which run the database for all the media that's on these hard drives and systems. We've got both low-res and high-res encoders and other servers keeping track of it all. When this server-based system came to WABC, it added over 150 computers to the building to support this new digital workflow. Now, if one machine has a problem, we sometimes end up rebooting to get everything to resync.

L: Whereas in the past, a Beta machine could have a head clog, and that was it.

K: Yes, you'd clean the tape machine and be done. Now, everything interacts with everything else, so there's no longer the isolated fixing of the individual box—it's all system-level maintenance. Before, if a tape machine broke, no big deal—you'd either swap that tape machine out with a spare, or take that edit room out of service and use a backup room. Now in the digital world, if a server goes down, and it could be one that keeps track of a lot of assets, you could have a whole system down. Here at WABC, we have an X system and a Y system—and they're parallel. So every job and process happens in parallel. If you're working on one, it gets copied to the other. So if one goes down, we have the other.

L: Are they both running simultaneously at all times?

K: Yes. And we always go with the n + 1, a third "Z" system, which is a small standalone system, so that if both my X and Y systems fail, I've got "Z" in a pinch.

L: Like a generator, so you can keep the food from going bad in the refrigerator.

K: Absolutely. So we have lots of redundancy. One major change caused by the transition to digital is that now the burden placed on the engineering department has shifted. We don't have engineers at work-benches fixing things that much anymore. Instead it's more system-level maintenance and diagnostics. We deal with vendors on a weekly basis, reporting software bugs and issues. That's one of the things about software—it's never the same from year to year, or even from month to month. With hardware, generally you reach a point where it's a fixed entity. Take tape machines for example. It's got x number of resistors and performs a function, and you reach a point where there are no significant developments going on with it. It's a reliable, stable piece of equipment that you can use for years, and you can continue to buy it. If you bought a mature product—a tape machine—10 years ago, and then another one 5 years ago, you were still buying the exact same machine. Not so with computer servers. You could buy a video server today from a manufacturer and 6 months from now place an order for another one, and they will likely have a different operating system, and a different version of the software—the software is constantly in flux.

L: How do you keep up? What has it done to your content?

K: We are the number one station in the number one market for news. We're still covering the same types of stories. One thing that has changed is that we're much more of a global news organization. It's faster, and more in real time. We see that now, day in and day out in Iraq. We're definitely seeing a lot more a lot faster.

L: How did you personally adapt to this transition? How do you keep up?

K: I attend trade shows and read write-ups in trade magazines and publications. I read *TV Technology, Broadcast Engineering, Cable News.* Technology is changing so rapidly that there's no school you can go to to stay current. The most important thing for any student in college to understand is that people may help you get your foot in the door, get an interview, an internship, your first job, but it's up to the individual to stay current. There is no one place to go, no one source of information that you can rely on. There are many things that you're going to have to research at least on the technical side. On the editorial side—if you're a writer, a producer, a reporter, anchor—obviously it's a very different world. You really don't deal as much with the technical issues, but even for them the world has changed. Twenty years ago, if you were hired as a writer, that's all you did, you wrote. You would work with an editor and write the text that the anchor or reporter would read on air. Now, because of technology, you can edit on the desktop. I'm quite sure that all the students in your classes know how to edit with some sort of nonlinear desktop editing system. And they're not expensive. For a few hundred dollars, you can buy something to edit video and audio. Even writers and producers have had to adapt to the new work world brought by technology.

KEY TERMS

QUESTIONS FOR REVIEW

Why do different video sources have to be made synchronous with one another? What machines accomplish the synchronizing process?

What are the differences between fading and dissolving video sources?

What are some of the effects possible with the special effects generator (SEG) on the basic video switcher?

What is the difference between internal and external keying?

What are some of the common uses for the downstream key (DSK) feature of the video switcher?

What special production considerations regarding lighting and set design would guide you in planning for a successful use of the chroma key effect? What would you tell the talent?

What is the cascading feature of multiple mix/effects bank switchers? How can digital video effects (DVE) machines enhance your video presentations? What are some of the effects you might use to shoot a music video?

NOTES

1. The number of available video transitions in today's video environment is enormous, raising questions about what transitions to use between video sources during a program. It's the director's call. Aesthetic decisions and judgment are shaped not only by what is possible but by what is appropriate. In general terms, it is recommended to keep it simple—that is, if the transition you have chosen gets in the way of the message or meaning of your program or sequence, you may want to reconsider the choice you have made. In some programs where the meaning of your show is more important than the pure perceptual stimulation it delivers (i.e., an instructional video vs. a music video), it may be wise to simplify the transitions you use—you may want to go with cuts and quick dissolves. If, on the other hand, you are going for the more dazzling display, then you may want to try more ornate approaches. Let the objectives of the program and consideration of the audience guide you. Keep in mind that the transition is part of your show and can convey different meanings. For example, simple cuts tend to indicate a change of viewpoint or a shift of attention within a scene without telegraphing a change of time and place, while dissolves and wipes often telegraph a change of time and place to the audience. These are vastly different effects, and when used properly, they can propel your show forward; when used improperly, they can confuse and distract your audience. Since the audience is of paramount importance, consider each transition in terms of how it will affect the viewer.

2. *Lever* and *toggle* are synonyms.

Chapter 11

FIELD PRODUCTION

An increasing amount of daily television fare currently originates from nonstudio locations, including news and sports programs as well as segments for sitcoms, dramas, reality shows, commercials, and variety programs. Increases in *field production,* as it is called, are largely due to breakthroughs in technology in two areas. First, because of the smaller size and weight of television equipment and improvements in technical performance, you can now collect video content under conditions that were once inaccessible to television. Second, once collected, you can now instantly transmit programs globally from any location through a variety of means. In short, advances have increased television's accessibility and transmission capability.

State-of-the-art field equipment is more portable, reliable, durable, efficient, and higher quality than ever before. Digital cameras use charge-coupled devices (CCDs), making field units lighter and smaller than their tube predecessors and therefore easier to pack and transport (see Photo 11.1). In addition, solid-state technology makes field cameras more durable; they are not subject to registration problems from getting knocked around.

Field cameras are also more light sensitive than ever, so they can work in lower light than was once possible. This means they can use denser lens systems, affording them greater focal range under more varied conditions. They also operate with lower energy demands for longer periods of time on batteries. Moreover, because of their greater light sensitivity, lights, if they are used at all, can now be used at lower power and illumination levels, making light kits smaller and lighter. The move toward lower power also means less intrusion and distraction for on-camera personnel—thus a more naturalistic atmosphere can be achieved.

Microphones have also become smaller while increasing in sensitivity and directionality. In addition, wireless systems have largely been perfected and now are quite reliable over longer distances in both studio and field settings.

Photo 11.1   This portable three-chip digital camcorder is less than 9 inches wide, less than 9 inches in height, and under 20 inches long (with the lens). Its total weight is under 8 pounds.

Once cameras, mics, and lights have been deployed in the field, the producer has the option of either transmitting to a home base from virtually anywhere on Earth for immediate live broadcast or recording material either on tape or disk or solid-state flash memory cards for later editing and/or broadcast. For delivering a signal to a home base, the methods include traditional coaxial cable and terrestrial (land-based) microwave relay links, newer fiber-optic lines, or even satellite *transponders* (radio devices aboard satellites that receive and then retransmit video signals originating on the ground).

This chapter explains how field production works and offers advice for executing successful field shoots. All the aesthetic and technical principles covered in earlier chapters remain important in field production, and you should review them when necessary. The topics covered in this chapter include the following:

Television war coverage: a case study in field production

Three basic concepts

Electronic news gathering
- The ENG mobile unit and equipment
- Signal transmission and relay facilities
- The ENG preproduction stage

- The ENG production stage
- The ENG postproduction stage

Electronic field production

- The EFP mobile unit and equipment
- The EFP preproduction stage
- The EFP production stage
- The EFP postproduction stage

Multicamera remote production

- The MCR mobile unit and equipment
- The MCR preproduction stage
- The MCR production stage
- The MCR postproduction stage

TELEVISION WAR COVERAGE: A CASE STUDY IN FIELD PRODUCTION

Perhaps no event in recent history more dramatically illustrates television's current robust field capability in terms of both immediacy and pervasiveness than the coverage of the war in Iraq. In addition to conventional broadcasting technology, television journalists rely on cellular telephones, satellites, computers, microwave relays, and fiber-optic technologies to cover global conflicts.

Through various configurations of these technologies, television news (however sanitized by the sources) is broadcast worldwide. News organizations such as CNN can now provide daily coverage of events *as they happen,* often using embedded reporters live on the scene. Television news may be viewed not just by audiences worldwide but by intelligence officers and military personnel on both sides of the battle.

What makes this possible is not just the technical capability of a single device, or several devices, but the *convergence,* or linking, of several media technologies with one another. Among the more advanced devices used is the **fly-away video satellite uplink,** a device that can be packed into a suitcase and then flown anywhere on a small commercial airplane. Upon arrival at a field location, fly-aways can be loaded on a truck and moved to anyplace the truck can go to provide global, live television coverage.

Laptop computers provide e-mail capability for field reporters, as well as access to the Internet and various databases, enabling reporters to file, read, and watch stories from around the world within moments of their creation. Laptops can also ingest, edit, and transmit the video shot by field reporters. Laptops and cameras that interface directly with computers are capable of replacing entire news vans as well as serving as a word processor for scripts.[1] News agencies can also share historical and archival data with field reporters. In addition, home base television stations and news agencies frequently forward news items from competitors to reporters for editing their own stories. Hence, the convergence of new media technologies makes global journalism more pervasive and immediate, even contributing to its content.

It is unlikely that you will be thrust into a field setting as an embedded reporter covering a war; more likely, you will have to cover an election campaign or a live sporting event for a local television station. Or you may work a live multicamera remote of some special event, such as a parade or a government official's inauguration. However, regardless of what you cover, the field production principles you use will be the same, and you may confront a similar variety of conditions. Some field reports may be broadcast live, and some may be taped, edited, and broadcast later. Some may be shot at night, some in the daytime. Some may be shot outdoors and some indoors. Some may be done under clear skies and bright sun and some under heavy clouds or in stormy weather. Some may feature professional talent and some the greenest amateurs. Some may have huge budgets, and some may be done on a shoestring. Many will have tight deadlines, and a few will have a luxury of time. Some will use radio energy (such as microwave links, satellites, and cell phones) to deliver live feeds from the field to the home base, while others will use fiber lines or some other physical connection. Finally, some hosts, subjects, or jurisdictions will impose few restrictions (legal or otherwise) on the use of the materials you shoot, while others will impose such severe limits that you may wonder whether it was worth shooting anything at all. *In all cases, you will be expected to act ethically and professionally with a finite supply of space, time, materials, and personnel.*

THREE BASIC CONCEPTS

To understand the media infrastructures relevant to field production, three general concepts are useful: **reach, range,**[2] and **interactivity.** The following sections describe these concepts and give examples of their application.

Reach. The term *reach* refers to the proportion of all relevant parties that can be connected to one another quickly and automatically by a communication technology. Ideally, maximum reach is attained when any relevant party anywhere can communicate with any other, as might be possible in a perfectly operating worldwide telephone or postal system. Reach relates to communication capabilities among production team members as well as communication with the audience.

For example, in producing a multicamera remote of a golf tournament, one group of relevant parties is the field crew, including the commentators, who may be deployed at some distance from one another and from the greens they must cover but who must be instantly informed about which player's shot will be taken next and when others must be recorded for later broadcast. To keep informed, the camera operators and other production personnel, many beyond earshot and out of sight of one another, need access to the director's voice. If voice contact is lost, the operation can grind to a halt. Hence, reach, at least in terms of voice contact, is critical.

Range. The concept of *range* refers to the different *types* of information (data, voice, live-action video, taped replays, etc.) that are handled by a given system. For example, the telegraph has great reach; however, since it uses Morse code but no voice or video, it has limited range. Likewise, the conventional telephone system has great reach, now made even greater by cell phones, and it also enjoys greater range than the telegraph since it can handle data transmissions such as e-mail and faxes in addition to voice communication. However, when the phone system becomes capable of transmitting live, real-time video—say, through the addition of handsets with video screens—we will then say that its range has increased.

The golf tournament example shows how the concept of range helps in understanding field production. Imagine a commentator having to describe different golfers' shots from distant locales. The commentator may be cued by a director's audio feed that it is time to describe actions at the ninth tee or the twelfth green, but audio alone would not be enough to show the commentator the action—that is, the audio feed can *reach* the relevant party, but it lacks the *range* to provide the necessary information, namely, the video feed the commentator needs to report intelligently. By adding a line monitor with the video feed, we increase the range of this communication system enough to make it fully functional.

Current growth in the range aspect of communication networks may be seen in the adoption of systems with digital platforms. By reducing all forms of messages (data, voice, and video) to series of 0s and 1s, digitalization makes them potentially universally compatible with one another. In theory, digitalization of information enables messages to be integrated and shared in all formats.

Interactivity. Finally, *interactivity* refers to the ability of a communication system to permit users to encode and decode messages simultaneously in real time. The telephone is an obvious example of interactivity, but how does the concept apply to video? Consider *The Larry King Show* on CNN, an interview show in which the host and guest take phone calls from viewers. This program has impressive reach (it is broadcast to dozens of countries) and some range (because it includes the viewers' telephone calls, though it does not carry video of the callers). It also has a limited amount of interactivity: It broadcasts calls in real time, providing live communication between host and caller, but only for one caller at a time. In the golf tournament example, interactivity in voice communication is provided by headset or phone connections for all relevant parties who must speak to and hear one another during a broadcast, including the field crew, commentators, the director, and other personnel at the home base.

These three concepts can help you plan and execute your live and taped field shoots. The proper configuration of communication systems linking relevant parties to one another in the field makes it essential for producing coherent field productions.

In the rest of this chapter, we will examine the major categories of field productions: the multicamera remote type of field production alluded to in the golf tournament example; electronic news gathering, as in daily coverage of a war; and electronic field production, such as might be used for a corporate video or a documentary featuring a series of location interviews with government figures offering solutions to some long-term problems (i.e., how to fix the health care system or revamp Social Security). These categories differ in emphasis, but they should not be viewed as entirely distinct from one another. Many principles apply to all of them, though each has unique qualities that make it appropriate to use different production strategies.

ELECTRONIC NEWS GATHERING

Roughly speaking, **electronic news gathering (ENG)** refers to that type of field production used for on-the-spot daily news coverage. Since news events happen in different locations without prior warning, ENG production is often marked by rapid response to fluid situations and by tight deadlines. In the news business, it is essential to be poised for mobility, to get the scoop, and to be first with the late-breaking story. As a result of severe time constraints, ENG production often has relatively rough (though still air-quality) production values, including handheld camera shots; imperfect lighting; simple, often unplanned blocking; and less-than-optimal audio. These imperfections are overlooked when the story is dramatic enough: For instance, when a war reporter describes bombs exploding outside his or her window, no one expects the audio to be flawless. On the other hand, difficult conditions are no excuse for sloppy work, and the quality expected in today's news operations is generally very high.

The ENG Mobile Unit and Equipment

The purpose of the ENG mobile unit is to enable crews to move and deploy video equipment quickly and efficiently to the site of a fast-breaking news story. At the

Table 11.1 Typical Contents of an ENG Mobile Unit

Cameras: at least one, preferably two

Camera tripods, body mounts, and/or shoulder braces

Lenses and lens shades

Flags and reflector boards

White balance cards and test equipment to set up and adjust transmission signals

Complete light kit (two-instrument minimum; three are better) with extra bulbs

Microphones: several wire and wireless lavs and handhelds, as well as a shotgun mic for more distant pickup, all with windscreens

Portable audio mixer and headset for monitoring audio levels

Batteries

An additional power source, such as a generator powered by the vehicle's engine

Two-way radio for communication with the home base

Walkie-talkies for on-site crew members

Microwave transmitter

Satellite dish for live transmissions (optional)

simplest level, the ENG mobile vehicle may be nothing more than a car into which a camcorder and microphone have been loaded, with a reporter, either alone or with an assistant who doubles (or triples) as driver and audio/video operator. Under more ideal conditions, the ENG crew will have two or three members (including an engineer who can be stationed inside the vehicle for operation functions and security needs); the vehicle will be a van or minibus equipped with all of the equipment needed to cover a story either live or on tape from the field under varied conditions (see Photo 11.2). The van or minibus is a good choice because it has enough room to carry what is needed for almost any situation while remaining small enough to park and maneuver with relative ease. Table 11.1 lists the typical contents of a fully loaded mobile unit.

In a well-outfitted vehicle, needed items are arranged in an orderly manner to make the setups and strikes efficient, including cables and miscellaneous items (gaffer's tape, clamps, extension cords, fishing line, etc.). Custom-made containers with safety straps for securing cameras and other major items may also be attached to specific locations in the van. In the glove compartment, it is a good idea to keep a flashlight and road map, as well as any police permits that the crew may need to gain access to restricted areas.

(a)

(b)

Photo 11.2   An ENG van with a transmitter on top (a) and ample video equipment stored safely inside (b).

Signal Transmission and Relay Facilities

A common method of delivering video signals (either live or on videotape) from a field location to a home base is through the use of microwave radio energy, which provides line-of-sight transmission from an antenna mounted atop the ENG van (see Figure 11.1).[3] The effective distance for microwave relay signals is roughly from 30 to a hundred miles, depending on signal power and terrain conditions. Once this distance is exceeded, a **repeater station** is used to boost the signal for another trip. With a series of about 30 repeater stations, television signals may be transmitted from coast to coast.

To link an ENG camera with a home base, two connections are needed: first, a connection between the camera and the antenna atop the mobile van; second, a link from the mobile van to the home base (see Figure 11.1). A physical cable can be used to link the camera with the van. In cases where this is not possible, a battery-powered microwave transmitter with about a one-mile range is connected to the camera. For reliable operation of this microwave transmitter, a clear path must be maintained from the camera to the van's antenna.

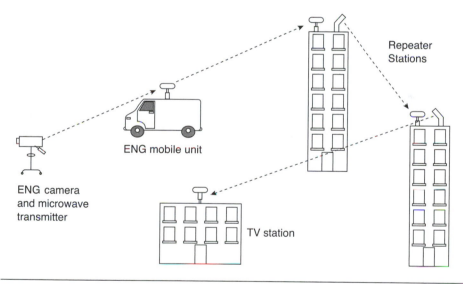

Figure 11.1   Typical microwave links in an ENG operation.

The link from van to home base is provided by the van's microwave transmitter. Sometimes, either the distance is too great or line of sight is too obstructed to permit successful transmission from the van directly to the home base. In such cases, repeaters are used to get the signal back to the home base for storage or broadcast. In most cities, repeaters are conveniently located at several geographical high points, atop tall buildings or hilltop towers. To get the best transmission, experienced crews carry a list of locations that have worked well in the past. Sometimes helicopters or tethered blimps, equipped with portable towers, can hover over news or sports locations to serve as repeater stations. A cheaper, though perhaps less reliable, way to get signals to receiving antennas is simply to bounce them off a nearby building.

When microwave delivery is not feasible because of distance, power, terrain, or other limitations, ENG transmissions can be sent using a satellite uplink (see Figure 11.2). Since the mid-1980s, **satellite news gathering (SNG),** as it is called, has extended the reach of ENG operations by using satellite **transponders,** which are orbiting microwave receiving/transmitting stations. A satellite uplink aboard an ENG van is aimed at a preassigned transponder aboard a satellite traveling in a geosynchronous orbit 22,300 miles above the Earth. (A satellite's orbit is geosynchronous when the satellite stays above the same spot on the Earth's surface throughout its orbit.) Aboard the satellite, microwave radio signals received by the transponder are converted to another frequency to avoid interference or jamming problems and then sent back to Earth. Since signals from orbiting satellites come from over 22,000 miles away, the coverage pattern, or **footprint,** blankets about a third of the Earth's surface. And because the coverage pattern from a satellite is so great, satellite communication is termed *distance insensitive.*

After determining the best position for the satellite uplink (through the use of a compass and an *inclinometer*), an engineer in the field immediately begins sending test and tone signals (usually video color bars and a 1,000-Hz audio tone) so that the home base can establish and adjust its connection. In addition to

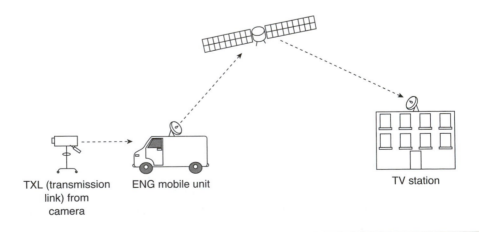

TXL (transmission link) from camera   ENG mobile unit   TV station

Figure 11.2   ENG connections using a satellite uplink.

providing a live television feed to the home base, satellite transponders are used to set up voice communication between field crews and selected personnel at the home base. This connection includes both telephone links and an **interruptible foldback (IFB)** circuit, a voice channel enabling the director to break into a program's audio feed to talk directly to the field reporter through the reporter's earpiece. IFBs also permit news anchors and other personnel to talk to field reporters without their conversation going out over the air about upcoming segments. In this way, satellites help establish the interactivity needed for a successful production. However, the time delay in these satellite-transmitted conversations is about a half second, a lag that can sometimes be irksome to the participants.

The ENG Preproduction Stage

Before leaving on a field assignment, the ENG crew should be thoroughly prepared. To paraphrase an old adage, *it is better to have gear and not need it than to need it and not have it.* In line with this advice, most serious ENG operations have a checklist of the most needed items to make preparation routine. In addition, it is useful for crew members each to have a press pass to enable them to cross police lines.

An *information log* listing the addresses and locations of valued conveniences is also handy. The log might include the locations of bathrooms and working phones, as well as names and numbers of key field contacts (the mayor's secretary, the police commissioner). It also helps to know key locations for getting the clearest line-of-sight microwave relay for the mobile van. In many ways, the information log serves the same purpose as the production book kept by the competent producer.

Cameras and Tape. Before and during the trip to the shooting location, you should consider the assignment objectives. Upon arrival, unpack and set up the equipment you intend to use. As far as the camera is concerned, if time and the nature of the job permit, use a tripod if at all possible to steady your shots. Remember to white balance the camera even if you have just done so at a previous location. The most popular cameras and tape formats for ENG operations currently tend to be Betacam or DVC-Pro 3-chip digital cameras with digital tape, although in some cases, other equipment may be in service. Depending on what you have, be sure to bring enough batteries and tapes or disks in the proper format to carry the day.

Before shooting begins, always record about 10 seconds of tape before cueing talent to ensure that you have tape up to speed and to provide enough control track for later editing. Shoot an additional 10 seconds of tape after each segment to give the editor enough control track to edit. When a tape cassette is finished, immediately label it. Identify each tape (and tape box) by date, time, and the event covered to reduce confusion. Bring a marking pen and stick-on labels for this simple accounting task. If you don't want to record anything else on a cassette, remove or adjust the "record" tab on the back panel to eliminate the risk of taping over crucial footage.

Lighting. If the shoot is to take place outdoors in daytime using available light, take note of the location of the sun and, if possible, place the camera so that the sun is behind you. If that is not possible, use lens shades to offset less-than-optimal angles of the sun. If the sun is extremely bright, use flags to reduce or eliminate contrast-ratio problems. Reflector boards can help fill in dark shadows. If it is windy, stabilize flags and reflector boards with clamps or with the assistance of utility crew to eliminate accidents and flickering effects. Better yet, try to use an area sheltered from wind and direct sunlight, such as the lee side of a building.

Rain may require the use of raincoats for cameras and other major equipment that needs protection. **Raincoats** are waterproof covers custom-fitted to cameras, recorders, and other key equipment. In the absence of custom-fitted raincoats, plastic garbage bags are a good substitute. With all electrical equipment, exercise extreme caution when operating in the rain, especially with lighting equipment—that means keeping things dry and not placing flammable rain protection gear so close to lights that you start a fire.

For night and/or indoor shoots where available light is not enough, artificial lights will be needed. The main goal is to provide adequate light for air-quality video. This can often be achieved using three portable instruments either on stands or clamped to available surfaces. The lights should be tunable so they can be used in spot or flood positions.

Most portable light kits feature lensless tungsten halogen lamps with barn doors, scrims, and gels for controlling spill and intensity. Wooden clothespins (the two-piece wire-loaded variety) are ideal for pinning filters and scrims to barn doors. Pack a pair of heat-resistant gloves for safe handling. Bring lights that run on batteries in case AC power is not available. In some cases, you may have to settle for a **speed light**, a single light mounted on top of the camera. While this alternative is not the best, it is sometimes all you have.

If possible, set lights according to the principles of good lighting design discussed in Chapter 5. Remember to light to create texture, depth, and acceptable contrast ratios. Lighting from above rather than below avoids unnatural, unflattering shadows. Use key, back, and fill light to achieve proper lighting effects.

If you can power only one or two instruments, you may be able to stretch your resources by using **bounce light**—that is, light reflected or bounced off a white wall, ceiling, or other reflective surface. Bounce light increases the amount of fill and even backlight on a subject and reduces contrast range. To use bounce light, position the subject near a white-colored wall or other such surface. If a wall is available but it is not white, you can tape white paper to it.

For outdoor night shoots, it is often desirable to find settings with illuminated backdrops. In reporting about the federal government, the White House and Capitol buildings are frequently used as backdrops, not only because they are important but because they are mostly white and are already lit. In the absence of prelit backgrounds, place the subject close enough to some background so that your lights spill light onto it. If none of these choices is available, expect the subject to look cameo lit (not necessarily bad).

If you shoot indoors in the daytime using tungsten halogen lights, they will be incompatible with natural light in terms of color temperatures, and you will need to decide how to deal with the natural light streaming in from windows. Draw the drapes, pull the shades, cover the windows with opaque paper, or coat the windows with filters that color-correct the natural light.

Finally, for daytime outdoor shoots, it is sometimes desirable to augment natural light with artificial lights: for example, to boost flat light conditions caused by cloudiness or to offset the light variations when a shoot takes place over several days. Under such conditions, if available, use hydrargyrum medium-arc iodide (HMI) lights to match the color temperature range of natural light. Alternatively, you can gel the lights to match the outdoor color temperature. A recent technical breakthrough in lighting is the introduction of high-efficiency HMI lights with much lower power requirements. There are even units that operate off the camera's battery.

Audio. Take audio levels as soon as possible, and shoot some test tape to make sure all systems are go. Use simple audio design—perhaps a single handheld mic for the reporter's speeches. For two-person interviews, the latest production approach uses a wireless lav for the reporter and a wireless handheld (held by the reporter) for the interviewee, but you can still do an adequate job sharing a single conventional handheld mic. For longer interviews, another approach is to have reporter and interviewee each wear a lav.

A shotgun mic can also be mounted on the head-end of the camera, and all audio can be recorded from there, but sound recorded in that way often lacks presence, and ambient noise can be distracting. Use this method only as a last resort, when crew or equipment is not available for other configurations.

For outdoor shoots, always use windscreens. Before or after taping, record room noise or nat sound for 20 or 30 seconds so that you have some for editing purposes if needed. Nat sound can also provide nice background for audio sweetening, which will often include postproduction voice-overs from studio announcers or news anchors.

Finally, monitor audio through a headset, and ride the gain throughout the taping to capture the best possible sound.

The ENG Production Stage

Of course, no matter how sophisticated telecommunications technologies are on land or in space, nothing can replace the intelligent use of facilities. At the site of a newsworthy event, the reporter and crew's journalistic experience, production and writing ability, editing knowledge, values, ethics, people skills, and even the organization's policies all influence the finished product. What principles and techniques can guide you in gathering air-quality footage? This section briefly outlines some key practices for single-camera field production to help you capture your story with the most professional results.

Sequential Thinking. Shot sequencing and visual continuity are natural by-products of standard multicamera studio production. The same action is viewed simultaneously by several cameras from different angles with different shot compositions, enabling you to cut from shot to shot without losing the normal flow of action. By contrast, in single-camera field production, matching action from different camera angles, positions, and compositions is not a natural by-product. Instead, segments must be shot at different times from different vantage points and must later be edited into final form in postproduction to simulate matched action. Simulating matched action is an essential ingredient of **continuity,** which we can define as the smooth flow of uninterrupted action from shot to shot. In single-camera field production, continuity between shots must be fabricated—it is an illusion.

Creating matched action is possible only with careful planning. You must think sequentially, planning the sequence of shots ahead of time.

Jump Cuts. Without sequential thinking, one of the problems you may encounter is a **jump cut,** an unnatural transition showing an abrupt change in the subject's location or appearance. Imagine a sequence beginning with a wide shot of a woman wearing a hat and preparing to sit down in a chair. The shot includes the entire body of the standing talent with a full view of the chair beside her. The next shot shows a close-up of the subject already sitting, no longer wearing the hat (see Figure 11.3). This sequence constitutes a jump cut because the viewer never sees the subject sit down or remove the hat.

Jump cuts are jarring to viewers because they telegraph the message that the viewer has missed part of the action. Jump cuts ruin the sense of continuity and smoothness. On special occasions, that may be just what the director wants, but usually jump cuts should be avoided.

(a)   (b)

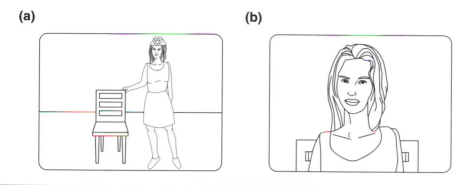

Figure 11.3   A jump cut. The transition from (a) to (b) involves a sudden "jump" because we never see the person sitting down or taking off her hat.

The way to avoid them is to shoot **overlapping action.** This means reshooting the same action again from a new camera position. For example, after shooting the move to the chair while in the wide shot, bring the camera in for the close-up, and then ask the talent to repeat the action of sitting down and removing the hat. Then match action in the editing suite by picking the frames in the medium shot and close-up that are most alike and edit them together.

Of course, in news coverage, it is not always possible to control actions to obtain overlapping footage. Some news groups prohibit **staging,** defined strictly as any act performed specifically for the camera. A more liberal definition permits having subjects repeat actions for the camera as long as those actions would normally have occurred in the absence of the camera. Depending on your news outlet's policy, if a repeating action is the subject of a story you are shooting, and you need several versions of it from different angles, you may have to wait until it comes around again to get overlapping footage. Or, if you are covering a unique event not likely to be repeated, such as a building demolition, and you wish to record it from more than one angle, you will have to shoot it simultaneously with several cameras.

Cutting on Action. To maintain smooth flow of motion, it is also best to **cut on action.** Think again about our example of the woman sitting down on a chair. Just as she is about to settle into the chair, you could cut to the close-up from the new camera position, capturing the subject an instant before she makes contact. Cutting on action results in smoother transitions because the viewer is more involved with following the action than with the edit itself or the camera's new position.

Cut-Ins or Inserts. After using an establishing shot to set the scene, it's a good idea to feature close-ups that carry forward the main action of a story. The **cut-in** or **insert** is a close-up that captures a key moment of visual business to drive home a story's main point.

Code of Broadcast News Ethics

To help deal with issues of staging and other ethical concerns, the Radio-Television News Directors Association has developed a Code of Broadcast News Ethics (see Walters, 1988, pp. 590–591), reproduced below.

The responsibility of radio and television journalists is to gather and report information of importance and interest to the public accurately, honestly, and impartially.

The members of the Radio-Television News Directors Association accept these standards and will:

1) Strive to present the source or nature of broadcast news material in a way that is balanced, accurate and fair.
   a. They will evaluate information solely on its merits as news, rejecting sensationalism or misleading emphasis in any form.
   b. They will guard against using audio or video material in a way that deceives the audience.
   c. They will not mislead the public by presenting as spontaneous news any material which is staged or rehearsed.
   d. They will identify people by race, creed, nationality, or prior status only when it is relevant.
   e. They will clearly label opinion and commentary.
   f. They will promptly acknowledge and correct errors.

2) Strive to conduct themselves in a manner that protects them from conflicts of interest, real or perceived. They will decline gifts or favors which would influence or appear to influence their judgments.

3) Respect the dignity, privacy, and well-being of people with whom they deal.

4) Recognize the need to protect confidential sources. They will promise confidentiality only with the intention of keeping that promise.

5) Respect everyone's right to a fair trial.

6) Broadcast the private transmissions of other broadcasters only with permission.

7) Actively encourage observance of this Code by all journalists, whether members of the Radio-Television News Directors Association or not.

Imagine you are covering an airport reunion of a soldier with his family after a long tour of duty (see Figure 11.4). You may start with a wide shot of the terminal, followed by a medium shot of a specific waiting area. Perhaps the camera then captures a group shot of his anxious family as the arrival is announced, closing on his daughter playing with a rag doll. When he arrives at the gate, you carry a two-shot of the first hug between the soldier and his daughter. At this point, you *insert* (or *cut-in*)

Figure 11.4   A shot sequence illustrating a cut-in or insert. (a) Start with a wide shot of an airline terminal. (b) Trim to a medium shot of a specific waiting area. (c) A family waits in an airport terminal for a soldier returning from duty. (d) Close-up of the daughter playing with a rag doll. (e) As the soldier arrives, a two-shot of the first hug between the soldier and the daughter. (f) Insert of a brief close-up on the doll. (g) Return to the two-shot of the hug.

a brief close-up of the rag doll carelessly slung behind the soldier's back to symbolize the child's joy in reuniting with her father. Then you cut back to the two-shot once again. If the story is carried forward to the next tour of duty, a cut-in of the departing soldier might include a close-up of the soldier's hands snapping a suitcase shut.

Cutaways. Cutaways are shots that lead the viewer's attention away from the main scene, often to related action outside of it. Cutaways provide bridges or transitions to subsequent scenes. For example, after the shot of the soldier and his daughter hugging, a cutaway might be a shot of a smiling flight attendant watching the action from nearby. In the subsequent part of the story, when the subject is getting ready to leave on another tour of duty, after the cut-in of his hands snapping shut the luggage, a cutaway shot might show his wife phoning the neighbor who will drive him to the airport.

Cutaways such as these, which relate closely to the story content, are sometimes called *motivated* cutaways. By contrast, *unmotivated* cutaways feature more neutral content. In general, motivated cutaways are more interesting than unmotivated ones. But even unmotivated cutaways can provide transition to the next scene. A simple example of an unmotivated cutaway used for transition is a wide exterior shot of a building where the next scene is to take place.

In addition to supplying transition, both cut-ins and cutaways do several things: They add pertinent visual information, they drive the story forward, and they compress time. Furthermore, from an editing perspective, cutaways provide a way to hide jump cuts. For example, cutaways can be used to connect interview segments that may have been recorded at different times.

The Reverse-Angle Shot. One of the most common cutaways is the **reverse-angle shot.** In a single-camera shoot of an interview, for example, the camera may be set up to capture a shot of the subject over the shoulder of the interviewer. From this position, the camera can zoom past the interviewer to feature a one-shot close-up of the subject. When the interview is done, for editing purposes, it is often helpful to shoot additional footage of the interviewer from the opposite perspective, or reverse angle—that is, from behind the subject (see Photo 11.3). From this position, you can zoom past the subject's shoulder to get a one-shot close-up of the interviewer, either pretending to listen to the subject's answers or repeating the questions as they were asked during the actual interview. In editing, these reverse-angle shots can be used to provide smooth transitions between different portions of the interview. They give the editor the flexibility to arrange responses in a different sequence, if desired, and to eliminate portions of the interview that may not be wanted. Of course, from an ethical standpoint, you should ensure that the views of the subject are not misrepresented; journalistic accuracy should be a constant concern.

Directional Continuity. Nothing confuses an audience more than watching footage of subject movement that illogically changes direction from shot to shot. The most common examples of this shoddy production practice are in covering horse races or parades. The action moves across the screen in one direction, followed immediately by footage of the same subject inexplicably moving in the opposite direction (see Figure 11.5). To eliminate such *false reversals,* as they are called, follow the axis-of-action rule.

According to the **axis-of-action rule,** you should establish an imaginary line (also called the *180-degree line*) along which the main action flows and *keep the camera on the same side of the line for all shots.* If you are shooting a parade with marchers moving from left to right in your viewfinder, the axis of action is parallel to the plane of your camera lens. You can move the camera to a new position as long as you do not cross that line (see Figure 11.5). Similarly, in an interview,

(a)

(b)

Photo 11.3   Sequence illustrating a reverse-angle shot in an interview. (a) Shot of the subject over the interviewer's shoulder. (b) Reverse-angle shot of the interviewer from behind the subject.

the axis of action may be thought of as the imaginary line connecting the subject and the interviewer's mouths. To avoid awkward pictures when shooting over-the-shoulder shots and reverse-angle shots, keep the camera on the same side of that line.

Of course, sometimes it is not possible to restrict all camera shots to the same side of the axis of action. What happens, in our parade example, if the police make you move to the other side of the street? In such cases, there are several ways to soften transitions between shots that change direction. One is to inject an intermediate shot (a cut-in or cutaway) that distracts the viewer and softens the change in direction. Handy cut-ins are the **head-on shot** and the **tail-away shot,** which, in

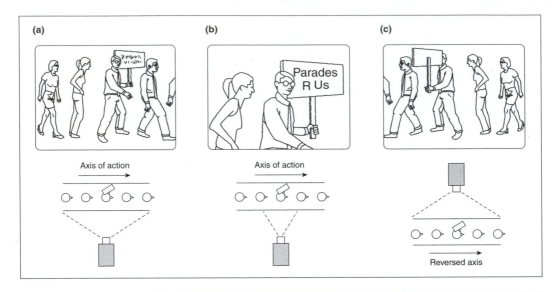

Figure 11.5 Sequence illustrating the axis-of-action rule. To cut from the wide shot in (a) to the close-up in (b) is fine because the axis of action has not been crossed. To cut from (b) to (c), however, would be a false reversal; the subjects would seem to have changed direction when they have not.

the parade example, are shots of the parade group either approaching or moving away from the camera, respectively (see Figure 11.6).

Another remedy is to take the viewer along for the ride. For example, in the case of a horse race, when the horses round the turn (thus changing direction), you may be able to follow them with a high-angle shot so the audience sees the change happen and accepts it readily.

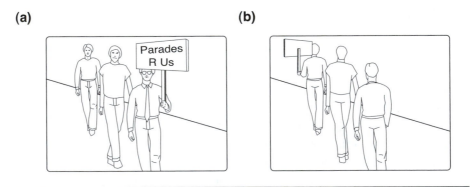

Figure 11.6 Shots that can help smooth out a transition involving a change of direction. (a) A head-on shot. (b) A tail-away shot.

Matching Camera Angles. The ENG camera operator must be sharply aware of the need to match camera angles when shooting segments that will be cut together later. Matching camera angles means following the line of action between two related shots so that when they are edited together, they appear consistent. For example, if you shoot a basketball player being interviewed by a shorter reporter, it is important to match the shot of the player with the reverse-angle shot of the reporter. If the camera angle on the subject is low, making the shot appear as if the interviewer is looking up at the subject, the reverse angle of the interviewer should be high to roughly the same degree, so that the subject appears to be looking down at the interviewer along the same axis (see Figure 11.7). If such consistency is lost, segments cut together can look jarring to viewers.

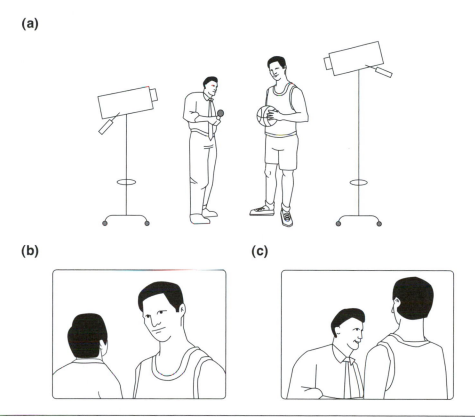

(a)

(b)   **(c)**

Figure 11.7 Matching camera angles. (a) Positioning of two cameras to capture a standup interview between a reporter and a taller basketball player. Note that one camera is pedded high, the other much lower. (b) The over-the-shoulder (OS) shot of the player being interviewed. (c) The reverse-angle shot of the reporter, which is angled down to the same degree that the player's shot is angled up.

Panning the Camera. Rough and unmotivated camera panning irritates viewers. Excessive panning takes attention away from the focus of your story and leads to dizziness when done in the extreme. In general, the rule is as follows: *Pan the camera to follow movement.* It is rarely justified to pan on a static scene. It is especially annoying to pan back and forth as if you were painting a fence. *Without question, 'tis better not to pan at all than to pan badly.* For more specific guidelines, check the list of Professional Pointers.

Panning the Camera in Field Production

➤ Avoid shaky, uneven movement. Work with a tripod whenever possible. If the camera is handheld, use your body as if it were a tripod, keeping your elbows tightly at your sides and your feet spread slightly wider than normal for added stability. To smooth out your panning motion, practice!

➤ Begin your pans by placing your feet in the position your body will be at the end of the pan, and twist your body to bring the camera to the beginning point. Then, when the shot begins, slowly untwist your body along with the action you wish to cover (see Figure 11.8).

➤ To increase steadiness, lean on a steady object such as a tree or car roof. You can even sit down.

➤ Slow down. No matter how slowly you think you are panning, it will always appear faster than you thought. Therefore, whenever you can, make the pan even slower than you think you need.

➤ Work at making the panning motion truly horizontal. If pans of the camera must leave the horizontal (as in following a plane taking off), keep the subject matter oriented in roughly the same portion of the screen space throughout the pan.

➤ Begin and end panning shots with static footage of the subject. This static footage will give the audience a chance to grasp the subject matter in the frame and to recover from the motion before a new shot or scene begins. It is jarring to the audience to cut from a still shot to a panning shot of different subject matter and vice versa.

➤ When possible, allow the subject to enter the frame before you pan to follow the action. This is known as anticipation. Likewise, when you finish covering an action, it is perfectly acceptable to steady the camera and let the subject exit the frame. Editors love this because it gives them a natural edit point for creating neat transitions between sequences. This approach is possible even when subject motion cannot be controlled, as in an airplane takeoff.

➤ Build your pans. Let the high point of subject action occur as the subject fills the screen. To do this, for example, you might position the camera at the finish line of a race. Also, begin covering action at a sharp angle to the subject rather than at a right angle. This gives viewers a chance to recognize the subject and orient their attention.

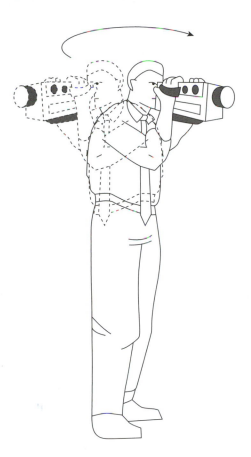

Figure 11.8 To pan a field camera with minimal jerkiness, start with your body straight, feet spread, elbows close to your sides, and the camera in the position it should be at the end of the pan. Then twist your body to move the camera to the starting position. To accomplish the pan, slowly untwist yourself.

Safety First. For all camera work in the field, if you bring the camera close to the action, train yourself to shoot with both eyes open. For example, if you are stationed on the sideline of a football game, use one eye to monitor the viewfinder and the other to watch the area around you. This way you can anticipate where to shoot next, but more important, you will be better able to tell when a 300-pound defensive tackle is about to crash into your camera.

ENG in Extreme Weather. Cold, wet, and windy weather conditions are a challenge to the ENG field crew. Covering major storms, hurricanes, tornadoes, and floods therefore requires special planning. If everyone has evacuated a dangerous weather zone, and you are assigned to cover the impending storm and its aftermath, you will need to adapt to extreme conditions while keeping yourself and your equipment safe. A good first principle is the following: *Use common sense, and don't be a hero.* Walking through a 3-foot-deep puddle in semi-darkness to get a key shot may not be a good idea if your next step is onto a hidden power line.

If the power is out, you will have to function without conventional electricity. You may also have to do without access to food or water for several days. Under such conditions, the ENG shoot soon begins to resemble a rustic camping trip or even a military operation. Plan accordingly. In addition to food and several changes of warm clothing, pack enough blankets, pillows, towels, and toiletries for several days. Depending on the area you are in, a snakebite kit may be a useful addition to standard first aid supplies. Flashlights and extra batteries are always useful. In addition to your cell phone, a multiband radio (battery powered) that can receive weather channels is also an obvious asset.

As for equipment, the main objective is to *keep it dry.* In addition to the raincoats already mentioned, additional waterproof barriers are invaluable. Plastic waterproof storage containers for tapes and batteries (and food) will keep them dry until you get back to the station.

When shooting in rain and wind, put the wind at your back to keep water off the lens. Keep soft dry towels handy to wipe the lens if necessary. If gale forces get too rough, shoot from inside the van for stability. Again, don't be a hero if the wind starts tossing street signs around as if they were Tinkertoys—at that point, you may have already gotten enough storm footage to permit you to retreat to a safe zone. A shelter is a good place to shoot additional storm footage and an even better place to begin shooting aftermath segments by interviewing people who are waiting out the storm. The human interest segment of the story can begin or continue there.

In extreme cold, keep camera batteries warm to extend their usefulness. Low temperatures can cut battery life to less than half. Store them under your clothes, next to your skin, to keep them warm until right before you use them. If available, use the electrical generator in your van to recharge them.

Going from a cold to a warm environment can promote condensation, which can paralyze mechanical parts of equipment. Some recorders have sensors that shut them off when the moisture level gets too high. If this happens, you simply need to wait until the machine dries out. Moisture can also be murder on flash cards and other digital equipment components.

Your job does not end when the storm ends. You still must shoot dramatic exterior aftermath footage to illustrate the storm's effects. Then you must get the story back to the station. If power is out, or if you are out of range of a microwave link, you will need an alternative method of reaching the station with your story. Some field crews arrange to feed video from local television stations—even competing ones.

Live ENG Communication Systems. As we saw in the earlier examples (i.e., the golf tournament), various communication systems are used to coordinate live field productions. These systems are best understood in terms of how their reach, range, and interactivity aspects connect different groups of relevant parties. The most obvious receivers of live video from the field are the end-users—namely, audiences, who see broadcast or cable feeds as part of regularly scheduled programming and special reports. However, earlier in the process, various production personnel exchange messages to help them produce and deliver finished programs. These include producers, directors, reporters, and crew members in the field, as well as directors, news anchors, and others at home bases that are often out of direct earshot and line of sight of one another.

Table 11.2 describes some of the communication devices used to connect relevant parties to one another, and Figure 11.9 diagrams the connections they establish. Without these systems, the smooth delivery of field coverage would be impossible. When working, these systems are invisible to the end-user. However, when breakdowns occur during live transmissions, such failures quickly become apparent to viewers in the way the end-product looks—viewers experience dead air, mismatches between audio and video, uncoordinated or missed coverage of key moments, embarrassing cutaways with apologies, and so forth. It is therefore little wonder that good field producers are committed to building redundancy into their communication systems to avoid catastrophe. Though these systems are especially important in live shoots, they are also used in many taped productions.

The double-headed arrows in Figure 11.9 indicate real-time interactive (that is, two-way) communication between relevant parties with a given communication system (voice, video, or data). The single-headed arrows indicate one-way message flow between parties. For example, the cell connecting off-air home base directors with on-camera field reporters contains an IFB entry because directors at the home base use IFBs to talk to on-air talent in the field. This link has a single-headed arrow because field reporters can hear messages from the directors but cannot use the IFBs to talk back to home base personnel. However, field reporters can send voice messages to home base personnel via the audio portion of the video signal. Hence, it is through two separate channels (therefore some redundancy) that interactive voice communication is established between these two relevant parties. If one of the two channels is lost, some communication is still maintained, a comfort to the field producer when Murphy's law kicks in.

Tape Logs. Much ENG-style raw footage is composed of interview segments, cover shots, cutaways and reverse-angle material, event coverage (also called *actuality* footage), and *standups* (direct-to-camera shots of the field reporter talking). Therefore, editing is often required to complete the program. Since time is of the essence in news, it is best to be poised for the postproduction editing from the start. For recorded segments, this means creating an accurate log of each recording as it is being shot, if possible, or shortly thereafter. The log should identify each clip in order, including its length in minutes and seconds, with SMPTE time

Table 11.2   Communication Devices for Field Production

Walkie-talkies	Establish voice contact among crew members who are out of earshot and/or line of sight with one another
Scanners	Permit news crews in the field to monitor police and fire department activities
Cell phones, two-way radios	Connect members of field crews and home bases with one another
Headset intercoms	Link field director and crew members
IFBs (interruptible foldback circuits)	Allow directors and other personnel to talk to on-air talent through an earpiece worn by the talent during a live telecast. The IFB system is commonly called a program interrupt (PI).
Video line monitors	Enable field personnel (both on and off camera) to see and hear a live feed of the program being transmitted from the home base
Battery-powered televisions	Serve the same function as line monitors
Camera-cable and wireless private lines (PLs)	Allow remote truck personnel and production crews to communicate with one another, as well as with other remote control rooms and home bases during all production phases
Pagers (beepers)	Provide data communications via radio transmission to alert personnel to contact someone
Megaphones	Enable field directors to communicate with nearby crew in the field during preproduction phases

code information if available. These accounting procedures are an invaluable aid to the postproduction process.

The ENG Postproduction Stage

Once production is complete, you will need to strike all of the equipment quickly, efficiently, and safely before moving on to the next location. You may wish to hold a postproduction meeting (a *debriefing*) to discover ways of doing better the next time. Usually the producer, director, technical manager, and assistant director meet to discuss any problems that were encountered. Sometimes, the technical manager's job includes feeding a daily "trouble report" to the home base. Besides helping to solve problems, the debriefing should build morale among the crew.

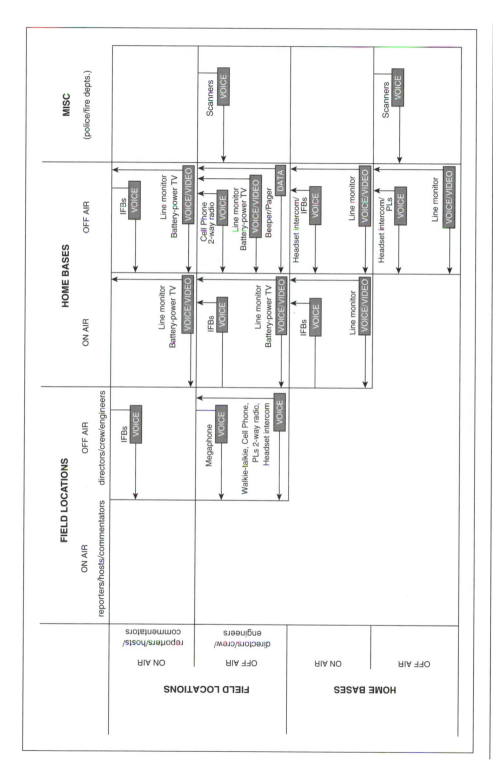

Figure 11.9 ENG communication systems. The diagram shows how selected communication devices establish links, either one-way (single-headed arrows) or two-way (double-headed arrows), between field locations and home bases.

Other postproduction chores include thanking all of the personnel in the field. In addition to the crew, others deserving of thanks (either in person, by phone, or by letter) include all support personnel and contacts that helped you set up and execute the shoot. It is not only the polite thing to do but wise also because the people you have just worked with may work with you again in the future.

Finally, for recorded material, the editing can begin, a process that we discuss in detail in the next chapter. If you have created an accurate log of each clip, the editing process will be greatly simplified.

ELECTRONIC FIELD PRODUCTION

Even stories that begin as breaking news can evolve into a different kind of field production. On the morning of the 9/11 attacks, viewers worldwide saw many shaky pictures of the Twin Towers' collapse and destruction of surrounding buildings shot from traffic helicopters. Later, however, much of the aftermath coverage was not nearly so spontaneous or rough in terms of production values. News crews camped for weeks, filing daily stories from lower Manhattan and Washington, D.C., locations. In the following months, reporters presented more carefully crafted feature stories for later broadcast. For example, later stories integrated retrospectives of events leading up to the attacks with interviews of friends and family members of the victims, as well as formal coverage of memorial services led by the mayor, and police and fire department officials.

For such stories, a more filmic approach is often taken, using a single camera with multiple setups. In particular, greater care may given to such production values as talent rehearsals, camera and subject placement, blocking, lighting, sound, continuity, scriptwriting, and editing. Roughly speaking, the shift away from spontaneity and rough production values to more planning and higher production values distinguishes ENG from what has come to be known as **electronic field production (EFP).**

Because of the advance-planning aspect of EFP, shoots can be better designed and more leisurely in their execution than ENG shoots. More sophisticated equipment is used. All in all, EFP aesthetics often match or exceed what is done in the studio. In this chapter, EFP refers to recorded single-camera production done in nonstudio locales. The multicamera remote (MCR), both live and on tape, is discussed later.

The types of programs produced using EFP techniques range from simple interviews done in people's offices to complex presentations shot in numerous locations. Commercials, corporate meetings, magazine programs, videos (instructional, educational, and industrial), promotional and public relations campaigns, even feature documentaries—all these may employ EFP techniques. They may feature almost no postproduction work, or they may use a wide variety of editing and sweetening techniques.

The EFP Mobile Unit and Equipment

The EFP mobile unit and equipment resemble that of the ENG operation with some notable exceptions. For example, since there is no need for a live feed from the field, the EFP mobile unit dispenses with microwave and satellite transmission hardware. Instead, the surface of the van's roof can be used as a camera platform to get high-angle shots. Without the transmission hardware, more room is available for additional camera, recording, lighting, and audio equipment. Of course, the well-equipped van has customized storage rigs to store and secure all equipment during transport. AC power connections and an electric generator that runs on diesel fuel are added advantages.

Cameras. Cameras for EFP can be higher-end models for added picture quality, with tripods and shoulder-mount accessories to match. Additional equipment can include an array of lenses and filters; a jib for high, sweeping camera movements; a portable dolly; and tracking equipment for sophisticated camera movements on the ground.

Higher-quality EFP productions currently tend to use Betacam cameras, with Betacam SP, Digi-Beta, or DVC-Pro-25 or -50. However, some work is still done using S-VHS, mini-DV, and even Hi-8 technology, though the latter two are often limited to in-house corporate and educational (closed-circuit) settings. The latest technology to gain prominence is the high-definition (HD) format. All these formats can run on batteries. However, it is always better to use AC power when available.

Lighting and Filters. Depending on the nature of the shoot, EFP lighting equipment can be as sophisticated as that found in a fully equipped studio. In fact, if the shoot takes place outdoors, the equipment can go beyond what is needed in the studio environment.

Filters are particularly important for EFP. Video cameras are made to operate without the need for color correcting under lighting with color temperatures in the 3,200 K range (as produced by tungsten-halogen lights). Under all other conditions, some filtering is necessary to maintain proper color. Table 11.3 lists the most common filters used to match color temperatures with lighting conditions you are likely to encounter on field shoots, including camera-mounted filters (mounted either behind or over the camera lens), light-mounted filters (mounted or clamped

Table 11.3   Common EFP Filters

Type of Filter	Function
Camera-mounted filters	
Neutral density	To reduce the quantity of light entering the camera. Reduced exposure permits the use of wider lens apertures, thus cutting depth of field.
Fluorescent	Correct for the greenish cast of fluorescent lighting, bringing it to 3,200 K. FLB filters correct for fluorescent lights with color temperatures of 4,500 K. FLD filters correct for "daylight" fluorescent lighting in the 6,500 K range.
Amber	Correct sunlight to 3,200 K. Also correct artificial light in the range of 5,600 K (HMIs) to 3,200 K.
Light-mounted filters	
Dichroic	Correct quartz-halogen light from 3,200 K to the 5,600 K range to make it compatible with sunlight.
Window-mounted filters	
Amber filter sheets	Correct incoming sunlight to 3,200 K range.

in front of the lighting instrument itself), and window-mounted filters (mounted on windows to correct to 3,200 K the color temperature of sunlight entering the production area).

Besides controlling the color temperature, filters also allow you to control the amount of light entering the camera. By controlling the light level, you can vary the aperture size you wish to use, thus making it possible to control depth of field. When filters are used to limit the amount of light entering the lens, a **filter factor** may be used to determine the amount of light lost because of filtering. For example, a filter factor of 2 cuts the amount of light entering the lens in half, which is the same amount that would be cut by reducing the lens aperture by one full f/stop. Using filters with known filter factors, you can control exposure levels and thereby control depth of field, even under extremely bright conditions. For example, using a neutral-density filter with a filter factor of 4, you can shoot at a lens aperture two f/stops wider than would be possible with no filter, resulting in shallower depth of field. For filters used in combination, remember to multiply filter factors to determine how many f/stops you have jumped.

Audio. The audio needs of an EFP production can go beyond the simple arrangements of the typical ENG shoot. In addition to those needs already outlined for ENG, you may need to include booms, wireless mics with RF transmitters, fishpoles, and shotgun mics. It is also common to use audio mixing boards with headsets for riding the gain during EFP productions. Furthermore, if audio foldback or playback is wanted, you will need to bring portable speakers and recorders. Of course, you must also supply enough cable to hook everything up, as well as gaffer's tape for securing cables.

The EFP Preproduction Stage

Perhaps one of the biggest differences between ENG and EFP shoots is the preproduction phase. The EFP crew has the luxury of scouting locations and planning all phases of the production before any shooting begins.

An EFP site survey should answer a wide range of questions, including the following: What is the site like? Can we get a location sketch? Is it indoors or outdoors or both? If outdoors, where is the sun? How will that affect the shots we need to get? How will time of day affect the nature of light during each shooting day? Is it always this quiet? Is the ebb and flow of people through this area uniform? It is always an advantage to do the site survey close to the day the shoot will begin to simulate the conditions as accurately as possible. If the site survey takes place 3 months in advance, much may have changed by the time the shoot occurs.

As for equipment concerns, the following questions are important: Where are our camera locations? What audio and lighting equipment are needed? Is there sufficient electrical power? Do all the outlets actually work? Which cable runs are shortest? Does that door open all the way? How and when can we gain access to the site?

In terms of scheduling, ask the following: What are the shooting dates? Can we get everything we need in the allotted time? What do we do if bad weather (or another problem) throws off our schedule? What kind of cooperation will we get from the jurisdiction or the property owner for additional use of space and facilities?

Practical issues also need to be worked out: Is parking available? Lodging? Food? Bathroom facilities? Telephones? Who pays for all that? Do we have the necessary security and insurance coverage to ensure that our equipment will be properly cared for and protected from damage and theft?

Finally, in terms of legal issues, ask what contracts, permits, clearances, and release forms are needed, and then plan accordingly. These and countless other questions should be answered during the preproduction phase of the EFP shoot.

As for voice communications among the crew, the EFP operation can make good use of cell and car phones for coordinating activities among crew members who may be arriving in separate vehicles. Once on location, crew members can communicate with one another with walkie-talkies. Battery-powered megaphones are also useful during rehearsals. Pagers, headset intercoms, and private lines may also become important during different phases of the production process.

The EFP Production Stage

An EFP shoot can mix all of the challenges of studio production with all of the unknowns of the field. Because of the varied types of programs that are handled in EFP, it is impossible to specify all the production situations you will encounter. However, it is possible to describe some of the more common production considerations for several leading program genres.

Meetings and News Conferences. Government hearings, news conferences, and similar indoor gatherings present unique problems. The subjects you are there to cover may be quite expert in their professional fields, but they may lack on-air experience and may not appreciate your production needs. On the other hand, if they are poorly covered, their insights may be lost. It is your job to keep this from happening.

More specifically, the subject may wander from a fixed microphone position, causing you to lose key audio. Or the subject may refer to graphic materials that are simply not air quality, such as thinly lettered charts on white reflective cards. Speakers may sweat profusely under hot lights after refusing to wear makeup. Or they may forget they have promised to stay in the lighted area for proper video coverage. They may turn away from the camera altogether.

As for the area where the coverage is to take place, it may be inadequately lit and lack adequate electrical outlets. The room may be too large to be lit well with the instruments you have. There may be room set aside for chairs to accommodate audience members but little or no space for cameras and lights. The room's decor—busy backgrounds, for example—may present extra problems for video coverage. The room may be echoey and boomy because of hard wall surfaces. The audience may be noisy. Other sounds from plumbing and nearby traffic may present additional audio problems.

Furthermore, audience participation in, say, a question-and-answer period during or after speakers' presentations may require lighting in two directions, presenting the possibility of glare problems. To solve such problems, it may be necessary to find alternate camera positions. Moreover, you will need to decide how speeches by audience members will be captured. You can hang an area mic over the group if it is small, but if that is not feasible, you may need to use a fish-pole mic carried by a production assistant. Another alternative is to use a mic stand for audience members to step up to when they ask questions. Or you can have someone at the speaker's podium field questions and then repeat them to obtain adequate audio coverage.

For all of these potential problems, preproduction planning is critical, but you will also need to arrive early at the site to begin working on problems that crop up at the last minute. If graphics are going to be used, try to prepare air-quality versions of them in advance. To integrate materials into the program, get a sequence of the events or discussion topics in advance and ask the on-air presenters to inform you of any significant changes.

Documentary and Magazine Features. Feature stories for television are infinitely varied in terms of content. Material can range from an exposé on police corruption to a soft piece concerning the latest grooming trends at a dog show. Length can also vary, from a 1-minute segment designed to fit into a larger show to an hour-long format. Regardless of the topic or length, here are some things to keep in mind to make the production run smoothly:

- Conduct a site survey and preinterview with all key personnel—clients, on-air talent, production staff, field contacts—before the first day of shooting.

- Finalize the script to reflect the approach you will be taking. Get it approved in advance by the client. Make sure it is understood by both talent and crew.

- Note the running time for each segment, and be careful to log each one for later editing. Label boxes, tapes, and disks so as not to confuse them with others you may be using. As with ENG operations, adjust the "record" tab from the back of finished tapes so they don't accidentally get recorded over at later shoots.

- Make a quick on-site review of each segment to be sure you have air-quality program material for each. This means reviewing a bit of every segment to ensure you have in fact gotten the clips you think you have gotten. Monitor the audio also to confirm that sound was successfully recorded.

- If you need to reshoot segments, be careful not to "burn out" your talent with too many retakes. There comes a time when you must decide that a certain level of performance is all you are going to get from someone. If possible, show the client the footage at a private meeting and offer your professional opinion. That is in part what you are being paid for.

- Don't forget to shoot transitional material for later editing, including master and establishing shots, close-ups, reverse angles, and cutaways. Record ambient sound also, for later editing.

- Check footage you have collected against a checklist to make certain you have indeed gotten the things you need.

- If you need to return for more shooting at a later date, take snapshots of the sets and costumes, if any, so that these can be replicated the next time. Similarly, if shooting outdoors, note the time of day and the weather conditions so that later shoots can match lighting conditions.

The EFP Postproduction Stage

At the conclusion of the production, your editing task may include additional audio and video sweetening, such as adding titles, credits, graphics, music, narration, and sound effects. However, the editing task is not the only postproduction concern. There may be promotional chores for getting the finished piece exhibited.

As with ENG operations, thank everyone involved. Finally, hold a debriefing meeting with the crew and other staff members to iron out problems that came up so that you can improve your future performance.

MULTICAMERA REMOTE PRODUCTION

Multicamera remote (MCR) production is, as the name implies, a production process done in nonstudio locations that uses more than one camera at the same time, permitting the director to cut between cameras exactly as is done in a conventional studio operation. Everything that can be done in a conventional studio can be done in an MCR operation. A mobile truck serves as the control room. Using ENG-type transmission facilities and intercom systems, the MCR operation delivers coverage to a home base for transmission to virtually any audience, potentially worldwide. Multicamera remote productions include live coverage of the Olympics and other sporting events, such as professional baseball and football and NCAA college basketball. MCR techniques are also used for political conventions, concerts, theatrical events, and major awards ceremonies.

Like EFP productions, MCR operations sometimes cover events staged primarily for television, making it possible to produce supporting material ahead of time. In these cases, event coverage can be integrated with prepared segments, feature stories, biographies, and interviews (*backgrounders*). Coverage is often carefully timed to accommodate cutaways for commercials and promotional announcements.

The MCR Mobile Unit and Equipment

In addition to using all the equipment already described for ENG and EFP operations, the MCR expands its arsenal to include banks of monitors and a production switcher.

In short, at the high end, all of the control room hardware found in the most advanced studio facilities is available. Some high-end units (trailer trucks over 40 feet long) even contain *more* equipment than is found in most studios (see Photo 11.4).

Photo 11.4   MCR facilities used at the Kemper Open golf tournament. These 46-foot MCR trailer trucks contain technical, maintenance, production, and transmission facilities.

For example, for units covering major sports, in addition to sophisticated transmission facilities, camera control hardware, character generators, still store machines, and a separate audio console, there are also a number of slow-motion replay recorders and laser disk machines. Power requirements for such facilities can easily exceed the load limitations of generators. For this reason, power needs may be supplemented with outside connections from local utility companies.

The MCR Preproduction Stage

The same concerns outlined in the preproduction phase of EFP operations are relevant to the MCR operation. In addition, the MCR preproduction phase should also be concerned with the following:

1. Since you will likely not rely solely on your own power and communications lines for service needs, be sure to establish reliable contacts for electricians, telephone company personnel, and any other maintenance services. During the site survey, power needs should be clearly established, and a decision should be made to go with either all generator-supplied power or all land-supplied power to eliminate phasing and grounding problems caused by two different sources.

2. Parking for the mobile vehicle may require special permissions from the local authorities. To ensure access to the remote site, arrange to get permits or reservations for entrance and parking.

3. Review the paperwork generated from the site survey ahead of time to establish the best location(s) for the vehicle(s) and equipment. Work out a plan that requires the shortest cable runs. For many events, such as established sporting events and concert venues, fixed (buried) cables may already be available. Inquire ahead of time to take advantage of them.

4. In addition to noting the location of each camera, be especially aware of the number of cameras you need to deploy, the mobility they are afforded by their locations, and the lens requirements each position demands as a function of the shots you want each camera to get. Select lens focal length ranges accordingly.

5. Audio needs are just as critical as video needs. Arrange to deploy mics near all the sounds you intend to collect. For example, for live coverage of an NCAA championship basketball game, separate microphones may be used to pick up sneaker squeaks, ball swishes through the nets, grunts of players, reactions of spectators, and the speeches of announcers and commentators.

These needs may require the use of headset mics, shotgun mics, parabolic mics, and wireless lavalieres with a variety of pickup patterns. You may also want to accept a direct audio feed from the arena's PA system.

6. In addition to intercom voice links among relevant parties via camera headsets, additional private lines may be added at selected locations for floor managers, assistants, and other production personnel. As with ENG operations, IFBs should be used to send voice cues from control room personnel to on-air talent.

7. Feeds for both program and preview video can be provided wherever needed by running cables from the truck's control room to selected field locations.

8. Establish security measures that protect equipment from theft and destruction.

The MCR Production Stage

Once the preproduction phase is completed, it is time to set up and rehearse. Arrive early. Review the schedule of events with the crew, and make sure that the sequence of tasks is correct. For example, if special platforms are needed to support cameras and other equipment, make sure they are ready when the cameras arrive. Many shops tack a handwritten schedule to the control room door of the remote truck.

Once everything is set up, the rehearsal phase parallels that in a regular studio production. Verify that all systems are up and running. For example, are transmission facilities functioning properly? Do you have reliable intercom connections and adequate video feeds for all crew and on-air personnel? Are all camera control units working properly? Are cameras color-balanced and shaded? Are microphones deployed where you need them? Have levels been taken? A facilities check is done by a broadcast associate and assistants who put on all the headsets and check all the monitors and audio lines.

Once all systems are go, conduct run-throughs. For events that can't be thoroughly staged in advance, such as sporting events, assign responsibilities so that camera and other production personnel know roughly what they will cover for a number of different scenarios. In baseball, for example, the camera located in center field can practice zooming and panning to capture the pitcher and batter, pop-ups behind home plate, and so forth.[4] During rehearsals, the crew should become accustomed to strange or awkward surroundings and any limitations presented by the site.

At show time, if you are broadcasting live, be sure to maintain contact with the studio, especially for time cues for commercial cutaways and other prerecorded inserts. Start times are strictly followed and must be coordinated carefully with the rest of the broadcast day. Promotional announcements and possible schedule changes should be monitored from the remote site. A line monitor in the remote truck carrying the station's broadcast feed is the best way to coordinate field coverage with the home base.

The MCR Postproduction Stage

The same postproduction chores noted in the ENG and EFP sections apply to MCR. In MCR productions, with their large amounts of expensive equipment, it is especially important to keep a checklist to make certain nothing has been left behind.

If the program is recorded rather than live, the editing tasks are likely to be larger and more complex than in ENG or EFP. In the next chapter, we will focus on the full range of editing processes that can be used for both studio and field productions.

INDUSTRY VOICES

Marc Wiener

On October 13, 2003, and then again in October 2005, I spoke with Marc Wiener, supervisor and assistant to the chief of engineering of WCBS television in New York. Wiener's 33-year career started at CBS-FM radio, where he went from broadcast engineer to production and assistant chief engineer, transferring to CBS television in 1983. Then he progressed from audio engineer to director of electronic news gathering and finally to assistant to the technical operations manager planning for new studio projects, rebuilding studio facilities to accommodate the digital transition, including the installation of video servers to enable television news operations to expand to Internet applications. Wiener talks about news gathering in New York City during 9/11. He also shares his insights concerning the impact of the changeover to digital technology in the television news business.

L: What happened on 9/11 in terms of news coverage?

M: We had another transmitter site—we were the only ones broadcasting over the air for a long time.

L: So tell us how that was done initially. It was 8:47 a.m. EST when the first attack occurred, then at 9:02 the second tower was hit. What was CBS transmitting, and how were they doing it?

M: Well at that point, we were still transmitting from the World Trade Center because even when the first plane hit, there was no collapse, and when the first plane hit, we weren't sure what it was. We looked up. Our helicopter was doing traffic news. No one actually saw what kind of plane it was. When we saw fire, we thought it was a Cessna or something and we said [sarcastically], "Oh, great, this is gonna be a lovely news day," because that was the day of the New York City mayoral primary. I had already given out equipment intended for election coverage that evening, with a plan already in place. We had done site surveys, paid for phone and video lines at various hotels around the city to cover the mayoral primary. I had given instructions of where the crews were to go that night, printed out sheets, and I had piled up equipment for the different crews to take. Then suddenly I'm looking up at the television behind me and saying, "What's that? Oh great, a Cessna or something hit the World Trade Center." And obviously, it is a major story, so now it's going to change everything as far as our coverage for the day. So I went up to the newsroom, across the street from where all the gear and trucks are kept. I saw the second attack on TV, because we had pictures—live pictures from our traffic helicopter.

L: And was what you were seeing being beamed to the network?

M: Well, CBS is unique among the three O and Os in New York, in that only the local station has ENG vans for live microwave pictures. The network did not own any satellite trucks in New York; the network has satellite gear, but until the advent of digital satellite news gathering (DSNG), satellite time was very expensive, so if the network wanted a live picture of New York City, they just hired Channel 2. So they have a history of taking our live shots for whatever they want. And our helicopter coverage is transmitted to our microwave room and can be routed to any division. So, basically, the CBS network can go live with our pictures.

L: To 220 stations around the country?

M: Right, whoever belongs to CBS network has access. If they want, they can feed our live shots from their C-band or KU-band satellite. They can either take a feed from the guy in the helicopter, or they can voice-over our live pictures with their own news anchors saying, "You're now seeing pictures of the World Trade Center live." When the second tower was attacked live on the air, we knew it was terrorism—our original plans for election coverage were out the window. I knew at that point all regular programming is cancelled, and this is it.

L: What did you do?

M: I went to the newsroom to talk to the news director about how we were going to cover the attack.

L: How many cameras and crews did you talk to that day?

M: It was all hands on deck with 12 microwave trucks (two of them combination microwave/digital satellite trucks), and an analog satellite truck, so that's 13, and a bunch of cars with camera crews that hook up with trucks to go live. We called all 26 crew members in who knew they were going to work overtime, and from that moment, we were on the air continuously for weeks. We were the only ones who had a transmitter.

L: What was your job title at that point?

M: I was director of electronic news gathering. I was overseeing acquisition, purchasing, capital planning, large project and event planning (for example, when the Yankees would win the World Series, I coordinated pooled coverage of the ticker-tape parades with all the other local TV stations). My work included handling everything from processing traffic tickets for our trucks to arranging for vehicle maintenance when they'd break down. I was in charge of press IDs, vehicle permits to go on parkways with trucks that weren't normally allowed on parkways, the whole gamut. It was a large job.

L: How did you personally feel that day?

M: I was continually adjusting my expectations. There were so many things to think of.

L: How were you communicating with all your crews?

M: We had Nextel phones with a walkie-talkie feature built in. Cell phone technology failed completely on 9/11, because the landline infrastructure of Verizon's main switching office was right across the street from the World Trade Center. The Nextel system uses both cell phone and land-line infrastructures for cell phone calls, but their direct connect feature uses a technology which is just now becoming known to the public called Voice-Over IP. Nextel's Direct Connect technology bypasses the landline system completely so even though the cell phone part of the system didn't work, the walkie-talkie feature did—flawlessly. CBS has also had its own two-way radio system for over 25 years, which functioned well within distance limitations so we could talk to all the crews with both the Nextel Direct Connect and our own two-way radios.

L: What kinds of things were you saying?

M: First we were finding out if everyone was safe. We had a truck crew at ground zero. We told them to get the hell out. I said "Leave the truck! Get out!" The truck was covered with rubble. And we lost a car, also. We didn't lose anybody on the ground, but we did lose two of our transmitter engineers when the buildings came down, because they could not get out, due to a fire below them. So we suffered losses on the television side, but not on the ENG side.

L: Did you attend any funerals?

M: Yes, I attended the funeral of one of the transmitter engineers. Then later, on the first anniversary, when they had the shaft of light installed at ground zero, and the Empire State Building observatory was closed to the public, the victim's family and CBS personnel were permitted access to observe ceremonies from the Empire State Observatory that night. Logistically, at the time of the attacks, we eventually began taking video from crews in New Jersey, as we were telling our New York crews near the attack site to just sit tight. We knew they'd have great pictures, but we still had to coordinate new feeds under new circumstances. We also had to decide who'd have the most important and dramatic sound and video.

L: Was everyone sending back live video, with you assessing what to put on the air?

M: Only a limited number of sources could put signals up simultaneously, because the World Trade Center had been one of our main receive sites, and it was gone. So we were left with just the Empire State Building as a receive site, and one in Plainview, and a place in Verona, New Jersey. And we couldn't have three trucks aiming at the same location and up simultaneously. The only way to decide what to carry was to have each source power up, then power down, to avoid interference. To coordinate who was going to feed what and when, was where the Nextel and two-way radio system came in. Two-way phone communication is essential for coordination, and coordination is the hidden component that television audiences don't realize or see. Crew members have IFBs in their ear, to listen to the director in the studio, or to someone in the microwave room receiving the signals. But without two-way phone connections, getting live television on the air is very difficult.

L: You said that emergency coverage went on "for weeks."

M: Yes.

L: Do you remember when there was normalcy again?

M: We were on the air continuously, 24 hours a day, for at least three weeks. There were no commercials; we had no regular programming. And we would cut away to Washington at times but we were still on the air continuously, and crews were doing 12-hour shifts for weeks. We would stay in a nearby hotel room, sleep for a couple of hours, and then go back to our posts. I didn't see my family, nor did I go home. I was up without any sleep for almost three days. I didn't go home at all to change clothes or anything for five days. There was no way out, anyway. Everything was shut down and you couldn't do anything. My wife knew—I've been in the business forever, so she knew, that my kids would not be seeing Daddy again until the next time we see him, whenever that is.

L: Perhaps nothing is "normal" again.

M: Right. We were doing 9/11 weekend newscasts for the next month or two. When there was no network programming, we came back to local news programming again, and we really didn't have any commercials; we had no commercials even past the three weeks. Even being a New Yorker has changed. As a New Yorker, you can't really think about it too much. You can't, you just have to live your life. It's the same as living in Israel, where a bus could blow up at any time. People say, "How do you live with that?" You just do it.

L: Changing topics. How in your view has the changeover from analog to digital technologies impacted the television business on your end of the industry?

M: At this point, although many stations have committed to some of the new formats, tape is still the dominant medium for field acquisition. Sony, Panasonic, and JVC all have new cameras, and some use recordable DVDs and some have solid-state chips while others use hard drives, but they're all expensive technology. The tape format is still in use because it is cheap. You can have workers ride around with 20 to 30 cassettes in their trunk with no more than $500 involved. That's low risk. By contrast, a hard drive may be over $100 for just 20 minutes. How many hard drives are you going to let a guy drive around in his trunk with?

L: With digital linear format tape, after you acquire material, what happens to get it to air? Do you send it digitally through a computer/Internet access?

M: Right now, there is a transition period going on at CBS where all of our new microwave trucks have digital microwave capability. Digital microwave has a waiver from the FCC and is not yet recognized as an official radio-type format, but CBS has digital microwave trucks. They roll the raw footage in the truck, and feed it back via either digital or ana-log microwave (it makes no difference to the receive site, either the Empire State Building or Plainview), and from there it's relayed, most of the time via microwave to the broadcast center, where it is re-recorded onto a 60- or 90-minute digital tape. Then the microwave room contacts the edit room and says, "The Marsha Kramer feed is coming in on Microwave 2." It can then be recorded or logged in real time in the edit room as it is being fed in or just recorded for later editing. Through this method, you have three or four copies. They'll roll two copies in the microwave room and one in the edit room, so there are three copies in house immediately, and when the crew comes back in to hand in the raw tape, that gets archived. The field tapes get saved on an average from two weeks to forever, depending on what it is. The stuff that comes in microwave is saved for a week and then recycled. All the tapes are dated, and after a year or so, they get thrown out. Eventually tapes get damaged, scratched, dropped, the magnetic oxide gets damaged so the tapes are eventually discarded. There are machines that do take evaluations of tape quality, but assessment is too manpower intensive, which makes it expensive. Because cassettes are only $10, you just toss them into the trash by date, basically.

L: So that's essentially the process in news these days. Thinking more generally, what would you say has been the impact of the digital transition on the television industry in broader terms?

M: In two words, the move to digital has led to media convergence and repurposing, faster than people would have anticipated. Repurposing means that video programs can now be used for both television and Web sites, or even cell phones or i-Pods at this point. As a result, they are produced with that idea in mind—to use the show for release on tele-vision, but then to make the program material, either in whole or in part, useful for Web distribution and other outlets. As for convergence, the equipment now used in television stations is not just video equipment. Because the hardware is computer-based, the same machines can be used in a research firm, a newspaper publisher, or in a video editing suite. That's convergence. At bottom, the information, whether visual, sound, or text, is binary code, and the computers process it the same way no matter what business is being served.

L: Which system does CBS use?

M: At the moment, WCBS uses a dedicated computer by Panasonic, the NewsByte, which features a deck that can do a transfer at four times normal speed. It also has a computer hard drive, and an interface with a Windows NT format, so they can do nonlinear editing. Of course, since it is a computer, it can crash, and when it does, it has to be rebooted, which is a real pain for old-time editors who say, "Why did we go to this? I'm in the middle of a news piece that has to be on the air in five minutes, and the whole computer's locked up. This is not progress." Beta machines never crashed. The worst you got was a head clog or something. So the old-timers are right in a sense. It is a step back, but it's the way the business has gone, and you have to live through these growing pains until it becomes more robust and reliable.

The Panasonic system WCBS uses is a dedicated video system. But Avid sells a system that is not dedicated—the same computer that does word processing for scripts also stores video, and has editing software built into it, and when you take a piece of video, not only can you put it onto video tape, you can distribute it directly to a Web site, with the script tied directly to the video so that if people click on a story, the video will come up on the Web site automatically. Then the user can see and hear it, and can even fast-forward and rewind. As for the producer-end, Teleprompter material is on there too. Finally, when the producer decides to edit or even kill a story, it can be edited or removed from the broadcast schedule. Scripts can be automatically changed, and in one stroke, so can the rundown, the prompter, the chyron, and hypertext links, all by one person. By contrast, in the past, if the director decided he wanted to change or drop a story, he'd have to tell the prompter operator to make the necessary changes, and operators in the newsroom and master control room would also need to respond. Now, one person does it, and everything changes at once.

L: The union must love that. Talk to me about the personnel side. What do you think of it?

M: These changes are inevitable. The impact on the major networks and affiliates is significant. For one thing, there is less production money available these days. TV and radio used to be a license to print money because there was no place else viewing audiences could go—advertisers had to buy advertising on TV and radio, because there were no other choices among nonprint media. Now, there are many more choices, with cable outlets, video games, DVDs, Internet Web sites, being on cell phones, even watching i-Pods.

Nowadays, you can watch 600 stations on satellite TV. The odds of a person watching a major network station are less—it's called fragmentation. There are only 24 hours in a day and there are only so many viewers at a given instant in time. So the money is not there as it once was. For all these reasons, there is tremendous pressure to reduce personnel costs, and using technology to enable one person to do more jobs is inevitable.

L: So what does a résumé say when they hire a person to come in and sit at the tower and type?

M: They're still called a newswriter. Right now, it's a transition period; most newsrooms don't have the money to put a fully versatile computer system in with the infrastructure to shuttle video around. But eventually, when it is universally deployed, writers won't have to go into the edit room. They won't have to leave their desks. They will see video in real time on a computer, which will be the same one used for word processing. And the writer will be able to mark in- and out-points on the video, and on the script, and tie it to time-code. Then machines will automatically edit the video, and tie it to words in the script. This is all possible now, but it's just expensive, because you need high-speed Ethernet running through the organization and servers which all store video. In the future, you'll be able to pull up video anywhere in the world with a Google-type search, and this is what is meant by convergence. It is this convergence technology that enables repurposing.

L: I'm fantasizing the possibility of using virtual actors and voice synthesis triggered by someone typing a story . . .

M: Look at the Lara Croft movie, where they had virtual actors, and look at the special effects where they have huge crowds of people that don't exist. It's technology that's definitely being worked on.

L: Do you still have to have a human in the field aiming the camera?

M: At this point, yes. But when ENG first started, it was a three-person crew, and now it's a one-person crew. A single person drives the truck, sets up a microwave signal, shoots the story, edits the piece in the field, then goes live. People used to say, "It'll never happen! They can't do it!" Well, they do it. CBS does it. All the trucks are one-person trucks, except at night. The only argument the union has at this point is personal safety. So you say thank God for lawyers. They won't send out a one-person crew at night, because there's nobody to watch the guy's back. But during the day, if safety is not an issue, it's all one-person crews.

L: What has this done to news judgment, and the quality of the product?

M: I think the combination of reduced crew size and the increasing pressure to go live on the air quickly has changed news judgment. You have much less judgment in terms of both accuracy and ethics, because those values have to take a back seat when the number one concern is being first, and there are fewer personnel on hand to cover the story adequately.

L: What about the impact of these changes on other electronic media fields?

M: In the movie industry, computer-cameras that record digitally are replacing film cameras, using 24 frames per second just like the film industry standard. A movie shot on video tape may then be edited on a nonlinear computer system. For example, I just saw the new Coen brothers movie (Intolerable Cruelty) with George Clooney, which was edited on Final Cut Pro, Apple's video editing software. It's only a thousand dollars, and major motion pictures are being edited on it using an Apple G5 computer. The last three Star Wars movies were all shot on video and edited in the computer. When created this way, a movie can be transmitted to theaters equipped with video projectors using Internet technology, not film, so it never has to be rendered onto celluloid and distributed in film canisters. Special effects can be handled with a computer, so in the Lord of the Rings movies, there were no sets with huge crowds; instead those shots were created in a computer.

As of today, there are not too many theaters that have electronic projection. But there will be, because that's what the film industry wants. They want to be able to shoot digitally, edit digitally, not make any prints at all, but rather distribute to movie theaters, digitally. And then they can monitor how many times a film is run, and how many tickets were sold. They can download the file to servers in theaters and show it via an electronic projection system, and when the movie run is over, there are no prints to mail back. The entire system will be run on fiber optic, on a Virtual Private Network, in effect barring illicit piracy.

L: But it might still be pirated, a la the Napster effect.

M: But the risk is worth it to reduce distribution costs, as well as the cost of making prints. If you have the movie showing on thousands of screens, that's thousands of prints not needed! Now, you have one file, you send it out simultaneously to all the theaters with no mailing cost, no print cost, and there are no prints getting lost or breaking or having to be replaced or getting noisy. In addition, movie theaters will have the technical capability of screening live events like concerts. The digital transition changes everything, including the entire economic model of the business, whether it's TV or film.

KEY TERMS

QUESTIONS FOR REVIEW

How do the concepts of reach, range, and interactivity help explain the way communication systems are set up to make field productions run smoothly? Give examples of each concept.

What similarities and differences are there between ENG, EFP, and MCR field productions? How does SNG differ from ENG in terms of the equipment and transmission methods used to cover news?

Why is satellite transmission called distance insensitive?

What preproduction planning might you do to execute a field shoot of a local neighborhood PTA school meeting?

How can continuity be maintained when editing footage from an EFP shoot? What techniques can be used to avoid jump cuts and distracting sound variations from one segment to the next?

What function does shooting inserts and cutaways serve in producing footage for field productions?

Why is the axis-of-action rule important for preserving directional continuity? Give some examples.

What kinds of filters can help maintain proper color temperature when shooting under varied lighting conditions?

NOTES

1. During the 2005 London train bombing, the BBC went live with cell phone video and audio.

2. The terms *reach* and *range,* as they are used here, were first introduced to the author by Calloway in her essay in McCain and Shyles (1994, pp. 56–59).

3. Newer COFDM units (which all microwave transmitters will soon be due to the mandate from the Federal Communications Commission to reassign 2-GHz Channels 1 and 2 to other communication services) no longer require line of sight.

4. Standard camera positions for most major sporting events are described in Catsis (1996).

Chapter 12

Editing

Aesthetics and Techniques

You are watching *The Nesters,* a sitcom about title characters Bill and Carol Nester, affectionate young newlyweds. Both work in different companies, not far from their home. Normally, they wake up and have breakfast together, then drive to work in separate cars. At lunchtime, they always meet at their favorite restaurant. They return to work at 1:00 and at 5:00 drive home. Such is their typical day.

But not today. In this episode, entitled "The Surprise," their afternoon is disrupted by Carol's plan to throw a surprise birthday party for Bill at his office. To stall him while his pals get the office ready, Carol calls the restaurant feigning car trouble and asks Bill to come get her. While polishing off two baskets of his favorite breadsticks, Bill has been worrying about her lateness and also about the big report his boss has demanded by the end of the day. He rushes to get Carol, but then she convinces him to wait while their mechanic, who is in on the deception, fakes an attempt to diagnose the car problem. After much delay, both call their offices to explain why they're late. Of course, Carol is really calling Bill's office to see if it's time to bring him back yet. Bill finally insists they go to his office together to "button up a few details." At 3:00 they arrive at last at Bill's office, where the party comes off as planned. He is relieved to learn his buddies have already printed his report and delivered copies to his boss. Along with other presents, Bill receives an extra-large basket of his favorite breadsticks.

If you were shooting a video of this episode, how much screen time would it take? Certainly not the 6 or 7 hours of clock time that elapse in the story. In terms of *screen time,* conveying all the details of this episode would require just minutes.

Imagine what viewing would be like if all television programs presented their subject matter in real time. Most of them would be too expensive to make and too tedious to watch. Instead, largely through *editing,* television programs routinely present stories that cover long time spans in a much shorter period.

On the simplest level, editing is the process of assembling video segments into a desired sequence after they have been shot. Aside from condensing the time span, editing permits scenes to be shot out of order, according to the most convenient schedule, and then rearranged afterward. Most important, editing is used to enhance clarity and add impact to programs. This chapter focuses on both the aesthetic principles and the practical techniques of editing, covering the following topics:

Editing aesthetics

- Continuity editing
- Classical editing
- Dynamic editing: thematic montage
- Pictorial complexity and mise en scène
- Editing *The Nesters*
- Editing sound
- Technical advances influence editing decisions
- Throwing out all the rules

Editing techniques

- Control track editing with the basic two-deck system
- Logging footage and making an edit decision list
- Frame counting
- Assemble and insert editing
- SMPTE/EBU time code
- The expanded meanings of "on-line" and "off-line" editing
- Multisource editing
- Analog and digital recording systems: tape and disk formats
- Nonlinear digital editing

EDITING AESTHETICS

It should be clear from our opening discussion that editing spares audiences the insult and inconvenience of having to watch the tedious aspects of real life. But life cannot be chopped and compressed arbitrarily. What are some of the principles that videographers follow to make compressed time seem as convincing as real time?

Continuity Editing

To condense time without confusing the audience, editing must maintain *continuity,* which we defined in Chapter 11 as the smooth flow of uninterrupted action from shot to shot. Editing that condenses exposition while preserving continuity is called **continuity editing** or cutting to continuity. Successful continuity editing depends largely on preserving cause-and-effect relationships and unity in space and time.

Shot Order and Cause-and-Effect Relationships. To achieve good continuity, the editor must understand what to include and in what order, so that the audience can comfortably follow the action. Imagine the meaning you might take from the following sequence: a low-angle shot of a safe plummeting to the ground from an office window, followed by a shot of a child's frightened face seen against the background of the same building, followed by a shot of the safe, now on the ground, with damaged concrete around it and a partial view of a child's limb protruding from underneath (see Figure 12.1).

Figure 12.1   Using shot order to influence the viewer's perception of cause and effect. (a) A sequence of a falling safe implying that a child has been crushed by the safe. (b) Exactly the same shots, but rearranged so that the child appears to be a witness rather than a victim.

The implication of this sequence is that the child whose face we have just seen has been crushed by the safe. But rearrange the order of these shots, so that the cause-and-effect relationships seem to be altered, and you get a very different meaning. For example, if the shot of the child's face came *after* the others, we would assume that the child had just witnessed the tragedy rather than become the victim of it.

Unity in Space and Time. Recall the example we used in the last chapter of the soldier returning from his tour of duty to be greeted by his daughter in the airport. In order to maintain *unity in space,* we might cover their reunion hug by starting on a wide establishing two-shot of the father and daughter seen from the side, with the daughter waving from the opposite end of a large airport waiting area, then cut to head-on close-ups of each subject running toward the other, followed by a final shot of the two seen from the side once again, this time in tighter close-up, just as their bodies meet (see Figure 12.2). In this way, the establishing shot captures the spatial relationship of the subjects for the audience. Having the subjects wave at each other in the same shot also telegraphs the message that the subjects are waving to each other at the same time. Thus, *unity in time* is also preserved.

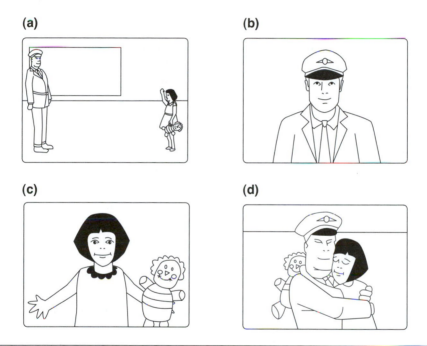

Figure 12.2   Creating unity in space and time. (a) Establishing shot of father and daughter waving to him shows their relationship in space and time. (b, c) Close-ups convey their emotions as they run toward each other. (d) A final two-shot as they meet rounds off the sequence in both space and time.

By contrast, if we used close-ups without an initial establishing shot, the subjects' relationship in space and time would remain unknown, and the exposition would be more confusing. Why are we seeing two different people in different places, the audience might wonder, and what do they have to do with one another?

Additional Continuity Concepts. In Chapter 11, we discussed cutting on action, shooting overlapping action when cutting from wide shots to close-ups, following the axis-of-action (the 180-degree) rule, and matching camera angles when shooting reverse-angle shots. All of these techniques, it turns out, are standard principles of good continuity editing.

One goal of continuity editing is to make edits as invisible as possible so that the audience is not distracted from the story. The Professional Pointers list provides some further tips. These pointers are not intended, though, to be applied dogmatically. Deciding how they should be used in different situations should depend on your program objectives.

Continuity Editing

➢ Match actions and subject matter between two consecutive shots in a single scene. In a given scene, the background, position, and wardrobe of the talent should be the same from shot to shot. For example, if a long shot of a room has a lighted chandelier, but the next shot shows the chandelier turned off, there may be a continuity problem. Similarly, if a talent is holding a drink in the left hand in the first shot but has it in the right hand in the next, or has no drink at all, that can be a jarring distraction (see Figure 12.3). Have a continuity person make notes on such details so that gaffes are avoided.

➢ Images cut together should be of sufficient difference in size, composition, and subject matter to appear motivated. Motivated cuts make a point, justifiably shifting the attention of the viewer from one place to another (see Figure 12.4). Avoid cutting between images that have small differences in image size or composition. Small changes will only irritate the viewer. If there is not sufficient reason to warrant a cut, don't make it.

➢ When cutting from wide to tight shots and vice versa within the same scene, keep the relative positions of objects in successive shots consistent. For example, if a wide shot of a subject contains a telephone pole on the right of the subject, keep the telephone pole on the same side when you cut to a tighter shot (see Figure 12.5).

➢ For moving talent, maintain motion vector continuity. That is, keep the screen direction of the movement constant, even when the talent moves in and out of frame. For example, if a talent moves out of frame to the right, it is generally most sensible to see the talent enter the frame in the succeeding shot from the left, moving in the same direction (see Figure 12.6).

➢ Besides motion vectors, consider graphic vectors as well. For example, when cutting from a wide to a tight horizon shot, the less jarring cut is the one that presents the horizon line at the same height in the close-up as in the long shot (see Figure 12.7). This is because the horizon line presents a strong graphic vector that is quite noticeable to the viewer from shot to shot. Graphic vectors include any strong lines that clearly define the screen space.

➢ Pay attention to index vectors. The term index vector refers to the screen direction implied by the physical orientation of people and things in the frame. For example, if two people are having a catch, the normal orientation of the bodies gives clues about (indexes) the action taking place (see Figure 12.8). Matching eye-lines when cross-cutting reaction shots is an example of an index vector concern.

➢ Preserve continuity as a function of developing narrative. When locales change or a new character is added to those already in a shot, it is generally advisable to establish such changes

> immediately through the use of wide (establishing and reestablishing) shots. This results in less jarring and more understandable story development.
> ➤ Edit scenes to emphasize significant events and to eliminate trivial details, even if minor physical inaccuracies result. If a scene is cut right, the audience will ignore small physical inaccuracies in favor of strong dramatic development.

(a)　　　　　　　　　　　　　　**(b)**

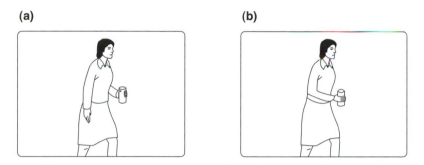

Figure 12.3　　Example of a continuity problem. If (b) directly follows (a), viewers will wonder how the glass suddenly jumped from one hand to the other.

(a)

(b)

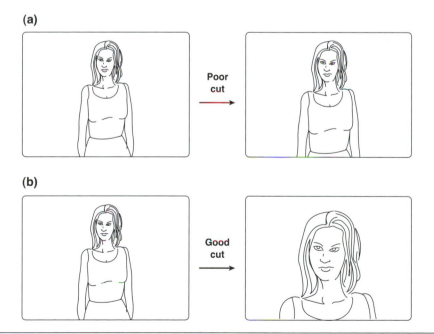

Figure 12.4　　Using motivated cuts. (a) Cutting from the left image to the right would be an unmotivated cut, annoying to the viewer, because the two images are only slightly different. (b) A motivated cut. Here the two shots differ enough to justify the cut.

(a)

(b)

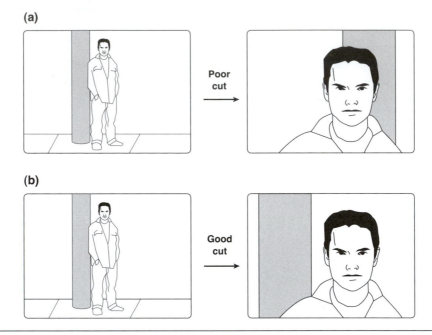

Figure 12.5   Keeping positions of objects consistent. (a) In this cut, the telephone pole appears to move from one side of the subject to the other, jarring the viewer. (b) A better cut: The pole stays on the same side.

(a)

(b)

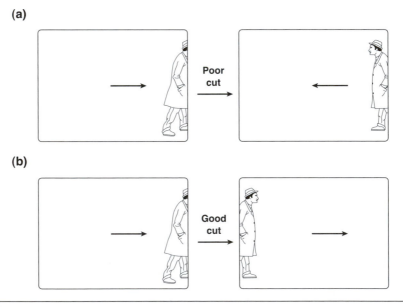

Figure 12.6   Maintaining continuity of motion vectors when talent moves in and out of the frame. (a) A cut in which the vector continuity is broken because the talent seems to reverse direction. (b) A better cut, in which the motion vector stays constant.

(a)

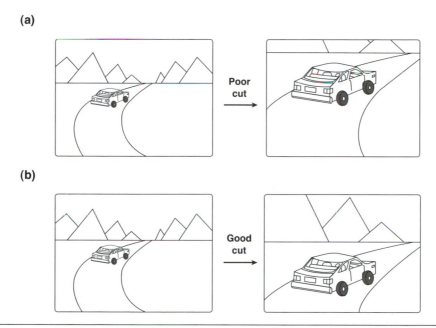

(b)

Figure 12.7 Maintaining continuity of graphic vectors. (a) Because the horizon changes level from one shot to the next, the cut jars the viewer. (b) A cut that keeps the horizon at the same level so that this graphic vector remains constant.

(a)

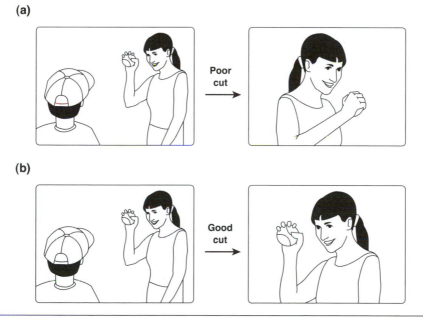

(b)

Figure 12.8 Picture elements that convey a direction of activity establish index vectors. (a) In the wider shot, the positions of the people's bodies and the angle of the throw create a clear index vector. But the cut to a close-up changes the screen orientation and thus breaks the index vector. (b) In a good cut, the index vector is preserved.

Of course, besides preserving continuity, editing determines timing and pace in a story. In general, the timing of cuts can add significant dramatic intensity. This leads us more deeply into the question of editing aesthetics.

Classical Editing

Editing can do much more than just provide clear, economic exposition. By changing camera location and framing, directors can accentuate parts of a scene, varying the intensity of the narrative accordingly. For example, it is possible to cover a boxing match with a single wide shot of the entire ring from a fixed camera position. That would provide lucid exposition. But imagine the same coverage accented with tight close-ups of each fighter's face as punches are landed (see Figure 12.9). Then intercut close-ups of ringside fans reacting to each barrage. Clearly, such editing would intensify the dramatic, physical, and psychological aspects of the story. Editing that intensifies the story in this way is called **classical editing.**

Reaction Shots and Parallel Editing. Many classical editing techniques were popularized by American film director D. W. Griffith in the first few decades of

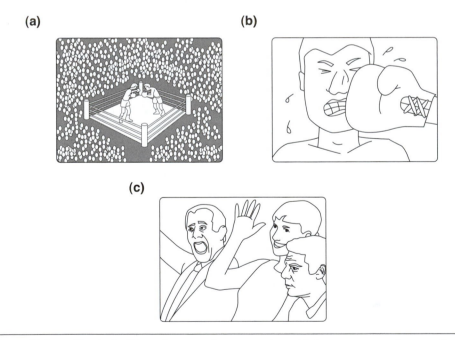

Figure 12.9 Classical editing often uses close-ups to intensify important story elements. In this sequence, to convey the drama of a boxing match, a wide shot of the entire scene (a) is intercut with (b) a close-up showing the boxer's face and (c) the screaming, gesticulating fans.

the 20th century, and they are still in wide use today. For example, Griffith intercut tight close-ups of talent reactions—*reaction shots*—to heighten the emotional impact of stressful or disturbing situations.

Griffith also popularized the practice of intercutting between events supposedly occurring at the same time but in different places. The most common example of such *parallel editing,* as it is known, is a sequence beginning with a shot of a damsel in distress, Little Nell, being tied to the railroad tracks by the evil villain, Snidely Whiplash (see Figure 12.10). The next shot shows a train approaching from right to left in the frame, getting progressively larger and louder, followed by

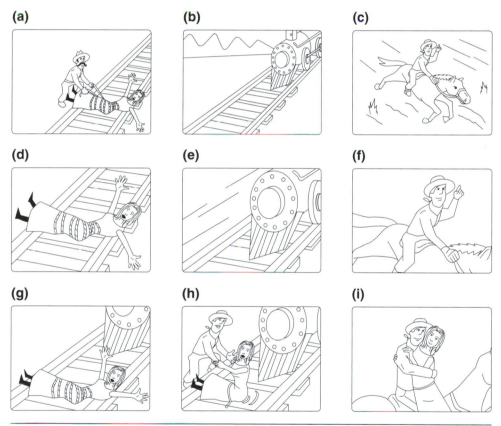

Figure 12.10 Parallel editing, a type of classical editing, cuts back and forth between events occurring in different places at the same time. (a) The stereotypical villain, Snidely Whiplash, tying Little Nell to railroad tracks. (b) A train approaching. (c) The hero, Dudley Doright, riding to the rescue from the screen direction opposite to the train. (d) Close-up of Little Nell struggling to free herself. (e) The train getting ever closer. (f) Dudley getting ever closer—can he outrace the train? (g) The locomotive almost upon poor Nell. (h) The hero arrives in the nick of time. (i) Hero and heroine reunited at last.

a shot of the hero, Dudley Doright, racing on horseback from left to right, also getting progressively larger and louder. Shots of Little Nell struggling to get free are then intercut with further shots of the train and the hero, both approaching ever closer. In successive cuts, each image is presented for shorter and shorter lengths of time. Ultimately, of course, the hero arrives to rescue Nell in the nick of time. In this way, three separate pieces of footage that may have been shot weeks apart are combined to increase the story's dramatic intensity and create a great deal of audience involvement and interest.

The Traditions of Formalism and Realism. Classical editing permits the director to create and control dramatic emphasis. Through the use of close-ups and multiple camera setups, the viewer is forced to see just the aspects of a scene the director wants seen and no others. This approach takes much control of dramatic intensity out of the hands of the on-camera performer. The style of editing that emphasizes selected elements of scenes this way to control and heighten audience attention is known as **formalism.**

Some view formalist editing as too controlling, too manipulative, and undemocratic. Critics say that formalist editing deprives audiences of the chance to make their own decisions about what to look at in the image. In contrast, offering the audience scenes edited for continuity only—or, better yet, one long master shot—would leave more choice in the audience's hands.

One leading critic of formalism was French film critic André Bazin. In sharp opposition to the formalists, Bazin took an approach often called **realism.** Bazin's theories stemmed from his view that one of the strongest elements of photographic art (including film and video) was its ability to capture realistic images of the world. Bazin thought that editing violated a connection to physical reality and could destroy a scene's impact. In place of editing, he advocated the use of deep focus, long takes, wide shots, and camera movement to follow key action through panning, tilting, and tracking.

In agreement with Bazin's views, it is easy to think of a situation where *not* editing adds dramatic impact to a scene. For example, imagine a story about a pilot who crash-lands in a desert. He hikes from the crash site in search of water, but his thirst becomes overwhelming and he collapses on a sand dune. Now the camera carrying the scene of his collapse slowly tilts up, and a tracking shot reveals that just on the other side of the sand dune is an oasis with plenty of fresh water. Obviously, the irony of such a scene might be lost if edits were made between the collapse and the oasis.

The extent to which the formal control of classical editing is praised or denigrated is probably a function of how it is used. It is up to you as the director to determine which edits are warranted and when it is better to leave the master shot alone so that audience members can choose which parts of the picture they want to see.

Dynamic Editing: Thematic Montage

In addition to continuity and classical editing, a radically different technique, called **dynamic editing,** is also widely used to shape program content. Largely developed by Russian filmmaker Sergei Eisenstein shortly after Griffith experimented with it in his 1916 silent-film epic *Intolerance,* dynamic editing, also known as **thematic montage** (from the French *monter,* meaning "to assemble"), stresses the association of ideas *but without regard to unity in space and time.*

In *Intolerance,* Griffith addresses the theme of man's inhumanity to man by juxtaposing scenes of the crucifixion of Jesus with conflicts taking place in ancient Babylon, 16th-century France, and 20th-century America. The segments that he intercuts are spatially, physically, and/or psychologically discontinuous but related in concept and theme.

Eisenstein further developed the technique of thematic montage in his 1925 movie masterpiece *Potemkin,* a film originally intended to tell the sweeping story of the Russian revolution of 1905. During filming, Eisenstein decided to limit its scope to a mutiny on board the battleship *Potemkin* and a massacre of peasants by the Russian army in the port of Odessa. During the mutiny scene, close-ups of the crucifix of the Navy priest (portrayed as a slovenly officer and an enemy of the abused sailors) are intercut with close-ups of a sword to underscore the ironic clash between the ship's religious authority and the rebellion. Similarities in the shape and the metallic appearance of cross and sword in these closely juxtaposed shots help Eisenstein make his ethical and political statements.

Since Eisenstein, thematic montage or dynamic editing has become a regular part of the filmmaker's and videographer's repertoire. The psychological associations induced in audiences can vary, depending partly on subject matter and the way images are juxtaposed. Sometimes the effect can be powerful and engaging. Some montages cause ironic tension, while others build complementary ideas.

One factor that influences how a montage is apprehended is the eye of the beholder. For example, in propaganda pieces (i.e., televised political advertising), montage is often used to associate political figures with one another, thereby making critical statements about them. Imagine juxtaposing shots of a presidential candidate giving a speech to a throng of supporters with similar shots of Hitler addressing Nazi crowds. To the candidate's supporters, such an association could be quite incendiary, whereas opponents might view the material as accurate and agreeable. In this way, besides making commentary on a subject relatively easy for the director-editor, montage can profoundly affect the audience—but in different ways.

Pictorial Complexity and Mise en Scène

In addition to audience-related factors, content factors also influence the effectiveness of editing. One of these is the pictorial complexity of the shots involved. The complexity of the image is a function of how much new subject matter is presented to the audience in a given amount of time. Editing pace should therefore be determined in part by the amount of new material being presented. Many experts feel that audience involvement seems to peak when viewers have been given enough time to absorb most *but not all* of the information in a shot before another shot is introduced of different subject matter. With the right pace of delivery, the audience maintains a satisfying curve of rest and excitement.

Another content factor to consider when determining editing pace is the arrangement of objects in the frame, known by the French term **mise en scène** (pronounced *meez on sen*). The editor should consider what and where the most important objects are in each shot and how easy it is to see them, so that editing pace can aid rather than harm story clarity and development. For example, to show that a main character is depressed and may attempt suicide, you might start with a wide shot of the subject in bed and then cut to a close-up of the bed and night table, revealing a gun on the table. If the gun is in clear view in the close-up, you will not need to stay on the shot as long as if the gun is partially hidden.

Editing *The Nesters*

To see how editing enhances storytelling, let us apply the editing techniques discussed so far to our imaginary episode of *The Nesters*. We will edit some scenes for continuity, simply to preserve lucid exposition, while others will get more complicated treatment using both classical and dynamic editing techniques. As you read these suggested treatments, think about other possible approaches that you might take.

Continuity Editing. Let's edit the opening scene to continuity. Our objective will be to present lucid exposition, as shown in Figure 12.11. We fade up on an opening shot of our young couple awakening in their bedroom as their clock-radio erupts with the 7:00 A.M. news, time, and traffic report (6 seconds). The next four medium shots show Bill in the shower, Carol brushing her teeth, Bill drying himself with a towel, and Carol rushing past him into the shower (14 seconds). The next shot is of Bill in his bedroom mirror, finishing tying his tie, and Carol entering the bedroom wrapped in a towel (6 seconds). A cut to the clock shows the time to be 7:25 (1 second); then we see Bill in the kitchen hastily pouring coffee and a fully dressed Carol slapping two plates of scrambled eggs and toast on the table (4 seconds). They sit at the breakfast table, gobbling their food and chatting in quick bursts (15 seconds).

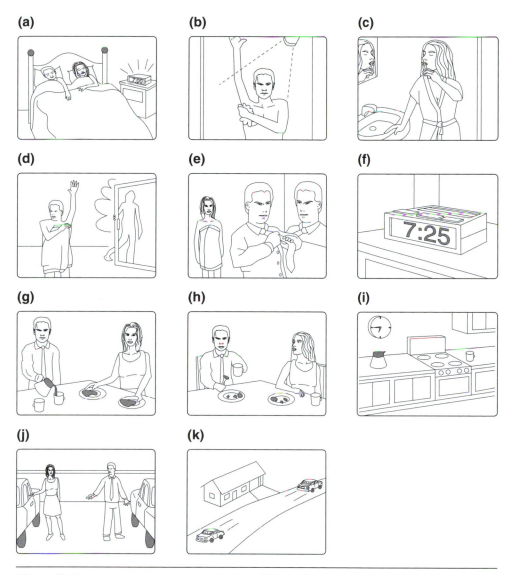

Figure 12.11 A sequence showing continuity editing in the opening scenes of *The Nesters.*

A glance at the kitchen clock reveals that it is now 7:45 (1 second). Next we see Bill and Carol in an exterior medium two-shot at eye level, snatching a good-bye kiss and jumping into their respective cars (4 seconds), followed by a wider aerial shot of their cars zooming out of the driveway and heading in opposite directions (4 seconds). Written out, the exposition sounds tedious, but the total screen time of this sequence is just 55 seconds. In less than a minute, we have established many of the basics of the Nesters' life together and allowed ample opportunity for comedy (Bill singing terribly in the shower, Carol's glasses falling off in the hasty kiss—whatever corny or original bits the scriptwriter might imagine).

Classical Editing. Classical editing may be used to emphasize more dramatic and psychological aspects of our story. For example, at the restaurant, to convey Bill's worry about Carol's unexplained lateness, we can do more than present a medium shot of Bill waiting alone at the table eating breadsticks. We can emphasize Bill's growing impatience by inserting close-ups of Bill's wristwatch from Bill's POV (see Figure 12.12). Such cut-ins drive home Bill's increasing concern about Carol and about his own tight schedule. Similarly, to convey Bill's growing discomfort, we could include increasingly frequent cutaway shots of the restaurant door from Bill's POV each time it opens.

(a) **(b)**

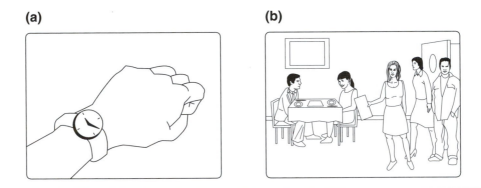

Figure 12.12 Classical editing of Bill's restaurant scene from *The Nesters* might use shots from his point of view to help convey his anxiety as he waits for Carol. (a) A close-up of his watch, as he sees it, can stress his concern about her lateness. (b) A shot of the restaurant's entrance, where the hostess is leading other people in, can emphasize that he keeps looking for Carol.

Dynamic Editing. Dynamic or montage editing could help us concentrate attention on Bill's feelings of loneliness and his worry about why Carol is late. While he waits in the restaurant, along with the POV shots of Bill nervously glancing at his watch, we might add shots of him looking out the window, noticing geese nuzzling each other in a park pond as well as several couples strolling together hand in hand (see Figure 12.13). These shots would drive home our theme of two young newlyweds deeply in love.

Editing Sound

Thus far, we have discussed editing without attending to the role of sound. Sound can motivate on-screen action, as well as cutting decisions, as much as any other

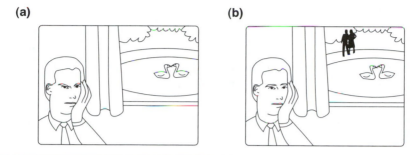

(a) **(b)**

Figure 12.13 Dynamic editing of Bill's restaurant scene in *The Nesters* might accentuate his apprehension with apparently unrelated shots that fit the theme of lovers being together. For instance, he could look out the window to see (a) two geese nuzzling each other and (b) a couple strolling by, hand in hand.

production or story element. In *The Nesters,* the sound of the clock-radio erupting with the news, weather, and traffic report motivates the characters to awaken and get out of bed. Clearly, soundtracks can help enormously, in many different ways, to set the scene. Yet, if sound is so important to the editing process, why have we not mentioned it until now?

The soundtrack is treated separately because the mode in which we apprehend sound differs from the way we see, and these differences have consequences for editing. In terms of our visual sense, we can justify the cut as the basic type of edit because cutting imitates important aspects of normal visual function. For example, if I am in bed reading a book and someone knocks on the door, my eyes (and perhaps my head) shift abruptly from the book to the door. I do not sweep my eyes gradually from book to door, focusing with equal sharpness on the entire transition. Rather, my eyes "cut" to the door, much like the way an edited video cuts between images.

By contrast, when sound enters my perceptual field, I need not shift my head to hear it or identify the direction it is coming from. Furthermore, I can select individual sounds for special attention from those present to me. As I am reading quietly in bed, I may become especially aware that my clock is ticking. And if a train approaches from a distance, gaining in volume gradually, my attention to the clock does not instantly "cut" to the train. Rather, it gradually shifts from one sound to the other, similar to the usual fading in and out of sound in a video. I can also shift my attention back and forth between sounds of roughly equal volume (in this case, the ticking and the distant train sounds), depending on which one I choose to concentrate on. Hence, "cutting" sound in and out of a program is unnaturally abrupt; it does not accurately simulate the way we normally attend to sound. Therefore, when editing, it is often necessary to treat sound differently from the way visuals are treated.

364 PART II: ELEMENTS AND TECHNIQUES OF VIDEO PRODUCTION

Synchronous and Asynchronous Sound. While sound is often a natural accompaniment to visual action, it is purely a matter of choice whether to include it with its corresponding visual on screen. When actions and corresponding sounds coincide, the sound is said to be **synchronous.** For example, seeing a gun being fired, with muzzle flash and smoke, and hearing the gunshot *at the same time* is an example of synchronous sound.

By contrast, hearing someone's voice while seeing the same person on camera with his or her mouth closed, indicating that the person is thinking, not speaking, is an example of **asynchronous sound.** In asynchronous sound segments, there is a discrepancy between what is seen on screen and what is heard. Often, asynchronous sound is used for dramatic effect, to fill in exposition, or to make ironic or psychological statements.

Beyond the artistic impact of using synchronous or asynchronous sound, knowing in advance whether you will use one or the other (or both) can have a significant impact on your editing decisions. For example, if a segment features a quick succession of cuts to build tension or excitement, you may decide that the abrupt synchronous sound changes that result from such a series of hard cuts would distract the audience. Instead of synchronous sound, therefore, you may decide to insert music, dialogue, additional sound effects, natural or ambient sound, or just plain silence. You may even decide to use a sound montage created from the original synchronous soundtrack, but sweetened with fades to soften or eliminate the abrupt changes. Whatever you decide, being aware of the difference between how we process visual and aural information can make the job of fabricating effective soundtracks easier. See the list of Professional Pointers for more suggestions about editing sound; again, these principles are offered as general guidelines, not as rules to follow slavishly in all cases.

Editing Sound

➤ In the absence of compelling reasons not to, use gradual fades rather than cuts to integrate sound into a program. Harsh, noticeable audio cuts draw attention away from the illusion of a continuous smooth stream of action and draw undue attention to technique.

➤ To enhance realism, it is not necessary to represent all sound as it occurs in real life. Rather, record only the significant sound. For example, the audience will not care if a fire in an on-screen fireplace does not crackle, as long as the fire is not a significant part of the story. If the fire later becomes a main part of the action—say, because an important letter has been thrown into it—a crackling sound can be used at that time. Use the same principle for handling sound for phone calls. Decide whether to have the audience hear the voice on the other

> end of the line on the basis of dramatic motivation, not realism. The audience will not question the choice you have made if the action on screen motivates the decision or attracts enough attention.

➢ Nat sound used to set a scene need not persist if it is too distracting. For example, if dialogue is to happen at an oil-drilling site, natural sound may be used to establish the location. But as the conversation gets going, it is acceptable to fade down the background noise. Of course, don't cut sharply from the noise of the drilling equipment to the dialogue track: Such abrupt change is unnatural, and the viewer will be sensitive to the lack of realism in it.

➢ Sometimes asynchronous sounds are more important than synchronous ones because they make the audience aware of something that was previously unknown.

➢ Sound quality, not just volume, can be used to add dramatic depth to a program. Even the simplest sound has many complex qualities associated with it. For example, a series of toots of a car horn, in addition to volume, has duration, presence (the quality of being on-mic or off-mic), tempo, rhythm, pace, pitch, timbre, overtones, attack and decay, dynamics, and even cultural and historical associations. If the sound you are dealing with is music, you may have the added dimensions of melody, harmony, and counterpoint.

➢ When adding music to dialogue, avoid using lyrics under voice-over, unless this technique is motivated by the program. Lyrics under dialogue can be distracting. If you are convinced that a certain lyric must be used with dialogue, make the volume levels different enough to offset audience distraction.

Technical Advances Influence Editing Decisions

Technical advances continually extend the mobility and capability of cameras. As you already know, today's cameras are lighter and smaller and can operate under a wider range of lighting conditions than ever before. The result is that cameras can now routinely capture actions that were once unavailable to television (skydiving footage is just one example). Advances in technology also influence editing decisions.

For instance, to show the flight of an arrow, typical editing might cut from a shot of the archer drawing back the bow and letting the arrow fly to a shot of the arrow hitting the target. The interim flight is not normally shown because it is too fast. However, if it were possible to mount an extremely durable, lightweight, and remarkably small battery-powered camera, equipped with radio signal transmission capability, on the arrow itself, imagine how we might shoot the sequence. Now we can cut from the shot of the archer to that of the arrow-mounted camera just as it leaves the bow. We could televise the entire flight to the target.

Digital editing now permits simulations of such imagery through the use of animation software; these options have unique looks and feels and, in some cases, can convincingly imitate the kinds of actions just described. Digital technology influences editing decisions and aesthetics in other ways. With digital technology, composite images from different sources can be edited into the same shot, not just in series with one another. Music videos offer many examples of digital compositing (see Photo 12.1).

Photo 12.1   Digital editing software now makes it easy to combine (composite) images from different sources into the same frame of film or video, as this example makes clear from Woody Allen's *Zelig*.

SOURCE: © Corbis.

Throwing Out All the Rules

Ultimately, editing technique must be judged in terms of the subject matter being presented, the context of the technology available at the time, and the goals of the programmer. Often, the principles set forth in this chapter are purposely violated, not only in music videos but also in avant-garde and experimental videos and even in television commercials. In the case of music videos, rather than exposition, narrative, or storytelling, the aesthetic goal is often to provide perceptual stimulation and sensual excitation. In such cases, smooth continuity may be neither desirable nor necessary. Yet it is still important to understand conventional editing principles. If you decide to ignore them, you need to know what you are doing and why.

EDITING TECHNIQUES

Before the advent of videotape in the mid-1950s, the only editing that went on in television production was done live, in real time, during the broadcast. The director watched a bank of monitors and called for shots from several cameras in the studio, and it was the technical director's job to cut, fade, or dissolve to the next shot while the show was airing. This type of editing, still practiced for live broadcasts, is called **on-line editing.**

Videotape, of course, greatly expanded the editing dimension of television, making video more like film in that footage could be shot, edited, and sweetened in postproduction before being shown. Editing done this way is called **off-line editing.** As postproduction editing practices have evolved, both of these terms have undergone changes in definition (discussed in more detail later in this chapter).

Off-line editing enables you to shuffle recorded program segments like a deck of cards. Furthermore, since all common videotape formats feature a video track and two or more audio tracks, all separate from one another, it is possible to manipulate any one of them independently from the others. This permits you to select, mix, insert, or assemble audio, video, or both for any program. Add to this the ability to digitally alter single frames of video with computer graphics software, and the postproduction suite offers nearly endless editing possibilities.

In addition to separate video and audio tracks, linear editing systems that use videotape (whether analog or digital) have a **control** or **pulse track,** a series of electronic signals that enables an editing system to mark every 30th of a second or each frame of video. The control track is used for locating specific frames for viewing and editing. The control track may be connected to a counter that displays total elapsed time by frame number, seconds, minutes, and hours; it can then be used to locate specific *in-* and *out*-points for editing purposes.

Unfortunately, control or pulse-track editing is not perfectly frame accurate. This is because the constant shuttling of tape back and forth through the system (as well as wear and tear of the tape, which can cause stretching) can result in some slight drifting of the pulse count over time. While this is not a serious problem for many editing jobs, when exact accuracy is required (i.e., when matching dialog with synchronous video of the speaker's mouth), control track editing is not ideal. A more accurate system uses *time code* to permanently assign a specific address to every frame of video. In time code editing, every frame of video is given a unique number, so that the address assigned to each video frame remains constant throughout the editing process.[1]

Control Track Editing With the Basic Two-Deck System

Although nonlinear digital editing (NLE) has become standard for video editing in recent years, knowing how to perform linear editing with a basic two-deck system is still important. This section explains the process for a basic two-deck system and then briefly describes how the same editing techniques can be used with expanded systems using multiple sources.

The basic videotape editing system (see Figure 12.14) consists of two tape decks. One is used to run *source* tapes, that is, unedited tapes. The other is used to run the *edit* tape, that is, the tape onto which you *dub,* or copy, the edited program. Monitors and speakers are provided for viewing each tape's video track and hearing its audio track(s). An **edit controller** enables you to coordinate the decks, search through tape, and execute edits.

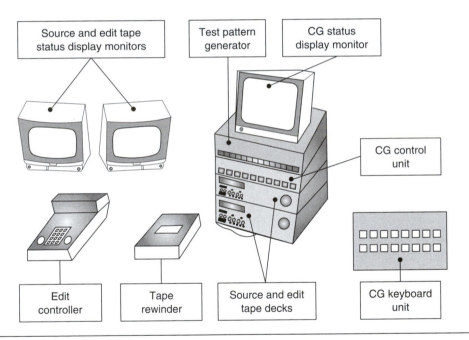

Source and edit tape
status display monitors

Test pattern
generator

CG status
display monitor

CG control
unit

Edit
controller

Tape
rewinder

Source and edit
tape decks

CG keyboard
unit

Figure 12.14   The components of a basic videotape editing system.

A **shuttle mode** on the edit controller allows you to quickly locate and view video segments on either source or edit tapes as they are run back and forth (*shuttled*) through their videotape decks. Since all segments are stored in series on tape, they cannot be randomly accessed; instead, individual segments are retrieved by shuttling back and forth through the tape until the desired segment is found. For this reason, the use of any tape-based editing system (whether analog or digital) is referred to as **linear editing.**

Most systems also allow tape to be more finely *jogged* for locating edit points more precisely within segments. Even single frames of video can be further trimmed or added using *trim* buttons. All of these electronic functions key off the tape's control track.

Logging Footage and Making an Edit Decision List

A written *log* can be kept of the raw footage, including the location and duration of each segment during the search process and while replaying tapes (see Figure 12.15). An **edit decision list** (EDL) can also be formulated before actual edits are performed. The EDL (Figure 12.16) is a written, rough-cut version of the proposed edited program, listing in order the beginning and end points for every segment. Many systems offer EDLs on disk so that edit decisions can be made without sitting at an editing console.

Writing an EDL is usually not optional except in the most basic editing situations. For simple assignments where the EDL phase is skipped, edits may be executed as soon as edit points have been selected. Time constraints often dictate whether you generate an EDL before performing actual edits.

RAW FOOTAGE TAPE LOG			
Counter/Frame #	Time	Description/Comments	A/V Quality
00:00:00:00- 00:00:30:00	30 sec	Nesters waking up (take 1)	audio noise from blankets; video good
00:00:30:00- 00:00:38:06	8 sec	Nesters waking up (take 2)	good A/V*
00:00:38:06- 00:00:42:19	4 sec	Close-up of clock (7:25 A.M.)	good (no audio needed)*
00:00:42:19- 00:00:52:11	10 sec	Carol Nester brushing teeth (take 1)	no toothpaste on brush (no good)
00:00:52:11- 00:00:04:12	12 sec	Carol brushing teeth (take 2)	good A/V*

Figure 12.15   Sample of the log of the raw footage from *The Nesters*. Here, the person who created the log indicated the best takes with asterisks in the *A/V Quality* column.

EDIT DECISION LIST

PROGRAM: THE NESTERS   DATE: November 15, 1998

Segment	Description	Tape #	EDIT IN				EDIT OUT			
			Hr	Min	Sec	Fr	Hr	Min	Sec	Fr
1	Nesters waking up to clock radio (take 2)	1	00	00	30	00	00	00	38	06
2	Bill Nester in the shower	1	00	17	21	18	00	17	25	18
3	Carol brushing teeth (take 2)	1	00	00	52	11	00	00	55	10

Figure 12.16   An edit decision list (EDL) for the opening shots of *The Nesters.* From the raw footage log shown in Figure 12.15, particular shots have been selected and placed in order as an initial guide to the editing.

Frame Counting

As tape advances or rewinds through each deck, a **frame counter** advances or reverses for each tape, wherever control track is recorded. The frame count is displayed as an eight-digit code arranged in four pairs of numbers referring to hours, minutes, seconds, and frames (see Figure 12.17). For example, if the source readout on the edit controller, starting from zero, counts frames from the beginning of the control track, the digital display after one minute of continuous control track would read 00:01:00:00, where the first pair of numbers (on the far left) designates the hour, the second pair the minutes, the third pair seconds, and the last (on the far right) the frame number. Assuming a stable and continuous control track, the readout of a continuous frame count after one hour, twelve minutes, and forty-five and a half seconds would be 01:12:45:15.

01:12:45:15

Figure 12.17   A frame counter.

Of course, the digital counter can be zeroed out at any time by the operator with the press of a button *(but this is not recommended if you want to retain the count for later searching),* and a new frame count can begin at any point that has control track. The major advantage of the digital display is that it makes it easy to log the location and duration of any segment of video. *Zeroing out the counter destroys this relationship.* From written logs, you can construct a rough EDL even without access to a videotape recorder.

Assemble and Insert Editing

Once edit points have been chosen for a series of segments, edits may be performed in a couple of different ways. Depending on your needs, you may choose to transfer *all* tracks from the source tape to the edit tape, including the video track, audio tracks, and the control track. This type of editing, called **assemble editing,** is most often done when raw footage must be put into final form quickly, as is often the case in ENG operations. In assemble editing, the edit controller must first be delegated to do such work by pressing the appropriate button on the console. Once in assemble mode, the edit deck erases all material (including the control track) on the edit tape ahead of the signal being laid down by the source deck.

Instead of assemble editing, you can transfer *selected* tracks of audio or video from the source tape to the edit tape. Transferring selected tracks is called **insert editing.** Insert editing is done when more extensive postproduction work is needed. For example, insert editing might be used to add asynchronous audio to a video track. It is also used to add video inserts and/or cutaways (called *B-roll* or *beauty* shots) to an interviewee's long speech (perhaps designated primary or *A-roll* footage). After selecting the insert mode on the edit controller, you need to specify the particular tracks of video and audio that you wish to transfer to the edit tape. For this there are usually three buttons—designated "video," "audio 1," and "audio 2"—that set up the edits so that just the requested tracks transfer when an execute command is given.

An important difference between assemble and insert modes concerns the way the invisible but critically important control track is treated. In assemble mode, all audio and video tracks, *plus the control track,* are transferred from the source tape to the edit tape. By contrast, in insert mode, selected tracks of audio or video are transferred, *but no control track.* This means that in insert mode, it is first necessary to lay down a control track on the edit tape (called *blacking the tape*) for either the length of the tape or the length of the program. Unfortunately, laying down control track can only be done in real time, and this can become a burden, especially when working on a tight schedule. For a 1-hour show, it would take an hour to lay down a complete control track on the edit tape. Because of this time requirement, some shops keep a supply of **preblacked tapes** (tapes with continuous control track already recorded on them).

Assemble mode has its own problems. Although the control track from the source tape should transfer to the edit tape whenever editing occurs, sometimes the source deck does not match the new control track exactly to the control track that has been laid down in prior edits. In addition, some dropout of the control track can occasionally occur between edits. When mismatches and gaps occur, some **tearing** of the video signal can result, causing picture roll, momentary glitches, loss of color, or other troubles. That is why assemble mode is best used when only a few simple edits must be performed for relatively long segments.

In summary, assemble editing is fast but sometimes results in an imperfect control track. Insert editing takes more time, but the unbroken, prerecorded control track avoids tearing the video signal.

Executing Assemble Edits. To execute assemble edits, begin by delegating the edit controller to assemble mode. Specify *in-points* on the source and edit tapes by pressing the appropriate buttons. Then specify an *out-point* on either the source or edit tape. If an out-point is not specified, the assemble edit will simply continue until you either stop the machine or the control track runs out.

Important: When performing assemble edits, the edit tape must have a little bit of control track recorded on it, just for startup purposes. Usually about a minute of control track is enough to get the process going. Control track is then transferred from the source tape to the edit tape as each edit is performed. To put the initial control track on the tape, simply record 1 minute of black onto it from a camera, or dub it from a preblacked tape. The system then has enough information to execute assemble edits.[2]

Executing Insert Edits. To perform insert edits, begin by delegating the insert mode on the edit controller. Be sure you have properly striped the edit tape with a continuous control track. You can confirm that you have a continuous control track by watching the action of the frame counter as the tape advances or rewinds through the edit decks. If you see moments when the frame counter stops counting, then you know there are segments on the tape that lack control track. If there are gaps, you will need to insert continuous control track on the tape before continuing.

When the tape is ready, specify which parts of the video signal you wish to dub. Remember the insert mode permits you to choose just the video track, one or both of the audio tracks, or any combination. Locate the beginning of the desired segment by shuttling through the tape, watching the monitor and listening to find it. Then jog and trim if necessary to locate precisely the frame you want to use as an edit point. When the desired frame is found, mark an in-point for the source tape by pressing the appropriate button on the console. Then repeat the process to locate the end of the segment and mark an out-point. Next, locate and select an in-point for the edit tape. You do not need to specify the remaining out-point because the editing system calculates it from the information you have provided.

If you like, you can specify in- and out-points for the edit tape rather than for the source tape. Then specify just an in-point on the source tape. The machine does not care which way it is done. This is known as *three-point editing*. Three-point editing specifies two in-points and one out-point.

Previewing and Performing Edits. In either assemble or insert mode, you can preview the edit you have requested by pressing the *preview button* on the edit controller. Previewing gives you a chance to see what the edit will look like before you accept it. If you decide you like it, you can execute the actual edit by pressing the *edit/perform button.* In edit/perform mode, the machine *dubs* (copies) the selected material onto the edit master, and when the preselected out-point is reached, the tapes come to a halt and the edit is complete.

Prerolling Tapes. When previewing or actually performing edits, the system automatically *prerolls* both tapes and then rolls them forward to their in-points. Usually a 3- to 5-second preroll time is programmed into the edit controller by the operator beforehand. Prerolling permits tapes to reach proper speed before passing the designated in-points so that edits can be produced cleanly.

SMPTE/EBU Time Code

Recall that control track editing is not perfectly frame accurate. This is because videotape can stretch or slip as reels of tape are spun back and forth during searches. In addition, during high-speed rewinds or fast-forward searches, so many frames are speeding past the tape heads that the machine can sometimes simply miscount frames. As a result, strict correspondence between frame numbers and specific video frames may be lost. In short, with control track editing, there is no guarantee that a particular video frame will have the same frame counter number throughout the editing process.

Even bigger discrepancies arise with control track editing because the frame counter can be inadvertently zeroed out at any time or can begin counting on tapes that have not been fully rewound. When this occurs, frame numbers appearing in early written logs or EDLs may be so different from subsequent numbers that searches based on them are no longer functional. One way to surmount these difficulties is to give every frame a unique and permanent address.

As mentioned in Chapter 8, as well as earlier in this chapter, a system for ensuring accurate coding of every frame of video has been developed by the

Society of Motion Picture and Television Engineers. It is called *SMPTE time code* or, since it was also adopted by the European Broadcasting Union, *SMPTE/EBU time code*. It is usually pronounced "simpty time code" for short.[3]

Time code may be recorded at the time tape is shot, or it may be added later. In-studio productions often record it during production. In field work, time code may be recorded as tape is shot if the camera is equipped with a built-in time code generator or if an external one is available. Of course, digital cameras all include time code capability.

Setting Time Code Before a Shoot. In setting time code for a shoot, it is generally advisable to start from zero and move forward continuously for each and every tape. This way, every frame of video for a shoot will have a unique address, and all frame numbers will be arranged sequentially without gaps. This is especially good for computer editing because any large gaps between segments or repeats of frame numbers may confuse the computer.

It is also possible and, under some circumstances, desirable to tie time code numbers to the time of day. This can be helpful if you wish to coordinate parts of your shoot with a studio clock or some other time source. It can also make it easier for production personnel to log segments and prepare EDLs.

Drop-Frame and Non-Drop-Frame Time Code. The original standard frame rate of 30 frames per second, adopted by the National Television System Committee (NTSC), was later changed to 29.97 frames per second to accommodate the chrominance signal needed for color television. This revised NTSC standard was adopted throughout most regions of North America, Japan, and South America. In other countries, where 50-Hz AC power is the standard, a different system, called *Phase Alternation by Line* (PAL), is used. The PAL system, which uses 625 lines, 50 fields, and 25 frames per second, is most prevalent in Great Britain, Europe, Africa, the Middle East, and the Far East. A third system, called *SECAM* (for *Système Electronique Couleur avec Mémoire*), which also uses 625 lines at 25 frames per second, is in place throughout much of the rest of the world.

As far as U.S. producers are concerned, the odd frame rate of 29.97 becomes important in longer programs because it can cause time discrepancies in edited material. For this reason, time code can be altered slightly to provide more accurate timing. **Drop-frame time code** compensates for the difference between 29.97 and 30 frames per second by ignoring frames 00 and 01 each minute except at every 10th minute. Actual video frames are not lost, but the frame numbers are dropped, thus eliminating discrepancies between actual time and time code values. For each hour of video in drop-frame time code, 108 frames of video are uncounted, amounting to a net correction in time code display of 3.6 seconds per hour.

For short programs, when the small discrepancy is hardly noticeable, **non-drop-frame time code** can be used. For each hour of non-drop-frame time code, 1 hour and 3.6 seconds of actual time elapses.

Time Code Readers. Time code recorded on tape can be read several ways. A *time code reader* can be used to see the frame numbers during playback and editing searches. With a time code reader, the time code may appear either on the top or bottom of the screen along with its corresponding video footage, or it may be fed to a separate digital readout.

Time code numbers can also be "burned in" to a video dub of footage and then viewed on a regular videotape recorder (VTR) or DVD player. This type of arrangement is called a **window dub** because the time code numbers appear in a small window on the screen (see Figure 12.18). Window dubs are useful for preparing logs and EDLs that can then be used to plan the editing. Working from a window dub is convenient because you can search and view the footage on a VTR or DVD player anywhere, without having to sit at an editing bench. Of course, window dubs cannot be used for actual editing because the footage contains time code display that cannot be erased.

Figure 12.18 A window dub showing the time code numbers "burned in" on a copy of the video.

The Expanded Meanings of "On-Line" and "Off-Line" Editing

The practice of generating detailed and accurate EDLs from viewing window dubs before entering the actual editing phase of a production has expanded the meanings of the terms *off-line* and *on-line editing*. Off-line editing now generally refers to the entire preparation phase after raw footage has been shot, when master tapes are viewed to prepare logs and/or EDLs and are searched for edit points prior to sitting at the editing bench to execute the final copy. Similarly, the term *on-line editing* has expanded to include more than just live cutting among several cameras during studio broadcasts. Now it includes editing on high-end equipment to bring the program into final form. Generally, the more editing work is done "off-line," in the new sense of the term, the less pressured the "on-line" phase is.

Multisource Editing

Expanding your editing facility by connecting more than one source of VTR to the editing system through a video switcher enables you to use more sophisticated transitions than just cuts (see Figure 12.19). With two or more source VTRs, each running a separate source tape, you can dissolve and fade between sources.

This arrangement also permits you to perform **A-B rolling**, creating an edit master from two video sources. For example, if two tapes (the A and the B sources) share a common time code, you can roll both tapes at the same moment from the same point and then treat them as if they were two video sources in a live studio production, cutting, dissolving, and wiping between them as you wish. The entire time, the edit master is taking the feed you send through the video switcher and rerecording it. The product that results is the mix of video signals you sent to the record unit. Of course, it is possible to use more than two sources. If three sources are used, the term is *A-B-C rolling*.

Another term to be aware of is **A-B roll editing**. If instead of doing the shot selection during an A-B roll, you delegate it to an editing control unit or a computer, you are performing A-B roll editing rather than simply A-B rolling. Why is this distinction necessary? In the case of A-B rolling, both sources are rolling from a common time code point, whereas in A-B roll editing, the sources do not have to be in sync with one another. One advantage of this latter system is that there is less work changing sources on the source machine(s). Of course, with multisource editing, other machines in addition to videotape players can also be configured to the system as video sources, such as special effects generators in video switchers and character generators.

Analog and Digital Recording Systems: Tape and Disk Formats

High-quality video recording once required 2-inch-wide videotape reels to store the audio, video, and control track information. Since its invention in the mid-1950s,

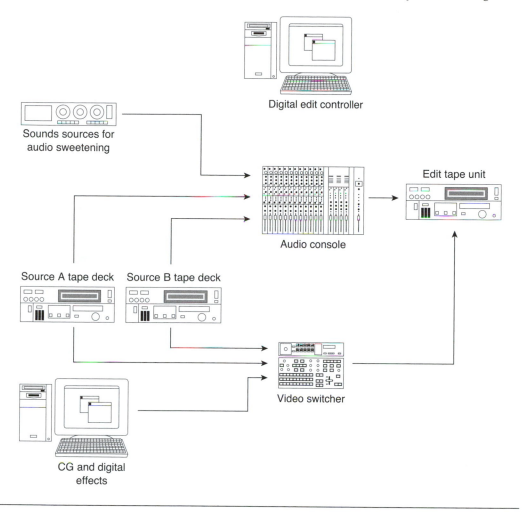

Figure 12.19 Schematic of typical components used in multisource editing. The edit controller, shown at the top of the diagram, mediates signal flow among components.

tape formats have continued to shrink in size and increase in capacity, so that now there are digital video cassettes that can record an hour of video on a cassette about the size of a standard audio cassette.

One of the major technical innovations that began the trend toward miniaturization in tape formats is **helical scanning,** which uses narrower tape widths for recording analog video. In this arrangement (see Figure 12.20), video information is recorded *on a slant* on the videotape rather than in perpendicular fashion, thus providing greater space for each frame of video on a given tape width. Since helical scanning was introduced, several narrower tape formats have been developed.

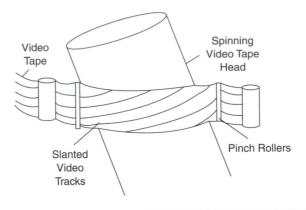

Figure 12.20 The helical scanning system. Because the tape runs across an *angled* head drum, the video information scans in a diagonal pattern on the tape. This way, video information can be recorded on a greater area of the tape, which enables the tape to store more information.

The trend from analog to digital recording has introduced a number of digital tape formats. In addition, disk-based recording now makes tapeless recording and storage of video content possible, eliminating the time-consuming step of transferring video from tape to disk before editing with a computer. Some video cameras designed for digital newsgathering (DNG) now use a digital hard drive for recording video and sound. Because it stores video on a digital hard drive, such systems allow you to edit shots right in the camera, making the camera itself a digital computer editing system. Another advantage of tapeless digital recording is that it saves time during the editing process since the editor no longer needs to search source tape for desired segments; the random-access feature permits you to select segments in any order and to call them up immediately. Nonlinear digital computer editing will eventually eliminate tape-based recording, though that reality is still some years away.

Whether recording is done on tape or disk or is in analog or digital form, the video signal may be recorded in either a component or a composite format. In **composite recording** systems, both color (chrominance) and brightness (luminance) parts of the television signal are recorded together using only one wire. As the original recording method standardized by the NTSC, composite recording is referred to as the *NTSC signal.*

By contrast, two newer **component recording** systems, called either *Y/C* or *RGB system* recording, have been developed. In Y/C system recording, the luminance (*Y* part of the signal) and the chrominance (*C* part of the signal) are recorded separately using two separate wires. In RGB system recording, the red, green, and blue portions of the video signal are recorded separately using three wires. The advantage of using separate circuits to collect the different parts of the video signal is that it yields a higher quality signal that loses less image quality when undergoing repeated dubbing during analog editing.

However, there is a downside to separating video signal components from one another. When the signal components are kept apart, they require more expensive circuitry in *all* the signal-processing equipment, including monitors, switchers, and editing decks. In addition, to be broadcast, the final product must eventually be made NTSC compatible through a conversion process.

Since many of the recording systems just described are incompatible with one another, it is important to know the different capabilities and limitations of the available recording formats before shooting and editing begin. Table 12.1 should help you recognize which tape formats are compatible with which recording systems.

Nonlinear Digital Editing

Table 12.1 lists a number of widely available digital formats. Videographers can record digital video on tape or disk, or digitize analog video and record it onto tape or disk, and then edit it on a computer equipped with digital editing software. Once loaded as computer files, digital video can be edited similar to the way word-processing programs edit words, paragraphs, and so forth in a written manuscript.

Digital editing offers major advantages over the analog process described so far. For one thing, unlike analog video, you can access digital video segments randomly; this random-access feature (called **nonlinear editing**) is faster than searching for shots sequentially along a tape. Digital editing is also frame accurate; you can move segments around repeatedly (and even make copies of copies) without dropping frames or losing signal quality. This last characteristic is a great improvement over analog video, which, as mentioned, loses fidelity with each successive copy; that is, with digital video, no matter how many edits you make, you are always working with first-generation quality video and sound.

You can also change your editing decisions by inserting or deleting segments without having to reedit work already done. By contrast, once analog sequences are edited, you cannot move them to make room for additional segments or expand them to fill spaces left by segments you might want to delete. With analog video, last-minute changes, depending on where they are needed, may require reediting the entire program, a time-consuming prospect. Time pressure could move you to consider using a partially edited program as the new master and rerecord it with new material. But with an analog recording, this approach bumps already edited portions of the final program another generation away from the original, further degrading overall signal quality. At times, the only solution is to start over from scratch.

Table 12.1   Analog and Digital Tape and Recording Formats

Tape Type (Name and Width)	Format Compatibilities	Recording Format	Production Applications	Comments
Analog				
VHS (½ inch)		NTSC composite[a]	Home video	Not for broadcast use.
S-VHS (½ inch)	Digital-S	Y/C[b] component, record as a composite signal	ENG, corporate, and closed-circuit applications	"Downward compatible" with VHS (lower-quality VHS can be played on S-VHS equipment, but not vice versa).
Betacam SP (½ inch)	Betacam SX, Digital Betacam	Y/C component	High-end studio, ENG, and corporate video	"SP" stands for superior performance. RGB signals are separate. Also has four audio tracks. Tapes cannot be played on other systems.
Hi-8 (8 mm)	Digital 8	Y/C component but can be rigged for NTSC output	Home video recording and professional use	High-quality recording, but should be transferred or "bumped up" to S-VHS or Betacam SP for editing work. Has three audio tracks.
U-matic (¾ inch)		NTSC composite	ENG and corporate video	Outmoded by ½-inch formats but still in use in some shops.
M II (½ inch)		Y/C component	Same as Betacam SP	Overshadowed by competition.
Digital				
Digital Betacam (½ inch)	Betacam SP, Betacam	RGB component	Studio and field production, professional quality	May be used for intensive editing and postproduction work. Also able to handle *compression* of the video signal, by which video information is digitally reduced for storage. Compressed.
DVC PRO/D-7 (¼ inch)	DV[c], DVCAM	RGB component	EFP, professional editing	Handles compressed video. Has stereo audio. Provides excellent quality, even after complex editing jobs. Compressed.
DVC PRO 50 (¼ inch)	DVCAM			Compressed.
DVCAM (¼ inch)	DVC PRO, DV	RGB component	Same as Betacam SP; extensive editing capability	Performs editing and dubbing with compressed video. As with most digital video, virtually no loss of signal quality. Compressed.

380

Tape Type (Name and Width)	Format Compatibilities	Recording Format	Production Applications	Comments
Digital-S/D9 (½ inch)	S-VHS	Y/C component	Professional-level video, comparable to Betacam SP	Downward compatible with S-VHS. Like DVCAM, permits editing with virtually no loss of signal quality. Compressed.
D-1 (¾ inch)		RGB component	Excellent professional quality	Excellent for postproduction editing. Often used in creating complex effects and animations. Not compressed.
D-2 (¾ inch)		NTSC composite	Excellent quality for broadcast and in-house, corporate, and closed-circuit settings	Since compatible with NTSC, it can be used with other broadcast equipment without extensive reconfiguring. Same tape shell as D-1 but not compatible with it. Not compressed.
D-3 (½ inch)	Data recorders	NTSC composite	Excellent quality, useful for both studio and field settings	Compatible with NTSC, so good for broadcast use. Small format makes it good for field production. Like other digital formats, permits extensive editing with virtually no loss of picture quality. Not compressed.
D-5 (½ inch)	D-3	RGB component	Superior quality	Excellent for postproduction. Contains four audio tracks, capable of CD-quality sound. Small format makes this an excellent choice for field production. Not compressed.
Betacam SX (½ inch)	Betacam SP			Compressed.
DV (¼ inch)	DVC PRO, DVCAM		Consumer use	Compressed.
Digital-8 (8 mm)	8 mm, Hi-8		Consumer use	Compressed.
DCT (¾ inch)				Compressed.
D-6 (¾ inch)	Digital HDTV recorder using D-1 tape			Compressed.

a. Composite systems encode the luminance (Y or black-and-white) signal information and the chrominance (C or color) signal information into a single signal and transmit it through a single wire.

b. Y/C analog component systems (also called S-Video) use two wires to keep the luminance (Y) signal separate from the chrominance (C) signal during encoding and transmission but combine them when edited onto videotape. RGB component systems are analog recording systems that keep video signals separate and are transmitted through separate wires throughout the entire recording process.

c. DV is the consumer digital video recorder format.

Digital video solves this problem. This shifting around of material to make room for late additions or deletions is called **rippling.** Together, the random-access and rippling features of digital editing provide major advantages over analog systems. They give you more technical freedom to create programs in any order you wish without worrying about where things will fit.

This section describes digital editing on a desktop workstation, with specific reference to some of the tools and options currently available in one of the more popular applications (see Photo 12.2); however, the procedures described here should be viewed as a general approach, similar to those you will encounter in other systems. It is intended as a primer to familiarize you with the fundamentals of digital editing, not to provide a complete manual.[4]

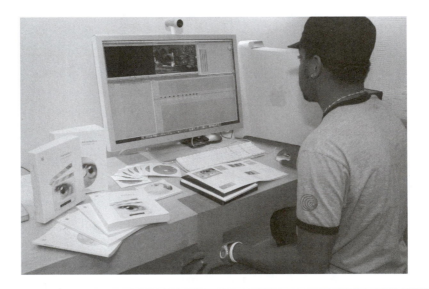

Photo 12.2   This basic, digital nonlinear system features a computer, a monitor, manuals and disks, and keyboard and mouse, all of the components necessary for producing high-quality video programs.

Before You Begin

In learning to use your editing suite, it is best to start with a small project and combine reading with doing. In this way, learning to use your digital editing application is like learning to cook a meal with a cookbook: You don't read the entire cookbook; rather, you decide on what meal you want to cook and then use a recipe from the cookbook as a guide in the kitchen with utensils and ingredients to make it. The same is true for editing: First decide what show you want to produce, and then use the manual with the workstation and the video files to make it.

Basic First Steps

Here are some of the basic steps in digital editing. The first time you open the application, you may be asked to specify certain settings to accommodate your camera and the most commonly used digital formats (i.e., DVC-PRO or DV-NTSC, etc.). Then you may be asked to specify a file or disk to store your video and then to "create a new project," which you can do with some clicking and typing to name it.

Your Editing Environment

Next, become familiar with your editing environment. In most cases, you will find controls for *organizing* the display itself (i.e., changing the size and location of windows to suit your taste). You will also find controls for *viewing, navigating,* and *marking* clips. Finally, you will find *editing* controls for altering and arranging clips into sequences.

In most applications, you will find close equivalents of the following windows: a *browser,* a *viewer,* a *canvas,* and a *timeline* (see Photo 12.3). There may also be a *tool palette* and an *audio meter* display.

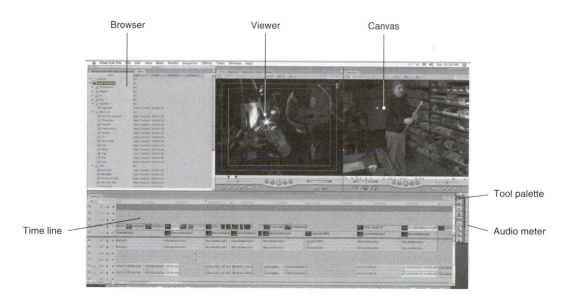

Photo 12.3   Screen display for a digital editing application. In addition to the four large windows (*browser, viewer, canvas,* and *timeline*), notice there is also a *tool palette* and an *audio meter* (small windows to the right of the timeline).

SOURCE: All screen shots reprinted by permission from Apple Computers, Inc.

The browser, located in the top-left portion of the screen shot in Photo 12.3, contains a list of the clips you have imported. As you capture clips from your camera, name them so that it is easy to remember what audiovisual material is on each one. Each line of text appearing in the browser represents a separate clip.

The viewer window (the top-center portion of Photo 12.3) is for watching clips to help you decide which ones, and/or which portion(s) of them, you wish to use. To place a clip in the viewer (among other ways), click and drag the clip name from the browser and drop it into the viewer area.

An array of *transport* and *marking* controls is featured around the viewer window, shown in detail in Photo 12.4; many are repeated in the canvas window, described below. The following is a summary of the controls featured in these windows and is also shown in Photo 12.4:

Tabs: Five tabs are available in the viewer, including ones for Video, Audio (two tracks), Filters, and Motion. Each one provides editing functions, some of which are described later.

Image area: View clips here

Playhead and scrubber bar: Allow you to move quickly to different parts of a clip (or sequence) in the canvas

Transport controls: See Photo 12.5

Jog and shuttle controls: Allow precise navigating within a clip

Marking controls: Set in- and out-points; also set markers for additional editing

In- and out-points: Show edit points selected for beginning and ending frames for each sequence

Zoom pop-up menu: Allows you to change the viewer's image size

View pop-up menu: Allows you to change the display that appears in the viewer

Playhead sync pop-up menu: Allows you to lock together playheads in both viewer and canvas while viewing clips

Generator pop-up menu: Allows you to select internally generated media such as color bars to apply to clips

Recent clips pop-up menu: Opens multiple clips in the viewer to aid modifications

Time code fields: Shows time code of current location of playhead

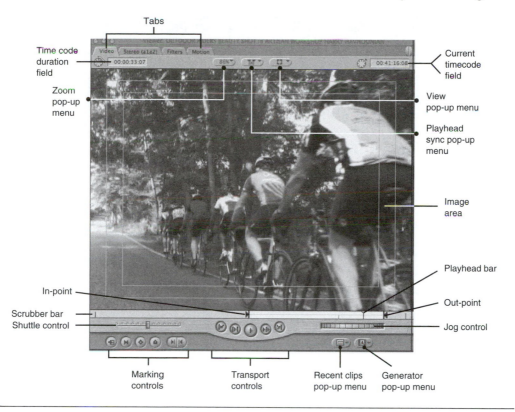

Tabs

Time code duration field

Zoom pop-up menu

In-point

Scrubber bar
Shuttle control

Current timecode field

View pop-up menu

Playhead sync pop-up menu

Image area

Playhead bar

Out-point

Jog control

Marking controls

Transport controls

Recent clips pop-up menu

Generator pop-up menu

Photo 12.4 Detail of viewer window with controls identified.

In addition, viewer transport controls include *go to previous edit, play in to out, play, play around current frame,* and *go to next edit* fields for viewing clip portions for possible inclusion as program segments. Photo 12.5 shows the viewer area in detail with the following transport controls for playing clips:

Go to previous edit: Moves the playhead of the viewer to a previous edit point if there is one or just moves the viewer playhead to the beginning of the clip

Play in to out: Plays a clip from an in-point to an out-point

Play: Plays a clip from the current location of the playhead to the end. Clicking the play button (or hitting the space bar) while a clip is playing stops the playback of the clip.

Play around current frame: Views material at the current position of the playhead

Go to next edit: Moves playhead to the next edit point

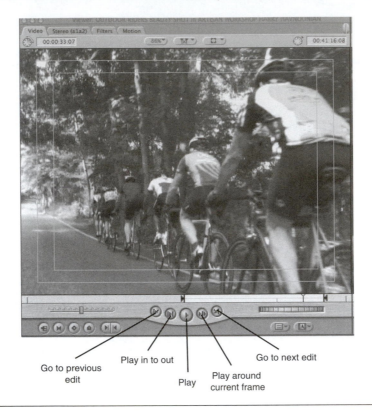

Go to previous
edit

Play in to out

Play

Play around
current frame

Go to next edit

Photo 12.5   Detail of viewer window with transport controls identified.

The *canvas* window features the same transport and marking controls just described for the viewer window, but it also features several editing buttons for taking clips prepared in the viewer and placing them into the timeline to build your program. The canvas and viewer windows are shown in detail in Photo 12.6. Use the canvas to play back changes you make to clips and to play back whole sequences as you build your project.

The controls unique to the canvas window include *editing controls:* The edit buttons and the edit overlay (see Photo 12.6) allow you to perform seven kinds of edits, including *inserts, overwrites, replace, fit to fill, superimpose, insert with transition,* and *overwrite with transition.*

When you click on a clip displayed in the viewer and drag it and drop it in the canvas window, *it instantly becomes a segment in your program and is added to your timeline.* A translucent edit overlay immediately appears in the canvas area (see Photo 12.6), inviting you to drop clips you select into one of seven choices offered.

Another way to add a clip to your program is to prepare the clip as you would like it in the viewer (review the clip and mark in- and out-points) and then click

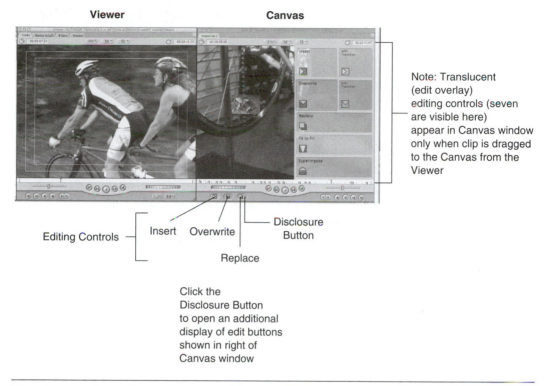

Viewer

Canvas

Note: Translucent (edit overlay) editing controls (seven are visible here) appear in Canvas window only when clip is dragged to the Canvas from the Viewer

Editing Controls

Insert   Overwrite

Replace

Disclosure Button

Click the Disclosure Button to open an additional display of edit buttons shown in right of Canvas window

Photo 12.6   Detail of viewer and canvas windows with edit overlay buttons visible in the canvas window and additional controls identified.

one of the three edit buttons indicated in Photo 12.6. They include an *insert* button, an *overwrite* button, and a *replace* button. There is also a *disclosure* button, which, when clicked, reveals additional edit choices, including *superimpose, fit to fill, insert with transition,* and *overwrite with transition.* Drag the mouse to the one you want and unclick it to perform the edit. The seven edits available (all shown in Photo 12.6) are defined as follows:

An *insert* edit pushes all clips after the edit point ahead to make room for your new clip. (The beginning of the edit point is located at the playhead.) The overall length of your program increases by the time of your added clip.

An *overwrite* edit copies over the material from the start point of the new clip to its out-point.

A *replace* edit overwrites a specific clip, without disturbing those next to it, and does so by filling in the exact time of the clip it is replacing, without leaving any gaps.

A *superimpose* places a title or other generated material over an existing clip or portion of a clip.

A *fit to fill* adds a clip to a given sequence that has a gap without disturbing any of the location or duration of the surrounding material.

An *insert with transition* performs an insert with a dissolve or other effect (i.e., wipe or fade).

An *overwrite with transition* performs an overwrite with a dissolve or other effect (i.e., wipe or fade).

The *timeline* window (the large window taking up most of the bottom half of Photo 12.7) displays the edited clips arranged into the sequence you want for your show. The timeline and canvas work together; that is, after a clip is edited and placed into the timeline, it can be viewed in the canvas (usually by clicking on the timeline and then hitting the keyboard's space bar to begin playing your video; hit the space bar again to stop playing). The canvas and timeline appear only when clips are selected for viewing. The timeline features display, navigation, and editing controls. Photo 12.7 shows the timeline area in detail, with the following display controls:

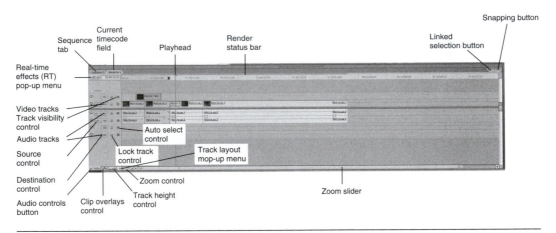

Photo 12.7   Detail of timeline window with display, navigation, and editing controls identified.

Sequence tabs: Each clip sequence has its own tab. The active sequence is displayed in the front position.

Video and audio tracks: The timeline is divided into audio and video tracks with a divider between them. Video tracks are above the divider and audio below. Additional video tracks move upward; additional audio tracks move downward.

Clip overlays control: These display either opacity overlays, seen as thin black lines over clips in the video tracks, to show how transparent each clip will be when played back, as well as audio-level overlays, indicating audio volume levels when played back.

Track height control: When clicked, this button changes the size of the track heights.

Track layout pop-up menu: This customizes track sizes for later editing sessions of selected sequences.

Linked selection button: This clicks either on or off to connect or disconnect, respectively, clip items such as an audio or video portion of a clip. It is useful for editing portions of clips separately from one another.

Snapping button: When clicked on, this button positions the playhead to edit points between clips, for editing between clips quickly without leaving gaps.

Render status bar: This color-coded bar indicates parts of sequences that need to be or have been rendered (see Note 2).

The timeline's navigation controls include the following:

Current time code field: This displays the time code for the current location of the playhead.

Playhead: This vertical line locates the current frame within a clip or sequence.

Ruler: This acts as a scrubber bar to show the duration of the total sequence.

Zoom control and zoom slider: Use these to show more or less of the current sequence.

The timeline's editing controls establish how clips will be entered onto timeline tracks and are located on the left of the timeline in a separate patch panel. They include the following:

Real-time (RT) effects pop-up menu: Lets you choose playback in higher or lower quality in exchange for lower or higher playback capabilities, respectively.

Track visibility control: Lets you enable or disable a track for seeing playback with or without it, respectively. Disabled tracks will not be output to tape when transferred.

Source and destination controls: Lets you select which track on the timeline a clip will be sent to when it is added to your program.

Lock track control: Prevents a track's content from being altered.

Auto select control: Limits the tracks affected by edit functions.

Audio controls button: Displays buttons used for muting specific tracks in the audio portion of the timeline.

Mute and solo buttons: Enables or disables audio playback for selected tracks; makes listening to selected audio portions of clips easy.

There are also two small windows located next to each other on the right of the timeline (see Photo 12.3). One is a *tool palette,* and the other is an icon representing *audio meters.* The tool palette is shown in detail in Photo 12.8, with nine tools visible. Some allow you to select a range of clips to move; others allow you to roll the location of an edit from its current position to refine its location (assuming the clips involved have enough time surrounding the location of the edit [or *handles*] to accommodate the change). Others allow you to cut a clip into separate pieces. The bottom icon looks like a pen and permits you to alter audio levels of clips displayed in the timeline. The audio meters icon next to the tool palette displays the volume levels of clips or sequences currently playing.

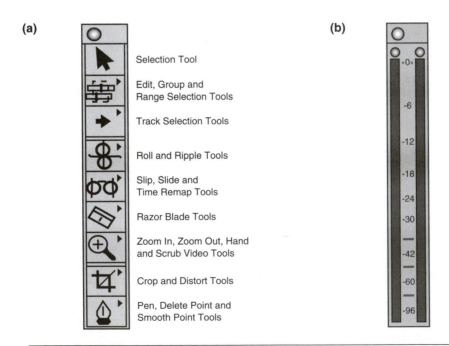

Photo 12.8   Detail of (a) tool palette and (b) audio meters icon, with each tool identified.

Additional Windows That Deserve Mention

Digital editing applications allow you to add text and special effects to your video programs. For example, Photos 12.9 (a and b) and 12.10 show the viewer window transformed to allow text to be composed and styled using a variety of choices.

(a)

(b)

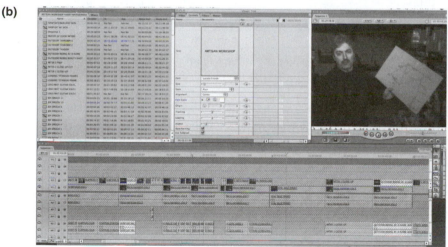

Photo 12.9   (a) Clicking the "A" under the viewer window's jog control opens further menus for adding text (and other things) to your program. (b) With a text selection, the viewer window transforms for composing and adding credits to your show.

Similarly, Photos 12.11 and 12.12 show the browser window transformed (by clicking on the tabs at the top of the browser) to allow special effects and transitions to be added to your program content.

Finally, Photos 12.13 and 12.14 show the viewer window transformed again, (by clicking on the tabs at the top of the viewer) this time to display in detail

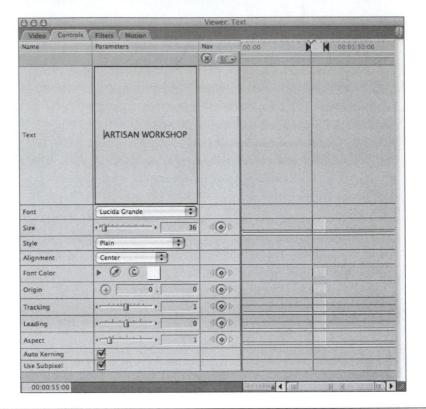

Photo 12.10   Detail of the text window shows items to select for font, size, style of text, and so on.

various aspects of the audio track of any selected clip or program segment. Unwanted audio portions of clips can be deleted; others can be altered with precision.

All of the modifications and effects made possible through the use of these additional windows can be easily tried; for all of them, and for edits in general, if you do not like the result, you can immediately access a drop-down menu to *undo* unwanted changes.

BASIC EDITING PROCEDURES

Once you have become familiar with the editing environment, you can begin building your show. In general, the process, or workflow, involves logging and capturing clips, editing and arranging the portions of them you wish to use in your finished program, audio sweetening, adding effects and titles to your video, and outputting your show for distribution and exhibition.

Some aspects of the workflow will vary in line with your editing style and with the shifting of your ideas as you go; other things must be done in a particular

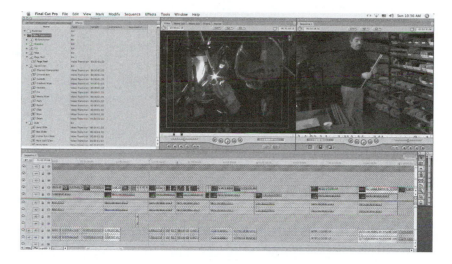

Photo 12.11   Clicking on the *effects* tab above the browser window transforms the window to allow you to access a number of effects and transitions for selected clips and sequences.

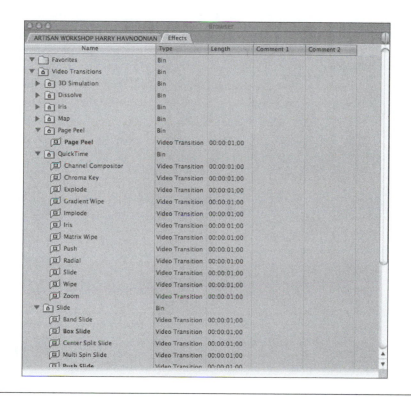

Photo 12.12   Detail of the browser window showing a variety of transitional and special effects available.

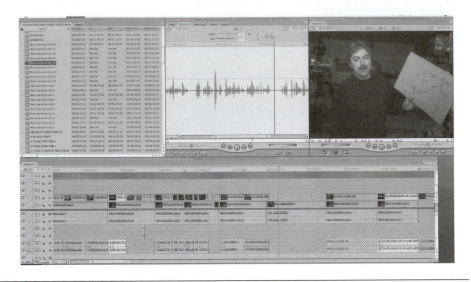

Photo 12.13   Clicking *audio tabs* at the top of the viewer reveals the audio waveform for selected clips or sequences. This graphic display of sound makes matching audio with video more precise.

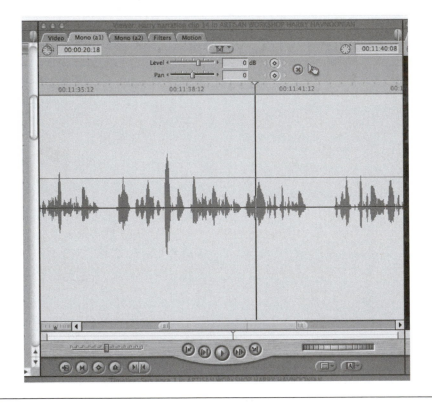

Photo 12.14   Detail of the viewer window showing the audio waveform with various controls used to alter a clip's soundtrack.

order. For example, you must first load the selected portions of video you have shot into the computer before you can begin editing them. As you already know, this will result in a set of video files, called *clips,* which will serve as the raw ingredients of your program.

One way to load clips is through the use of a *firewire* cable, known more formally by electricians as an IEEE 1394 cable. The firewire connects your camera (or other device containing your video raw footage) to the computer. The cable's terminals are different on each end and only fit into the camera and computer one way.

Once the camera and computer are connected and turned on, the computer senses that the camera is there and becomes ready to import video. It is best to transfer footage to your computer after reviewing it to determine which parts you want to import. By transferring only the desired portions, you save valuable disk space. As you capture footage, log the clips and give each a name to make it easy to remember what each clip contains. The browser window will then display a list of each clip you have logged. Once captured, you will have clips you can then assemble into your program.

Once computer and camera are connected, the computer establishes communication with your digital video (DV) camera and displays a set of transport controls

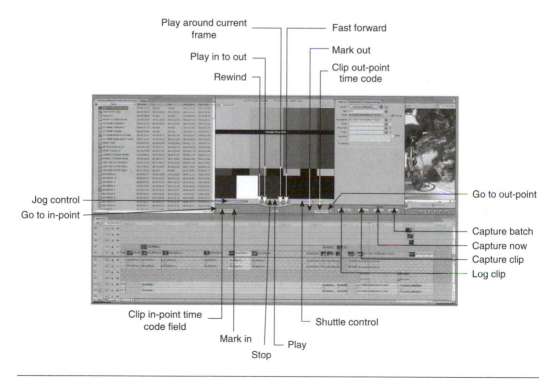

Photo 12.15   Screen display of the log and capture window with transport, marking, and log and capture controls identified.

for shuttling through your raw footage so that you can specify the portions of footage you want to capture. Transport controls include *stop, play, jog and shuttle, rewind, fast forward, play in to out,* and *play around current frame* fields for controlling your camera; in addition, there are *marking controls,* which permit you to mark in- and out-points on your raw footage for capture. The log and capture window (see Photo 12.15) features the following transport control functions:

Play: Plays your footage

Stop: Stops your footage

Rewind: Rewinds your tape

Fast forward: Advances your tape

Play in to out: Moves tape to the current in-point of a clip and plays it to the out-point to allow you to view the segment you have selected for possible capture

Play around current frame: Allows you to view footage at the local time code position

Jog and shuttle controls: Allows more precise navigation within selected clips

The marking controls include the following:

Go to in point: Brings the tape to the current in-point

Clip in point time code field: Displays time code location of selected in-point

Mark in: Sets a start frame for capture

Mark out: Sets an end frame of the capture you have planned

Clip out point time code field: Displays time code location of selected out-point

Go to out point: Moves tape to the current out-point

Log and capture buttons also appear, at the bottom of the log and capture window, and include the following:

Log clip: Click this to log a clip for later capturing

Capture clip: Captures the video for the selected clip or portion

Capture now: Captures an entire tape or live video

Capture batch: Captures several clips at once

Determining if you have enough disk space for capturing the footage you want depends on the quality of the video you wish to import and the length of your program. DV-format video transfers data at 3.6 MB/second. This means that a 30-second commercial requires 108 MB, a 5-minute show requires 1.08 GB, a 30-minute program requires 6.5 GB, and so on. If you intend to include graphic files in addition to video footage, you will of course need more space.[5]

The general rule of thumb is to have about five times the disk space required by the length of the finished program.

Log and Capture Phase

The typical steps in capturing footage for editing include the following:

- Connect your camera to your computer and turn it on.
- Insert your tape of raw footage.
- Choose File>Log and Capture.
- Play the raw footage and set in- and out-points.[6]
- Click the capture button.

Throughout the log and capture process, you will see clips added to the browser. You may add descriptive information to clips later to ensure that you remain aware of what each contains. As you add more clips, it becomes more important to keep track of what each contains to avoid problems remembering what you have logged. Other typical problems involve breaks in time code, which can result in the application stopping capturing at inconvenient moments. To ensure that this does not happen, you should record unbroken time code on each tape before recording footage you wish to use in your program (use *pre-blacked* tapes).

Editing and Arranging Phase

The typical steps involved in editing and arranging, while variable in line with your personal style, are as follows:

- View clips and mark in- and out-points for selected portions.
- Drag them from the viewer to the canvas, where they are automatically entered into the timeline. *They will enter the timeline at the playhead.*
- Arrange selected clip portions in the order you want.
- Select and apply the transitions you want between selected portions.

Audio Sweetening Phase

Audio sweetening entails modifying volume levels associated with the sounds you wish to retain (or deleting others) and adding music and/or voice-overs and sound effects. The audio files used to add sounds can come from other clips or from any other source available to you. Some applications include copyright-free music sampling programs that allow you to compose music bits and then import them as audio files.

Special Effects Phase

Adding special effects may be done at any point in your production, but it is usually done after most of the program has been built. There are endless possibilities, including ornate titles featuring drop shadows and artful spins of the letters, more complex transitions and blur effects between and within shots, and even electronic rain and snow. Many effects require additional disk space and time to perform *rendering* functions. Here you must weigh carefully whether the choices you are making are integral to your program objectives. Here is some advice: *If in doubt, leave it out.*

Outputting Phase

When your show is complete, it is time to share your work. This can be done a number of ways. You can send your finished work back to your camera and then use that tape to load into another computer for viewing (or further editing). Or you can export the work to a DVD authoring tool. Or you may export it as a QuickTime file or some other cross-media platform multimedia technology for distribution over the Web.

Finally, in all cases, it is highly recommended that you archive your work by saving the original media (i.e., the videotapes). Save the project file and the original videotapes of your project to make it easy to alter the program in the future. After your project has been archived, you can delete files from your hard drive to make room for your next project.

INDUSTRY VOICES

Paul Wilson

On March 30, 2005, I interviewed Paul Wilson, who runs the Digital Media Lab at Villanova University after a 40-year career in freelance video and film production. From the mid-1990s until the early 2000s, Wilson sold, installed, and serviced Avid editing systems in the Philadelphia area. His views on the impact of the digital transition on the video and film industries are therefore informed by his extensive knowledge of both the production and business sides of the television industry and digital media.

L: *Paul, you seem to be the master of the domain, running about 20 video workstations here.*

P: Correct. This facility is brand new this year. Until last year, we had 10 editing stations over in the live production suite. Now, we have a larger space with better quality control and more software, all networked so we can control updates and repairs.

L: How many cameras do you have?

P: About 20 small three-chip SONY 950s and PDX-10s, which are the cameras many journalists use. We also have some Canon GL2s, which are moderate in quality in our stock, and some better quality Canon XL-1s, and a few Panasonic DV-100As, which can shoot in 24-p.

L: How long have you been involved in video production?

P: Since the late '60s, early '70s. I worked on the first Bill Cosby specials when they were in Philadelphia, then I went out to L.A. and did work there, had been doing still photography, celebrity shoots, record album covers, and music videos. I also shot movie food up in New York. At that time, video wasn't capable of doing luscious colors, so ad agencies wanted food shot on film.

L: You worked for an advertising agency?

P: No, I was a freelancer—for TV Guide, for Campbell's Silver Cosby Corp., which did Cosby's three specials. Then I had my own studios in Philadelphia and New York where I did food, celebrity, fashion, and film work.

L: Born and raised in Phila?

P: No, I moved from New England in the late fifties to study economics at UPenn and Wharton undergraduate, then Annenberg for graduate work. I studied at Temple, and moved around a lot to pick up digital and film work, mostly in New York and L.A. I wanted to get into editing, because I wanted to shoot films. In those days, there was only one off-line editor, a system made by EMC, which could transfer video onto a black and white proxy, then edit it and transfer it back into tape using time code to make a finished tape. Then Avid came along with a low-res editing system. I went up to New York and watched their new suite and they had machines that allowed you to put video in, and you could see a grainy, pixilated view of the video with time code so you could transfer the finished edit to a high-end Sony BetacamSP or Digital Betacam, machines costing at that time several hundred thousand dollars, and the edit suite would do the finishing. That fascinated me, and I went to an Avid show in Philadelphia, and I met a guy who said we need someone to sell Avids in Philadelphia. And I said, "Give me a system and I'll learn how to use it, and I'll sell it." So they did.

I loved using it and I started to sell big-dollar volume. For a while I put aside my filmmaking because I was making lots of money selling, servicing, installing, teaching, proselytizing, evangelicizing Avid. It was a great product. It went from a niche product back in 1972–1973 to where, let's say in 2000, 98% of the film and video in the world was edited on it. They owned the market. And they also had the service locked up, and you could only get parts from them and you could only use certain computers, and everything was certified this and certified that. It was Mac-based to begin with. And then they had an argument with Apple, so they turned to IBM, and IBM provided them with some high-end IBM dual Xenon-processing behemoths. And lo and behold, under Windows, Avid became more stable and worked even better.

L: I see your lab here is largely Mac-based. How come?

P: Life is a cycle. Apple adopted a Unix-based system, which is more stable than the competition. It's also buildable; it is what the government uses for all their mission-critical stuff. It's what all the great servers are fueled by. Even Pixar began using Unix-based systems with a Mac interface, a really powerful and very stable system, especially for graphics applications. Currently, Mac still has only 5% to 6% of the market. And at last calculation, I think about a third of their profit is in i-Tunes and i-Pod. But their video editing system is very stable, and it isn't bloated, which means that in contrast to Windows, which works on dozens of different types of computers and boards, Mac works on only one system: Apple Macintosh. So you can run the system and it's very stable—rock solid. If something crashes, you can quit the program, reboot it, and you're back in business. You don't need to rebuild the desktop, maybe go find the pieces of the program like the old days. Now, Apple users have become a cult, as Avid people have become a cult.

L: But it doesn't appear that you are a cult person for Avid, even though you used and sold that system for over 10 years.

P: No. While Avid's certainly a good program, Apple developed Final Cut Pro (FCP), which is now an industry alternative. Compared to FCP, Avid is a huge engineering machine. It does things very technically and very perfectly. But, do most jobs need Avid? No. Even the most demanding editing jobs use only 50% to 60% of what Avid can do. But most of today's daily editing work, importing footage, layering a couple of tracks, doing some dissolves, laying in titles, cleaning up sound, adding some music, uses only about 15% to 20% of Avid's capability. And that takes care of 95% of the broadcast day. For the typical job, the videographer does the shoot, imports it into an editing workstation, edits it, puts in dissolves, uses a few effects, with not much fancy titling—it's rudimentary really.

L: And so the editing need for the average editor can be handled by FCP adequately?

P: More than adequately. You can do very creative things. What finally happened was, someone needed to make the commitment to use Final Cut on a major film and tell the world about it. The film Cold Mountain was edited using FCP, as was Full Frontal and

The Corpse Bride. It's become more prevalent to see editing using FCP, even for Hollywood films. You can have five such systems networked for the price of an Avid Symphony. And if the system goes down, you plug in another for $3,000 to 4,000, no big deal. So now, with a Final Cut HD Production Suite, you can edit very high-tone projects.

L: What is the HD Production Suite?

P: HD stands for high definition, but it's a bit of a misnomer. With HD, you can get throughput of fantastic capacity—400 to 600 Mbps, which is enough to get fantastic detail. It's higher definition than what was previously available, so the video you are working with is closer to film than video.

L: And you mentioned before the full throughput of a DV is 3 to 4 MB per second.

P: Well, that's DV. If you do HD, you need special HD editing equipment. Real HD is not processed on these machines. The real HD in real time is edited on machines that are $600,000 to $2.5 million.

L: And does Apple do that too?

P: No, they don't. Avid has one—it's called Digital Studio.

L: Who uses them?

P: Big studios. If you want to watch in real time and need to do a film that has a lot of matte work like Star Wars and Lord of the Rings, then you need to get very high-speed computers, and those are Suns and SGIs. But HDV, which is in between, which does 720 progressive scan, you can do on a Mac with a couple drives hanging on the outside.

L: All these developments sound impressive, especially for the independent producer.

P: I think PCs may be faster, but the Mac is integrated and has made a commitment to doing multimedia, including editing video, producing for the Web, special effects, even animation. That's where Apple's niche is. Every independent editor now has a G5. Every wedding photographer who used to have a myriad of boxes that you hooked up to a VHS is now using a Mac.

L: So it's not just 7% to 10% of the market anymore?

P: Well, in video editing, it's made significant inroads. I'd say that—and it's a rough guess—that Mac now accounts for probably close to 15% of the video production market, especially in the independent field. Almost all my old clients now are beginning to switch over as their 3- to 4-year leases on Avid run out. They're saying, "Why should I spend another $95,000 when I can do essentially the same thing for $30,000?"

L: Besides lower cost, you said earlier that you thought Final Cut Pro was more intuitive to use. Why?

P: With Final Cut Pro, I can bring up a clip, and as I click the mouse cursor, I can drag it from the browser to the canvas, or towards the timeline, and as I drag, it automatically gives me a bunch of choices—to insert, insert with transition, overwrite, overwrite with a transition, vary the speed, fit to fill, which are normal choices for an edit, right there on the screen. Avid doesn't allow that. Avid is a multistep process. For instance, with Avid, I have to move the playhead to where I want it, then drag it down, and then, once I get everything on the timeline, I must access a trim mode to do all the trimming. With Final Cut, I can do most of the trimming before I get it on the timeline, so there's less work to do later. Another thing is, with Avid, if I have audio, and I double-click it, I get an empty window and can't see a waveform, so I can't tell where I am or even that I've loaded the audio until I press play. Then I can only hear it, until I put it down on a timeline. By contrast, Final Cut assumes that if I am clicking on audio, I naturally want to do something with it, so it automatically displays that audio segment's waveform. That way, I can instantly see whether the sound is too big or too small. It instantly shows me whether I am cutting on someone's breath or a sound. So when I trim audio, I can see what I'm trimming, and I can alter the volume at the same time, or alter the pan in that same window. In Avid, if I want to do that, I have to take the video, then put it back down on one of the lines, and if I have two audio tracks, I first have to create separate audio tracks and then make the alterations I want, one by one; it won't automatically create more tracks; instead, it'll overwrite the audio I have. With Final Cut Pro, I simply drag tracks down to wherever I want them and it automatically activates those tracks. It's just simpler; it anticipates the things I want to do. In Final Cut, if I want to access some effect, in the same window on top of my gallery where I keep all my clips, I can click an effects button, pick the effect I want, drag it onto the clip where I want to use the effect in the timeline. Then I can double-click the clip in the timeline, open up all the effects in the viewing window, and tweak the clip as I wish, altering the time of a clip or its brightness, or whatever, all in one pass. If it's an audio track, I can clip what I want from the waveform, resize it to make the sine wave bigger or smaller to see it better, and make as many changes as I want in one pass. With Avid, everything must be done in single steps, so I have to go to another place in the program for each step involved. The good news with Avid is I can work frame by frame and do things very precisely. But only 10% of people really work that way.

L: So even though you learned on Avid, do you find as a teacher people pick up Final Cut Pro more easily?

P: I even find myself picking Final Cut Pro these days. I spent about 8 years with Avid, and it's become a habit, like skiing or something—you tend to do it the same way all the time. And in some ways, I still miss it. But Final Cut has incorporated many of the same modes that Avid popularized. For example, there are the JKL keys, which allow you to shuttle back and forth through a clip. Final Cut Pro now has that. Avid permits the user to assign keys certain functions, so if you're left-handed or right-handed, you can actually modify the keyboard. Final Cut Pro now has that. As a matter of fact, there are programs that allow you to take Avid settings and import them to Final Cut Pro to make it look and feel exactly like Avid. So if you've edited for 5 years, and you're used to certain keys controlling certain functions, and you can transfer them from Avid to Final Cut, you lose absolutely nothing except the weight and cost.

L: How do you like what you've seen happen in the industry during the last 20 years of your career?

P: Everything has changed. The biggest impact has been the democratizing of audiovisual production and editing. It means instead of having to have a $30,000 camera and a $95,000 editing suite, you can now buy a $5,000 camera and a $10,000 edit suite and you can potentially make professional-quality films and videos.

Of course, just because I can buy my own scalpel and forceps doesn't make me a competent surgeon—I'm not qualified to take out my own appendix, or yours. The problem is what has happened is you have a lot of people who own a camera and think having is being. But it's not that simple. You can't take someone seriously who says, "I own a camera, and I own an edit system, therefore, I am a filmmaker, editor, videographer." But, if you have proper training and expertise, and you are a Cecil B. DeMille, it makes it much easier to realize your ideas. And the last few years of growth in video production capability is the same as what happened 20 years ago when Apple revolutionized desktop publishing. Apple produced the first desktop publishing program so people could produce their own manuscripts, do their own brochures, set their own type, make fancy advertising. Did it mean that there were more high-quality books published? No. It meant that those people that were good at typesetting no longer needed the $100,000 typesetter—they could do that kind of thing for less money. It made it possible to bring down the cost of typesetting and rendering graphics. But access cannot guarantee traditions of excellence.

L: So production may be more accessible, but access doesn't guarantee quality.

P: True. Distribution opportunities have also changed. The Internet has democratized distribution as never before; that is, anyone can make his or her own Web site, and can then make their own music or music video and hype it on the Net and sell downloads to anybody.

L: So in a nutshell, the big change you see is democratization for both production and distribution.

P: Yes. Increased access and lower prices for both.

L: *Then the issue comes back to the idea that owning a scalpel and forceps doesn't make you a surgeon.*

P: *There is also the question of who will watch all the content that is produced—who and how big is the audience going to be for future programs? Once upon a time, in the analog world, you'd have to fast-forward through a whole tape to find that little part where Aunt Betty blew out the candles. Now, you can mark that little part as a segment, and anytime you want to watch it, you can access it in an instant from a DVD. And the potential is much greater for business and education. Content can be loaded on your laptop and fed to a projector to a small group of people. Distance learning, telecommuting, teleconferencing are all feasible for companies large and small. With DV, it means that you can take some inexpensive camera, shoot material, edit together a great presentation, and send it out either on the Web, or as a CD or DVD, even as an e-mail.*

KEY TERMS

QUESTIONS FOR REVIEW

What are some practical and aesthetic reasons for using editing in video production?

Define *continuity, classical,* and *dynamic editing.* Compare and contrast them, and give examples of each.

How does shot juxtaposition affect audience interpretation of cause and effect in an edited sequence? Use an example to illustrate.

Describe the formalist and realist traditions and how they influence editing decisions in different situations.

Generally speaking, how do pictorial complexity and mise en scène affect editing pace?

In what ways might technology development affect editing aesthetics? What recent developments have had the most impact on editing practice?

Why is the control track important in both analog and digital editing?

What advantages does time code editing offer over control track editing?

What are the differences between assemble and insert editing?

What advantages does nonlinear editing offer over linear editing?

NOTES

1. The time code system most widely adopted by the video industry is called SMPTE/EBU time code (pronounced "simpty time code"). It stands for the Society of Motion Pictures and Television Engineers/European Broadcasting Union, which are the professional organizations that set standards for this function.

2. Remember also that as you perform assemble edits, the erase head is erasing the tape in front of the edit, eliminating the control track just ahead of the new material. This means that if you want to perform another edit, you will need to allow the last edit to continue past the point where you want the new edit to begin so that you have enough control track for the new one to align with properly. Forgetting this can be frustrating and time-consuming.

3. Two types of SMPTE time code can be recorded on videotape. One, called longitudinal time code (LTC), is recorded lengthwise on either the audio or cue track. The other, vertical interval time code (VITC, pronounced "vitsee"), is recorded in the vertical interval for each frame in the video track. For some grades of tape, LTC may be found in a special address track. On analog VHS tape, for example, LTC is located on an audio track. When LTC time code is recorded on an audio track, it must be recorded at a high enough level to be read clearly, but not so high that it causes audio problems such as cross-talk or squeals. You must also guard against the possibility of losing it by overdubbing audio.

An advantage of VITC time code over LTC is that it cannot be lost when audio tracks are added in postproduction. A disadvantage is that VITC records only when video is recorded and cannot be read when the tape is fast-forwarding.

4. Manuals describing all the functions and capabilities of the most popular digital video editing applications are available from the manufacturers and may include multiple volumes, in some

cases totaling well over a thousand pages of guidelines. Other single-volume "quick" guides are also available from independent authors. For example, for the system presented here, see Brenneis (2004).

5. Some applications use additional disk space for rendering files, which means that they perform additional processing of audio and video (i.e., adding effects and motion to titles like drop shadow, blur effects, etc.).

6. At this stage, it's a good idea to import clips with a bit of extra footage at the beginning and end of each desired portion, leaving some material available for transitions that require extra time, such as dissolves and fades. The extra few seconds of time at the beginning and end of desired clips are called *handles*.

PART III

PRODUCTION ROLES

Chapter 13

WRITING AND SCRIPT FORMATS

The art of writing is the art of applying the seat of the pants to the seat of a chair.

—Mary Heaton Vorse

How vain it is to sit down to write when you have not stood up to live.

—Henry David Thoreau

To write well, there are required three necessaries—to read the best authors, observe the best speakers, and much exercise of his own style.

—Ben Jonson

If you wish to be a writer, write.

—Epictetus

The advice from these veteran authors is invaluable for video scriptwriters. They know good writing is best learned by doing: by living, observing, reading, and writing. Furthermore, it helps to be realistic about one's abilities, as well as tenacious and able to take rejection. But what in particular do you need to know to write for video, as opposed to writing a play, a novel, an essay?

Since video writers may deal with a great number of topics and quite different types of subject matter, both fiction and nonfiction, this chapter cannot cover all the situations you may encounter. What it will do is offer some valuable guidelines for video writing and prepare you for using basic script formats. The topics include the following:

Principles of video writing
- Characteristics of the medium
- Characteristics of audience and genre
- Characteristics of the competitive market

Basic script formats

- The rule of pragmatism
- The director's working script
- News scripts
- Scripts for commercials
- Full-page scripts
- Scriptwriting software

PRINCIPLES OF VIDEO WRITING

Certain features of video writing make it different from other types of writing. The nature of the medium itself, the audience and genre, and also the competitive market influence the scriptwriter. In the most obvious sense, the work of the television writer never comes to the audience on paper. Rather than being read, the writing is heard, after being embedded in a program along with other sounds, images, and actions. This has strong implications for the writer.

Characteristics of the Medium

Television can deliver sounds and images live as they occur, as in news and sports. It can also present performances repeatedly, thanks to storage media such as film, tape, and disk. Either way, there is a quality of natural immediacy and action to video programs. Video's strength lies in its ability to convey human action through real-time audiovisual displays. Even computer systems have only just begun to render human action at a comparable level of picture quality, immediacy, and pervasiveness.

What writing styles fit best with these characteristics of the medium? Most television writers advise using simple, concise language, in a direct, natural, conversational tone, in the present tense. Such language works well on video because it fits video's active, immediate, and dynamic nature; it is also quickly and easily comprehended. Unlike narrative writing, it emphasizes showing over telling, revealing over describing, and demonstrating over explaining, taking advantage of the medium's ability to showcase processes as they unfold. Imagine the squandered opportunity of a cooking program that spent its precious airtime talking about recipes but never actually preparing one.

Pictures, Sound, and Words: The Goal of Synergy. Though it may be humbling for the television writer to admit, it is likely that the dramatic, arresting images of video are remembered more than the words that accompany them. Therefore, there may be great sense in letting words play a supporting role to pictures. Decide what parts of the story will be conveyed by nonverbal elements, and then write to support the program as a whole. Let the words provide what the other program elements fail to provide.

This does not mean that words play a minor role. In fact, in the well-written television program, words and pictures frequently codetermine one another. In radio, you might write a line like "Why don't you wear this red polka dot dress to the party?" Those words would give the listener a mental image of the dress. However, on television, where the dress might be perfectly visible in a close-up or medium shot, a better line might be, "Why don't you wear *this?*" These simplified words demand a picture to back them up, and the picture in turn calls for words that are simple and direct.

Pictures often serve to support the claims made by the words. For example, if an announcer's voice-over claims that microwave oven X brings water to a boil faster than its chief competitor, it is more persuasive if the claim is accompanied by a visual demonstration of the claim. As another illustration, imagine the difference in impact between merely hearing about a plane crash and hearing about it while seeing graphic video of the disaster. Such *synergy,* where the combination of program elements has a greater impact than any individual element alone, is one main goal of the television writer.

In addition to visuals, the writer can sometimes rely on sounds to replace or reduce the need for verbal description. In news coverage of an intense forest fire, if location sound features loud crackling and wind, it may be superfluous to include verbal descriptions of the noise. In fact, injecting surplus verbiage over the natural sound would risk drowning out the very noise that generated the description.

The Impact of Editing. Besides the effects of shot content and nonverbal portions of the soundtrack, the writer's task is influenced by the extensive editing often done in video. For example, television writers providing commercial and promotional copy often write scripts for 30-second spots that may be reduced to 10-second versions known as **liftouts.** To provide coherence in either version, writers work to preserve sense and provide smooth transitions from sentence to sentence, regardless of which version is used.

More generally, since videotape editing often condenses stories into their highlights, the pace and order of shots and sequences may change during the production process. Such changes can affect the sense, flow, rhythm, tempo, and tone of the written material. For this reason, writing changes are often needed to preserve meanings lost or changed by program editing. Experienced video writers know to prepare for this possibility and not become overly frustrated by it.

Fixed Program Time and Order. With newspapers, magazines, and books, time spent with a particular story may differ widely among audience members. Different people have faster or slower reading speeds; they read for different purposes, and they have different amounts of time available. Readers can also skip around if they choose or review items of interest a second or third time. In short, with print, readers have a great deal of control over the amount of time they spend with the material and the order in which they attend to different items.

By contrast, viewers of live television are tied to a fixed schedule. Even with prerecorded programs, when they are seen the way they are meant to be seen, viewers are exposed to sequences in a predetermined order, each for a predetermined amount of time.[1] Once a speech is spoken, it is gone. What are the implications of this for the writer?

As mentioned, it helps to keep the language simple and conversational. Avoid long sentences. Try to present your ideas clearly the first time. Furthermore, it is particularly important to *pace* speeches for television at an acceptable rate for the majority of the audience. Material presented too slowly can bore viewers or, worse, insult their intelligence, motivating them to tune out. On the other hand, if material is presented too quickly, viewers can become confused. Try to present speeches with a pace that keeps your audience interested while not confusing them.

Telegraphing what is coming next is often useful. **Telegraphing** involves warning the viewers about upcoming topics so that they are prepared to receive the ideas more easily. A common example is when the program host tells viewers to get a pencil and paper ready for an important phone number or address. Another useful technique is **recapping,** restating important ideas to refresh the audience's memory. This may be especially appropriate when the material is complex, and it also helps late tuners-in to catch on to what is happening.

To check the pace and the need for telegraphing or recapping, gauge how the script works in real time. Read lines aloud to time them and to assess their sound, sense, and clarity. For more difficult segments, you may need to slow down or recap key statements. Don't be satisfied with merely adequate results. Rework lines to make them more understandable and functional. Then be dissatisfied again. Continually demand more of your writing.

Characteristics of Audience and Genre

As Chapter 1 notes, video programs are usually tailored for particular audiences. As a writer, you should bear in mind the audience's maturity level, values, opinions, social history, interests, needs, and so forth in deciding how to write your copy.

On the most basic level, a video writer considers how much knowledge of the program's subject matter the audience already possesses. What information can be taken for granted so that program time is not wasted? What information must you provide to bring the audience along at a comfortable pace? Where do you risk boring the audience? Such information may not always be available, but it certainly helps to have as much of it as possible so that you can pitch your script properly.

Consider the U.S. Army's original radio and television advertising campaign and the slogan they made so popular upon becoming an all-volunteer force in the early 1970s. The slogan did not say, "Aspire to achieve all of your yearnings." Instead, it said, "Be all you can be."[2] Why is the shorter slogan better? Among other reasons, it is probably understood by more of the army's target audience, American high school seniors. Similarly, a program about AIDS prevention would be written more simply for a target audience of elementary school children than if the audience were an international conference of biomedical professionals and health workers.

As a video writer, you should also be attuned to the needs of the particular *genre,* that is, the basic type or category of the program. There are major differences in the writing of fiction and nonfiction, comedy and drama, variety and quiz shows, sitcoms, and soap operas, to name but a few. The differences involve not only subject matter but also the overall approach that you take with the script, including language usage, level of difficulty, diction, dialect, pace of delivery, and demands for factual accuracy. The audiences for different program types may vary in age, socioeconomic status, values, and so on, and audience members may have particular expectations for each genre. Thus, to prepare for writing in a particular genre, you should steep yourself in examples of that type of program. For instance, what vocabulary could you use in a period western that you couldn't use in a contemporary police drama, and vice versa? How might the pace of a sitcom differ from that of a tragedy?

Recognizing genre differences does not lock you into imitating exactly what has come before. If that were the case, there would be no innovation. While much programming is derivative, there is always room for ground-breaking ideas that develop new program forms. Knowing about genre differences allows you to conform to accepted practice when you want and need to and, conversely, to depart from it for special impact. With a strong understanding of genre differences, you can use them to your own advantage.

Characteristics of the Competitive Market

In addition to being influenced by the medium, the audience, and the genre, the video writer must also respond to the demands of the competitive market. One obvious effect of the market is that a video script often develops through a number of stages as the financial backers decide whether the program deserves their commitment.

The first stage, as discussed in Chapter 1, is often a **proposal** for a new program, whether it be a comedy, variety special, reality show, game show, a drama for public television, or a more specialized work for an industry client. The purpose of the proposal is to convince a production company or client that the concept has merit, especially audience appeal. The proposal should describe the program's premise, introduce the central characters or talent, and describe the main program segments.

If the proposal is approved, you may be asked to write a **treatment,** a narrative version of the program designed to give the reader a feel for the characters, setting, and action that takes place. Then, once the format and subject matter of the program and the main characters or talent have been described, you may be asked to go beyond the treatment stage to show how they all function in a pilot episode. A **pilot** is a test episode used to gauge the value of the program idea.

In both fiction and nonfiction programs, the proposal and treatment stages are designed to convey an idea of the subject matter and tone of the program. They may also convey typical elements of the action, the pacing, the set design, and any other key features that give the reader insight about the show. The focus especially is on identifying the program's audience appeal.[3] In the current market, which is rife with choices, especially as more wire and wireless digital outlets become available for exhibiting programs, competition can become so intense that the need for strong proposals and treatments is greater than ever.

In short, competition affects the way scripts are written. For example, video writers feel strong pressure to engage the viewers' interest quickly. In past decades, network series invariably started with title, theme, and credits, but many of today's start "cold," with script material presented even before the credits and theme song (if there is one at all). This **cold start** is designed to grab an audience that is also being wooed by cable and satellite programs, streaming videos delivered via the Internet, DVDs, and numerous other independent programming sources. Therefore, an arresting lead is crucial: A program's opening words should command attention and create immediate audience interest. Then the follow-up should hold that interest, so that the viewer does not start clicking the remote control or computer mouse in search of other options.

Today's successful television writers know that they must deliver story interest within seconds, not minutes, and that any lag can result in lost audience. Such intense market competition influences the writer to cut to the chase, so to speak, without wasting time.

BASIC SCRIPT FORMATS

Television scripts[4] assign speeches to particular talent. However, scripts that do *only* this are far from complete. The extra-verbal information in television scripts includes cues for music and other background sounds, camera assignments, talent blocking, microphone cues, and notations describing special effects and transitions. Information about lighting and facilities needs, set and prop lists, floor plans and lighting plot diagrams, and other production elements may also be included.

Of course, some programs cannot be fully scripted in advance because not all of the words spoken during the show are known in advance. Programs that feature ad-lib or off-the-cuff remarks may be written in a **semiscripted format.** Still other programs may be handled using an even less detailed **rundown sheet,** which is little more than a list of a program's major segments in proper order with approximate running times. While semiscripts and rundown sheets do not include all of the words that are spoken, they can still provide as much of the nonverbal information as full scripts. In other words, the fact that a program uses a rundown sheet is no reason to omit support documentation such as set and prop lists, a list of facilities, and so on.

Examples of semiscripted shows include interviews, reality shows, musical variety programs, and sports coverage, for which some but not all of the materials have been prepared in advance. Such scripts indicate the order of presentation of segments (if it is known beforehand), and they often contain **in-cues** and **out-cues** for each segment—that is, phrases preceding or ending talent speeches that alert production personnel when it is time to move to the next segment.

News shows may be fully scripted. However, if they feature late-breaking stories or live segments, a semiscripted format may be the most sensible one. For semiscripted news, the script may include notations to alert the director and crew about when and where transitions between stories occur. There may also be notes indicating the technical source for each story (for instance, studio VTR or live feed from the field). Furthermore, the notes can say whether the upcoming story is presented with sound on tape (SOT) or with a reporter's voice-over (VO) and when a segment is to be accompanied by character-generated text (CG) or chroma key inserts (C/K).

The least structured script format, the rundown sheet, is used for such programs as *The Tonight Show, The Daily Show,* and other night-time talk shows, audience participation programs (i.e., game shows), and variety formats, where the order, general content, and approximate running time of each segment are set in advance, but the actual words spoken are not known until they are uttered. Figure 13.1 shows an example of a rundown sheet for a 3-minute, stationary-talent interview program.

Title: *BOOK LOOK*

Date: November 20, 2006

0:00–0:10	OPENING SHOT: HOST AND GUEST CHAT W/ TITLE AND MUSIC
0:10–0:30	HOST INTRO OF GUEST
0:30–0:45	GUEST SAYS HELLO
0:45–2:30	HOST AND GUEST CHAT ABOUT AND SHOW BOOK
2:30–2:45	HOST MOVES TO CLOSE, ANNOUNCES NEXT GUEST
2:45–3:00	TALENT SAYS GOODBYE, MUSIC AND CLOSING CREDITS ROLL

Figure 13.1   Rundown sheet for three-minute interview program.

Successful programs that start out using a semiscripted format can develop such a regular rhythm over the years that eventually the veteran director and crew become comfortable with just a simple rundown sheet. *The Tonight Show* (now with Jay Leno), which ran for 30 years with Johnny Carson as host, is an example of such a program.

The Rule of Pragmatism

The only rule that should govern what script to use, as well as what information to include in it, is the rule of pragmatism: *Use what works.* What this principle means is that the finished script should answer most if not all the questions the crew might have, so that the director can concentrate on the most important functions, including clearing up last-minute problems and conducting run-throughs.

To the extent that the script acts as a proxy for the director, providing answers for the crew, the script is doing what it is supposed to do. Therefore, it is a good policy to ask yourself these questions: Have I included everything I can to make every element of the production clear to all involved? Have I eliminated uncertainty and ambiguity so that everyone knows what is supposed to happen and when? Have I made the script so complete that if, by some twist of fate, the entire cast, crew, and director were suddenly removed from the production, a new group could execute the show from the information in the script? While this last question may exaggerate what a good script can provide, it represents the ultimate goal for every scriptwriter.

The Director's Working Script

If we wanted to convert the rundown sheet in Figure 13.1 into a full script for the 3-minute interview program, what might the script look like? Figure 13.2 provides an example. The script shown in the figure contains a number of elements designed to reduce uncertainty and ambiguity to a reasonable level, making it possible to execute the program with a minimum of misunderstanding. Let's examine some key features of this script.

Starting at the top of the first page, note that the pages are numbered using an inclusive numbering system: "p. 1 of 4," "p. 2 of 4," and so on. This numbering allows all crew members to see whether they have a complete version of the script in proper order *without having to ask the director.* Next, notice that the script has a title. Every script should have a title, even if it is only for a 10-second announcement. If you are producing a series of spots, the titles permit each one to be identified without ambiguity.

Similarly, notice the date and client name. Including this information ensures that crew members can know which version of the script they have and who the

P. 1 of 4

Date: November 20, 2006

Client: Bio-Pic Productions

Title: ***BOOK LOOK***

<u>VIDEO</u>	<u>AUDIO</u>

Op. Shots

     C 1, Title card

     C 2, 2-shot, host and guest chatting

(ready Q Biz)

(ready open mics)

(ready f/2)

(ready Key 1/2)

(ready music up and under)

(ready Q tal)

       Q BIZ

       HIT MUSIC

       F/2

       OP. MICS

       Q TAL

       MUSIC UNDER   <u>HOST:</u> Welcome to *BOOK LOOK*.

       (KEY 1/2)————————————

(ready lose 1)   Our guest is _____. Today we are

       LOSE 1, MUSIC OUT

(ready C2, on-air, Z in CU Host)   going to talk about _____. How

(ready 1, CU guest)   are you today?

                         <u>GUEST:</u> Hi. I'm fine and happy to be here.

       (1)————————————

(ready 2, CU host)

(ready intercut 1 and 2)

       INTERCUT 1 AND 2   ((HOST AND GUEST CHAT))

(ready C 2 Z out on air to a 2-S)

(ready pull card for close)

(ready Q Host's wrap)   <u>HOST:</u> Well, we're out of time.

      (C 2 Z)————————————

       PULL CARD

Figure 13.2   A director's working script for the same 3-minute interview program shown in Figure 13.1.

P. 2 of 4

(ready C1 on card)

Thanks for joining us. Next time, we'll be
(ready K 1/2)

interviewing _____, so don't forget to join

KEY 1/2

(ready sneak in music)

SNEAK MUSIC IN

us again for another edition of *BOOK*

LOOK. So long.

(ready lose key)
LOSE KEY

(ready f/blk)

((HOST AND GUEST CONTINUE

F/BLK, F/AUDIO

CHATTING)).

–CLEAR–

THANKS EVERYONE

P. 3 of 4

SUPPORT DOCUMENTATION FOR *BOOK LOOK*

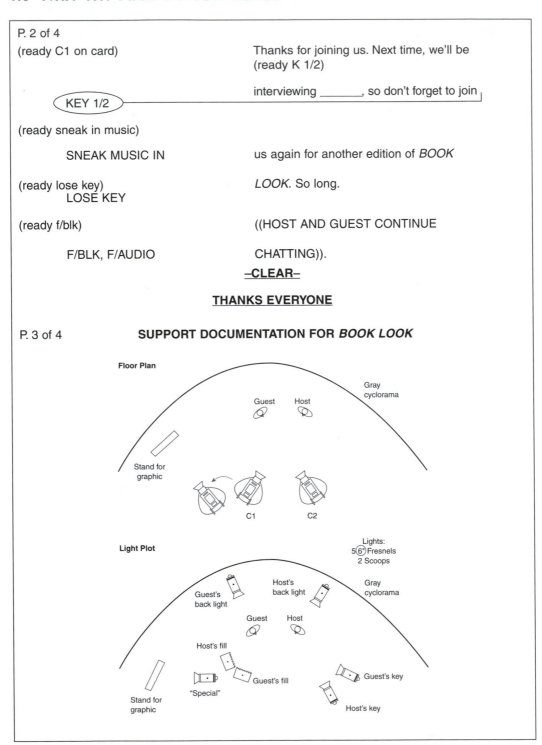

Figure 13.2 (Continued)

P. 4 of 4   <u>FAX LIST</u>

| <u>Graphics:</u> | <u>ESS:</u> | <u>Mics:</u> | |
| 1 title card *(BOOK LOOK)* | none | 2 lavs | |

<u>Other audio:</u>	<u>Props:</u>	<u>Set:</u>	<u>CG:</u>
cassette for op. and close	book	2 chairs	1 credit
			graphic
		cyclorama (gray)	

<u>Costumes:</u>	<u>Other notes:</u>	<u>Lights:</u>
casual wear (no white,		5 six-inch Fresnels
no black, no intricate		2 scoops
patterns)		

<u>Key</u>

Op. Shots	Opening shots
C 1, C 2, etc.	Camera 1, camera 2, etc.
Q Biz	Cue business. In this case, host and guest pretend to chat, but in general, a business cue is any activity talent is given to do before fading up their camera, so that the effect is created of having come in on action (wiping a bar with a rag, dialing a phone, etc.).
Op. mics	Open microphones
Q Tal	Cue the talent to begin the show or some other action
f/2	Fade Camera 2
Key 1/2	Key Camera 1 over Camera 2
Z in	Zoom in
1	Take Camera 1 (arrow indicates a specific word or syllable where the take occurs)
F/AUDIO	Fade audio

Figure 13.2 (Continued)

client is. Some production companies even use different-colored paper to signal when a new version of a script has been written.

Next, notice the **split-page format,** which lays out the audio content on one half of the page and the video content (with other cues) on the other half. This layout makes it easy to link the words in the script to other program elements. In multi-camera productions, a split-page format aids in coordinating different camera shots with specific speeches and scenes. This format is standard in most types of video production, although some types, such as single-camera EFP-style production, may use a full-page format like that used in the film industry. The Professional Pointers feature lists a number of other characteristics of the split-page format. In reviewing Figure 13.2 and the pointers, consider what other elements you might add to the script to make it better than it is now.

Preparing a Split-Page Script

➤ You do not need a vertical line between the video and audio columns. Leaving the line out keeps the copy cleaner and reduces the idea of a barrier between video and audio elements.

➤ The speaker of each and every speech is identified in the audio column by a name or role.

➤ Speeches are double or triple spaced to allow for easy reading.

➤ Speeches on the first page begin at the halfway point on the page, or lower down, in order to leave room for intro or ready cues, music cues, and any others that might be needed to start the show.

➤ In order to limit confusion for the talent, spoken lines are distinguished from other verbal entries in the audio column by a difference in type face, type case, or other attributes. For instance, it's far better to write "HOST: Welcome to the show" than "Host: Welcome to the show."

➤ The first entry in the video column lists opening shots for every camera. Even if the third camera in a 30-minute show is not used for the first 25 minutes, it still has an opening shot listed at the beginning. With this format, camera operators know which shots to prepare for openers without having to ask the director.

➤ After the opening shots, the left half of the split page contains all the ready cues, in order, in lowercase letters, in parentheses, flush left in the column. Then it shows the actual commands, in uppercase letters, at the right of the column. This arrangement makes it easy for the director to see both ready cues and commands in order at a glance.

➤ The video column also contains cues referring to nonvideo elements, including mic and music cues and talent cues.

➤ Horizontal arrows (as shown in Figure 13.2) are often drawn from circled camera commands to speeches in the script where camera changes are meant to occur. This method of connecting camera commands to specific speeches is more accurate than simply writing "Take 1," for example, on the line where you want to use that camera.

Notice that the script in Figure 13.2 continues after the split-page section for the verbal content. The script goes on to include a floor plan, a light plot, and a facilities (*fax*) list that indicates set, lights, graphics, mics, props, costumes, and so forth. Set and light lists are provided *in addition to* the floor plan and light plot because the lists make it easy to gather the items needed for a shoot. This portion of the script can list any information that will be important for the crew. For example, notice that the cyclorama on our floor plan is labeled not just "cyc," but "gray cyc." Get as specific as you need to be.

One great advantage of developing a thorough script is that you can place the floor plan and the verbal text side by side during the preproduction phase, confirming whether the shots you have planned are indeed possible. By developing commands with the floor plan as a guide, you guard against the possibility of asking for things that are simply not possible (e.g., having a camera in two places at once).

Depending on the company you work for, the crew you work with, and the genre of program you are producing, the level and type of detail provided in the scripts may vary tremendously. You may work with scripts that are quite sketchy compared to the detailed treatment presented here. You may work with some that are even more detailed. In addition, some program genres have unique demands in terms of script preparation. The following sections examine a few different script formats associated with specific kinds of programs.

News Scripts

Television news scripts may use the split-page format, clearly indicating the production process for each story. Figure 13.3 shows a typical news script. In this example, a live intro by the studio news anchor is followed by taped ENG video of auction activity with continued voice-over by the anchor. A *font,* or CG-generated line of text, identifies the location shown in the video by name. Next, the news anchor is shown on camera again, providing a bridge to the next part of the story, contained in a *news package,* or prepared tape, featuring an on-the-scene reporter's narration and video of an inventory of jewelry items. Notice that the right-hand column describes the package only in terms of length. The left-hand column identifies the in-cues and the videotape machines to be used. In our illustration, the package uses B-roll and A-roll tapes, each with a separate in-cue. At the end of the package, the reporter appears briefly on camera to sign off, with a font identifying her. Finally, the studio anchor's tag closes the story.

Notice these other features of the news script in Figure 13.3:

- Each story is headed by a *slug,* a one- or two-word identifier—in this case, "ONASSIS AUCTION." Also included are the date and time, the writer's name, page length for the story, and running time.

Slug: ONASSIS AUCTION	Talent: F.J. Writer: Fred Jones Q: 5PM

Printed by: Fred Jones at 4:10:30: P.04-29-06   pgs: 2   time: 50 sec.

TALENT: ANCHOR   ((ANCHOR))

ON CAM   AUCTIONING OFF MOM'S BAUBLES AND KEEPSAKES,
                                 CAROLINE KENNEDY OFFERS THE PUBLIC AN
                                 OPPORTUNITY TO PUT A PRICE ON FAME . . .

ENG/VO   THE VALUE OF CAMELOT SEEMS TO EXCEED EVEN
                                 THE WILDEST PREDICTIONS OF THE PROS

FONT: SOTHEBY'S   AT SOTHEBY'S AUCTION HOUSE. JACKIE O'S
                                 CELEBRITY SEEMS TO HAVE SEEPED INTO HER
                                 FAMILY TREASURES.

TALENT: ANCHOR ON CAM   CINDY STANDUP WAS ON THE
                                 SCENE AT SOTHEBY'S TO FILE THIS REPORT

B-ROLL: TO FILE THIS REPORT

ENG SOT   ((PKG-30 SECONDS))
                                     A CARTIER NECKLACE WENT FOR EIGHT
                                 HUNDRED TWENTY FIVE THOUSAND DOLLARS,
                                 A HARRY WINSTON PENDANT FOR EIGHT HUNDRED
                                 EIGHTY THOUSAND.

(MORE MORE MORE)   THIS RUBY, SAPPHIRE, EMERALD,
                                 AND DIAMOND CLIP IN THE SHAPE OF A
                                 FLAMINGO WENT FOR EIGHT HUNDRED AND
                                 SIX THOUSAND DOLLARS. WHAT THIS MEANS
                                 TO SOME OBSERVERS IS

A-ROLL: PRICE OF FAME IS HIGH   THAT THE PRICE OF FAME IS HIGH. IT ALSO MEANS
                                 THE DESIRE

ENG SOT   TO CAPTURE A PIECE OF THE BELOVED KENNEDY
                                 PAST IS PERHAPS STRONGER NOW THAN IT WAS
                                 THIRTY YEARS AGO.

FONT: CINDY STANDUP   AT SOTHEBY'S THIS IS CINDY STANDUP REPORTING . . .

                                 ((ANCHOR))

TALENT: ANCHOR   THANKS FOR THAT REPORT, CINDY . . . WELL
                                 I WONDER HOW MUCH I COULD GET FOR
                                 MY EMERALD TIE PIN . . . BACK WITH MORE NEWS
                                 AFTER THIS

Figure 13.3   A sample news script.

- The split-page portion of the script clearly identifies the copy to be read and the reader for each speech. Transitions to new story segments are also clearly indicated.
- Transitions among video sources (in-cues for both A-roll and B-roll tapes) are clearly marked to alert crew about what sources to cue and when to take them.

Some additional hints about preparing news scripts are included in the Professional Pointers list.

Preparing News Scripts

➢ Each story should start on a separate page.
➢ If a story runs longer than one page, use inclusive numbering so that each page shows both the number of the current page and the total number of pages in the script. Also, for multipage stories, write "MORE" at the bottom of each page before the last page.
➢ To get an accurate idea of running time for each story, establish a standard for margins, type size, and number of lines per page. You may find, for example, that each page equals about 30 seconds of running time.
➢ The paper used for on-air scripts should generally be some color other than white to reduce light reflection.
➢ On-air script pages should not be stapled together. Unstapled, they can be put aside when they have been read without unnecessary rustling.

Newswriting, Ethics, and the Law. The news writer must be acutely aware of legal and ethical concerns relevant to the journalism profession. Beyond First Amendment guarantees of freedom of the press and speech, you should also be familiar with the rights of privacy of individuals under the Fourth Amendment, as well as protection from libel, slander, defamation, and trespass. Laws related to transgressions in these areas affect the way news is gathered and reported. Several of these terms are defined in Table 13.1.

In addition to federal law, state laws also dictate journalistic practices related to rights of access to restricted areas, the use of surveillance equipment, the recording of telephone conversations without proper notice, and access to juvenile trials. The use of cameras in the courtroom may also vary depending on state law. To avoid costly litigation and to protect yourself and the news group you work for, become thoroughly familiar with the laws in your state. Check with your legal department if possible in order to minimize problems.

Table 13.1   Some Journalistic Legal Terms Defined

Defamation	Any statement that harms a person's reputation, name, or character.
Libel	Malicious defamation in written or graphic form. Libel may include any false statement that damages an individual's reputation. A person's business or property can be libeled, as can an institution. To avoid making libelous statements, restrict claims to statements that are true. Furthermore, evaluate the source of a damaging remark to eliminate malice from the motive. Reporters can avoid charges of libel if they express their thoughts in the form of opinions.
Slander	The defamation of a person through oral speech. Guidelines are similar to those for libel. Usually broadcasters are charged with libel rather than slander because their oral presentations generally originate in written notes.
Trespass	Illegal entry into another party's property, land, or premises or unlawful injury to a person or to a person's rights or property.

Besides legal restrictions, a news writer encounters questions of ethics. Ethical questions involve balancing the need to promote an informed citizenry and increase the general welfare against the need to maintain fairness to news sources.

Questions of taste, values, and cultural norms may also arise. As a news writer, you may have to decide whether to use illegally obtained information in preparing a story; whether or how to televise an execution, suicide, or hostage crisis; whether a special favor from a news source compromises your objectivity; and whether you can use staged reenactments of crucial events.

The Code of Broadcast News Ethics of the Radio-Television News Directors Association (see Walters, 1988), reproduced in Chapter 11, is a useful guide in such decisions. Your news organization may also have its own guidelines. Even so, you will need to reflect on ethical matters yourself, drawing on your own experience and common sense.

Scripts for Commercials

Scripts for television commercials are among the most detailed. Much care is put into them for a number of reasons. First, costs for both production and airtime can be expensive. Second, since commercials are usually short messages, sponsors have no time to waste. Finally, since commercials are totally planned in advance, they can be meticulously designed.

Running times for segments within a spot may be specified to the second, as well as the images for each moment of airtime. To convey this information, a storyboard is often used. A **storyboard** is a cartoon panel or sequence of drawings that shows the main shots of a story. Each image in the storyboard sequence may feature corresponding audio material.

Figure 13.4 shows a script with a storyboard for a 30-second political commercial for a fictitious candidate. The spot fades up from black (F/Blk) onto a text crawl with an announcer's voice-over. Next we see a dissolve (DIS.) to a medium shot (MS) of the candidate (CAND.) in an interior locale (INT.). The storyboard shows a cozy office with a desk and fireplace. The storyboard also reveals the candidate speaking directly to the camera, in a business suit, sitting on the edge of his desk. As he reaches the middle of his speech, the camera zooms in (Z-in) to a close-up (CU) of the candidate, as shown in the next storyboard image. As he concludes his speech, the CU dissolves to a closing graphic with the text "BURGER-HEAD: LEADERSHIP FOR THE MILLENNIUM." At the end of the 30 seconds, the spot fades to black (FTB).

Notice these other features of the script in Figure 13.4:

- The script lists the name of the production company; the client's name; the date of production; the date of release; the spot number, title, and length; and locations where the spot is to be shown.
- The storyboard provides a visual display of all the spot's main shots. In addition, the script includes the order and duration of shots and the overall running time.
- From this material, the producer, director, and crew can see what the main camera shots and other visuals (such as the CG text) look like. They can survey the camera angles, shot size, shot content, and so forth.

Full-Page Scripts

Instead of the split-page script, film productions of screenplays often employ a **full-page format,** and this practice is also common in certain types of video (i.e., feature-length drama). The full-page format is often found in single-camera EFP productions, made-for-TV movies, television dramatic programs, and documentaries. Programs that originate as a series of separate scenes or camera shots—that is, programs whose scenes are shot out of order and then assembled in postproduction—are quite amenable to the full-page script format. This can even include commercials.

POLLY TITIAN ADVERTISING COMPANY

Television script: Title: *"Leadership"*

p.1 of 1

Client: Linden Burgerhead for President Campaign
Production Date: October 10, 1998
Air Dates: November 5, 2006.
Cities: N.Y., L.A., Chi., Phila., Boston.
Length: 30 seconds
Spot Identification #: x-15

VIDEO		**AUDIO**
(0:00–0:10) F/Blk text		**ANNCR:** Some Senate leaders say our country has stopped growing, that we must adapt to a lower standard of living than we've had in the past. Linden Burgerhead disagrees.
(0:10–0:25) Dis. MS CAND. INT.		
Z-in CU CAND		**CAND:** We live in the greatest country on earth. Throughout our history, we have managed to solve our education problems, our social strife, and even our economic problems. With our talent, energy, and commitment, all we need is effective leadership.
(0:25–0:30) Dis. ID Graphic	BURGERHEAD: LEADERSHIP FOR THE MILLENNIUM	
"BURGERHEAD: LEADERSHIP FOR THE MILLENNIUM" FTB. F/AUDIO		

Figure 13.4 A sample script for a commercial, with a storyboard.

Figure 13.5 offers a sample of a full-page script illustrating many of the characteristics common to the format. Notice the following features:

- A title page bears the writer's name, as well as the producer's name if separate. It also provides copyright information (optional) and revision dates. Immediately after the title page, there may be pages describing the main characters, their physical attributes, their wardrobes, and so forth.

- All pages are numbered with inclusive numbering, and the date of last revision appears on every page. New pages containing revisions may be on different-colored paper so that they stand out for cast and crew.

- Descriptions of scene locations, time of day, and camera directions are given in capital letters, as are names of characters, actions, sound effects, and music.

- Single spacing is used within paragraphs, double spacing between paragraphs. Double spacing is also used between scenes, between different characters' speeches, and to set off transitions such as "CUT TO" and "FADE OUT."

- Dialogue is typed in a column centered on the page, about 3 inches wide. The character's name is centered in capital letters above each speech. Stage directions, indicating how the talent is to deliver the lines, are presented in parentheses after the character's name.

Scriptwriting Software

Computers are not yet capable of writing Emmy-winning television programs; they can't even write serviceable flops—people must still do that. However, word-processing programs make script formatting easier than ever. Software also makes it easy to count words, set margins, use a thesaurus, check spelling, move copy, and perform other editing functions. For these reasons, word-processing programs are especially helpful in news organizations, where copy must be revised and produced quickly.

For screenplays and other scripts that require a standard format, script-processing programs such as Final Draft and Scriptware are popular. They attempt to make the formatting even easier than a regular word processor. Check with your software supplier to find the software best suited for the work you intend to do.

A FINAL NOTE

The writing tips and examples of script formats presented in this chapter provide some useful guidelines for preparing scripts for most television productions.

Sample of Full-Page Script Format

FOUND MONEY

An original screenplay by: Len Shyles

Copyright 2007. Registered with WGAE

Revised: February, 2007

P. 1 of 4

Main Characters:

Father McElroy:

A young priest, recently ordained, shy, innocent, and ignorant of the real-world problems that beset him. He is pathetically unprepared for the work of running the AIDS hospice in south-central L.A. to which he has just been assigned, yet run it he must. He is even less able to supervise his newly inherited underling, Sister Mary Elizabeth, who seems to know more than he does about everything. He is daunted by the hospice; the task is simply too big for him to handle. Aside from providing care and counsel to his patients, he must also raise money to keep it open. He is minister, fundraiser, and bookkeeper.

Sister Mary Elizabeth:

A middle-aged nun, strong, attractive, serving the community for the last five years by working the AIDS clinic. The sister is fervently committed to finding ways of making her hospice work more fulfilling by increasing the number of beds available to the community, which is suffering from a lack of funding and an increasing need as the epidemic continues to rise. She has been toiling in the vineyards long and hard, and knows her time is limited.

1   FADE IN.   1

   INT. SOUTH-CENTRAL COMMUNITY AIDS CLINIC—NIGHT

   SISTER MARY ELIZABETH finishes her phone call to the convent, telling SISTER FRANCINE that she is leaving to come home. She notices the clock and

Figure 13.5   Sample of full-page script format.

(5/20/06) p. 2 of 4

calendar on her plain metal desk. It's eight P.M., Friday, and she looks tired. Just as she hangs up, she notices that FATHER McELROY has entered looking dejected. She has never seen him looking quite this bad.

SISTER MARY

Good evening Father. You don't look

very happy tonight. What's wrong?

FR. McELROY

(with despair)

I feel like I've been brushing back the

waters of the ocean with a broom.

Between trying to comfort dying patients and

their family members, and trying to raise money

to cover the bills due tomorrow, I feel

like I've been torn in two or four major pieces.

SISTER MARY

(gentle yet firm)

Well this is just one more normal day . . .

You need some rest. You'll be fresh

when the relief staff arrives, giving us

both a well-earned weekend off.

FR. McELROY

Look, don't tell the relief this, but you

Figure 13.5 (Continued)

(5/20/06) p. 3 of 4

        see, we're out of money. If we don't pay the bills that

        come due tomorrow, especially rent and phone,

        this place gets shut down. I hope you have carfare.

                SISTER MARY

          (turning toward him)

        You mean we're evicted???

        McELROY shakes his head in agreement. He steps aside as

SISTER MARY heads for the door.

                SISTER MARY

           (resolutely)

        We'll get the money. We'll get by.

2   EXT. THE BUS STOP ON THE STREET—NIGHT   2

     SISTER MARY steps on board and pays the L.A. bus fare with the last bit of change in her modest plastic purse. The bus is empty, since the rush hour has ended over two hours ago. The camera outside the bus PANS with her as she makes her way to the rear of the bus. As she plops down with a THUD, the bus moves away from the curb, the street noise of boom box RAP MUSIC quickly fading. As the GRIND of the bus engine begins to invade her brain as welcome white noise, her tired eyes soon light upon a soft leather wallet lodged between the seats. The twenty thousand dollars in it in large bills shocks her to attention.

Figure 13.5 (Continued)

(5/20/06) p. 4 of 4

CUT TO

3 INT. SISTER MARY'S BEDROOM—NIGHT 3

SISTER MARY tosses the wallet onto her bed, then flops down next to it, flips it open, and pulls twenty Gs onto the bedspread. She reaches over to the night table for her bedside Bible, opens it up to her favorite psalms, mouths some prayers, and quickly falls asleep.

FADE OUT

END ACT 1

Figure 13.5 (Continued)

However, these ideas are just a start. More in-depth treatment of these topics is available in texts dealing with screenplay writing, news reporting, advertising, and, more generally, broadcast writing and writing for the mass media. If you are at all interested in writing for video, make it a point to seek further information as well as practical experience.[5]

KEY TERMS

liftouts 411
telegraphing 412
recapping 412
proposal 413
treatment 414
pilot 414
cold start 414
semiscripted format 415
rundown sheet 415
in-cues 415
out-cues 415
split-page format 420
storyboard 425
full-page format 425

QUESTIONS FOR REVIEW

How do characteristics of the television medium, audience, and program genre influence the writer's task?

What is meant by the idea that content carried in the video and audio track "codetermine" one another? Give some examples.

What aspects of the competitive video marketplace influence television writing?

What differences are there between fully scripted and semiscripted shows? Between rundown sheets and other script formats? When is it appropriate to use each?

What advantages does a split-page format offer the director?

What are some of the legal and ethical concerns involved in newswriting?

How might a storyboard be used in a 30-second commercial for an exercise machine?

NOTES

1. Of course, with videotape or disk, it is possible to skip chunks and go back and forth as in a book or magazine. However, the pace of presentation within selected units of material will still be important to consider.

2. The current slogan is "Army Strong," which is short and sweet but does not yet appear to have caught on to the same degree as the original.

3. For a full description and detailed examples of different types of program treatments and proposals, see Blum (2000).

4. Detailed examples of script formats for both fiction and nonfiction television programming abound on the Web. For example, typing *video script formats* into the subject line of the Google search engine results in a rich listing. In current news operations (i.e., CNN's newsrooms), scripts may be sent electronically through prompters directly to distant news desks and anchors for immediate use.

The scripts presented here are designed to illustrate how directors can conduct efficient rehearsals and are not intended to exhaust all script formats. For additional examples, see the sources listed later as well as those available on the Web.

5. For further examples of scriptwriting formats, see Blum (2000), Haag (1985), Cole and Haag (1989), Brady and Lee (1988), Walters (1994), and especially Wolff and Cox (1991). For more on storyboards and their use, see Walters (1988) and Orlik (2003). For more on screenplay writing, see Armer (1993), Blum (2000), Brady and Lee (1988), and Lucey (1996). For more on writing and reporting the news, see Shook (1996), Stephens and Lanson (1994), and Mencher (1994). For more on writing copy for a variety of media forms, see Walters (1994), Newsom and Wollbert (1988), Mencher (1994), and Orlik (2003). For more on legal and ethical issues in news reporting, see Shook (1996), Mencher (1994), and Walters (1994). For manuals and handbooks on writing style for broadcasters, see the *UPI Stylebook* (Cook & Martin, 2004) and MacDonald (2002).

Chapter 14

PRODUCING AND DIRECTING

Producing and directing for video are highly varied activities. For the most part in this chapter, we discuss producing and directing as separate roles. In many cases, however—especially early in your career—you may find yourself filling both roles on the same project, becoming a *producer-director*.

It takes skill, talent, and an aptitude for handling details to manage the job of the producer-director. Of course, having broad experience helps also. The producer-director wears many hats, as the cliché goes, coordinating a video project, to bring it from the concept stage through to the completed program or series, at times even planning its distribution and exhibition. Famous producers and/or directors in television include Norman Lear, Marta Kaufman, Aaron Spelling, James L. Brooks, and Larry David, to name but a few.

The purpose of this chapter is to explain the responsibilities, roles, and tasks of the producer and the director in the making of video programs. The topics covered in this chapter are the following:

Producing

- Different producer levels
- Producing in the preproduction stage
- Producing in the production stage
- Producing in the postproduction stage
- Dealing with artistic and technical unions
- Audience measurement and ratings

Directing

- Qualities of directors
- Directing in the preproduction stage
- Directing in the production stage
- Directing in the postproduction stage

PRODUCING

Depending on the nature of a project, the producer's job can vary tremendously. For example, while a theatrical program may require the producer to spend much time hiring talent, this task may be quite small for the news or sports producer, perhaps even nonexistent. Conversely, while a news or sports producer may routinely have to rent satellite facilities, a theatrical producer who tapes fiction dramas may spend no time at all dealing with satellite transmission.

Other tasks of the producer may include writing program proposals and budgets, approving scripts, renting or building sets and studio space, getting copyright clearances, working with union contracts, and marketing, distributing, and exhibiting the finished program, including arranging distribution rights and syndication deals. Of course, if the producer is acting as a producer-director, the list can be even longer. Table 14.1 lists some of the typical concerns of producers, classified according to the five crucial factors of space, time, equipment, money, and personnel.

Once personnel are hired, the producer's job involves *coordinating* crew and talent and *delegating* responsibilities, knowing that the team members know their jobs better than the producer does. Then mutual trust and respect between the producer and a talented team become the producer's greatest assets.

Different Producer Levels

Just as the producer's job may vary according to the type of program being made, so the scope of the job may vary depending on the level of producer you are. In a program of sufficient complexity, producing responsibilities may be differentiated according to a hierarchy. Some of the titles used to define different producer positions include *executive producer, staff producer, agency producer,* and *freelance producer.* Additional titles include such refinements as *associate producer* and *coexecutive producer.* These terms are used to differentiate levels of responsibility roughly as follows:

Executive Producer. The *executive producer* may be involved with originating project ideas but does not get into specific details. Rather, the executive producer is responsible for funding and budgeting projects and then supervising production. In addition to approving projects, the executive producer may check in from time to time to make sure everything is on schedule. To handle the daily details of particular projects, the executive producer often assigns a staff producer.

Staff Producer. The *staff producer* is responsible for the overall production of a particular project. On that project, the staff producer may be in charge of all

Table 14.1   Typical Concerns of Producers, Classified in Terms of Space, Time, Equipment, Money, and Personnel

Space	Time	Equipment	Money	Personnel
Studio	Schedule	Facilities	Budget	*Above the line:*
Field locations	Order	Artwork	Salaries	Director
Equipment storage	Overtime	Cameras	Union fees	Writers
Parking	Calendar	Lights	Insurance	Producers
Rehearsal rooms	Hours	Microphones	Parking fees	Talent
Meeting rooms	Rain dates	Cables	Hotel bills	Art directors
	Rehearsals	Audio mixers	Food costs	Scenic designers
	Shooting	Videotape	Overtime	Graphic designers
	Editing	machines	Equipment rentals	Musicians
	Clock time	Costumes	and purchases	*Below the line:*
	Backtiming	Graphics	Studio rental	Technical director
	Front timing	Script		Floor manager
	Deadlines	Floor plan		CG operator
	Meetings	Props		Videotape
	Appointments	Sets		technicians
	Program length	Vans		Engineering
	Pace	Satellites		Editors
	Time slots	Phone lines		Assistant director
	Air dates	Intercoms		Camera operators
		Music		Audio technicians
		Sound effects		Utility crew
		Walkie-talkies		Lighting director
		Catering		Set construction
		Hotels		Props
		Transportation		Wardrobe
		Clearances		
		Release forms		

production decisions. It is the staff producer's responsibility to ensure the highest possible quality for the project.

Agency Producer. Sometimes an advertising agency assigns a producer (sometimes called the *agency rep*) to a production being done by a station or a production house. The agency rep works for the advertising agency's client, making sure the program accomplishes the client's objectives. The agency rep may execute the contract, and depending on the deal, the production company or another outside source may provide the facilities and crew. Frequently, the agency provides the script and audiovisual materials. Talent and locations may also be provided by the rep. In determining who should produce the program, the rep may entertain several bids from various production houses.

Freelance Producer. *Freelance producers* work for production companies or agencies on a single-project basis. This arrangement saves the agency or production house a full-time salary and makes it possible to bring in specialists on an as-needed basis. The daily cost for a freelance producer is usually higher than it would be for a regular employee, but it is worth it because the overall cost is still lower than employing a full-time staff person all year long. The level of work is expected to be of the highest quality since the freelancer is brought in as a specialist. In such cases, it is routine for the producer to handle such diverse responsibilities as financing, budgeting, hiring, production scheduling, and, of course, the execution of the production itself.

Associate and Coexecutive Producers. As these titles imply, *associate* and *coexecutive producers* share the burden of the production, often taking on a predetermined set of responsibilities. Large productions such as network sports productions and large-scale theatrical performances may warrant having several individuals involved in producer roles to handle various aspects of the production, from financing script development to acquiring talent and crew, from scheduling production tasks to arranging hotels and food. During the postproduction phase, the editing, distribution, exhibition, and syndication rights may also be handled by associate and/or coexecutive producers. Of course, in such situations, it is essential for all involved to have a clear idea of who is supposed to do what and in what order.

Producing in the Preproduction Stage

One way to view the producer's job is in terms of the different roles producers play in bringing a program idea into final form, including those of aesthetic judge, technical expert, psychologist, business manager, sales agent, audience analyst, marketing master, legal authority, organization executive, and detail virtuoso. Depending on the type of program being made, more or less energy may be used in each of these roles. To get a more detailed idea of how such talents may be used, we now look at how they come into play during each production phase, beginning in this section with preproduction.

Concept Development. Among the first concerns of the producer in the preproduction stage is to develop a program proposal from a concept deemed to have some audience interest. While ideas can come at any time from almost anywhere, at the concept stage, it is wise to take an inclusive approach. During preliminary brainstorming sessions, write every idea down, no matter how unlikely it sounds at first. As a project develops, it is always easier to eliminate ideas than to invent new ones.

Next, a winnowing process occurs, selecting the best idea from the list of possibilities. Your selection should be determined by the intrinsic quality of the idea, by the availability of an audience for it, and by analysis of production feasibility (cost and availability of talent, space, and facilities). During this phase, strategies and compromises are made as you entertain different approaches. Some approaches may offer advantages in terms of audience appeal, while others may be more attractive from the standpoint of scheduling and budget. When the program idea becomes more stable and clearly defined, you are ready for the next step.

The Program Proposal. After making a firm commitment to a particular program idea, the producer usually must develop a full-blown proposal to convince a production company or sponsor to finance it. The program proposal should specify needs with respect to the five key factors listed in Table 14.1: space, time, equipment, money, and personnel. Furthermore, the program's objectives and target audience should be clearly identified. While formats for program proposals can vary, here are some of the elements to include:

- *Title.* As mentioned in the last chapter, all programs should have a title from the outset. The title identifies the program so you can refer to it without ambiguity during production meetings (a real help when you are working on several projects simultaneously). *Most important, titles should capture the subject matter, content, and tone of the program for the sponsor, crew, talent, and eventually, of course, the audience.* (Even tentative titles should do this.)

- *Program purpose.* The goal(s) of the program should be briefly stated. This can be done in a single sentence, as in the following example: *The purpose of this program is to demonstrate to students at the Culinary Institute how to prepare filet mignon.*

- *Intended audience(s).* This part of the proposal clearly identifies the group(s) of people you wish to reach with your program (the *target* audience). The audience can be mentioned elsewhere, as in the statement of program purpose, but it should be clearly identified in its own right as well. It is regular practice to identify audiences in terms of sex/age categories (women ages 18–34, teenagers, etc.), but that is by no means the only way to do it. Try also to identify the audience in terms of the variables most relevant to the program you are producing: for example, all viewers who have purchased a General Motors car in the past 5 years.

- *Program treatment.* The treatment is a narrative description of a program written to convey a feel for the characters, setting, and action. Though the treatment is sometimes handled as a separate stage, it may be included in the original proposal. If so, it should briefly describe the program's content, subject matter, length, pace, style, and any other aspects that telegraph the nature of the program to the prospective sponsor. The treatment should also tell whether you intend to shoot in studio and/or on location, using film or tape, in or out of sequence, with one or several cameras. You can include a bit of dialog to convey a sense of the characters to the reader, but in general, it is better to leave such detail to the script stage.

- *Preferred date, time, and channel (if appropriate) for showing the program.* This information tells how you intend to reach the target audience. Obviously, a show can succeed in reaching its audience only when they are available to see it. For a children's program, for example, you would probably specify an after-school hour on weekdays, or perhaps Saturday morning.[1] Identifying the date, time, and channel has the added effect of forcing you to think more clearly about the competition.

- *Budget.* Include a budget so the client can see how you have computed all expenses. A sample budget form is shown in Figure 14.1. Costs can often be determined using **rate cards** (see Figure 14.2) that list prices for services, materials, and labor; these are available from various production houses and unions. In your budget, try to show the price for every conceivable item, whether purchased or rented. Consider script preparation, talent and crew salaries; rental of equipment and studio space; fees for location shoots; expenses for costumes, sets, props, and makeup; editing time; and videotape. Include also estimates for food, transportation, lodging/hotel accommodations, insurance, copyright fees, and parking. Include some elasticity to accommodate extra charges that inevitably result, such as additional equipment rental expenses if a day of location shooting is lost to bad weather. It is reasonable for an actual budget to go over the original estimate by 10%, but coming in under budget is always preferable from the sponsor's standpoint. One traditional budgetary practice in television is to arrange costs in terms of above-the-line and below-the-line expenses (discussed in the next section). Other budgets arrange costs in terms of preproduction, production, and postproduction expenses. It is wise to ask the client what is preferred and present the budget accordingly.

- *Schedule.* The schedule should indicate the time involved for completing the production. Try to show order as well as duration for each production element. If specific dates and times are known in advance, as is often the case with programs about public events, indicate them.

Production co.:_____   Bid by: _____

Address:_____   Client: _____

Telephone number:_____   Bid date: _____

Contact:_____   Client contact: _____

Director:_____   Tel: _____

Producer:_____   Fax: _____

Writer:_____   Project title: _____

\# preproduction days:_____

\# build/strike days:_____

\# studio shoot days:_____

Location sites:_____

Summary of estimated costs:

CREW	DAYS	RATE	OVERTIME	TOTAL	ACTUAL
Producer					
Assistant director					
Camera op.					
Technical director					
Utility					
Audio					
Boom op.					
Makeup					
Hair					
Playback					
Wardrobe					
Script clerk					
VTR op.					
Teleprompter op.					
Scenic design					
Postproduction coord.					
Other					

Preproduction materials and expenses:

	UNITS	RATE	TOTAL	ACTUAL
Auto rental				
Airfare				
Lodging				
Camera rental				

Figure 14.1   A partial budget form.

Taxis
Telephone and fax

Location expenses:

	UNITS	RATE	TOTAL	ACTUAL
Permits				
Car rentals				
Parking, tolls, and gas				
Air freight				
Food				
Limousines				
Cabs				
Gratuities				
Misc.				

Studio rental and expenses:

	UNITS	RATE	TOTAL	ACTUAL
Rental for build days				
Rental for shoot days				
Rental for strike days				
Meals for crew and talent				
Set guards				
Total power charges and bulbs				
Stage manager				
Misc.				

Equipment rental:

	UNITS	RATE	TOTAL	ACTUAL
Video cameras				
Lighting				
Sound				
Crane				
Generator				
Videotape				
Teleprompter				
Walkie-talkies				
Cellular phone				
Misc.				

Talent:

	NO.	DAY RATE	WORK DAYS	TRAVEL DAYS	OVERTIME	TOTAL	ACTUAL
Principals (category I)							

Figure 14.1 (Continued)

Principals
  (category II)
Narration
Spokesperson
General extras
Voice-over
Audition fees
Fitting fees
Agency commission
Workers' comp.
Misc.

Videotape and postproduction:

	UNITS	RATE	TOTAL	ACTUAL
Window dubs				
Off-line logging				
EDL conversion				
Editing				
Stock rental and purchase				
Audio mixing				
Audiotape costs				
Dub protection master				
Betacam dubs				
Video effects and animation				
Misc.				

Total Miscellaneous Expenses:

SUMMARY:

	Estimated	Actual
GRAND TOTAL:		

Comments: _____

_____

Figure 14.1 (Continued)

Equipment	Rate
Videotape machines:	
D-2 VTR	$150.00/hr
D-1 VTR	$100.00/hr
Cameras:	
BetacamSP	$50.00/hr
Camcutter	$100.00/hr
Editing suite (on-line editing):	
2 VTR D-2	$350.00/hr
3 VTR D-2	$500.00/hr
Editing (off-line):	
AVID and EDL	$650.00/day

Figure 14.2   Sample rate card for equipment and editing services.

Planning Meetings and Script Preparation. Once the proposal has been approved, you need to plan the practical aspects of the production. This means coordinating all personnel, informing them about the program and how it is to be executed.

The people involved in initial planning meetings should largely come from the creative team of the production, the *above-the-line* personnel, as they are called. These include writers, directors, talent, art and graphic designers, executive and associate producers, and music composers and musicians, if any.

Initial planning meetings should be used to develop a script everyone can use to transform the project from paper to the screen. One practical way to prepare the script is to have the writer write the words while the director comes up with accompanying images. Working with the producer, the entire creative team should suggest ways to reflect the essence of the treatment in the script so that it delivers what was promised. At this stage, the producer should also be working with the art director to plan sets and graphics that fit the tone of the project.

As producer, it is your job to keep the creative team on track. Keep in mind the program objectives, intended audience, style, length, tone, and pace of the show— and everything else you have promised to the client. After the script is completed or at least brought into working shape, it is possible to hire the crew, the *below-the-line* personnel, including technical directors; camera, lighting, and audio operators; as well as recording technicians, production assistants, floor managers, and so forth.

Facilities Requests. At this stage, you can also finalize the scheduling of equipment. Use a facilities (fax) request form, such as the one shown in Figure 14.3, to list all of the equipment you need, including cameras, mics, sets, props, lights, and graphics. The fax sheet should also include the date, time, and place each piece of equipment will be needed. To determine exactly what to order or rent and when, confer with the rest of the staff.

Remember to avoid using the latest equipment just for its own sake. Nothing can be more unprofessional than to waste space, time, material, money, and personnel this way. The rule for selecting equipment should be to pick only what you need to get the job done, and no more.

Of course, knowing when equipment and personnel are needed and for how long is a function of the schedule you have devised. Be sure to allow some flexibility in case of delays. Communicate the final schedule in writing to all parties to reduce confusion and misunderstandings.

Keeping a Production Book. As producer, it is essential to keep an up-to-date, accurate, and thorough production book listing everyone's phone number (fax and e-mail too), hours of availability, best times to reach the person, and any other information helpful for getting the job done. Besides the cast and crew, include key field contacts, such as the police commissioner's secretary and the caterer. Also note the flight schedules of out-of-town talent and their hotel information. Furthermore, the production book should list possible sources of last-minute equipment. Keep the rehearsal and production schedules in the book, as well as a set of release forms, clearances, and permits to cover copyright and other legal needs. Being a consummate detail person is invaluable.

Release Forms and Copyright Clearances. Finally, be sure to get release forms signed and any final music clearances approved. This is best done in the preproduction stage to avoid the nightmare of not being able to use the program after investing time, money, and effort in its production. Figure 14.4 offers a sample of a standard release form.

Both pictures and musical works (including lyrics) may be copyrighted. Therefore, it may be necessary to pay a fee for the use of such materials. In the music industry, two organizations collect fees for music performance rights: the American Society of Composers, Authors, and Publishers (ASCAP) and Broadcast Music Incorporated (BMI). Virtually all music written is registered with one of these organizations. By paying for the rights to use their catalog, you are legally covered when you use their members' works.

Photographs and motion images may also be copyrighted, making it illegal to use them without permission. Such materials can be used in your programs if fees

Date: _____   Submitted by: _____

Production Title: _____

Producer: _____   Director: _____

Recording date: _____   Air date: _____   Time: _____

Studio or field: _____

Location address: _____

EQUIPMENT LIST:

a)

b)

c)

d)

e)

f)

g)

h)

(Include all audio, video, lights, graphics, editing, cables, intercom, transmission, vans, etc.)

Requestor's signature: _____

Approved by: _____
                         (producer's name)

Approved by: _____
                         (engineer's name)

Date of approval: _____

Figure 14.3   Sample facilities (fax) request form.

I hereby give permission to _____ Production Company and
_____, their agents, successors, assigns, clients, and purchasers of their services
and/or products, to use my photograph (whether still, motion, or television) and recordings of
my voice, and my name in any legal manner whatsoever.

(1) I fully and irrevocably release and hold harmless _____ and
_____ Production Company and their respective
employees, agents, and contractors from all liability, loss, claims, demands, and actions
arising directly or indirectly out of my appearance in the Program, which was videotaped
on [date].

(2) Further, I irrevocably authorize _____ Production
Company to use my voice, likeness, and appearance in the Program for educational
purposes and for other noncommercial purposes.

(3) I irrevocably assign to _____ Production Company
the following:

   (a) all of my right, title, and interest in the copyright and any other property interest I
   may have in the Program; and

   (b) all of my right, title, and interest in any proceeds or royalties from the sale, rental,
   loan, publication, license, or other disposition of the Program.

(4) I irrevocably grant to _____ Production Company
total ownership of the Program; the right to edit, exhibit, or otherwise communicate the
Program; the right to secure a copyright in the Program; the right to sell, publish, and
advertise the Program; and the right to license or assign to others the foregoing rights
enumerated in this Paragraph 4.

Intending to be legally bound hereby:

Date: _____

Signed: _____

Parent or guardian: _____

Address: _____

City: _____

State: _____

Phone: _____

Figure 14.4   Standard release form.

are paid in advance. Photo libraries are good sources for such materials. Check with the organization from which you solicit the materials to make sure you have proper permissions. In some cases, especially if you can use older images, you may be able to find good noncopyrighted material at the Library of Congress and at state or local historical societies.

Producing in the Production Stage

Once a script has been developed and approved and the five key factors listed in Table 14.1 have been determined in sufficient detail, it is time to enter the production phase.

Coordinating and Delegating Responsibility. The producer's role during the production stage is to coordinate and delegate responsibility, making sure that the production stays on schedule. Check actual progress against the proposed schedule to stay reasonably close to what was originally promised. By keeping careful tabs on each day's work, you can evaluate the progress and make adjustments as you go. Treat the proposal as a template of the actual program and try to match your production to it.

In delegating work, be as explicit and specific as possible. For example, while it is obvious that the writer is responsible for the writing, it may be less clear whether you want the art director or the floor manager to design the floor plan. Similarly, other duties may not be clearly defined until you tell people what is expected of them.

To answer questions regarding task assignments, hold production meetings. Indicate a chain of responsibility in case a crew member takes ill and cannot participate. Keep the operation running smoothly by providing contact information for every crew member to all involved so everyone can be reached if need be. Communication is crucial. At the end of each rehearsal and production day, conduct a short status meeting to iron out problems and realign tasks and schedules.

Publicity and Promotions. The producer should also notify the public about the upcoming program. To do this, work through your company's promotion and publicity department, or similar channels outside your company, to make the public aware of the show. After all, your program can have no impact if no one sees it.

At the network level, publicity efforts include the production and distribution of press kits for new shows. Press kits contain glossy promotional brochures that showcase the program and talent. The kits are sent to newspaper, broadcast, and other media outlets. If your publicity budget does not permit you the luxury of a flashy press kit, you can always resort to a short telephone campaign and a less sophisticated press release, such as a one-page announcement emailed in advance to various media outlets in the market where the program is about to air.

Observing and Taking Notes During Shooting. During rehearsals and production, the producer should let the director call the shots. The producer's job is now to observe and take notes. If you have concerns or suggestions, write them down and discuss them with the director and crew during rehearsal breaks. During the broadcast or recording, do not interfere. You as producer have assembled all the elements. Now let the director and crew do their work.

Producing in the Postproduction Stage

Depending on the show you are producing, the postproduction phase can include editing, perhaps both off-line and on-line. If it does, you will need to arrange editing facilities. You may wish to be involved in the process or leave it to the director and editor. You may also have to show the rough cut (the off-line edited product) to the client before final approval is given to complete the job.

Aside from such production concerns, the postproduction phase also involves recordkeeping and accounting tasks that must be handled competently. For example, there may still be bills to pay. Pay them promptly to preserve good will with outside agents who may be needed for your next project. Remember also to thank everybody in writing, by phone, or in person and to complete the publicity effort for the debut of the show. Finally, keep a copy of your program as well as the production book on file for archival purposes. You never know when a past effort or some portion of it may become useful in the future.

Dealing With Artistic and Technical Unions

One of the producer's responsibilities at all stages of production is to deal with the appropriate unions. In the media industries, unions have long worked to improve working conditions, salaries, and benefits. For example, in 1933, film actors were lucky to be paid $15 for a day's work ($66 for a 6-day week). Unregulated hours and working conditions were often viewed as a greater problem than the pay. In March of that year, producers unilaterally enacted a 50% pay cut for all actors under studio contracts. With no organization or collective bargaining power, the actors had no means of maintaining their wages.

As a response to the producers' decree, a small group of Hollywood actors formed a self-governing group called the Screen Actors Guild (SAG) to give actors a stronger voice. A 4-year struggle ensued for union recognition and better contracts with producers. In 1937, the actors voted to strike if necessary to win union recognition. More than 95% of the major stars involved threatened to walk off the job. Faced for the first time with an effective threat, the producers agreed to improve both working conditions and wages.

The formation of a strong union was a powerful means of protecting actors from unfair labor practices, as well as a potent instrument for promoting their future interests. Today, video producers often deal with unions that represent and protect the interests of television workers. Union rules and regulations can have a significant impact on work schedules, hourly pay rates, overtime, holidays, and many other working conditions that can directly affect budgets, schedules, and therefore programs.

Depending on the type of work people do during a show or rehearsal, they can be classified as performers, guests, or crew members. These distinctions are important because if a worker's efforts go beyond normal duties, you as the producer may be subject to talent fees and even legal penalties from unions not covered in your budget. To avoid problems and unanticipated expenses, be aware of the various labor boundaries that have become the province of each of the major unions involved in television work. Using nonunion labor in a union setting also requires the proper clearance.

In television work, there are unions for creative personnel (such as writers, directors, performers, musicians) and technical employees (electrical workers, camera operators, etc.). Table 14.2 lists the most prominent unions, with pertinent information on each.

Audience Measurement and Ratings

Since the producer must convince a client that a suitable audience can be reached, it is important to know how audiences are measured. Audience measurement is critical for commercial television because a commercial station's revenue, which comes mainly from the sale of commercial time, is primarily determined by audience size.

In measuring audiences, levels of audience attention or involvement are rarely determined. Rather, surveys are used to estimate the number of households or viewers tuned to a program. Two such estimates are often computed: ratings and shares. The **rating** for a program is the proportion of all television households (TVHHs) in a market tuned to a particular program. The **share** is the proportion of homes tuned to a particular program among all households *using* television (HUTs) at the time.

Knowing both the TVHHs and HUTs tuned to a program allows one to judge both its overall popularity and its performance against its immediate competition in the same time slot. For example, in a market with 1,000 households (assuming, for simplicity, 1 set per household), if 20% of all TVHHs are tuned to a program, that program gets a 20 rating. If all 1,000 households have their sets turned on, then the share will also be 20. However, if half the sets are off, leaving only 500 sets in use, then the rating of 20 will mean that 40% of all HUTs are tuned to that program, giving that program a 40 share.

Table 14.2   Major Unions for Television Workers

Unions for Creative Personnel

American Federation of Television and Radio Artists (AFTRA)	Founded in 1937 to represent the interests of professional broadcasters. Today, AFTRA ensures fair contracts for radio and television workers, sets minimum pay scales, ensures safe and equitable working conditions, and provides legal representation in case of disputes. It also offers health and retirement plans, credit unions, scholarships, and other services. AFTRA has over 77,000 members, including network news anchors and correspondents, announcers, actors, and other on-air talent. Its National Code of Fair Practice lists pay scales for talent working in various programs in various capacities.
Screen Actors Guild (SAG)	SAG represents over 84,000 actors (including singers, dancers, models, and extras) working for producers of motion pictures and video programs. Its employment contracts govern wage scales, holidays, meal periods, overtime, parking, residuals, rest periods, reuse of photography, script readings, stunt coordinators, safety regulations, travel costs, and more.
Writer's Guild of America (WGA)	WGA represents professional writers in motion pictures, television, and radio. Membership is acquired only through the sale of literary material or through employment for writing services in one of these areas. The guild is divided into two membership corporations, one on each coast, but for practical purposes, it is a single national organization. The WGA protects its members' rights with Minimum Basic Agreements that cover fees, payments, rights, and credits for authored material. The guild also offers pension and health benefits and a registration service to protect the rightful ownership of literary material.
Director's Guild of America (DGA)	Formed in 1960 by a merger of the Screen Director's Guild and the Radio and Television Director's Guild and enlarged since then by mergers with other creative organizations, the DGA now represents the interests of directors, associate directors, stage managers, and production assistants working in live and taped television.
American Federation of Musicians (Musician's Union Local 47)	Organized in 1894 as the Los Angeles Musical Association, the AFM today has over 9,000 members. Its pay scale agreements set the pay rates for musical performances used throughout the television and movie industries. AFM bargains collectively for members involved in musical performances on network radio and television, videotape, educational television, music videos, electronic transcriptions, commercial advertisements, cable and pay TV, nontheatrical and non-TV documentary and industrial films, and traveling theatrical productions, among others.

(Continued)

Table 14.2 (Continued)

Unions for Television
Technicians

National Association of Broadcast Employees and Technicians— Communications Workers of America (NABET–CWA)	Formed in 1994 by the merger of NABET and CWA, the combined organization represents the interests of broadcast engineers, technicians, news writers, announcers, photographers, and stage service workers, among others. Most of the 10,000-plus members work for two of the major television networks, ABC and NBC, and over 50 private radio, TV, film, and videotape companies in the United States and Canada. The areas in which NABET–CWA has improved working conditions for its members include work schedules, compensation for travel time, meal periods, holidays, vacations, on-camera appearances, retirement plans, and sick leave.
International Brotherhood of Electrical Workers (IBEW)	The IBEW, formed in 1891, negotiates contracts for technical staff involved in broadcasting work, including camera operators, videotape and audio personnel, editors, and maintenance workers. IBEW has national agreements with the CBS and Fox television corporations, as well as local agreements governing daily hires (per diem contracts) for freelance technicians performing television work. Currently, IBEW has over 800,000 members, only a small proportion of whom work in broadcasting.
International Alliance of Theatrical Stage Employees (IATSE)	IATSE was formed in 1893 to represent behind-the-scenes workers in theater production. Today, IATSE includes behind-the-scene workers in the television industry as well. With over 85,000 members, including wardrobe and makeup artists, camera operators, prop, sound, and grip personnel, IATSE represents people involved in television series, commercials, and made-for-TV movie productions.

A late-night show usually has a relatively low rating because the number of sets in use is generally lower than during prime time. However, the show must still compete with others available at that time, and this is where knowing the share becomes important. In late night, a program with a 5 rating (5% of all TVHHs are viewing it) and a 40 share (40% of HUTs are tuned in) may easily win its time slot and therefore remain on the air. By contrast, a program in prime time may get a rating of 10 but only a 13 share and be canceled because it fails to compete well against other shows that air at the same time.

Of course, in addition to learning *quantitative* audience information, you could also learn valuable *qualitative* information, including demographic audience characteristics (age, sex, educational level, race, income), psychographic measures (attention level to your program, favorite characters, motives for watching), and lifestyle characteristics (hobbies and interests). As Chapter 1 made clear, such knowledge can provide a solid basis for program planning.

In nonbroadcast settings, audience measurement can also help in making programming decisions. With the advent of wireless media (i.e., video i-Pods, cell phones with Web capability for streaming video, etc.), the arrival of the untethered video user challenges the validity of traditional ratings measurement methods. In this brave new world of media choices and opportunities for attending to new digital video platforms, ratings and shares become much harder to measure. The brute proliferation of choices fractionalizes audiences as never before, making measurements of smaller slivers of available viewers even more problematic. As a result, audience measurement has become more complex than ever.

In an effort to increase accuracy in audience measurement in such a new market, diaries and electronic monitoring devices attached to receivers (called *audimeters*) to record tuning behavior in sample households is not enough, especially in multiset households. Among the approaches being used to rectify measurement deficiencies is to use *peoplemeters,* devices designed to capture not just information about which channels televisions are tuned to in a household but also *who* is watching by having viewers "check in" by pressing a button to announce themselves, or through the use of passive devices designed to identify particular viewers through pattern recognition techniques. Another approach uses questionnaires designed to tap audience members' reactions to programs they have just watched; such postprogram evaluations can be used to determine the effectiveness of entertainment programs on a number of dimensions, as well as measuring the effectiveness of instructional videos, training tapes, information campaigns, and so forth. There are also informal avenues for audience feedback, including letters, phone calls, e-mail, and computer Web sites and bulletin boards.

DIRECTING

Once the basic conceptualization and planning are done, it is the director's job to execute the production. But directing is so critical to the success of a video program that it is essential to involve the director from the earliest planning stages, not just when the program is ready to shoot.

Just as the activities of the producer vary depending on the type of program, so may the director's. For example, live broadcasts place different demands on the director than programs shot in the field and edited in postproduction. Program genres may also influence the directing effort: A sitcom requires different treatment than a musical variety show, a sports program, or an instructional video.

Qualities of Directors

For all directors, communication, preparation, vision, flexibility, and tact are essential. The competent director must be able to communicate clearly what is wanted, solve problems as they arise, and deal effectively with temperamental people. Maintaining group unity and cohesion, as well as promoting a positive attitude among talent and crew, can be difficult when the group is a disparate collection of tender egos.

Good directors must also be demanding, have high standards, and know which things are going right as well as wrong. Of course, a vision of the final product must first exist in the mind's eye (and ear) of the director so that it can be conveyed clearly to the talent and crew. Only then can quality be maintained as the script gets translated from paper to the screen. If the concept of the show is not clear to the director, it cannot be communicated to the team, and there will be little chance of making a successful program.

Another way to think about the director's talents is in terms of the many roles the director has to play. The following sections look at the director as artist and technical expert, psychologist, manager, organizer, coordinator, and leader.

The Director as Artist and Technical Expert. As artist, the director determines the sequence of the shots and their duration. The director must call for every audiovisual change or transition. The director must constantly assess whether what is seen and heard is necessary and appropriate to the goals of the program and whether it will maintain audience interest.

As technical expert, the director must be familiar with the capabilities of each piece of equipment used in the production. The director should be able to judge whether the equipment selected for a particular job is the best available for the task in light of the budget.

The Director as Psychologist. As psychologist, the director must be sensitive to the needs of the crew and talent, recognizing that human beings deserve dignity and respect. (Translation: Remember the Golden Rule, and treat others as you would like to be treated.) In addition, directors must recognize when talent are performing to the limits of their abilities, when they are about to burn out, and when they need rest. The director should try to create an esprit de corps, conveying to the crew the importance of teamwork and the value of putting the goals of the production first.

The Director as Manager, Organizer, and Coordinator. As manager, organizer, and coordinator, the director schedules the tasks to be performed and delegates some of them to others. The director's immediate support staff includes the assistant or associate director (AD), the technical director (TD), the floor manager, a production assistant (PA), and perhaps a lighting director (LD). By delegating tasks to these people, the director maximizes efficiency.

In practice, appropriate delegation means that the director shouldn't climb a ladder to adjust lights if the lighting director can take care of it. Similarly, the director shouldn't stop a rehearsal to pin a mic on a talent if the audio operator (or a utility person) can do it. Of course, in a union shop, such actions could be in violation of the union contract, in which case the director should not be doing such work in the first place. The key point is this: The director must delegate specific tasks to others so that he or she can perform the more general task of running the production.

The Director as Leader. Finally, as leader, it is the director's job to supervise the production, making sure all program elements, crew, and talent are brought into play when and where they are needed. In this way, the director is like the conductor of an orchestra, and the crew and talent are like the musicians.

Directing in the Preproduction Stage

The preproduction stage is arguably the most important part of the television production process since it is here that the most time is spent formulating and perfecting the program concept, working out details, and solving production problems. Without a fruitful preproduction stage, there is virtually no chance of succeeding in the production stage. And with a bad production stage, no amount of postproduction manipulation will, as the saying goes, make a silk purse from a sow's ear.

One main goal of the preproduction stage is to finalize the script and floor plan since these documents anchor the entire production. These documents are to the program what a recipe is to the food a chef prepares. The director's other preproduction objectives include conducting production meetings and read-throughs, refining and marking the script, preparing storyboards and shot sheets if needed, and, in studio productions especially, working out talent movements, working out camera shots and camera movements, conducting rehearsals, and making the final adjustments and corrections clear to talent and crew. At this stage, the director's job differs from that of the producer because the director focuses on bringing the program into final form rather than gathering and arranging production elements and personnel. The following sections look at these preproduction tasks in greater detail. Though some tasks must precede others, many of them can be done simultaneously.

Conducting Production Meetings. Prior to actual rehearsals, it is useful to conduct production meetings on an as-needed basis to communicate with crew and talent, answer questions, iron out difficulties, and communicate last-minute changes. Depending on the type of show being produced and how it will be shot, the amount and type of preparation can vary tremendously, and thus the detail handled at the meetings will also vary. Even for simple productions, however, production meetings should be conducted as needed throughout all the production stages.

Refining the Script and Floor Plan. When you are directing, it is helpful to visualize the shot sequence as you read through the script. Read through several times to finalize your camera shots, camera angles, and microphone and talent positions. For studio productions, place the floor plan beside the script as you read to confirm that everything you want to do is physically possible. For your purposes as director, the script should be, insofar as possible, a written sequence or timeline of every audiovisual element that will be used, in order, from the first fade-in of a program's opening shot to the last fade-out of its closing credits. Similarly, the floor plan should provide a complete map of the program, showing the positions of all set pieces and talent, as well as all relevant off-air production elements such as crew members, cameras, lights, and booms.

Also, mentally listen to the dialog in the script to "hear" what it sounds like. Are there some lines that could be improved? Do they say everything that needs to be said? Are the speeches delivered by each talent consistent with their characters? Can some speeches be deleted without sacrificing the overall meaning of the program?

Think through your rationale for each production decision, justifying why you have decided to shoot things the way you have. Does each decision fit with the overall concept of the show? Is there a better way to do it? If you think of a better way to go, is it feasible to make the change, or will your late inspiration require such radical revision that it is better to leave well enough alone?

Script Marking. After the script has been finalized, mark up a fresh, final copy that is legible and accurate. Set off all speeches and dialog clearly. Include all transitions and descriptions of shot content, music, and sound effects. Be as complete as possible. See Figure 13.2 on pages 417 to 419 for an example of a director's working script. Above all, this copy should be so clear and easy to read that you can tell what's happening at a glance without having to search for any information.

Preparing Storyboards and Shot Sheets. As mentioned in Chapter 13, a storyboard is often used in fully scripted shows, especially in commercials, to precisely convey the content, appearance, order, and screen time of a program's main shots. If a storyboard is being prepared, the director will make certain it is complete and accurate. In other cases, though, a **shot sheet** (see Figure 14.5) can serve a similar function. The shot sheet provides a list of shot descriptions for each camera by number. The shot sheet conveys to camera operators which shots they will be responsible for and the order in which shots will be called. One advantage of a shot sheet is that it enables the director to call for a particular shot by number, so that ready cues are faster than they might be if they had to be described. For example,

Camera Three	
Shot number	**Description**
1	Close-up host and guest
3	Extreme close-up product shot
6	Bust-shot host holding product
8	Two-shot host and announcer tasting food

Figure 14.5   Sample section of a shot sheet.

saying "ready Camera 2, Shot 12," is faster than saying "ready Camera 2, close-up head shot of host, please."

Talent and Camera Blocking. Blocking is the process of coordinating the movement of talent and cameras through space to achieve the desired appearance on screen. Blocking rehearsals are crucial to cover talent movement on air because without practice, it may be impossible for camera operators to carry talent smoothly from one point to another, especially if they don't know where or when talent will be moving.

Before an actual rehearsal, you can use the floor plan to help you visualize and plan the moves you want the talent and camera operators to make. The floor plan will help you confirm that certain movements are possible in the space constraints.

In the blocking rehearsal, at first let the talent perform their moves as they would do them normally. This will give you an idea of how to block them more naturally. After seeing how they perform and taking time to consider how the blocking can best serve the program, make the talent aware of any adjustments or modifications you need.

As they perform the adjusted moves, make them aware of the framing, shot size, and camera angles you intend to use for each camera. If talent must cross from one set area to another, make them aware of which camera will carry them and whether they should address the camera directly. If they are to handle props, let them know which camera will be used for prop shots so that they can maneuver the props without hiding them from view and without losing focus or framing.

To rehearse blocking in studio, use the floor plan, a program monitor, and headsets if needed to communicate with talent and crew. With the floor manager and relevant crew members on headset, you can verbally cue talent and cameras to move to desired locations. Alert talent and crew that you may need them to perform certain movements repeatedly until key shots are mastered. If need be, mark the floor with tiny pieces of masking tape to indicate places where talent *and* cameras need to go. During the blocking rehearsal, note the amount of time needed to perform transitions so that you know which changes are reasonable to ask for and which ones are not.

Depending on the time available, the complexity of the moves, and your personal directing style, you may wish to conduct blocking rehearsals from the studio floor rather than from the control room. Doing it from the studio is usually faster because it eliminates the need to work through the floor manager. If you do it this way, have the technical director operate the video switcher for you in the control room. Set up a line monitor in the studio so that you can see the shots you are calling and a live studio mic so that control room personnel can hear your commands. After ironing out the major problems, conduct the last blocking rehearsals from the control room through the floor manager.

Early Rehearsals. The rehearsal stage is the time when all production elements are integrated into the finished product, a video program. Rehearsals are often known as **run-throughs,** though the early, rough passes can look more like tumble-throughs!

To avoid wasting valuable studio time and to reduce crew salaries, equipment costs, and rental fees, preliminary rehearsals are often conducted outside the studio facility or field location. For the early stage, often called a **dry run,** the director and talent may assemble in a meeting room to read through the script and discuss the approach they will take. Questions are answered and problems are worked out. Such preliminary meetings are often conducted for dramas, comedies, and musical variety programs. For blocking, the dimensions of the space where the actual program will be shot may be simulated in the meeting room with chalk or masking tape. Sets may also be simulated with available furniture and materials.

When the rehearsals are held in the actual studio or field location, some directors prefer to split them into phases, each focusing on a different level of activity. For example, **primary movement** includes the motion of the talent and other things in front of the camera. A primary rehearsal, therefore, could just concentrate on directing talent to move to their various locations as they say their lines. After such a practice of *marks and lines,* another primary rehearsal could be held to layer in the timing and props.

When the talent can perform these elements successfully, the director can then move to the next level of rehearsal, dealing with secondary movement. **Secondary movement** includes camera movement, framing, focus, zooms, and so forth. When this phase is mastered sufficiently, the director may tackle **tertiary movement**—namely, the control room activities such as cuts, wipes, keys, special effects, and other transitions.

The advantage of working in phases is that the crew as a whole will need fewer full rehearsals. This method can cut expenses, including unnecessary wear and tear on personnel. It also increases the chance for the director to work personally with each individual in the production, and it increases the crew's confidence that the production is being built on one solid foundation after another.

Full Studio Rehearsals. Depending on the type of show being produced, the director might choose to perfect and then tape a single segment before going on to the next. Some EFP single-camera programs lend themselves to this approach. Alternatively, the director may decide to rehearse the entire show from beginning to end several times, bringing it up to speed and polishing it more with each pass. Live-to-tape studio productions might reasonably be done this way.

In **interrupted run-throughs,** the participants may spend most of the rehearsal time practicing complicated transitions between segments and very little time rehearsing the program segments themselves. For example, if a live shot in a 10-minute interview is to carry the host from the interview set to a separate area for a commercial, the director might spend only a few seconds rehearsing the interview itself and use most of the time perfecting the more challenging move from one set to the other. Interrupted run-throughs cut to the chase, so to speak, using rehearsal time to solve the most pressing and complex production problems.

The seasoned director distinguishes between major problems, which may require calling a cut and bringing everything to a screeching halt, and minor errors that can be fixed later. Not every mistake is worth killing the rhythm of a rehearsal to fix. Sometimes it is better to let the talent and crew go for a while to get a feel for the project and to give you a sense of the pace and timing of the show. If you work this way, have your production assistant or the assistant director write notes as the run-through progresses so that you can recall later what you wanted to fix. On the other hand, you must not accept garbage, nor do you want the cast and crew to memorize a string of mistakes that will be hard to change. Deciding how to treat problems in rehearsals is a critical judgment call the director must make.

Dress Rehearsals. The final studio rehearsal should be a **dress rehearsal,** a replication of the actual show, including every production element—every sound effect, music cue, credit, down to the last detail. Dress rehearsals are sometimes taped in case segments go better than in the actual program. Then it may be possible to cull the best bits from the dress rehearsal and combine them with the best from the actual show to make the final product even stronger.

Before airtime or final tape, the director should communicate any last-minute suggestions, corrections, or changes. Any such items the director thinks of (as well as meritorious contributions by others) should be noted during the rehearsal period and communicated to the crew and talent before show time.

Directing in the Production Stage

During the production stage, the director orders every audiovisual change that occurs by issuing commands to crew members. To do this, the director usually delivers verbal cues through a headset from the control room to the crew in studio or field. The director may also speak to the master control room to let technicians know when to begin rolling in recorded segments before the show begins.

Techniques for Delivering Director's Cues. Several techniques can help you deliver cues effectively. First, speak clearly and succinctly to keep confusion to a minimum. Second, to improve crew members' poise in executing the commands, deliver each cue in two stages: first give a **ready cue,** then give a **command:**

"Ready take Camera 1. Take 1."

(This is usually shortened to "Ready 1. Take 1.")

"Floor manager, ready cue talent. Cue talent."

Third, since many different people may hear your voice, it helps to specify *who* is being addressed as close to the beginning of the speech as possible:

"Camera 1, when we get off you, please break to commercial set for product shot. OK 1, break."

This technique alerts the proper crew member to listen to the command, and it frees up others so they do not have to listen to the entire cue.

Finally, keep verbiage to a minimum. For example, it is better to say "Ready Take 3. Take 3" than to say "Ready *to* Take 3. Take 3" because the word *to* may be misunderstood as a camera number.

The Importance of Anticipation. In whitewater rafting, it is critical to anticipate the rocks that lie ahead of you to avoid being bumped or tossed from your craft. Rocks already passing by are of no concern at all. Similarly, for the director, it is important to concentrate on what lies ahead, not on what has just been broadcast. What has already been broadcast can never be called back; therefore, from the director's standpoint, it is useless to worry about it.

To deal effectively with both planned and unplanned situations, the director should become adept at anticipating future conditions. In terms of planned situations, anticipation involves the ability to deal with normal, moment-to-moment program changes, including setting up the next shot, knowing where the script is headed, and being aware of the preview and off-air monitors. Familiarity with the script and thorough rehearsal prepare the director for just such professional performance.

In terms of unplanned situations, the director must be a contingency thinker, considering in advance what to do in case of disaster. Much of this thinking should be done during the preproduction stage so that if disaster strikes during production, you have already prepared ample fall-back positions. Ask yourself plenty of questions and work out the answers:

Question: What if Camera 1 goes down while on air during the interview?

Answer: Cut immediately to the cover shot on 2 while we reposition Camera 3.

Question: What if the talent gets sick and fails to show at the last minute?

Answer: Shoot other segments that do not require the absent talent.

At times like this, the poise you show as director will go a long way toward building confidence among the cast and crew. By contrast, if you lose your cool, the entire production can grind to a halt.

The Director's Use of Time. Time pressure is inherent in directing. Since facilities are in demand, often rented for a fee, their use is always limited by budget constraints. Time is money, and making good use of production time is essential. Furthermore, program time is often determined in advance, making it necessary to time each program segment precisely so the show comes out to the required length. To use production time wisely, set up a production schedule and *stick to it.* Figure 14.6 shows a simple production schedule set up in blocks of time.

Production schedule	
8:00-9.00 A.M.	Production Meeting
9:00-11:00 A.M.	Equipment setup and lighting
11:00-11:30 A.M.	Technical Meeting
11:30-12:30 P.M.	Talent and camera blocking rehearsals
12:30-1:00 P.M.	Notes and reset
1:00-1:30 P.M.	Lunch
1:30-3:00 P.M.	Dress rehearsal
3:00-5:00 P.M.	Tape
5:00-5:30 P.M.	Strike

Figure 14.6 Sample production schedule.

The major advantage of a production schedule is that it provides a blueprint for getting the job done in the allotted time. Of course, the schedule is useful only if it is followed. Therefore, avoid the temptation to sacrifice time blocks to perfect the work you are doing at the moment. It is generally better to move along and stay on schedule.

One reason strict timing is so important in commercial television is that programs and commercials that a station runs may originate from different sources, making it necessary for stations to switch program feeds repeatedly throughout the broadcast day. If programs were not of a set length, synchronous switching between sources would be impossible. By contrast, with precise timing, stations can switch from one source to another without losing part of either message, thus increasing their revenue.

In controlling program time, several concepts are helpful. **Clock timing** refers to the use of a separate clock in the control room (usually a digital clock or a stop-watch) to time a program or program segment during run-throughs and actual recording. This tells the director exactly how long each segment takes. For every run-through, the clock can be reset.

Backtiming is a means of determining how much time is left in a show by subtracting a program's present time from its total length. As we saw in Chapter 8, backtiming can be especially useful when you need to figure out when an audio or video source should begin so that it ends precisely at a desired moment. For example, imagine that you have a 48-second piece of music that you would like to use to close your half-hour show. If you have the AD cue the audio operator to roll it at precisely the 29-minute, 12-second mark, then regardless of when you fade that music in, it will end exactly as your clock reaches 30 minutes. This use of backtiming can give a professional, polished quality to your program.

With **front timing,** you add the running times for specific audio or video segments to the starting time of a program, so that you can compute when to run certain inserts. Front timing is especially helpful in news programs, in which pre-pared packages of known length are frequently inserted. If you find that an insert comes up later than it was supposed to, you know immediately that the show is behind schedule.

Directing in the Postproduction Stage

Immediately after the appropriate thank-yous, the director often calls a "post-mortem" meeting with the crew to discuss problems that arose during the production and how they might be solved in the future. Then, during postproduction, the director supervises editing, if needed. This process (described in detail in Chapter 12) begins with viewing all unedited tape and deciding what is usable. To temper your judgment, it may be wise, if time permits, to get some distance from the project for a while, at least for a few days.

When you finally do sit down to watch, remember that the editing process lets you shuffle reality like a deck of cards. You may be able to use some shots in ways that were unanticipated. Listen to the audio with a critical ear, and don't forget that visuals can be salvaged even if the accompanying audio must be discarded and vice versa.

A FINAL WORD

As the beginning of this chapter pointed out, today's video industry often allows people to work as producer-directors, combining the two roles into one. But even in a large, traditional setting where the two jobs are distinct, they are inextricably bound together. The director fundamentally depends on the producer to gather and arrange all production elements so that the project can be put into final form. Conversely, the producer depends on the director to do justice to all of the elements placed at the director's disposal. Only through a professional effort by both parties can they hope to achieve their mutual objective: the creation of a successful video program.

KEY TERMS

rate card 438	tertiary movement 456
rating 448	interrupted run-through 457
share 448	dress rehearsal 457
shot sheet 454	ready cue 458
blocking 455	command 458
run-through 456	clock timing 460
dry run 456	backtiming 460
primary movement 456	front timing 460
secondary movement 456	

QUESTIONS FOR REVIEW

What activities does the producer get involved with during the preproduction stage of a video project? The production stage? The postproduction stage?

What should you include in a program proposal to maximize the chances of getting your project approved?

What information should be included in a production book to make the producer's job run smoothly?

Name the major unions for television workers, and discuss the impact they have on video production. What should producers know about union rules to stay on schedule and budget during a production?

Define *ratings* and *shares,* and explain why it is useful to compute both. Besides ratings and shares, what other quantitative and qualitative measures can help you assess the success of a television program? What approaches might enable researchers to measure audience viewing of new digital wireless video devices?

What main roles does the director play? How does the director work with the script and the floor plan?

What are the usual stages of rehearsals, and what typically happens in each?

How should director's cues be delivered to minimize confusion?

NOTE

1. Of course, with alternative digital platforms making it possible to shift viewing times, recording for later viewing, and so on, the actual times a program is seen may vary. Nevertheless, traditional outlets are still sensitive to schedules depending on the intended audience for a program.

Chapter 15

PERFORMING

Performing as video talent covers a wide range of activities. But whether you are acting in the role of a fictional character, performing as yourself as a sports commentator or interview guest, or working with talent as a producer-director, there are basic guidelines that you should know.

If you appear as a video talent, you should consider how technical, social, and aesthetic aspects of video production affect the way you look and sound as you communicate with your audience. Since television presents live human action within certain technical limitations, it is important to craft your presentation accordingly. After all, what good is a key speech if it is delivered off mic, or a product demonstration if done out of frame and out of focus? Furthermore, since video production is a collaborative effort, it is important to understand the social aspects of performing—your best performance may be lost if you miss the floor manager's cues. Finally, it's important to consider the aesthetic dimensions of the program, including its content, meaning, tone, and purpose. As an obvious example, your favorite comedic impressions may have little place in a serious drama. Moreover, to make the best possible appearance, you need to know how to select the proper wardrobe and use makeup.

The purpose of this chapter is to explain how technical, social, and aesthetic aspects of video production affect the look, sound, and performance of television talent. The chapter includes these topics:

Technical aspects of video performing

- Scanning system
- Color, contrast ratio, and lighting
- Depth of field and framing
- Orientation and movement of talent
- Using microphones

Social and aesthetic aspects of video performing

- Auditioning
- Performer and director
- Performer and floor manager
- Performing with other talent
- Performer, audience, and program content
- Video makeup

TECHNICAL ASPECTS OF VIDEO PERFORMING

Since video presents material composed of sound, images, color, and motion, it is important to consider each of these in performing. The following sections examine several technical characteristics of the medium that affect the way your performance appears on the screen.

Scanning System

Remember from Chapter 3 that the National Television System Committee (NTSC) standard for American television is still in wide use throughout the country. As we make the transition to high-definition (HD) television, we still need to be aware that the current television system produces a relatively low-resolution image. For the video performer, this means that wardrobe must be selected not on the basis of how it looks to the naked eye but on the basis of how it appears on screen after being rendered by the camera. As the medium transforms to HD, the range of acceptable wardrobe choices will expand. However, unless you are performing as a clown or a space alien, it is best to wear clothing free from intricate patterns that challenge the camera's imaging capability.

Small and intricate clothing patterns such as herringbone, houndstooth, and narrow stripes are generally poor choices for video (and could remain so even in a fully HD environment) because they can create a distracting *moiré* effect, or color vibration, that results from the interaction of the clothing design and the scanning lines of the television system. Solid colors, which avoid this problem, are generally better choices.

Color, Contrast Ratio, and Lighting

Wearing clothes similar to or the same color as the sets and backgrounds in which you appear makes it difficult for viewers to see where your form begins and ends. Worse, wearing clothing the same color as the chroma key effect can result in losing portions of the image of your clothing. To present yourself clearly, find out beforehand what the set looks like in terms of color, and then try to wear something different that fits the situation. Furthermore, highly saturated colors, such as deep reds and other primary colors, can command the viewer's attention, perhaps distracting the audience from your performance. For this reason, seasoned performers often avoid highly saturated colors unless they are justified by the program.

Clothing choices should also be conditioned by the contrast range of the video camera. *Contrast ratio,* as we saw in Chapter 4, refers to the difference between the brightest and darkest portions of the picture that the camera can accurately reproduce. In video, a contrast range of about 40:1 (50:1 in many CCD cameras) is common, so that the brightest portion of the picture is at most 40 or 50 times brighter than the darkest portion. In practical terms, this means that if you wear a dark blue hat with black lettering on it, the lettering may be too difficult to read on screen. Furthermore, a completely white outfit can cause tonal compression or reduction (*clipping*) in the contrast range of the television image (even digital ones), resulting in an unrealistic darkening of the face. Conversely, a pure black velour suit can cause the iris to open wide, making faces appear washed out and overexposed. To avoid contrast range problems caused by your wardrobe, the best color choices are those that avoid these extremes, such as mid-range colors and muted pastels.

Jewelry can also be a problem in the presence of bright studio lights. Shiny jewelry can cause distracting reflections. To reduce or eliminate them, apply dulling spray to the jewelry's surface or rub it with a bar of soap or, better yet, don't wear it.

Finally, most experts agree that the television image tends to add weight to the performer. This may be due in part to the camera angle used to picture talent, as well as to the fact that video renders three-dimensional objects on a flat screen. Or perhaps the illusion of added weight arises because the body is enclosed in a tight visual frame. Whatever the reason may be, you can offset the illusion of added weight by wearing well-tailored clothes that fit properly and by avoiding horizontal stripe patterns.

Choosing a Video Wardrobe

➤ In the absence of compelling reasons to the contrary, choose fabrics in solid colors.
➤ Wear mid-range colors, not highly saturated ones, bright whites, or pure blacks.
➤ Choose colors that do not match the set, background, or the planned chroma key effect.
➤ Do not try for wardrobe effects that rely on subtle contrasts in tone.
➤ Avoid horizontal stripe patterns (unless you want to look chubbier).
➤ Avoid shiny jewelry and other appurtenances, such as large belt buckles, that could cause strong reflections.

Depth of Field and Framing

Television's technical limitations with respect to framing and shot composition directly affect what talent can and cannot do. The fact that video reduces three dimensions to two makes it critical to block positions precisely. If you are standing further back in the set than another talent, the camera's rendering of the distance between you and the other person may differ greatly from your own perception. Moreover, depending on the camera's depth of field, a small movement toward or away from the camera can take you out of focus. Sometimes, if you are not the center of attention, it may be proper to move out of focus, but at other times, it is obviously not proper.

In terms of framing, as you already know, a camera shot can vary from an *extreme close-up* (ECU) to an *extreme long shot* (ELS). For television talent, it is important to know the framing at any particular time to judge how much lateral movement is possible. If, while you are carried in a tight headshot, you extend your arms to show the size of the fish you recently caught, the gesture may be lost (along with the information about the size of the fish) when your arms go out of frame. This can happen whether the aspect ratio is 4:3 or 16:9. If a shot is tight enough, just shifting weight slightly can move you out of frame. Therefore, it is often necessary to remain more still than you would in real life. Also, if you are going to move or gesture, it helps to telegraph that fact to the director in the control room. For instance, you might use a verbal cue ("Let me show you how big this fish was") as you slide to the edge of your chair. The verbal cue and the preliminary movement signal that you are about to do something different and give the director time to request a wider shot.

Framing also affects the way you handle and move props. For example, if you are cued to show an item featured in a tight shot—say, a dish of pineapple cubes to be used in a drink recipe—it may be better to point to the dish while discussing it rather than picking it up from the table. Picking it up can move it out of frame, nullifying the shot the camera operator has just set up.

Though tight framing is a constraint, it also has its advantages. It enables you to convey a wide range of emotions with very little movement. For example, in a close-up, a mere tilt of the head or shifting eyebrow can speak volumes about what you are thinking. In close-up, remember that exaggerated movements and expressions are usually not needed; instead, rely on more subtle indicators.

Orientation and Movement of Talent

When you make eye contact with the camera lens, your orientation to the camera is called **direct orientation.** Many performers use a direct orientation, including newscasters, announcers, hosts, and speech makers. The direct orientation is appropriate for addressing the home viewer in the most intimate manner, with no intermediaries.

In many cases, though, it is more appropriate to avoid direct eye contact with the camera lens. Such an **indirect orientation** to the camera is usually preferable in a sitcom or fiction drama, where the characters are supposedly unaware of viewers. Likewise, in an interview, it is more natural for the host and guest to look at each other than at the camera. The indirect orientation conveys the sense that talent are primarily involved in action on the set. Some notable exceptions to this rule include the pioneering *George Burns and Gracie Allen Show* and the *Gary Shandling Show,* where the title characters occasionally break through the mythical *fourth wall,* as it is known in theater, to address the audience directly.

For the director, deciding whether the talent's camera orientation should be direct or indirect helps determine where to place prompting devices or cue cards. For example, if the director wants to use an indirect orientation, a Teleprompter attached to the front of the camera would be useless. The prompting device would have to be placed in some other off-camera location so that the talent's performance could appear as natural as possible.

Camera Switching. Newscasters often must deal with on-air camera cuts. Imagine that you are a sports reporter appearing in a two-shot with the news anchor. The anchor tosses you the story with an "intro" line, and as you begin your report, the director cuts to your one-shot on another camera. When this happens, it is important to know exactly when the cut occurs so that you can maintain eye contact with viewers.

To make smooth transitions, you need to follow the floor manager's cue or watch for the tally light change indicating when the cut occurs. A common trick is to glance down for a beat as if you are checking your notes, and when you look up, reorient yourself to the on-air camera. This method of changing cameras appears more natural and fluid than simply turning your head on air from one camera to the other. If many cuts are planned, you may wish to mark your script for them in advance.

Blocking and Pace. As noted earlier, an unexpected movement, even a relatively small one, can take you out of focus or out of frame. Moreover, shots intended to be combined with graphic inserts in postproduction may be spoiled if you fail to hit your marks precisely and at the right moment.

To turn in the most professional performance in terms of blocking and pace, work hard to match your actual performance to what was rehearsed. Do not deviate from what was agreed on in rehearsal, and be sharply aware of running times for each segment so that the show times out properly. On the other hand, in the back of your mind, always consider the places in the script where lines, business, or movement can be padded or shortened to accommodate last-minute changes. In other words, if you are performing, be precise and consistent in your moves and delivery, and don't surprise the director, but prepare to be flexible if the need arises.

Cheating to the Camera. To accommodate the camera, it is often necessary to position talent differently from the way people might be positioned in real life. For example, when two people talk to one another, it is generally normal for them to face each other. On video, though, to get the best coverage of their faces, it is often better to twist each talent's position slightly toward the camera. Shifting talent to enable the camera to capture a fuller view of faces is called **cheating** to the camera. This often occurs in soap operas: Two actors, engaged in dialog with one another, are positioned with both faces toward the camera, with the shorter person in the foreground, the taller one behind.

Sometimes people speak of cheating props and display items to the camera, too. To determine whether and how much talent (or a cereal box) should be cheated to the camera, assess their appearance on the line monitor.

Controlling Dead Space. Television often uses close-ups and tight framing to provide greater picture detail. What this means for video talent is that performers shown together in the same shot may need to be closer together than would be normal in real life. Under daily circumstances, when you talk to a friend in a face-to-face conversation, you might stand several feet apart, but on television, this could result in too much dead or wasted space between you. To get the desired level of picture detail in an attractively composed two-shot, talent are sometimes placed just a few inches apart. At first, this kind of invasion of talents' personal space may be discomforting, but as a performer, you need to adapt to accommodate the camera.

Performing in Edited Productions. Frequently, video acting requires performing in scenes that are shot out of sequence and edited later in postproduction. When this style of production is used, it is difficult to maintain continuity in both your appearance and your intensity level. If you shoot a crying scene in which you are being led away from a hospital room, and the next scene shows you, still weeping, being helped into a car to be driven home, you need to maintain the same demeanor even if the scenes are shot days apart.

In such cases, it helps to take a snapshot or shoot some video of the final moments in the first scene and write notes about your acting during that scene. Studying these materials will help you guard against obvious discontinuities in terms of props, clothing, and hair and make it easier to recapture a similar level of intensity when the follow-up scene is shot.

Using Microphones

Whether your voice is carried on a lavaliere, desk, boom, handheld, or other mic, visible or concealed, you must be close enough to maintain the quality of being "on mic" as you deliver speeches. To turn in an air-quality performance, be aware of where your microphone is when you speak, and speak clearly.

In rehearsals, speak at the same intensity you intend to use for your opening speech. Then trust that the audio technician has taken proper levels during rehearsals and has placed the mics used to cover you in the proper position. The technician will "ride the gain" to accommodate varying intensity levels as your performance continues.

If you must handle or move your microphone, do so gently. Also, do not pull a mic cable by the microphone—pull the cable itself to reduce the danger of damaging the connections. If you must move from one set to another with a hand mic and cable, make sure you have enough cable to make the transition. Practice making transitions and crossovers without getting tangled in furniture and other talent.

If you must move from one area to another with a wireless mic, confirm in rehearsal that the equipment can capture the audio at each location. To do this, the audio technician may ask for a voice check at each location.

It is also important to control unwanted and incidental noise resulting from props, costumes, and jewelry. For example, if you are handed stapled copy to read on air, remove the staple in advance and then place pages gently to the side as you finish reading them. Noise from other paper props, such as newspaper and construction paper, can be reduced by spraying them slightly with a water mist shortly before airtime.

As for costumes, assess the fabrics you select not only for their visual compatibility with the camera but also for their noise level. Crinoline and other coarse, stiff fabrics may look all right on the line monitor but may sound terrible. Remember that lavaliere mics are especially susceptible to rustling noise from clothing.

Finally, the best test for jewelry is to wear it in rehearsal to determine whether it causes an audio problem. If you detect a problem, you may be able to correct it with some bits of masking tape in a few strategic places. If you can't keep the jewelry from rattling or clanging, consider eliminating it from your wardrobe.

SOCIAL AND AESTHETIC ASPECTS OF VIDEO PERFORMING

Auditioning

If you wish to be considered as talent for a video production, the first step will often be an audition. Audition calls are posted in talent agencies, advertised in trade papers or newspapers such as *Variety,* and advertised on radio or television.

How should you prepare for an audition? To make the best showing, bring a portfolio of your past work, especially recordings and photos (*headshots*). Next, be ready to perform, either acting, reading, singing, or dancing. If possible, prepare in advance a piece similar to the one for which you will be auditioning. (Some auditions, though, are nonspecific *cattle calls,* making it impossible for you to prepare anything in advance.) Finally, leave your name, address, e-mail address, and phone number(s) so that you can be called back if you are judged right for the job.

If you are called back, remember that you may not be the only one still under consideration. You may be asked to demonstrate your skills once again. Be prepared to delve further into the part, and, if asked, be ready with suggestions about how the job might be done better.

Those who assess your performance will likely look for several characteristics, including the way you look and sound, your **range** (ability to handle different types of material), your pace and delivery, your **flexibility** (ability to give more than one type of performance), your ability to take direction, and your **consistency** (ability to repeat key parts of your performance exactly the same way each time).

Performer and Director

Aside from being involved with technical matters, scheduling, logistics, and content issues, the director must also work to get the most out of the talent. It is the director's job (and sometimes the producer's) to assess the performances, note weaknesses, and make improvements.

However, it is common for television directors to have little time during production to work with talent. In many cases, the director is too busy in the control room with other production matters. For these reasons, the production period is not always the best time for meeting with the director. Even during rehearsals, the talent generally works with the floor manager and crew. It is early in preproduction that the director is most able to give you the attention you may need to answer questions about your upcoming performance.

If you are employed as talent, work hard in preproduction to prepare your presentation. If you have lines to memorize or ask questions about, the earlier you do it, the better off you will be. If there is a product you are supposed to demonstrate, practice beforehand to perfect your pitch. Practice with the props you will use, and notice any problems that need the attention of the director. Then, when you do have a chance to meet with the director and discuss your role, have your questions ready.

Performer and Floor Manager

In general, the crew member you will interact with the most is the floor manager. If you are not able to hear the director's voice through an earpiece, the floor manager may be your only link to the director. Therefore, it is critical to understand the silent hand signals the floor manager uses to cue your performance. During preproduction, learn the set of hand signals the floor manager will use so that you have a clear understanding of what each gesture means. The floor manager should be able to cue you to slow down or speed up, go to a commercial, wrap up a segment, speak louder or softer, get closer to a microphone, and many other things. Photo 15.1 displays a number of hand signals commonly used by floor managers to communicate with on-air talent.

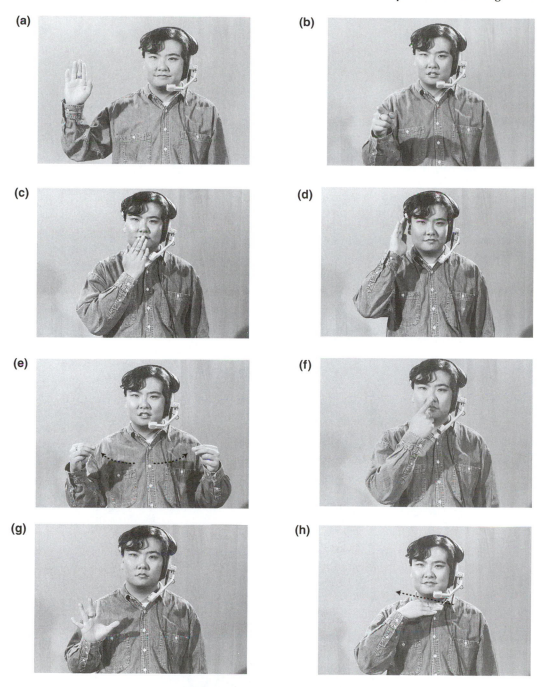

Photo 15.1   Hand signals typically used by floor managers to cue talent. Although the ones shown here are fairly common, anything that communicates successfully is acceptable: (a) stand by, (b) cue (you're on), (c) speak more softly, (d) speak louder, (e) stretch (slow down to fill time), (f) we're on schedule, (g) 5 minutes left, (h) cut, (i) move back, (j) come closer, (k) walk (move to the next performance area), (l) go to station break, (m) and (n) two ways to signal "go to commercial," and (o) everything is okay.

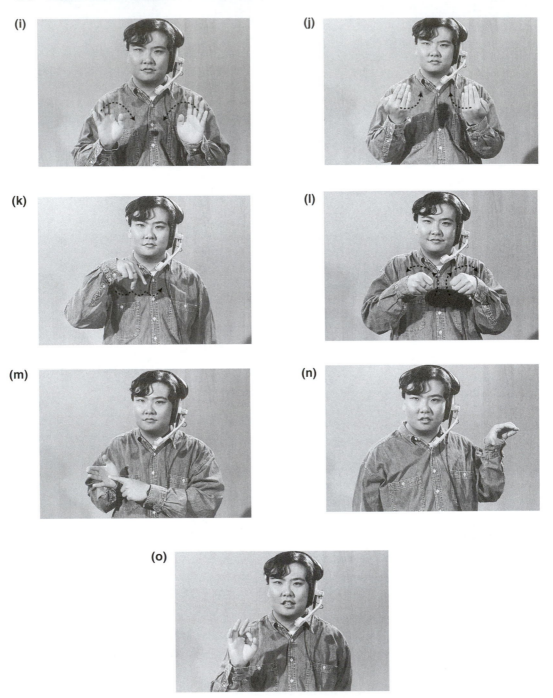

Photo 15.1 (Continued)

In acting assignments, when you are playing a fictional character in a fully scripted and blocked production, your communication with the floor manager may be more limited than if you are performing as yourself in the role of host or announcer. Nevertheless, some cueing may still be necessary, so it is wise to come to an understanding with the floor manager even in these instances.

Performing With Other Talent

As television talent, you may find yourself working with others from all parts of the performing spectrum, including experienced professionals, newcomers, major stars, and prima donnas. The people you work with may come from drama, comedy, talk shows, news, the music industry, and numerous other parts of the entertainment and nonentertainment worlds. How can you craft your performance to make working with others most rewarding?

First, be dependable. Show up on time since a great number of individuals may be relying on you for getting the show produced. Also, be sensitive to time constraints. There is usually a limited time available to get the program made.

Second, know your assignment. Be familiar with the script. Remember there is no substitute for thorough preparation. Remember also that at times, during rehearsals, it is better to listen than perform.

Third, don't throw curve balls. Be consistent. Do not deviate from the rehearsal and script so much that it throws off your coworkers. While ad-libbing may appear to be the bread and butter of a Robin Williams, most of the time, a polished ensemble performance is carefully plotted out in advance. Stick to the script.

Try also to get a sense of the overall pace, tone, and meaning of the production. Tune your delivery and intensity level to the program, and permit other performances to come through as well.

Finally, be sensitive to the vast range of skill levels and temperaments of your coworkers. Some may be consummate professionals with years of experience, while others may be the greenest amateur first-time guests with no clue about how to be television talent. Some may detest small talk; others may make you detest it. Getting to know the skill levels, backgrounds, and personalities of your coperformers can help you understand production needs and simplify the entire process.

In general, try to make the experience of performing together fun. Be respectful of others, for aside from the intrinsic social rewards gained from enjoying people enjoying themselves, you never know when you will have to work with someone again in the future. The good will you cultivate is invaluable.

Performer, Audience, and Program Content

Ultimately, your objective in being a video performer is to communicate some message to an audience. But the vast majority of the target audience is usually not present while you are performing. While there is always some crew around and sometimes a studio audience, home viewers and other audience members are not there to react to you, making it difficult to assess your effectiveness. This means relying on your own concept of the audience and your sensitivity to the material.

One way to surmount the difficulty of the absent audience is to imagine the camera lens not as a proxy for potentially millions of faceless viewers but rather as a small group of close friends, or even a single best friend. The quality of intimacy achieved from this approach may be exactly what you need to be most effective.

Finally, remember that viewers' expectations are often strongly shaped by program genre. Try to get some sense of the program's genre and its main objectives. Steep yourself in prior examples of the genre, and then pay attention as well to the program objectives. Some programs are made to entertain while others are intended to educate, to inform, or to persuade. Some programs have multiple goals. The purpose behind the program should shape the tone, pace, and other aspects of your performance.

Video Makeup

Makeup can improve, control, or change the way you look on camera. If used properly and in keeping with your program purpose, makeup can be one of the cheapest and fastest ways to benefit your video appearance.

The video camera unflinchingly captures faces, often in extreme close-up and under bright lights. Under such conditions, the television system may reveal and even emphasize blemishes, blotches, and other minor skin imperfections (see color insert photo C4). The adoption of HD standards emphasizes this intensity more than ever. While minor defects might not be noticeable under normal conditions, they can detract from your television appearance.

In male talent, the darker appearance of the face in the beard area, even after a recent shave, can be distracting. Some people's skin is more translucent than others, resulting in uneven lighting effects when two or more people are pictured together in the same shot. Being subjected to hot lights causes some performers to perspire and release oils to the surface of the skin, resulting in distracting shine when photographed by the camera. Skin color also varies across subjects, sometimes making it necessary to use makeup to offset unflattering color distortion or contrast range problems that result.

Of course, if talent looks good in tight close-up (the acid test) without any makeup at all, then none may be needed. However, if close-ups reveal unwanted or distracting effects such as those described, the proper application of makeup is often the solution.

Using Makeup to Control Shine and Uneven Skin Tone. To control shine caused by perspiration and oil on the skin and to hide minor blemishes, apply a **foundation** or **base makeup** to cover the skin and give it a more even appearance. Foundation makeup is also used as a background for all other makeup applications.

Foundation makeup comes in fluid form, cream, or cake. If you use foundation, it is generally considered best to match the color to the skin you are covering. For men, though, it is sometimes desirable to use a foundation one or two shades darker than the skin you are covering to maintain a masculine appearance. For women, lighter colors should be used only for very light-skinned subjects.

Fluid foundations are best for video work and are available in oil-free formulas for oily skin. Cream foundations are available in stick form, compact, or case. Among the brands most widely available are Bob Kelly Creme Stick and Kryolan Paint Stick. Product lines by Mirage and Joe Blasco have also been developed for television. Water-based cake foundations have been developed for face and body makeup by Max Factor, Bob Kelly, and Kryolan. A basic beauty kit, used for both male and female talent, is illustrated in color insert photo C5.

Dealing With Color Distortion. Skin tones differ from person to person across a wide range of colors, from very light to very dark. In addition, television viewers judge the accuracy of their color reception using skin tone as a reference point. Therefore, it is important to render skin tones accurately.

In darker faces, the television system may overemphasize cooler hues (blues and greens). You can offset this with foundation makeup that contains more of the warmer colors. Similarly, in light faces, when the television system overemphasizes the warmer hues (reds and oranges), you can counteract this effect with foundation of a cooler color. Judge the makeup on the basis of how it looks on screen and under the actual lighting conditions that will be used during the production.

Powdering. All cream foundations require powdering after the foundation has been applied. Without powdering, the skin will appear shiny, especially under bright lights. Powdering provides a matte finish that helps show off the features of the face. Powder also sets and holds the makeup during your performance. The most useful powder is loose, translucent powder with no color value. To apply it, press it into the foundation using a cotton ball or smooth, flat sponge. If applied properly, there will be no extra to brush away after it is applied.

Shading and Highlighting. After applying foundation, **shading** and **highlighting** makeup can be used to define or de-emphasize facial features. Shading makeup darkens areas of the face that would fall into shadow under natural lighting conditions. Highlighting makeup helps emphasize natural highlights of the face.

Shading is done first with darker colors using powders and creams, applied with brushes and worked in with the fingers. *Grease liners* that resemble pencils may be used for more precise shading work. Highlighting is done last with lighter colors, also using creams and grease liners. Use the fingertips to blend in the makeup to eliminate noticeable edges or abrupt color differences. When the shading and highlighting additions have been made, use powder to set the work.

Shading and highlighting may be used to thin or broaden the face, to change the appearance of the nose, to reduce tired-looking shadows around the eyes, and to emphasize facial structures such as cheekbones and eyes. In general, follow the principles of naturalism discussed in Chapter 5. Remember that we are accustomed to seeing human faces the way they look when lit from above by a single main source of light—namely, the sun. Therefore, when using makeup to achieve natural effects, it makes sense to sculpt the facial features by adding shading where natural light is most likely to cast shadows—namely, under eyebrows and under cheekbones. Table 15.1 lists the most widely used shading and highlighting applications along with the effects they produce.

Rouge. Rouge is a powder or blush of red, peach, or rust color used to offset the uniform appearance of foundation makeup and for emphasis on the face. Female talent usually use lighter colors of rouge and male talent darker colors. For lighter skins, lighter peachy tones of rouge generally work best, especially on women and children. For darker skins, deeper, rust colors work best.

For video, cream rouges are better than powders since creams provide more of a glow to the skin. The rouge should be applied to the area where the cheeks

Table 15.1   Shading and Highlighting Applications and the Effects They Achieve

Application	Effect
Shading	
Shade under the eyebrows	Emphasizes the eyes
Shade under the cheekbones	Thins the face, deepens facial structure
Shade the point of the chin	Shortens long faces
Highlighting	
Highlight eyelids	Emphasizes the eyes
Highlight cheekbones	Emphasizes natural facial highlights
Highlight middle of nose	Emphasizes natural highlights of nose

appear full when smiling. A touch can also be applied to the center of the forehead and nose. After applying the rouge, use a soft brush to fade the edges of the color into the surrounding area.

Eye Makeup. *Eyeliner, shadow,* and *mascara* provide emphasis and definition to the eyes and should be used for both male and female talent. Normal street makeup may be used, especially brown tones that tend to provide the most natural appearance on television.

Makeup Procedures

➢ Makeup area: Set aside a separate, well-organized makeup area with a chair, table, and large mirror. The area should be well lit so that you can see the work as it takes shape. If possible, to accommodate the color temperatures that will be used in the production, match the lighting conditions in the makeup area to the actual studio or field lighting. To further reduce color temperature problems, the makeup area should be decorated with neutral colors.

➢ Washing and drying the face: Before applying makeup, wash thoroughly with soap and water to remove dirt, oil, and perspiration from the skin. Then dry the face thoroughly with a towel.

➢ Protecting your clothes: Use an apron to keep stray smudges of makeup from getting on your clothes or costume.

➢ Applying foundation: As the first step in applying makeup, foundation should be applied with a sponge to the face, neck, and ears. On bald men, apply to the head also. After applying, gently sponge off excess foundation to avoid streaks and smears.

➢ Applying powder: Always set the work with a coating of colorless, loose powder. Use a cotton ball to press on the powder gently and lightly—do not rub.

➢ Applying rouge: To break up the flat look of the foundation and powder, use rouge to bring out the natural glow of the skin. Use a brush to apply rouge to the cheekbones, center of forehead, and nose.

➢ Defining the eyes: Use mascara and eyeliner to define the eyes clearly. Use just enough to reveal the eyes to the camera. Remember that in tight close-up, only a little is needed to get the job done. In general, especially for men, it is better to err on the side of too little rather than too much. In women, more eye makeup is acceptable because many women use such cosmetics in everyday life. If eye shadow is used, stick to the medium browns rather than blues and greens, which look less attractive on television.

➢ Lipstick for women: Have a selection of natural colors. Use lip liners for improving the definition of the shape of the lips. Top off with lip gloss to add a moister appearance if desired.

➢ Hair care: After preparing a careful makeup job, it helps to keep the hair off the face so that the camera and audience can see it. To keep unwanted hair from flopping in front of the face, use hair spray or some strategically placed pins.

➢ Makeup removal: Removal is best done with cold cream and a soft cloth. Soap and water are less effective and can be harsh on the skin.

(a)

(b)

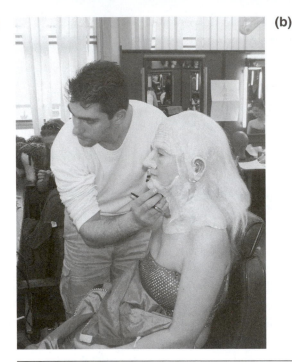
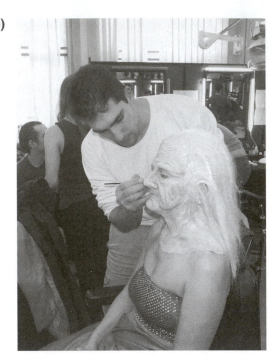

Photo 15.2   An example of what can be done with special effects makeup.

SOURCE: Reprinted with permission of Dubi Preger.

Advanced Makeup Materials. So far, our discussion of makeup for television has focused on enhancing the talent's natural appearance. However, more extensive makeup may also be used to alter your appearance entirely, as is often done on sci-fi television programs (see Photo 15.2).

Special effects makeup is commonly used for aging, providing special effects such as wrinkles, cuts, stitches, scars, and black eyes, and rendering characterizations in period and fantasy productions. Among the most widely used materials for such makeup jobs are *latex* for age wrinkles, *collodion wax* for scars, *spirit gum* for securing hair pieces (wigs, mustaches), *mortician's wax* or *putty* with red liners for cuts and stitches, and dark liner colors for black eye effects. For more on using makeup for special effects, see Swinfield (1994).

Makeup Equipment. Most makeup equipment is available from cosmetics counters in department stores, but some of the more exotic equipment may be available only from theatrical suppliers. Here are the basics:

- *Tissue and cotton balls:* 100% cotton is recommended for applying powder and foundation.

- *Brushes:* A variety of different sizes is useful for different jobs, from applying rouge to shading to highlighting.
- *Sponges:* These are useful for powdering.
- *Pencils and grease liners:* These are useful for eye makeup and for providing detail.
- *Cleansers:* To maintain good skin condition, do not use soap and water to remove makeup. They will not do a thorough job, and they can leave old material on the skin that can eventually clog skin pores. Instead, use a good cleansing cream or lotion, available at most cosmetics counters.
- *Additional musts:* The basic makeup kit should also include combs and brushes, scissors, hair spray, a razor, and false eyelashes.

KEY TERMS

direct orientation	466	consistency	470
indirect orientation	466	foundation (base) makeup	475
cheating	468	shading	477
range	470	highlighting	477
flexibility	470		

QUESTIONS FOR REVIEW

What technical characteristics of video affect talent's on-air appearance? Describe how the television system influences the selection of wardrobe in particular.

What technical characteristics need to be considered when working out blocking for on-air talent?

When is it advisable for talent to use direct and indirect orientations to the camera? Describe several situations when it is appropriate to have talent "cheat" to the camera.

How do framing and depth of field affect the location of talent with respect to one another?

What special performing problems are involved in acting in edited productions?

What are some good points to remember about using microphones?

What are the main purposes of makeup in video performing?

Describe the various types of makeup available and their functions.

GLOSSARY

A-B roll editing Editing two tape sources through an edit controller.

A-B rolling Running two synchronized tape sources through a video switcher and treating them as if they were two live sources, editing them on the fly.

amplitude Maximum value reached by a current or voltage in an electric circuit.

amplitude modulation (AM) Using sound to vary the amplitude of a radio carrier wave.

angle of view The horizontal and vertical area captured by a camera lens.

antialiasing In character generators and other digital text displays, a function that reduces or eliminates the stair-step or jaggy appearance of the curved parts of letter forms.

aperture Opening through which light passes in a camera.

artificial intelligence The capability of computer systems to control complicated and varied sets of conditions.

aspect ratio Width-to-height proportion of the television screen, currently set at 4 units by 3 for NTSC video and 16 units by 9 for high-definition television.

assemble editing Transferring all tracks of audio and video from a source tape to an edit tape, including the control track, in order. Assemble editing is most often done when raw footage must be put into final form quickly, as is often the case in ENG production.

assistant director (AD) Crew member who assists the director in all phases of a production.

asynchronous sound Sound featured in the audio track that does not coincide with the image presented on screen.

audio console Audio mixing board or audio mixer that provides access to each audio source, provides volume control, allows cueing and monitoring of each source before it is used, allows you to modify each source during production, blends and mixes various sources during production, and provides an air-quality output signal.

audio sweetening Making audio corrections, changes, and additions in post-production. It is best done in an audio production studio.

audio technician Plans the audio treatment, deploys all the audio materials for the program, operates the audio console and executes the director's audio cues, and helps with the editing process.

axis-of-action rule Imaginary line along which the main action of a scene takes place. As a rule, to avoid false reversals of action, keep all shots on the same side of the line throughout your shoot.

back light Light that illuminates the back of a subject.

backtiming Determining how much time is left in a show by subtracting its running time from its total length.

bandwidth The frequency range of a radio signal between its lowest and highest frequencies.

base light Diffuse, even light level required for optimal operation of a television camera.

binary code A communication system that uses just two symbols to record information.

blocking Rehearsing and marking the movements of talent and cameras through space.

body mounts Mounts that include (a) shoulder mounts and (b) body braces that use a harness or belt. Shoulder mounts place most of the camera's weight on the shoulder, freeing the hands for framing and focusing work. Body braces provide greater stability than shoulder mounts but may restrict freedom of movement and may prove uncomfortable.

boom mic Any microphone extended over a set on either stationary or mobile extension.

bounce light (1) Light reflected off a wall, card, or other flat surface behind talent to create backlight. (2) Light reflected as above to soften lighting on talent.

broadband High-speed communication network with large bandwidth.

cameo lighting Lighting that illuminates the subject but leaves the background dark.

camera control unit (CCU) Equipment that allows a video technician to adjust the video signal during a program or taping, including contrast and brightness, color rendition, and picture registration.

camera operator Prepares and operates the camera, following the cues of the director received over a headset or earpiece, during both rehearsal and shooting.

cardioid mic A microphone with a typical pickup pattern that is somewhat heart shaped. Cardioid mics may be further classified as *supercardioid, hypercardioid,* or *ultracardioid,* each of which describes progressively more directional sensitivity.

cascading Principle whereby the composite video signal flows from the top mix/effects bank downward, much like a stream of water flowing downstream.

cassettes Use a reel-to-reel format encased in a plastic housing to keep the tape free from dirt. Cassettes permit record and playback functions in two directions. They also use narrow tape and slower speed than open-reel tape, yielding longer playing time.

CCU See *camera control unit.*

CG See *character generator.*

character generator Computer with keyboard used to type electronic letters and numbers for text graphics.

charge-coupled device (CCD) Solid-state electronic circuit containing thousands of discrete picture elements (pixels) used to transform light into electrical energy. CCD cameras are also called *chip* cameras.

cheating Shifting talent or objects to enable the camera to capture a fuller view of the subject.

chroma key Special effect that replaces a video signal of a preselected hue (usually blue) with a signal from another source.

chrominance Color or hue information of a color television signal.

classical editing Editing to emphasize and vary the intensity of a narrative. Dramatic, physical, and psychological story aspects may be manipulated with classical editing techniques.

clip (1) To close someone's microphone. (2) To limit the black and/or white levels of a video signal.

clock timing Using a separate clock in the control room (e.g., digital or stopwatch) to time a program segment during rehearsal or taping.

close-up Camera shot picturing the subject at close range.

cold start Opening a program with the first scene, even before credits and theme song. Cold starts have become more common in recent years in the television industry as a means of adapting to fiercer competition from cable channels and independent program suppliers.

color temperature The relative amount of a given color (red, blue, etc.) exhibited by a light source, measured in degrees Kelvin. Television studio lighting is in the 3,200-degree range, and normal daylight is in the 5,600-degree range.

command Instruction issued by the director.

component recording In a Y/C format, a recording system in which the luminance and chrominance parts of the signal are recorded separately using two separate wires; in an RGB format, the red, green, and blue portions of the signal are recorded separately using three separate wires. The advantage of separating out signal components is that many more dubs are possible without appreciable signal loss. However, the disadvantage is that more expensive circuitry is required to process the separate signals.

composite recording Recording system in which both color and brightness information are recorded together. Composite recording is the original recording method standardized by the National Television System Committee (NTSC).

computer-aided design Computer software programs that simplify and speed up the process of creating floor plans, light plots, and other drafting materials.

concealed mic A microphone that is hidden anywhere on the set, such as in a vase of flowers, under a sheet of newspaper, or taped to the edge of a table or to a telephone handset.

consistency The ability to repeat key parts of your performance exactly the same way each time.

continuity Preserving a smooth flow of uninterrupted action from shot to shot in an edited scene or program.

continuity editing Editing to maintain the smooth, uninterrupted flow of action.

contrast ratio Difference in brightness between the darkest and lightest parts of a television picture, measured in foot candles of reflected light. For most cameras, the contrast range of light to dark is roughly 30 or 40 to 1.

control (pulse) track Part of the videotape used to record sync pulse information and keep a count of each frame of video; also called *pulse track*.

convergence Term describing the growing intercompatibility of different mass media technologies. For example, the ability to use a cell phone to transmit computer data over a modem combines the once autonomous technology of the telephone with the computer.

cue cards Poster cards with lines of copy printed on them used to deliver scripted copy to on-air talent.

cueing Readying an audio or video source for use in a program.

cut An instant change from one video image to another; also called a *take*.

cutaway Shot that leads the viewer's attention away from one scene and links it to another. Cutaways provide bridges or transitions between unrelated scenes. A common cutaway uses a wide exterior shot of a building in which the next scene is to take place.

cut-in (insert) Close-up that captures a key moment of visual business to emphasize a story's main point.

cut on action Going from one shot of an action to another before the action is completed to provide a smooth, uninterrupted flow. Cutting on action generally holds audience interest more than cutting to the next bit after the first action is finished.

cyclorama Continuous stretched curtain running from the floor to the top of the set area in a studio; used to provide a backdrop for sets and talent. Also called a *cyc* (rhymes with *bike*) for short.

decibel A value that expresses the ratio of two sound or voltage intensities.

demodulation Process of recovering signal intelligence from a modulated carrier wave.

depth of field In a camera, the range of distance within which objects appear to be in focus.

desk mic Microphones clipped to desk stands.

digital audiotape A superior form of recording compared to analog tape because it offers a wider dynamic range and lower noise level on playback.

digital audio workstation (DAW) A facility for digitally manipulating audio segments.

digital television (DTV) Also called HD or HDTV. A video signal that is rendered into digital information at a higher level of resolution from the analog.

digital video effects Turn video signals (both analog and digital) into digital graphics. Once captured, the images are subject to virtually infinite manipulation without losing signal quality.

dimmer board Lighting console that enables an operator to control intensities of individual lighting instruments with a series of faders. Many dimmer boards are now automated.

director Is involved in all meetings of the creative team and has input into the program format, content, and treatment, including the script, lighting, sets, and audio. In consultation with the producer, the director also works out crew and talent assignments.

direct orientation Orientation in which the performer makes eye contact with the camera.

dissolve Gradual transition from one nonblack video source to another nonblack video source.

downstream key Component of the special effects generator of a video switcher that the technical director uses to key in a video source (usually the CG) without using a key bus.

dress rehearsal A replication of the actual show, including every production element—every sound effect, music cue, credit, down to the last detail.

drop-frame time code Time code method used to adjust for discrepancies caused by the need to change from the original standard frame rate of 30 to 29.97 frames per second to accommodate the addition of a chrominance signal for color television. To keep time code in step with real time, drop-frame time code ignores frames 00 and 01 each minute except at every 10th minute, amounting to a net correction in time code display of 3.6 seconds per hour.

dry run Meeting of director, talent, and crew to read through the script and discuss the approach they will take.

dynamic editing (thematic montage) Using editing to stress the association of ideas but without regard to preserving unity in space and time.

edit controller Enables you to coordinate the decks, search through tape, and execute edits.

edit decision list See *EDL*.

EDL (edit decision list) Written log of proposed edit points for constructing a program by time code numbers in sequence. The EDL can also specify shot content and desired transitional devices to be used (e.g., cut, wipe, dissolve).

electromagnetic waves Radio energy transmitted through space at the speed of light, making radio and television broadcasting possible.

electronic field production (EFP) A mode of television production using a single field camera with multiple setups, with care given to such production values as talent rehearsals, camera and subject placement, blocking, lighting, sound, continuity, scriptwriting, and editing.

electronic news gathering (ENG) A mode of television field production characterized by rapid deployment of equipment to the site of a fast-breaking news story. ENG coverage is usually done with a minimum of preproduction planning.

electronic still store Digital device for storing individual video images.

ENG See *electronic news gathering.*

ESS See *electronic still store.*

essential area Part of the television screen in the center of the scanning area that is most likely to be seen by the home viewer; also called the *safe title area.*

establishing shot Shot used to establish setting, talent relationships, and/or situation in a scene or program.

ethos Source credibility; the degree of believability attached to a message source (e.g., a speaker) by the audience.

fade Gradual transition from black to a nonblack video source or from a nonblack video source to black.

feedback Sound from speaker feed into the microphone, causing squealing.

field Each successive scan of 262.5 lines.

fill light Light directed at the subject from the opposite side of the key light to add illumination to shaded areas, reducing shadows. Soft lights are most often used as fills.

filter Pieces of clear or colored transparent material (either glass or plastic) for eliminating unwanted wavelengths of light while permitting others to pass.

filter factor Measure of the quantity of light lost when a filter is added to a lens or lens system. Each factor of 2 reduces the amount of light entering the lens by half.

flat Standard set piece used to form backgrounds for interior sets, made of either canvas on wood frames (softwall flat) or particle board (hardwall flat).

flatbed scanner Machine used to digitize two-dimensional graphics.

flat lighting Lighting that provides uniform illumination for talent throughout the acting or performing area. Flat lighting minimizes jarring discrepancies in light levels when cutting between cameras shooting the same subject from different angles. Flat lighting is often used in sitcoms.

flexibility The ability to give more than one type of performance.

floor manager Coordinates activities in the studio, feeding cues from the director to the talent. The floor manager is the director's main connection to the talent and studio crew. The floor manager also supervises set and costume changes during production.

fly-away video satellite uplink A satellite station that can be packed into a suitcase and then flown anywhere on a small commercial airplane. Upon arrival at a field location, fly-aways can be set up on a truck and moved to any place the truck can go to provide global, live television coverage.

f/number (1) Standard numerical value expressing the amount of light admitted by a lens at a given aperture setting. (2) The ratio of aperture diameter to the focal length of a lens, in millimeters. Also called *f-stop number.*

focal length Distance in millimeters between the optical center of a lens or lens system and the plane on which the image of an object at infinity (or greater than 50 feet, practically speaking) is in sharpest focus.

focus Adjusting a camera's lens system to achieve a sharp, clear image of the subject.

footprint Coverage pattern of a satellite signal on the Earth.

formalism Production style that emphasizes selected elements of scenes to heighten audience attention to particular parts of the story.

foundation (base) makeup Makeup that covers the skin and gives it a more even appearance.

frame (1) A single picture in a motion picture. (2) One complete scanning cycle in a video presentation, occurring every 30th of a second. Two fields equal one frame of video.

frame counter Keeps track of every frame of the video signal. The frame count is displayed as an eight-digit code arranged in four pairs of numbers referring to hours, minutes, seconds, and frames.

frame grabber Device used to capture and store single frames of video.

frame synchronizer Device used to synchronize video signals from various video sources.

framing Selecting the perimeter around the picture to limit the field of view. Extreme close-ups of a subject are said to be tightly framed.

frequency The number of cycles per second exhibited by a radio wave. Frequency is inversely related to wavelength; that is, the higher the frequency of a given wave, the shorter its wavelength.

frequency modulation (FM) Using sound to vary the frequency of a radio carrier wave.

Fresnel spotlight Pronounced "fra-nell," the most commonly used light in television production; features a lens with stepped concentric rings, enabling it to throw a directional light onto the subject. The spread of the beam may be adjusted with a focusing knob.

front timing Adding the running times for specific program segments to the starting time of the program to compute when to begin certain segments.

full-page format Script that is common in certain types of video (i.e., feature-length drama). The full-page format is often found in single-camera EFP productions, made-for-TV movies, television dramatic programs, and documentaries.

gain (1) Volume level of an audio source. (2) Level of amplification of a video signal.

gel Colored filter that may be fixed to the front of a light to give it a desired hue.

geosynchronous Satellites stationed 22,300 miles above the equator that stay above the same spot on Earth at all times.

graphic artist Consults with the creative team about the graphics that will be used and then prepares them either electronically or mechanically, makes any necessary changes and operates the graphic equipment on cue from the director or the assistant director, and supplies any additional materials that may be needed during editing.

hand mic Microphones held in hand to afford mobility and control to program hosts who use them on audience participation programs, as well as to news and weather reporters in the field.

hanging mic Any mic hung over a set.

HDTV See *resolution*.

head-on shot Shot featuring the main action of the scene coming directly toward the camera.

headroom Screen space above the talent's head.

headset mic Allows the users to position the mic extremely close to the mouth while maintaining constant distance even when the head is turning.

helical scanning Diagonal arrangement of video frames on a videotape to increase the surface area of the tape as it appears to record or play back heads of a video-tape recorder. Helical scanning makes it possible to use narrower tape formats to store video information with less signal loss or deterioration. Also called *slant-track* video.

high-definition television (HDTV or HD) See *DTV*.

high fidelity Audio signals featuring the full range of frequencies.

highlighting Makeup that helps emphasize natural highlights of the face (e.g., rouge).

HMI lamp Highly efficient, high-intensity light that produces hard shadows; used to simulate the effect of sunlight in field productions. HMI lights operate in the 5,600-degree Kelvin range, using an additional piece of equipment called a *ballast*. The letters HMI stand for hydrargyrum medium-arc iodide.

interruptible foldback (IFB) Audio system that allows voice communication (usually instructions from the director or other production personnel) with an on-air talent through an earpiece. Also called *interruptible feedback*.

in-cue Notation on a script indicating the phrase or moment where a new segment is to begin. In-cues help maintain continuity and reduce dead air and choppiness.

indirect orientation Orientation in which the performer avoids eye contact with the camera.

insert See *cut-in*.

insert editing Transferring selected tracks of audio and/or video from a source tape to a preblacked edit tape. *Preblacked* means the edit tape has a continuous control track laid down in advance. Insert editing is done when extensive postproduction work is needed (e.g., when adding additional audio or B-roll "beauty" shots to raw footage).

interactivity The ability of a communication system to permit two-way communication among relevant parties in real time.

interrupted run-through A run-through in which the participants may spend most of the rehearsal time practicing complicated transitions between segments and very little time rehearsing the program segments themselves.

inverse square law The principle that light intensity decreases as distance from the source increases. The rate of fall-off is inversely proportional to the square of the distance.

jack (brace) A triangular wood or metal unit joined at a right angle to the back of the flat with either a clamp or a pin and hinge.

jib Camera support that permits a single operator on the ground to raise and operate the camera at heights of about 25 feet.

jump cut Abrupt transition between shots that violates smooth flow of uninterrupted action, often involving the same subject presented in slightly different screen locations.

keyhole A video source used to cut a hole into a background.

keying Replacing part of one video signal with part of another.

key light The main source of light used to illuminate a subject. Usually the key light is a "hard" light with a directional throw.

lavaliere mic Small microphone worn on the lapel or other clothing on the front of talent below the chin; also called *lapel mic.*

law of reflection Physical principle in which the angle of incidence equals the angle of reflection.

leadroom Screen space located in front of talent moving across the screen from right to left or vice versa. Usually leadroom should be greater than the space behind the subject, unless it is desirable to create a sense of entrapment for the subject. Such framing decisions should be determined from the subject matter of the program and from consideration of the effect the director wishes to create in the audience.

letterboxing A technique used to preserve the original aspect ratio of a film by blacking out portions of the screen, usually at the top and bottom.

liftout Portion of video copy that may be used as a stand-alone, shorter version of a message. For example, if properly written, a 10-second spot may be lifted out of a 30-second spot and used by itself without any alteration.

light meter Device used to measure the light intensity falling on a scene, usually measured in lux.

light plot Two-dimensional plan, similar to a blueprint or floor plan, depicting the location, wattage, and aim or direction of all of the lighting instruments used in a television production.

lighting director Consults with the entire creative team (including the producer, director, costume designer, makeup artist, and scenic designer) to develop the best lighting approach.

lighting grid Support pipes used to secure lighting instruments from the ceiling.

limbo lighting Illumination of a subject with plain light background to create the feeling of endless space behind the talent.

linear editing The use of any tape-based editing system (whether analog or digital).

logos Pronounced with an *s* rather than a *z* sound, logos refers to rational appeals a message source offers to an audience.

long shot Camera shot featuring the subject occupying a small portion of screen space.

lossless compression A compression algorithm that must be capable of retrieving the original signal in its entirety.

lossy compression Digital compression that results in some loss of information when a data file is retrieved.

lower-third Presentation of text material in the bottom one third of the screen. Lower-thirds frequently present the names and affiliations of interviewees.

LS See *long shot.*

luminance The amount of brightness information presented in a video signal; usually measured by its location on a gray scale.

luminance (insert) keying Method in which background video is electronically replaced by a second video source.

master shot Widest shot used in a scene or program. It is useful to see the master shot on the line monitor during setup and rehearsal to plan the locations of lights and booms. Also called *cover shot.*

medium shot Camera shot devoting roughly one half of the screen space to the subject.

mise en scène Pronounced "meez-on sen," the arrangement of objects in the frame.

mix/effects bank A set of buses above the program bus that can handle complex transitions with multiple sources.

motivating light Illumination conveying the presence of a light source in a scene or program (the sun, a flashlight, a lamp, etc.).

mounting head Device used to support a camera on a tripod or dolly.

MS See *medium shot.*

multicamera remote (MCR) production Type of field production done in the style of a studio production from a complete control room facility and a number of live camera feeds, usually from the site of a major sporting or public event scheduled in advance (e.g., a political convention). Often involves a truck with either satellite or microwave transmitters.

narrowband A telecommunications channel with limited bandwidth.

nat sound Natural sound that adds sonic texture, helps identify the location for the audience, and helps smooth out the transitions when segments are shot out of sequence.

naturalism Lighting approach advocating that, in the absence of compelling reasons to do otherwise, one should imitate the effect of sunlight by providing lighting that simulates a single main source of light from above.

noise Any part of a signal that is unintended by the source and can distract the receiver from the intended meaning.

non-drop-frame time code Time code method that displays 1 hour of time for each 1 hour and 3.6 seconds of real time. See *drop-frame time code.*

nonlinear editing Editing in which segments can be manipulated out of sequence with the same flexibility now available for word processing.

noseroom Amount of screen space in front of the subject when turned to the side. Usually noseroom is greater than the space behind the head. This norm is often violated to convey a sense of entrapment of the subject.

off-line editing Editing preparation phase after raw footage has been shot, including viewing master tapes to prepare logs and/or EDLs and searching for and selecting edit points before entering the editing suite to cut the final copy of a scene or program.

one-shot Camera shot featuring a single subject.

on-line editing (1) Editing a live broadcast or a live-to-tape program by calling shots among multiple cameras in a studio or remote truck. (2) Editing a program into final form in postproduction using high-end editing equipment.

open-reel tape A thin ribbon of magnetic tape wound onto an open spool. Also called *reel-to-reel tape.*

operating light level Minimum amount of light required for the camera to function.

out-cue Notation on a script indicating a phrase or moment where a segment is about to end. Out-cues help maintain continuity and reduce dead air and choppiness.

overlapping action Action in one shot repeated in another shot to provide a logical and continuous edit point.

over-the-shoulder (OS) shot Camera shot from a position behind and above a subject that includes one of the subject's shoulders; often used in interview programs to establish the relationship of the host (interviewer) to the guest (interviewee).

packet switching A form of data handling in which signals do not require dedicated lines to carry them.

paintbox An editing system that allows video graphics to be generated out of whole cloth, using a *stylus* and a *bit pad.*

parabolic mic Microphone that uses a dish or bowl-shaped reflector to direct sound from distant sources to a pickup element located at its focus.

patch panel To transfer any audio source with any output destination.

pathos Emotional appeals that a message source offers to an audience.

period The time it takes for one cycle to occur in any sine wave.

persistence of vision Tendency for the human perceptual system to retain an image for a short period of time after it is no longer present to the eye.

perspective The illusion of depth in a two-dimensional image, which can be formed by *linear perspective,* where apparent distance is conveyed by the relative size and location of objects.

phase Indicates the time relationship between two waves with alternating voltages and currents. Two waves are said to be in phase with each other when they reach maximum and minimum values at the same time.

photoconductivity See *photoelectric effect.*

photoelectric effect Effect exhibited by materials that emit electrons when light strikes them; also called *photoemissive effect.*

photoemissive effect See *photoelectric effect.*

pickup tube Device in a video camera that permits an image to be captured for transmission.

pilot Prototype of a series episode. A pilot story is an outline of all the visual sequences of the initial episode.

pitch Perceived highness or lowness of the tones of a particular sound.

pixel (1) Short for picture element, the light-emitting points arranged on a grid of a CCD used to compose video images. (2) Discrete points arranged on the face of a television receiver or computer monitor to register video images when scanned with an electron gun.

point-of-view (POV) shot Camera shot from the angle or perspective of the subject, showing the audience a scene as it would be seen from the subject's perspective.

polarizing filter Filters that are constructed to pass only wavelengths from a light source that vibrate in a particular plane or reflect at a particular angle, reducing glare.

postproduction Production phase devoted to evaluating and/or editing the program and the marketing, publicity, distribution, and exhibition of the finished product.

preblacked tape Tape that already contains a control track; essential for performing insert editing.

preproduction The planning and development phase of a video production.

pressure zone mic Microphone equipped with a sound-reflecting surface designed to receive sound from varying distances at the same time. Used in roundtable discussions and to cover audience sound. Also called a *boundary microphone.*

preview (preset) bus Contains the same sources as the program bus in the same order. Sources punched on the preview bus are *always off air.*

primary movement Movement that takes place in front of the camera (e.g., talent walking through a set area).

producer Develops the program concept, outlines the budget, and selects the crew. The producer approves the script and the director's treatment of it and supervises and coordinates personnel, scheduling, and payroll. The producer also handles all contracts and other legal matters, including the necessary permits and releases.

production Stage that includes all of the activities designed to produce the actual program, including setup, rehearsals, and shooting.

program bus Row of buttons on the video switcher used to put pictures from various video sources on the program or line monitor.

program (line) monitor The monitor that shows the actual output that the audience will see.

progressive scanning Each line scanned in order, with no skipping, of 60 frames per second

properties (props) Items held in the hand and set dressings to fill out a scene.

proposal Convinces a production company or client that the concept has merit, especially audience appeal. The proposal should describe the program's premise, introduce the central characters or talent, and describe the main program segments.

quantizing Assigning a value to the amplitude or other aspects of a video signal at a particular instant.

raincoat Cover for a field camera or other production equipment used to protect it from moisture.

range Refers to the different types of information and media that can be shared in a communication system (e.g., voice, image, data, motion visuals).

rate card Cards that list prices for services, materials, and labor.

rating Proportion of all television households in a given market tuned to a particular program.

reach The universe of relevant parties that can be connected to one another by a communication system.

ready cue A director's instruction to alert a crew member to be prepared to execute a command.

realism Production style that advocates the use of deep focus, long takes, wide shots, and camera movement rather than editing to offer the audience more choice in what to look at in the video image.

recapping Restating important ideas to refresh the audience's memory.

repeater station Ground station that receives, amplifies, and retransmits radio signals.

resolution Level of picture detail possible with a television system. Currently, picture resolution in the American television system is limited by the 525-line standard set by the NTSC. In the near future, that standard will be replaced by a 1,080-line standard (now called HDTV or high-definition television). Picture resolution is also affected by the lens system used and the presence or absence of filters.

reveal Camera shot that gets progressively wider, showing more and more of a scene. Reveals should increase audience interest by giving them more relevant information.

reverse-angle shot Footage of a scene from an opposing perspective, useful for editing purposes. Reverse-angle shots are commonly used in interviews, where footage of the interviewer from over the interviewee's shoulder provides transitions between different portions of the interview.

rippling In nonlinear editing, the term describing the ability to shift material around to make room for late additions or deletions without having to reedit material already laid down.

riser Platform used to bring seated talent to eye level with the camera.

rundown sheet List of each program segment in order with approximate running times. Rundown sheets can take the place of full or semiscripts in productions where the program format is well known to a seasoned crew, such as in late-night talk shows, where the show is roughly the same night after night.

run-through A rehearsal.

sampling A process of selecting instants of a video signal for processing.

satellite news gathering See *SNG*.

saturation Degree of purity of a color, free from white light.

scenic designer Works with the creative team in preproduction to develop the sets and set dressings, prepares scale drawings and floor plans that illustrate where all set pieces will go, and supervises set construction and makes changes as needed.

secondary movement Movement of the camera itself (panning, tilting, zooming, trucking, etc.).

semiconductors Devices capable of conducting an electric current, performing the same work as vacuum tubes but without the heat and with far less electricity consumption.

semiscripted format Script that features some but not all of the words to be spoken during the program. News shows that have late-breaking news stories often use semiscripts.

shading Adjusting the electronic levels of the camera to provide the desired contrast range and color reproduction. Shading is done by a technician in the studio at the camera control unit (CCU).

share Proportion of all television households with sets in use in a given market tuned to a particular program.

shotgun mic Microphone with a long tube casing designed to pick up sounds from a long distance.

shot sheet Provides a list of shot descriptions for each camera by number. The shot sheet conveys to camera operators which shots they will be responsible for and the order in which shots will be called.

shot sweetening Making final adjustments in a shot while it is still on the preview monitor.

shuttle mode In video editing, allows you to quickly locate and view video segments on either source or edit tapes as they are run back and forth (*shuttled*) through their videotape decks.

signal-to-noise (S/N) ratio The ratio of the strength of the intended signal to the amount of interference that accompanies it.

SMPTE-EBU time code Frame-accurate system for coding videotaped footage. SMPTE-EBU time code gives each video frame a permanent "address" throughout the entire editing process. Pronounced "simpty time code" for short.

SNG (satellite news gathering) Use of a satellite to transmit live and/or recorded audio and video material from a remote location to a home base (e.g., a news station).

sound effects (SFX) Sounds that are neither music nor speech, used to provide clues about location and context in a TV program.

sound envelope Changes in the loudness of a sound through time.

special effects generator (SEG) The part of a video switcher used to provide internally generated graphics involving two or more sources (i.e., keying, wiping).

speed light Small lighting instrument clipped to the top of a camera to provide illumination of on-air talent in ENG productions.

split-page format Scripts that place audio content on one half of the page and the video content (with other cues) on the other.

staging Having on-air talent perform action they might or might not perform if the camera were not present in order to capture it for a news story. Depending on how staging is done and presented to the audience, ethical issues of misrepresentation may arise. Different news organizations have different policies regarding staging and should be consulted to follow accepted guidelines of journalistic integrity.

storyboard Panel of drawings showing the main shots of a scene, story, or program. Storyboards are especially useful in television advertising, where precise picture content and running time are crucial.

studio (camera) card Cards that are used to present titles and credits.

studio pedestal Camera mount that is more versatile than tripods in that it permits you to raise and lower the camera while on air.

super beam mic A row of microphone elements that pick up sound from distant sources.

superimposition Mixing two video sources on the same screen at the same time, where the picture strength of each source is less than 100%.

surround sound (1) Sound created through speakers set up at the front, sides, and back of a room. (2) Term referring to Dolby Stereo.

synchronous sound Sound featured in the audio track that coincides with the visual action seen on screen.

tail-away shot Shot featuring action of the scene moving away from the camera.

take See *cut*.

talent Performers and actors who appear on camera, including reporters, newscasters, program hosts, guests, singers, comedians, and so on.

tally light Red light on the front and/or back of a studio camera or on the inside of a field camera's viewfinder that indicates when that camera is on the air.

TBC See *time base corrector*.

tearing Breaks between two video signals when mismatches or gaps occur, causing picture roll, momentary glitches, loss of color, or other troubles.

technical director (TD) Crew member who operates the video switcher. The TD may also be responsible for the overall quality of the video images during the production.

telegraphing Informing the audience in advance about upcoming program segments.

Teleprompter Electronic device for feeding script material to on-air talent; located on the front end of a television camera.

television gray scale A multistep scale (usually 7, 9, or 11 steps) that is used to determine differences in reflectance values between different parts of a video image.

tertiary movement Movement on screen created by control room manipulation (e.g., wipes, keys).

thematic montage See *dynamic editing.*

three-point lighting Most commonly used lighting scheme for illuminating stationary talent. Three-point lighting features a key light, a fill light, and a back light to provide an attractive, sculpted look to the talent while adding depth to the video image.

three-shot Camera shot featuring three subjects in the frame.

throughput A measure of the amount of bandwidth carrying *meaningful* data compared to the overall information capacity of a device or channel.

time base corrector Device used to stabilize video signals from video tape recorders.

transducer Device that changes one form of energy into another.

transponder A receiver/transmitter aboard a satellite.

treatment Narrative version of a proposed story, presented as a means of generating interest in a producer to produce a pilot of the program.

trim (1) Camera shot featuring a zoom-in to reduce the area captured in the frame. Trim shots should be motivated and should direct the viewer's attention to important picture information relevant to the subject. (2) Device on an audio console that reduces volume levels at the mic or line input.

tripod Camera support with three legs that can be placed on a dolly for easy movement.

two-shot Camera shot featuring two subjects in the frame.

vectorscope Device used by a video technician to adjust color levels for studio and field cameras during rehearsal and production.

video switcher Device that routes, controls, and shapes video images during a television production.

video technicians Help maintain picture and transmission quality, adjusting cameras to maintain technical and aesthetic picture quality. They may also help with special effects if needed.

viewfinder TV monitor on the back of the camera used by the operator to see the image captured by the camera.

voice-over Script notation indicating that a piece of tape will be accompanied by an announcer's voice-over.

volume unit (VU) Measure of the relative loudness of a sound, or the percentage of modulation of an audio signal.

VU (volume unit) meter An audio measure that displays volume intensity leaving the console. It is calibrated in both volume units (decibels) and (in the case of a transmitter) percentage of modulation.

waveform monitor Device that displays a graph of a television signal electronically; used for setting optimal video levels from black to white.

wavelength The distance a radio wave travels in the time it takes to complete one full cycle. Since light travels at about 300 million meters per second and radio waves travel at the speed of light, the wavelength in meters of a radio wave of a given frequency equals 300,000,000/frequency.

white balance Adjustment of a television camera to produce an accurate rendition of white when the camera is focused on a white field. White balancing is necessary to avoid inaccurate color reproduction.

window dub Time code display "burned in" to a video dub of raw footage, which may then be viewed on a regular videotape player; useful for preparing logs, EDLs, and off-line editing. Window dubs cannot be used for on-line editing because the time code display cannot be erased.

wipe Video effect that looks as though one video source is pushing another off the screen. Wipes can have a variety of patterns (e.g., checkerboard, circle).

writer Works with the producer and director to develop the script and format of the show. The writer writes, edits, and revises the script until it is approved.

Y/C recording See *component recording.*

z-axis Depth dimension of the video image going from foreground to background. Action along the *z*-axis may keep talent in a tight, stationary frame and in focus throughout the entire depth of field.

zoom lens A variable focal length lens. *Zooming in* means moving the lens elements to a narrow angle of view, making the scene appear to move closer to the viewer. *Zooming out* means moving the lens elements to a wide angle of view, making the scene appear to move farther away.

BIBLIOGRAPHY

Adams, Michael H. (1992). *Single camera video: The creative challenge.* Dubuque, IA: Brown.

Alten, Stanley A. (1994). *Audio in media* (4th ed.). Belmont, CA: Wadsworth.

Andrews, Bart. (1985). *The* I love Lucy *book.* New York: Doubleday/Dolphin.

Armer, Alan A. (1993). *Writing the screenplay.* Belmont, CA: Wadsworth.

Augarten, S. (1984). *Bit by bit: An illustrated history of computers.* New York: Ticknor and Fields.

Bannan, Karen J. (2003, June 12). Between 2 sheets of glass, a million flashing lamps. *New York Times.* Retrieved June 16, 2003, from http://www.nytimes.com/2003/06/12/technology/circuits/12howw.htm

Bazin, Andre. (1967). *What is cinema?* Berkeley: University of California Press.

Bellman, W. F. (1974). *Lighting the stage.* San Francisco: Harper & Row.

Belson, Ken. (2004, October 26). F.C.C. approves Cingular deal to buy AT&T Wireless. *New York Times.* Retrieved October 26, 2004, from http://www.nytimes.com/2004/10/26/business/27cellcnd.html

Belson, Ken. (2005, December 25). Fiddling with formats while DVD's burn. *New York Times.* Retrieved December 26, 2005, from http://www.nytimes.com/2005/12/25/technology/25cnd-format.html

Bentham, Frederick. (1980). *The art of stage lighting* (3rd ed.). London: Pitman.

Bettinghaus, Erwin P. (1973). *Persuasive communication.* New York: Holt, Rinehart & Winston.

Blum, Richard A. (2000). *Television and screen writing: From concept to contract.* Boston: Focal Press.

Boxer, Sarah. (2005, May 16). Arial, Mon Amour, and other font passions. *New York Times.* Retrieved May 16, 2005, from http://www.nytimes.com/2005/05/16/arts/Design/16typo.html

Brady, Ben, & Lee, Lance. (1988). *The understructure of writing for film and television.* Austin: University of Texas Press.

Brenneis, Lisa. (2004). *Final Cut Pro for Mac OS X.* Berkeley, CA: Peachpit Press.

Captain, Sean. (2005, August 4). Just the right digital camera for you. *New York Times.* Retrieved August 15, 2005, from http://www.nytimes.com/2005/08/08/technology/circuits/04basics.html

Catsis, John R. (1996). *Sports broadcasting.* Chicago: Nelson-Hall.

Cohler, David K. (1985). *Broadcast journalism: A guide for the presentation of radio and television news.* Englewood Cliffs, NJ: Prentice Hall.

Cole, Hillis R., Jr., & Haag, Judith H. (1995). *The complete guide to standard script formats: Part I. The screenplay.* North Hollywood, CA: CMC.

Collins, Glenn. (2005, June 8). Lights, camera, Brooklyn! *New York Times.* Retrieved June 8, 2005, from http://www.nytimes.com/2005/06/08/nyregion/08studio.html

Cook, Bruce. (Ed.). (2004). *United press international stylebook: The authoritative handbook for writers, editors, and news directors.* Lincolnwood, IL: National Textbook Co.

Cook, Bruce, & Martin, Harold. (2004). *UPI stylebook.* Herndown, VA: AL Books.

Cooper, Lane. (1960). *The rhetoric of Aristotle.* Englewood Cliffs, NJ: Prentice Hall.

Coyle, K. (1996). *Copyright in the digital age* [Talk given at the San Francisco Public Library]. Retrieved from http://www.kcoyle.net

Cremer, Charles F., Keirstead, Phillip O., & Yoakam, Richard D. (1996). *ENG: Television news.* New York: McGraw-Hill.

Cronkhite, Gary. (1969). *Persuasion: Speech and behavioral change.* New York: Bobbs-Merrill.

Darling, Damon. (2005, August 20). Falling costs of big-screen TV's to keep falling. *New York Times.* Retrieved August 22, 2005, from http://www.nytimes.com/2005/08/20/technology/20tv prices.html

Darling, Damon. (2006, January 2). Data, music, video: Raising a curtain on future gadgetry. *New York Times.* Retrieved January 2, 2006, from http://www.nytimes.com/2006/01/02/technology/02electronics.html

Davies, H., & Wharton, M. (1983). *Inside the chip.* London: Usborne.

DeFleur, M., & Ball-Rokeach, S. (1989). *Theories of mass communication* (5th ed.). New York: Longman.

Dewey, J. (2000). *Democracy and education.* Philadelphia: Pennsylvania State University, Electronic Classics Series. Retrieved from www.hn.psu.edu/faculty/jmanis/johndewey/demded.pdf

Dominick, J. R., Sherman, B. L., & Copeland, G. A. (1996). *Broadcasting/cable and beyond: An introduction to modern electronic media* (3rd ed.). New York: McGraw-Hill.

Dominick, J. R., Sherman, B. L., & Messere, F. (2000). *Broadcasting, cable, the Internet, and beyond: An introduction to modern electronic media* (4th ed.). New York: McGraw-Hill.

Dmytryk, Edward. (1984). *On film editing.* Stoneham, MA: Focal Press.

Dmytryk, Edward, & Dmytryk, Jean Porter. (1984). *On screen acting.* Stoneham, MA: Focal Press.

Drude, P. (1922). *The theory of optics.* New York: Longmans Green.

Elliott, Stuart. (2005, November 25). Placing ads in come surprising spaces. *New York Times.* Retrieved November 25, 2005, from http://www.nytimes.com/2005/11/25/business/25adcol.html

Faigin, Gary. (1990). *The artist's complete guide to facial expression.* New York: Watson-Guptill.

Fasoldt, Al. (1991). As new digital audio tape formats shape up, the analog cassette keeps its lead. *The Syracuse Newspapers.* Retrieved January 5, 2006, from http://aroundcny.com/technofile/texts/newtapeformats91.html

Fink, Donald J. (1957). *Television engineering handbook.* New York: McGraw-Hill.

Fink, Donald J., & Lutyens, David. (1960). *The physics of television.* New York: Anchor.

Fischer, C. S. (1992). *America calling: A social history of the telephone to 1940.* Berkeley: University of California Press.

Fleishman, Glenn. (2005, July 28). Revolution on the radio. *New York Times.* Retrieved July 28, 2005, from http://www.nytimes.com/2005/07/28/technology/circuits/28basics.html

Furman, Phyllis. (2005, November 22). TiVo bringing TV shows to your iPod. *New York Daily News.* Retrieved November 22, 2005, from http://www.nydailynews.com/Front/v-pfriendly/story/368097p-313108c.html

Gaskill, Arthur L., & Englander, David A. (1967). *How to shoot a movie story.* Hastings-on-Hudson, NY: Morgan Press.

Gates, B. (with Hemingway, C.). (1999). *Business @ the speed of thought: Using a digital nervous system.* New York: Warner.

Gaunt, Leonard. (1981). *Zoom and special lenses.* New York: Focal Press.

Gilpin, Kenneth N. (2003, June 2). F.C.C. votes to relax rules limiting media ownership. *New York Times.* Retrieved June 2, 2003, from http://www.nytimes.com/2003/06/02/business/02 cnd-rule.htm

Gorman, R. (1998). Intellectual property: The rights of faculty as creators and users. *Academe, 84*(3), 14–18.

Greenhouse, Linda. (2003, June 24). Justices back law to make libraries use Internet filters. *New York Times.* Retrieved June 24, 2003, from http://www.nytimes.com/2003/06/24/politics/24INTE.htm

Greenleaf, A. R. (1950). *Photographic optics.* New York: Macmillan.

Gustin, Sam. (2005). IPod is making a 'seen.' *New York Post.* Retrieved October 18, 2005, from http://www.nypost.com/php/pfriendly_new.php

Haag, Judith H. (1995). *The complete guide to standard script formats: Part II. Taped formats for television.* North Hollywood, CA: CMC.

Hansell, Saul. (2005a, January 6). Breaking free of cable's stranglehold. *New York Times.* Retrieved January 6, 2005, from http://www.nytimes.com/2005/01/06/technology/06cablebox.html

Hansell, Saul. (2005b, August 1). More people turn to the Web to watch TV. *New York Times.* Retrieved August 2, 2005, from http://www.nytimes.com/2005/08/01/technology/01video.html

Hansell, Saul. (2005c, October 6). Smaller video producers seek audiences on Net. *New York Times.* Retrieved October 6, 2005, from http://nytimes.com/2005/10/06/technology/06video.html

Hansell, Saul. (2005d, October 6). Online pioneer sets out to shake up TV. *New York Times.* Retrieved October 6, 2005, from http://www.nytimes.com/2005/10/06/technology/06bright.html

Hansell, Saul. (2005e, October 21). Profit rises sevenfold at Google. *New York Times.* Retrieved October 22, 2005, from http://www.nytimes.com/2005/10/21/technology/21google.html

Hansell, Saul. (2006, January 6). Google and Yahoo aim at another screen. *New York Times.* Retrieved January 6, 2006, from http://www.nytimes.com/2006/01/06/technology/06online.html

Harris, Tom. (2006). *How plasma displays work.* Retrieved October 10, 2002, from http://www.how stuffworks.com/plasma-display2.htm

Head, Sydney W., Sterling, Christopher H., & Schofield, Lemuel B. (1994). *Broadcasting in America* (7th ed.). Boston: Houghton Mifflin.

Hedgecoe, John. (1992). *The book of photography.* New York: Knopf.

Hewitt, John. (1995). *Air words: Writing for broadcast news.* Mountain View, CA: Mayfield.

Hilliard, Robert L. (1997). *Writing for television and radio* (6th ed.). Belmont, CA: Wadsworth.

Holson, Laura M. (2003, September 25). Studios moving to block piracy of films online. *New York Times.* Retrieved September 25, 2003, from http://www.nytimes.com/2003/09/25/business/media/25STUD.htm

Junnarkar, Sandeep. (2005, June 23). A dizzying array of options for using the Web on cellphones. *New York Times.* Retrieved June 23, 2005, from http://www.nytimes.com/2005/06/23/technology/circuits/23basics.html

Kehoe, Vincent J.-R. (1985). *The technique of the professional make-up artist for film, television, and stage.* Boston: Focal Press.

Kehr, Dave. (2005, February 22). New DVD's: 'Edison: The invention of the movies'. *New York Times.* Retrieved February 22, 2005, from http://www.nytimes.com/2005/02/22/movies/HomeVideo/22dvd.html

Kingslake, Rudolf. (1978). *Lens design fundamentals.* San Diego: Academic Press.

Kingslake, Rudolf. (1989). *A history of the photographic lens.* San Diego: Academic Press.

Krantz, Michael. (2005, July 3). Television that leaps off the screen. *New York Times.* Retrieved July 3, 2005, from http://www.nytimes.com/2005/07/03/arts/television/03kran.html

Kurzweil, R. (1999). *The age of spiritual machines: When computers exceed human intelligence.* New York: Viking.

Labaton, Stephen. (2003, May 16). U.S. moves to allow trading of radio spectrum licenses. *New York Times.* Retrieved May 16, 2003, from http://www.nytimes.com/2003/05/16/technology/16SPEC.htm

Leeds, Jeff. (2005, August 27). Apple, digital music's angel, earns record industry's scorn. *New York Times.* Retrieved August 29, 2005, from http://www.nytimes/2005/08/27/technology/27apple.html

Levin, Robert E. (1984). *Sylvania GTE lighting handbook for television, theatre, and professional photography* (7th ed.). Danvers, MA: GTE Products Corporation, Sylvania Lighting Center.

Levy, Steven. (2005a, February 28). Ma Bell's kids will live on the Net. *Newsweek.*

Levy, Steven. (2005b, May 16). Thinking outside the (music) box. *Newsweek.*

Levy, Steven. (2005c, May 30). Television reloaded. *Newsweek.*

Levy, Steven. (2005d, July 11). The Supremes hit the pirate ships. *Newsweek.*

Levy, Steven. (2005e, November 28). Sony gets caught with slipped discs. *Newsweek.*

Lohr, Steve. (2005, December 11). Can this man reprogram Microsoft? *New York Times.* Retrieved December 12, 2005, from http://www.nytimes.com/2005/12/11/business/yourmoney/11micro.html

Longhurst, R. S. (1957). *Geometrical and physical optics.* London: Longman.

Lu, C. (1998). *The race for bandwidth: Understanding data transmission.* Redmond, WA: Microsoft Press.

Lucey, Paul. (1996). *Story sense: Writing story and script for feature films and television.* New York: McGraw-Hill.

MacDonald, R. H. (2002). *A broadcast news manual of style* (2nd ed.). New York: Longman.

Magid, Larry. (2005, February 10). Mac meets PC and both learn to share. *New York Times.* Retrieved February 10, 2005, from http://www.nytimes.com/2005/02/10/technology/circuits/10basi.htm

Manly, Loren. (2005, April 5). As satellite radio takes off, it is altering the airwaves. *New York Times.* Retrieved April 5, 2005, from http://www.nytimes.com/2005/04/05/national/05satellite.html

Markoff, John. (2004, June 9). New service by TiVo will build bridges from Internet to the TV. *New York Times.* Retrieved June 9, 2004, from http://www.nytimes.com/2004/06/09/technology/09net.html

Markoff, John. (2005a, February 7). Smaller than a pushpin, more powerful than a PC. *New York Times.* Retrieved February 7, 2005, from http://www.nytimes.com/2005/02/07/technology/07chip.html

Markoff, John. (2005b, August 1). New file-sharing techniques are likely to test court decision. *New York Times.* Retrieved August 2, 2005, from http://www.nytimes.com/2005/08/01/technology/01file.html

Markoff, John. (2005c, August 19). 14,159,265 new slices of rich technology. *New York Times.* Retrieved August 22, 2005, from http://www.nytimes.com/2005/08/19/technology/19google.html

Markoff, John. (2005d, December 29). Chip industry sets a plan for life after silicon. *New York Times.* Retrieved December 29, 2005, from http://www.nytimes.com/2005/12/29/technology/29nano.html

Markoff, John, & Lohr, Steve. (2005, June 6). Apple's decision on chips is applauded by programmers. *New York Times.* Retrieved June 7, 2005, from http://www.nytimes.com/2005/06/06/technology/06cnd-apple.html

McAdams, Katherine C., & Elliot, Jan Johnson. (1996). *Reaching audiences: A guide to media writing.* Boston: Allyn & Bacon.

McCain, Thomas A., & Shyles, Leonard. (Eds.). (1994). *The thousand hour war: Communication in the gulf.* Westport, CT: Greenwood.

McCandless, Stanley R. (1958). *A method of lighting the stage* (4th ed.). New York: Theater Arts.

McNichol, Tom. (2004, October 28). Pluggin into the Net, through the humble wall outlet. *New York Times.* Retrieved October 28, 2004, from http://nytimes.com/2004/10/28/technology/circuits/28howw.html

Mencher, Melvin. (1994). *News reporting and writing* (6th ed.). Madison, WI: Brown and Benchmark.

Mencher, Melvin. (1995). *Basic media writing* (5th ed.). Burr Ridge, IL: McGraw-Hill.

Merritt, Douglas. (1993). *Graphic design in television.* Oxford, UK: Focal Press.

Meyrowitz, J. (1985). *No sense of place: The impact of electronic media on social behavior.* New York: Oxford University Press.

Minnick, Wayne C. (1957). *The art of persuasion.* Boston: Houghton Mifflin.

Montefinise, Angela. (2005). Shut the cell up. *New York Post.* Retrieved February 21, 2005, from nypost.com

Mott, Robert L. (1993). *Radio sound effects.* Jefferson, NC: McFarland & Co.

Myleaf, Harry. (Ed.). (1966). *Electricity one-seven.* Rochelle Park, NJ: Hayden.

Myleaf, Harry. (1976). *Electronics one-seven.* Rochelle Park, NJ: Hayden.

Napoli, Lisa. (2003, September 22). Think debate on music property rights began with Napster? Hardly. *New York Times.* Retrieved September 22, 2003, from http://www.nytimes.com/2003/09/22/technology/22tune.htm

Neblette, C. B. (1965). *Photographic lenses.* Hastings-on-Hudson, NY: Morgan and Morgan.

Neblette, C. B., & Murray A. E. (1973). *Photographic lenses* (2nd ed.). Dobbs Ferry, NY: Morgan and Morgan.

Newsom, Doug, & Wollbert, James A. (1988). *Media writing: Preparing information for the mass media.* Belmont, CA: Wadsworth.

Nice, Karim. (n.d.). *How DVDs and DVD players work.* Retrieved July 6, 2001, from http://www.howstuffworks.com/dvd.htm

Noll, A. Michael. (1988). *Television technology: Fundamentals and future prospects.* Norwood, MA: Artech House.

Noll, A. Michael. (1998). *Introduction to telephones and telephone systems.* Boston: Artech House.

O'Brien, Timothy L. (2005, August 28). King Kong vs. the pirates of the multiplex. *New York Times.* Retrieved August 30, 2005, from http://www.nytimes.com/2005/08/28/business/media/28movie.html

Orlik, Peter B. (2003). *Broadcast cable copywriting* (4th ed.). Boston: Allyn & Bacon.

Parker, W. Oren, & Harvey, K. Smith. (1979). *Scene design and stage lighting* (4th ed.). New York: Holt, Rinehart & Winston.

Penzel, Frederick. (1978). *Theatre lighting before electricity.* Middleton, CT: Wesleyan University Press.

Petzold, C. (1999). *Code: The hidden language of computer hardware and software.* Redmond, WA: Microsoft.

Pogue, David. (2005a, January 20). New ways to manage your photos. *New York Times.* Retrieved January 20, 2005, from http://www.nytimes.com/2005/01/20/technology/circuits/20stat.html

Pogue, David. (2005b, January 27). Videotape to DVD, made easy. *New York Times.* Retrieved January 27, 2005, from http://www.nyties.com/2005/01/27/technology/circuits/27stat.html

Pogue, David. (2005c, February 24). The big picture: Megapixel race at milestone 8. *New York Times.* Retrieved February 24, 2005, from http://www.nytimes.com/2005/02/24/technology/circuits/24stat.html

Pogue, David. (2005d, June 16). A pro camera that amateurs can afford. *New York Times.* Retrieved June 17, 2005, from http://www.nytimes.com/2005/06/16/technology/circuits/16pogue.html

Pogue, David. (2005e, June 23). Beyond wi-fi: Laptop heaven but at a price. *New York Times.* Retrieved June 28, 2005, from http://www.nytimes.com/2005/06/23/technology/circuits/23pogue.html

Pogue, David. (2005f, October 18). An iPod worth keeping an eye on. *New York Times.* Retrieved October 20, 2005, from http://www.nytimes.com/2005/10/18/technology/circuits/10web-pogue.html

Pogue, David. (2005g, December 8). A camera that has it all? Well, almost. *New York Times.* Retrieved December 8, 2005, from http://www.nytimes.com/2005/12/08/technology/circuits/08pogue.ready.html

Pogue, David. (2006, February 2). Pixel counting joins film in obsolete bin. *New York Times.* Retrieved February 2, 2006, from http://www.nytimes.com/2006/02/02/technology/circuits/02pogue.html

Rai, Saritha. (2005, September 7). A tutor half a world away, but as close as a keyboard. *New York Times*. Retrieved September 8, 2005, from http://www.nytimes.com/2005/09/07/education/07tutor.html

Ray, S. (1979). *The photographic lens*. New York: Focal Press.

Rees, Terence. (1978). *Theatre lighting in the age of fas*. London: Society for Theatre Research.

Richtel, Matt. (2005, May 16). Makers of cellphone video games suddenly find great expectations. *New York Times*. Retrieved May 16, 2005, from http://www.nytimes.com/2005/05/16/technology/16cell.html

Richtel, Matt, & Marriott, Michel. (2005, September 17). Ring tones, cameras. Now this: Sex is latest cellphone feature. *New York Times*. Retrieved September 20, 2005, from http://nytimes.com/2005/09/17/technology/17porn.html

Rivituso, Monica. (2005, August 26). *Sirius unveils its latest products*. Retrieved August 29, 2005, from http://www.smartmoney.com/Techsmart/index.cfm?story=20050826

Robischon, Noah. (2005, February 15). Thanks to cellphones, TV screens get smaller. *New York Times*. Retrieved February 15, 2005, from http://www.nytimes.com/2005/02/15/arts/television/15cell.html

Ross, Raymond S., & Ross, Mark G. (1981). *Understanding persuasion*. Englewood Cliffs, NJ: Prentice Hall.

Rowland, W. (1997). *Spirit of the Web: The age of information from telegraph to Internet*. Toronto: Somerville House.

Rubin, Joel E., & Watson, Leland H. (1954). *Theatrical lighting practice*. New York: Theatre Arts.

Ryan, Rod. (Ed.). (1993). *American cinematographer manual* (7th ed.). Hollywood, CA: ASC Press.

Schellhardt, Laura, & Logan, John. (2006). *Screenwriting for dummies*. Hoboken, NY: John Wiley.

Schwartz, John. (2003, September 22). Music's struggle with technology. *New York Times*. Retrieved September 22, 2003, from http://www.nytimes.com/2003/09/02/technology/22neco.htm

Sellman, Hunton D., & Lessley, Merrill. (1982). *Essentials of stage lighting* (2nd ed.). Englewood Cliffs, NJ: Prentice Hall.

Settel, Irving. (1983). *A pictorial history of television* (2nd ed.). New York: Frederick Ungar.

Shiers, George. (1977). *Technical development of television*. New York: Arno.

Shook, Frederick. (1996). *Television field production and reporting*. White Plains, NY: Longman.

Shyles, L. (1990). *Improving pilot efficiency in the age of the glass cockpit: Designing intelligent software interface for the military aviation setting*. Dayton, OH: U.S. Air Force Office of Scientific Research, Wright Patterson Air Force Base.

Shyles, Leonard. (Ed.). (2003). *Deciphering cyberspace: Making the most of digital communication technology*. Thousand Oaks, CA: Sage.

Siklos, Richard. (2005, November 8). NBC and CBS to sell reruns for 99 cents each. *New York Times*. Retrieved November 8, 2005, from http://www.nytimes.com/2005/11/08/business/media/08demand.html

Smith, Roberta. (2005, December 16). It's a Pixar world. We're just living in it. *New York Times*. Retrieved December 16, 2005, from http://nytimes.com/2005/12/16/arts/design/16pixa.html

Spottiswoode, Raymond. (1965). *Film and its techniques*. Berkeley: University of California Press.

Spottiswoode, Raymond. (1969). *A grammar of the film: An analysis of film technique*. Berkeley: University of California Press.

Stephens, Mitchell, & Lanson, Gerald. (1994). *Writing and reporting the news*. New York: Oxford University Press.

Stross, Randall. (2005a, July 31). Why Bill Gates wants 3,000 new patents. *New York Times*. Retrieved August 2, 2005, from http://www.nytimes.com/2005/07/31/business/yourmoney/31digi.html

Stross, Randall. (2005b, November 20). How Google tamed ads on the wild, wild Web. *New York Times*. Retrieved November 21, 2005, from http://www.nytimes.com/2005/11/20/business/yourmoney/20digi.html

Swinfield, Rosemarie. (1994). *Stage makeup step by step.* Cincinnati, OH: Betterway Books.

Taub, Eric A. (2004, November 29). Signs of a glut and lower prices on thin TV's. *New York Times.* Retrieved November 29, 2004, from http://www.nytimes.com/2004/11/29/technology/291cd.html

Taub, Eric A. (2005a, May 16). HDTV is a new reality for game developers. *New York Times.* Retrieved May 16, 2005, from http://www.nytimes.com/2005/05/16/business/16game.html

Taub, Eric A. (2005b, December 8). In judging DVD players, performance is in details. *New York Times.* Retrieved December 8, 2005, from http://www.nytimes.com/2005/12/08/technology/circuits/08basics.html

Tedeschi, Bob. (2005, November 14). The trail of a clicked-on ad, brought to you by Google. *New York Times.* Retrieved November 15, 2005, from http://www.nytimes.com/2005/11/14/business/14google.html

Walters, Roger L. (1988). *Broadcast writing.* New York: McGraw-Hill.

Walters, Roger L. (1993). *Computer telephone integration.* Boston: Artech House.

Walters, Roger L. (1994). *Broadcast writing* (2nd ed.). New York: McGraw-Hill.

Weiner, Tim. (2005, February 16). A new model army soldier rolls closer to the battlefield. *New York Times.* Retrieved February 16, 2005, from http://www.nytimes.com/2005/02/16/technology/16robots.html

Wilkie, Bernard. (1979). *The technique of special effects in television.* London: Focal Press.

Willis, Edgar E., & D'Arienzo, Camille. (1993). *Writing scripts for television, radio, and film.* New York: Harcourt Brace Jovanovich.

Wolf, Ben. (2005, April 18). CNET review: Camcorders. *New York Times.* Retrieved June 2, 2005, from http://cnet.nytimes.com/Canon_XL2

Wolff, Jurgen, & Cox, Kerry. (1991). *Successful scriptwriting.* Cincinnati, OH: Writer's Digest Books.

Zeller, Tom, Jr. (2005, February 7). As piracy battle nears Supreme Court, the messages grow manic. *New York Times.* Retrieved February 8, 2005, from http://www.nytimes.com/2005/02/07/technology/07sharing.html

Zernike, Kate. (2005, February 19). Tired of TiVo? Beyond blogs? Podcasts are here. *New York Times.* Retrieved February 24, 2005, from http://www.nytimes.com/2005/02/19/technology/19podcasting.html

Zworykin, V. K., & Morton, G. A. (1954). *Television* (2nd ed.). New York: John Wiley.

Zworykin, V. K., & Ramberg, E. G. (1949). *Photoelectricity.* New York: John Wiley.

INDEX

ABOUT THE AUTHOR

Leonard Shyles (Ph.D., Ohio State University) has been an Associate Professor in the Department of Communication at Villanova University since 1989. He served as the Director of the Video Production Lab until 2000. His research focuses on the transition from analog to digital platforms across media and telecommunications institutions. He is also an expert in both qualitative and quantitative research methods. He has taught research methodology in the Communications Department since 1989 and has published widely in the fields of political communication, public communication campaigns, and military propaganda analysis, including *The 1000 Hour War: Communication in the Gulf* (1994). In addition, he has contributed to a wide selection of book chapters, collected works, and journal articles in both the communication and political disciplines. His most recent publication includes *Deciphering Cyberspace: Making the Most of Digital Communication Technology* (2003).